RECENT ADVANCES IN CANINE AND FELINE NUTRITIONAL RESEARCH:

Proceedings of the 1996
Iams International Nutrition Symposium

RECENT ADVANCES IN CANINE AND FELINE NUTRITIONAL RESEARCH:

Proceedings of the 1996 Iams International Nutrition Symposium

Edited by
Daniel P. Carey, DVM
Director, Technical Communications
The Iams Company

Sharon A. Norton, PhD
Manager, Technical Communications
The Iams Company

Susan M. Bolser
Technical Writer
The Iams Company

ORANGE FRAZER PRESS
Wilmington, Ohio USA

Mission Statement

*Our mission is to
enhance the well-being
of dogs and cats
by providing world-class quality foods.*

ISBN 1-882203-09-7
Printed on recycled paper

Published by
ORANGE FRAZER PRESS
37¹/₂ West Main Street
Wilmington, Ohio 45177
USA

Dedicated to
the advancement of
dog and cat nutrition.

Table of Contents

RECENT ADVANCES IN CANINE AND FELINE NUTRITIONAL RESEARCH

Gastrointestinal Health

Dietary Fiber for Dogs and Cats:
An Historical Perspective

Gregory D. Sunvold, PhD
Research Nutritionist, Research and Development
The Iams Company, Lewisburg, Ohio

The gastrointestinal (GI) health of dogs and cats can be influenced by disease state, physiological status, and components of the diet. A specific dietary ingredient, fiber, has been shown to influence GI health in many species. This manuscript will provide an historical perspective on dietary fiber research in ruminants and humans and then give an overview of fiber research regarding dogs and cats. In addition, the effect of dietary fiber on ameliorating certain diseases and recommendations regarding the use of dietary fiber will be discussed.

Introduction

Dietary fiber generally is defined as structural carbohydrates and lignin resistant to digestion by mammalian intestinal enzymes. Previously, fiber was thought to have little, if any, value as a dietary component. This is not the case as evidenced by research delineating many benefits of fiber inclusion in diets of animals and humans.

Definition and Components

Fiber is an amorphous structure whose chemical composition varies widely depending on source. Most commonly, the main chemical components of fiber include pectin, hemicelluloses, cellulose, and lignin, with hemicellulose and cellulose found in the greatest quantity. Additionally, unique compounds such as fructooligosaccharides (FOS) are not included in any of these categories but still act as fiber sources since they are not digested by mammalian enzymes. The chemical composition of fiber is important because it influences how fiber can affect the host animal.

Fibrous feedstuffs can provide over 70 percent of a ruminant (e.g., cattle, sheep) animal's energy requirement. These feedstuffs are made useful to the host by the symbiotic action of gut microflora with the host animal. This aspect of ruminant nutrition has been studied for several decades. Several benefits of fiber in the human diet were proposed over 25 years ago.[1,2] Early reports related western world diseases (e.g., coronary artery disease, appendicitis, diverticular disease of the colon, gallbladder disease, varicose veins, deep vein thrombosis, hiatus hernia, and large bowel tumors) to dietary fiber intake by humans.[1,2] Studies of people consuming low amounts of dietary fiber (Europeans) and high amounts of dietary fiber (Afri-

Dietary Fiber Research Background

cans) revealed negative correlations between the incidence of these diseases and dietary fiber intake. Since that time, researchers have investigated diverse subjects such as the effects of fiber on stool bulk and consistency, intestinal cancer, heart disease, and diabetes in humans. Thus, one could consider that the area of fiber research is somewhat unique in that it has been influenced from two very different perspectives — production agriculture and human nutrition.

In the last five years research with dietary fiber for dogs and cats has been actively pursued. Prior to this, fiber was primarily added to commercial dog and cat diets for two reasons: to alter stool consistency and to provide indigestible components (up to 30%) in weight loss products. Unfortunately, human nutrition concepts regarding dietary fiber have been misused in dog and cat diets. For example, if an adult human consumes 2000 kcal per day, that individual should consume 25 grams (g) of dietary fiber (current average consumption is between 13 and 17 g). Based on a diet providing 37 percent of its calories from fat (average fat intake of adult humans in USA), that individual should consume approximately six percent of their diet as fiber. This is in contrast to high fiber dog and cat foods that contain up to 30 percent fiber. Thus, a relatively high fiber diet for humans contains only one-fifth the amount of fiber in a high fiber dog or cat food. Side effects of dogs and cats consuming high fiber diets are constipation, excessive stool output, decreased nutrient digestibility, and a decline in the visual appearance of the animal's skin and haircoat. Literature is also not available as to the long term effects of these high fiber diets on mineral balance. Therefore, a great opportunity exists for researchers interested in dog and cat nutrition to improve the diet of these animals by disproving some of the conjecture with nutritional truths. The following section will review controlled research experiments published in the last five years that document further benefits of fiber in the gastrointestinal tract of dogs and cats. *Table 1* outlines these benefits.

Overview of Research with Dietary Fiber for Dogs and Cats

As mentioned previously, few controlled experiments regarding dietary fiber for dogs and cats have been conducted until recently.[3-5] These experiments evaluated the effects of various fiber sources and(or) concentrations on nutrient intake, digestion, passage, and metabolism. Results from this research indicated that different sources of fiber vary in their digestibility, and total dietary fiber (TDF) characterized fiber digestibility much better than crude fiber. Adaptation of TDF methodology originally developed for human foods has further enhanced the ability to determine in vivo fiber digestion. The next major advancement in fiber research documented that intestinal microflora from dogs and cats could ferment various fiber sources.[6-7] Followup experiments involved feeding dogs and cats diets formulated on the basis of fermentability, and research documented the potential usefulness of fiber blends.[8-9]

Other recent experiments evaluated the effect of diets formulated to provide different amounts of fermentability on colonic weight, microstructure, and morphology to determine the influence of short chain fatty acids (SCFA) resulting from in vivo fiber fermentation on intestinal health.[10] These results demonstrated that an optimal amount of fermentable fiber in the diet is necessary to maintain a healthy intestine in dogs. Other work reported the effect of FOS on intestinal bacteria populations in the fluid and tissues in the small intestine. These efforts documented that a novel fiber source, FOS, can alter the population of intestinal bacteria.[11] The previously mentioned research will be discussed in greater detail in the next several sections, as well as in other chapters of this book. In certain research areas, experiments with dogs and cats are not available; therefore, information from other species is discussed. *Table 2* summarizes the various biological response factors to dietary fiber that have been documented in dogs and cats.

Year	Topic	Reference
1990	Documented Usefulness of Beet Pulp in Dog Diets	Fahey et al. (1990a)[4]
1990	Documentation of the Superiority of Using Total Dietary Fiber vs. Crude Fiber to Measure Fiber Digestibility	Fahey et al. (1990a,b)[3,4]
1990-1993	Documentation of Digesta Mean Retention Time as Influenced by Different Fiber Sources in Dogs	Fahey et al. (1990a,b; 1992; Sunvold et al., 1993b)[3,4,5,8]
1993	Documentation of Fiber Fermentation by Colonic Microflora from Dogs	Sunvold et al. (1993a)[6]
1993	Evaluation of Various Fiber Blends Formulated to Provide Desired Fermentability for Dogs	Sunvold et al. (1993b)[8]
1994	Documentation of Fiber Fermentation by Colonic Microflora from Cats	Sunvold et al. (1994a)[7]
1994	Documentation of the Effect of Dietary Fiber on the Fermentative Activity of Colonic Microflora from Dogs	Sunvold et al. (1995d)[30]
1994	Documentation of the Effect of Dietary Fiber on the Fermentative Activity of Colonic Microflora from Cats	Sunvold et al. (1995d)[30]
1994	Documentation of the Ability of FOS to Alter the Composition of Small Intestinal Microflora in Dogs	Willard et al. (1994)[11]
1994	Documentation of the Effect of Fiber Fermentability on Colonic Mass and Intestinal Morphology in Dogs	Reinhart et al. (1994)[10]
1994	Documentation of the Effect of Fiber Fermentability on Intestinal Histopathology in Dogs	Reinhart et al. (1994)[10]
1995	Documentation of Similar Potential to Ferment Fiber by Gastrointestinal Microflora from Dogs, Cats, Humans, Pigs, Horses, and Cattle	Sunvold et al. (1995a)[29]
1995	Evaluation of Various Fiber Blends Formulated to Provide Desired Fermentability for Cats	Sunvold et al. (1995c)[9]

Table 1. Highlights of research with dietary fiber for dogs and cats.

Biological Response Factor	Dog	Cat
Stool consistency	Sunvold et al. (1995a)[29]	Sunvold et al. (1995c)[9]
Nutrient Digestibility	Fahey et al. (1990a,b; 1992) Sunvold et al. (1995a)[3,4,5,17]	Sunvold et al. (1995c)[9]
Intestinal Passage	Fahey et al. (1990a,b; 1992)[3-5]	N/A*
Fermentation	Sunvold et al. (1995a,c,d)[17,29,30]	Sunvold et al. (1995c)[9]
Colonic Mass	Reinhart et al. (1994)[10]	N/A
Intestinal Morphology	Reinhart et al. (1994)[10]	N/A
Intestinal Histopathology	Reinhart et al. (1994)[10]	N/A
Intestinal Bacteria Composition	Willard et al. (1994)[11]	N/A

*N/A = Not available.

Table 2. Documented biological response factors to dietary fiber consumed by dogs and cats.

Stool Bulk and Consistency

The amount of fiber in the diet can influence stool bulk and consistency in dogs and cats. Dogs fed diets varying only in the concentration of oat fiber exhibited increased wet fecal output as dietary oat fiber increased.[5] Cats consuming diets with supplemental fiber had increased wet fecal output as compared to unsupplemented cats.[9] Stool consistency for dogs and cats also can be influenced by type of dietary fiber.[6-9] For example, a diet containing a blend of highly fermentable fibers (i.e., pectin, carob bean gum, locust bean gum, gum talha, and/or guar gum) resulted in liquid, unformed stools while a diet containing a poorly fermentable fiber (i.e., cellulose) resulted in hard, dry stools. Inclusion of a moderately fermentable fiber (i.e., beet pulp) resulted in moist, well-formed stools. Therefore, dietary fiber is important for dogs and cats to provide stool bulk and maintain optimal consistency.

Nutrient Digestion

The source of fiber greatly influences its digestibility in dogs and cats. Indeed, TDF digestibility of dog diets containing different sources of fiber has been shown to range from 4.1 to 60.8.[8] An evaluation of soybean sources that varied in their concentration of oligosaccharides revealed that diets containing the lowest concentration of oligosaccharides (i.e., stachyose, raffinose) had improved apparent nutrient digestibility.[12] Source of fiber can influence the digestion of dry matter, nitrogen, and lipid across the total GI tract.[8-9]

These differences in apparent digestibilities may or may not be indicative of differences in the digestibility of various diet components. For example, if the fiber type influenced intestinal secretions, the apparent (total GI tract) lipid digestibility could vary while the actual digestibility of the lipid component of the diet may not be different. Further research in this area is needed to better understand the influences of fiber on nutrient digestibility.

Intake of diets containing different amounts or types of fiber was measured in several studies with dogs.[3,4,8] Intake of DM was slightly increased (4.5%) while ME intake remained constant when dogs consumed diets with increasing levels (from 2.5 to 12.5%) of beet pulp. Intake of DM and ME was less (>11%) when dogs consumed diets containing no supplemental source of fiber. Other research suggests that high concentrations of fiber in the diet may impair intake. Cats fed diets containing 20% celluflour[13] or up to 40% kaolin[14] consumed a similar amount of food as cats fed the same diets without these indigestible substances. Therefore, these indigestible substances limited the intake of the digestible portion of the diet. An explanation for these results is that diet palatability may be decreased by high concentrations of dietary fiber.[15]

Lag time in the recovery of a polyethylene glycol (PEG) hydroxypropyl-methylcellulose (HPMC) solution administered by oral gastric tube at the duodenum and mid-jejunum of dogs was positively correlated ($r = 0.701$; $P < 0.001$) with solutions of higher viscosity. Also, when dogs consumed solutions containing HPMC, flow rate constants were decreased several fold compared to dogs consuming solutions without HPMC. Therefore, transit time may be increased in the upper small intestine by dietary fibers with higher viscosity and confirm the observation that certain fiber sources can increase the length of time that food resides in the small intestine.[16]

Contrary to this study, mean retention time of chromium mordanted beet pulp administered to dogs fed different sources of fiber indicated that intestinal passage of beet pulp tended ($P = 0.19$) to be fastest (21.0 h) while a diet containing a blend of fibers (75% cellulose, 25% gum arabic) was slowest (32.3 h).[17] These results do not support the theory that insoluble and nonfermentable fibers speed digesta passage. Further research in the area of digesta passage in the intestine of dogs and cats is needed.

Correct estimation of intestinal transit time is important when one considers the fermentation potential of dietary fiber. Longer residence times in areas of the intestinal tract that contain anaerobic microflora will promote greater extents of fiber fermentation. One problem with quantifying the fermentation of fiber to SCFA, however, is that SCFA are continually absorbed. This process probably is accomplished through passive diffusion.[18] Additionally, utilization of SCFA by colonocytes makes measurement of portal blood levels useless as an indicator of SCFA production in the colon.[19,20] Thus, several groups of researchers have used in vitro fermentation techniques to quantify both substrate degradation and SCFA production.[21,28] Several of these techniques have been derived from in vitro fermentation techniques used to evaluate ruminal fermentation.[21,22,25,27]

The goal of in vitro technology is to simulate in vivo conditions in the colonic environment. Major characteristics of these procedures include: 1) maintenance of anaerobic conditions; 2) provision of adequate nutrients (e.g., vitamins, minerals) so that growth of the many and varied microbial species is not inhibited; 3) maintenance of an appropriate and constant temperature; and 4) use of defined fermentation times. Several experiments utilizing an in vitro technique have been adapted for use with intestinal microflora from dogs and cats.[9, 17, 29, 30] These results will be discussed by Gregory Reinhart in another chapter of these Proceedings.

Role of
Short Chain
Fatty Acids

As mentioned earlier, predominant end-products of substrate fermentation are the SCFA, acetate, propionate, and butyrate. These account for 85-95% of the SCFA in the human colon.[31] Short chain fatty acids are important to the integrity of the intestine as they supply possibly 60-70% of the energy requirement of mucosal cells. Up to 30% of the total energy requirement of some nonruminant species may be met by SCFA.[32] Nonruminant species that have been shown to extract the greatest amount of energy from SCFA are the rabbit[33,34] and pony[35] whose intestinal tracts consist of a large and complex hindgut.[32] Short chain fatty acids also have been shown to have a trophic effect on the colonic structure during total parenteral nutrition of rats.[36] Furthermore, sodium and water absorption by the colon is promoted with SCFA administration[37-38] so these metabolites may play a role in controlling diarrhea.[39] The presence of SCFA also may be responsible for altering colonic weight, microstructure, and histopathology.[10]

Short Chain
Fatty Acid
Production

Because many potential effects of SCFA on the host individual exist, it is important to consider the potential sources of these metabolites. Several substrates enter the large intestine and are available for fermentation under normal conditions.[31] In the nonruminant, these include: 1) starch that is resistant to digestion; 2) non-starch polysaccharides; 3) sugars and oligosaccharides (e.g., lactose, raffinose, stachyose); 4) mucins (secreted by the colonic epithelium); and 5) protein and nitrogen (from the diet or endogenous secretions). Experiments regarding the fermentation of different sources of dietary fiber in dogs and cats are scarce.[9, 17, 29, 30]

Effect of Fiber
Fermentation on
Gastrointestinal
Microflora

The presence of several genera and species of intestinal bacteria in dogs and cats has been reported.[40-42] Bacteria found in the human gastrointestinal tract have been categorized into beneficial and harmful/pathogenic groups.[43] Beneficial bacteria: 1) inhibit the presence of harmful bacteria; 2) stimulate immune function; 3) aid in digestion and(or) absorption of food; and 4) synthesize vitamins. Harmful bacteria can produce 1) toxins; 2) carcinogens; and 3) putrefactive substances. Several genera found in the human intestine are also found in the gastrointestinal tract of dogs and cats. Therefore, manipulating the composition of intestinal microflora could benefit dogs and cats as well as humans.

Recent research has indicated that the source of dietary fiber can influence the fermentative activity of intestinal microflora.[30] Therefore, either the composition of the intestinal microflora and(or) the enzymatic activity of the existing microflora can be altered by dietary fiber. Other research has evaluated the dietary addition of oligosaccharides which are resistant to digestion (e.g., FOS, lactosucrose). Mixed cultures of bacteria readily ferment FOS.[17, 30] Evidence from several experiments indicates that FOS are selectively utilized by certain species of intestinal bacteria. The number of *Bifidobacteria* has been shown to be significantly higher in feces from humans after consuming four grams per day of FOS for 14 days.[44] Pathogenic bacteria are also decreased in the presence of dietary FOS. When chickens were stressed by limiting feed and water intake and being exposed to *Salmonella*, fewer were infected with *Salmonella* in the cecum when a diet containing 0.75% FOS was consumed.[44] These novel fiber sources, fed to dogs and cats, result in changes in the composition of intestinal bacteria.[41, 42]

Dogs and cats are affected with a number of intestinal diseases similar to those in humans. Intestinal diseases/conditions in dogs and (or) cats include diarrhea, constipation, small intestinal bacteria overgrowth (SIBO), inflammatory bowel disease (IBD), colitis, and megacolon. It is often suggested that these diseases may be ameliorated with dietary fiber. Dietary fiber has also been suggested to ameliorate other diseases (e.g., hyperlipidemia, obesity, and diabetes). Unfortunately, dietary fiber was touted as a "wonder drug" for treating these diseases in humans, and the euphoria that resulted carried over into dog and cat diets. While some theories regarding dietary fiber for humans have held true, caution is advised in extrapolating these theories to dog and cat diets.

Potential Diseases in Dogs and Cats That May Be Ameliorated with Dietary Fiber

---

Table 3 outlines several biological response factors to dietary fiber. Some intestinal diseases may be improved through the application of the dietary fiber research that was previously discussed. Current clinical studies show a high percentage of dogs presented with chronic diarrhea are SIBO-positive[46] with coliforms, *Staphylococci*, *Enterococci*, *Clostridium* and *Bacteroides* being the predominant species of bacteria isolated. Clinical diagnosis of SIBO has also been reported in cats which otherwise appeared healthy.[47] The most common bacteria isolated from the duodenal fluid were *Bacteroides*, *Eubacteria*, *Fusobacteria*, and *Pasteurella*. Therefore, FOS may have widespread potential for modifying the composition of intestinal microflora associated with bacterial overgrowth in cats and dogs.

Application of New Nutritional Technology

Under diarrhea conditions, absorption of water from the lumen of the colon appears to be mediated by SCFA. Supplementation of fermentable fiber such as beet pulp to provide SCFA could help increase water absorption and ultimately stabilize diarrhea conditions.[48]

While the use of SCFA as an energy source by colonocytes is well documented, the importance of SCFA in intestinal disease states is understood to a lesser extent. Provision of additional butyrate from fiber fermentation may be of benefit to individuals with ulcerative colitis as the rate of butyrate oxidation appears impaired in human patients with ulcerative colitis.[49]

Disease	Biological Response Factor
Colitis	Colonic Mass, Fermentation, Intestinal Morphology, Intestinal Histopathology
Constipation	Stool Consistency, Fermentation
Diarrhea	Stool Consistency, Intestinal Bacteria, Intestinal Morphology, Intestinal Histopathology
Inflammatory Bowel Disease	Fermentation, Intestinal Bacteria, Intestinal Morphology, Intestinal Histopathology, Nutrient Digestibility
Megacolon	Stool Consistency, Intestinal Passage
Small Intestinal Bacteria Overgrowth	Intestinal Bacteria, Intestinal Morphology, Intestinal Histopathology, Fermentation

Table 3. Biological response factors to dietary fiber which may influence disease.

Recommended Uses of Dietary Fiber

Because of the diverse physiological actions of different sources of dietary fiber on the host animal, the question is not whether fiber should be included in the diet but rather what is the most appropriate source and at what level should it be provided. Evidence in normal, healthy dogs and cats supports the use of a moderate amount of moderately fermentable fiber to maintain stool consistency and intestinal morphology. The use of excessively high amounts (up to 30 percent) of dietary fiber in weight loss diets results in a high amount of fecal output, decreased nutrient digestibility, a decline in the visual appearance of the skin and haircoat, and may decrease diet palatability. Sources of fermentable fiber provide SCFA which are important energy sources for intestinal cells. Novel fiber sources such as FOS appear to be important in altering the composition of intestinal bacteria in vivo and, therefore, are likely to be important dietary components during intestinal disease (e.g., SIBO). High fiber diets for diabetics are based on the concept of nutrient dilution and are accompanied by several side effects. Hyperlipidemia can be managed through reduced fat diets, regardless of the amount of fiber. An important consideration when using dietary fiber as an adjunct therapy in treating a disease is to consider all aspects of the animal's physiology. For example, an animal with hyperlipidemia should be fed a low-fat diet but still needs a moderate amount of a moderately fermentable fiber to maintain intestinal health.

Summary of Current Knowledge Gained from Research with Dietary Fiber

The previously discussed research has indicated the diverse nutritional role of fiber. In sum, fiber provides stool bulk, a dietary source of SCFA, and an ability to modify the composition of intestinal microflora (*Figure 1*). However, the source of dietary fiber greatly influences its ability to perform these functions.

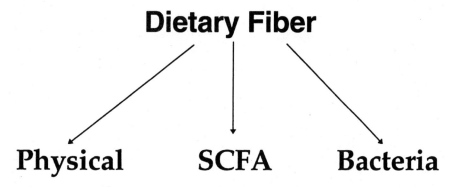

Figure 1. Routes by which dietary fiber influences the health of dogs and cats.

Future research with dietary fiber must further evaluate how fermentation processes influence the host animal through SCFA production and alterations of intestinal microbial populations. Dietary fiber research with dogs and cats must continue to utilize sophisticated technologies to allow more in depth study of diseased and healthy animals. The study of GI health as influenced by dietary fiber will become more challenging as research attempts are made to study the whole animal rather than a single aspect. Undoubtedly, future research with dietary fiber for dogs and cats must set forth new nutritional truths at the expense of antiquated dogmas. The final application of nutritional truths, however, rests with the formulators of these foods to make the proper adjustments to commercial diets. Without the pursuit of this endeavor the greatest scientific advancements regarding dietary fiber provide no benefit in improving the health of dogs and cats.

*Future
Dietary Fiber
Research*

References

1. Burkitt DP, Walker ARP, Painter NS. Dietary fiber and disease. *J Am Med Assoc* 1974; 229:1068.

2. Burkitt DP. Epidemiology of cancer of the colon and rectum. *Cancer* 1971; 28:3.

3. Fahey Jr GC, Merchen NR, Corbin JE, Hamilton AK, Serbe KA, Hirakawa DA. Dietary fiber for dogs: II. Iso-total dietary fiber (TDF) additions of divergent fiber sources to dog diets and their effects on nutrient intake, digestibility, metabolizable energy and digesta mean retention time. *J Anim Sci* 1990; 68:4229.

4. Fahey Jr GC, Merchen NR, Corbin JE, Hamilton AK, Serbe KA, Lewis SM, Hirakawa DA. Dietary fiber for dogs: I. Effects of graded levels of dietary beet pulp on nutrient intake, digestibility, metabolizable energy and digesta mean retention time. *J Anim Sci* 1990; 68:4221.

5. Fahey Jr GC, Merchen NR, Corbin JE, Hamilton AK, Bauer LL, Titgemeyer EC, Hirakawa DA. Dietary fiber for dogs: III. Effects of beet pulp and oat fiber additions to dog diets on nutrient intake, digestibility, metabolizable energy, and digesta mean retention time. *J Anim Sci* 1992; 70:1169.

6. Sunvold GD, Bourquin LD, Titgemeyer EC, Fahey Jr GC, Reinhart GA. Fermentability of various fibrous substrates by canine fecal microflora. *FASEB J* 1993a; 7:4276.

7. Sunvold GD, Titgemeyer EC, Bourquin LD, Fahey Jr GC, Reinhart GA. Fermentability of selected fibrous substrates by cat fecal microflora. *J Nutr* 1994a; 124(Suppl.):2719S(Abstr.).

8. Sunvold GD, Fahey Jr GC, Merchen NR, Bauer LL, Brown LS, Reinhart GA, Hirakawa DA. Evaluation of nutrient digestibility, passage, and fecal characteristics of dogs fed fiber-containing diets. *J Anim Sci* 1993b; 71(Suppl. 1):159(Abstr.).

9. Sunvold GD, Fahey Jr GC, Merchen NR, Bourquin LD, Titgemeyer EC, Bauer LL, Reinhart GA. Dietary fiber for cats: In vitro fermentation of selected fiber sources by cat fecal inoculum and in vivo utilization of diets containing selected fiber sources and their blends. *J Anim Sci* 1995c; 73:2329.

10. Reinhart GA, Moxley RA, Clemens ET. Dietary fibre source and its effects on colonic microstructure and histopathology of beagle dogs. *J Nutr* 1994; 24(Suppl.):2701S(Abstr.).

11. Willard MD, Simpson RB, Delles EK, Cohen ND, Fossum TW, Kolp D, Reinhart GA. Effects of dietary supplementation of fructo-oligosaccharides on small intestinal bacterial overgrowth in dogs. *Am J Vet Res* 1994; 55:654.

12. Wiernusz CJ, Shields Jr RG, Van Vilerbergen DJ, Kigin PD, Ballard R. Canine nutrient digestibility and stool quality evaluation of canned diets containing various soy protein supplements. *Vet Clin Nutr* 1995; 2:49.

13. Kanarek RB. Availability and caloric density of the diet as determinants of meal patterns in cats. *Physiol Behav* 1975. 15:611.

14. Hirsch E, Dubose C, Jacobs HL. Dietary control of food intake in cats. *Physiol Behav* 1978; 20:287.

15. MacDonald ML, Rogers QR, Morris JG. Nutrition of the domestic cat, a mammalian carnivore. *Ann Rev Nutr* 1984; 4:521.

16. Reppas C, Meyer JH, Sirois PJ, Dressman JB. Effect of hydroxypropylmethylcellulose on gastrointestinal transit and luminal viscosity in dogs. *Gastroenterology* 1991; 100:1217.

17. Sunvold GD, Fahey Jr GC, Merchen NR, Titgemeyer EC, Bourquin LD, Bauer LL, Reinhart GA. Dietary fiber for dogs: IV. In vitro fermentation of selected fiber sources by dog fecal inoculum and in vivo digestion and metabolism of diets containing selected fiber sources and their blends. *J Anim Sci* 1995b; 73:1099.

18. von Engelhardt W, Busche R, Gros G, Rechkemmer G. Absorption of short-chain fatty acids: Mechanisms and regional differences in the large intestine. In: Roche, A.F. (Ed.) *Short-Chain Fatty Acids: Metabolism and Clinical Importance*. Report of the Tenth Ross Conference on Medical Research. Columbus: Ross Laboratories. 1991:60.

19. Roediger WEW. Utilization of nutrients by isolated epithelial cells of the rat colon. *Gastroenterology* 1982; 83:424.

20. Marty JF, Vernay MY, Abravanel GM. Acetate absorption and metabolism in the rabbit hindgut. *Gut* 1985; 26:562.

21. Ehle FR, Robertson JB, Van Soest PJ. Influence of dietary fibers on fermentation in the human large intestine. *J Nutr* 1982; 112:158.

22. McBurney MI, Horvath PJ, Jeraci JL, Van Soest PJ. Effect of in vitro fermentation using human faecal inoculum on the water-holding capacity of dietary fibre. *Br J Nutr* 1985; 53:17.

23. Mortensen PB, Holtug K, Rasmussen HS. Short-chain fatty acid production from mono- and disaccharides in a fecal incubation system: Implications for colonic fermentation of dietary fiber in humans. *J Nutr* 1988; 118:321.

24. Stevens BJH, Selvendran RR, Bayliss CE, Turner R. Degradation of cell wall material of apple and wheat bran by human faecal bacteria *in vitro*. *J Sci Food Agric* 1988; 44:151.

25. Adiotomre J, Eastwood MA, Edwards CA, Brydon WG. Dietary fiber: in vitro methods that anticipate nutrition and metabolic activity in humans. *Am J Clin Nutr* 1990; 52:128.

26. Vince AJ, McNeil NI, Wager JD, Wrong OM. The effect of lactulose, pectin, arabinogalactan and cellulose on the production of organic acids and metabolism of ammonia by intestinal bacteria in a faecal incubation system. *Br J Nutr* 1990; 63:17.

27. Bourquin LD, Titgemeyer EC, Garleb KA, Fahey Jr GC. Short-chain fatty acid production and fiber degradation by human colonic bacteria: effects of substrate and cell wall fractionation procedures. *J Nutr* 1992; 122:1508.

28. Guillon F, Barry JL, Thibault JF. Effect of autoclaving sugar-beet fibre on its physico-chemical properties and its in-vitro degradation by human faecal bacteria. *J Sci Food Agric* 1992; 60:69.

29. Sunvold GD, Hussein HS, Fahey Jr GC, Merchen NR, Reinhart GA. In vitro fermentation of selected fibrous substrates by gastrointestinal microflora from dogs, cats, humans, pigs, horses, and cattle. *FASEB J* 1995a; 9:A740(Abstr.).

30. Sunvold GD, Fahey Jr GC, Merchen NR, Reinhart GA. In vitro fermentation of selected fibrous substrates by dog and cat fecal inoculum: Influence of diet composition on substrate organic matter disappearance and short-chain fatty acid production. *J Anim Sci* 1995d; 73:1110.

31. Cummings JH, Macfarlane GT. The control and consequences of bacterial fermentation in the human colon. *J Appl Bacteriol* 1991; 70:443.

32. Wrong OM, Edmonds CJ, Chadwick VS. *The Large Intestine: Its Role in Mammalian Nutrition and Homeostasis.* Lancaster England: MTP Press Ltd. 1981.

33. Hoover WH, Heitmann RN. Effects of dietary fiber levels on weight gain, cecal volume and volatile fatty acid production in rabbits. *J Nutr* 1972; 102:375.

34. Parker DS. The measurement of the production rates of volatile fatty acids in the caecum of the conscious rabbit. *Br J Nutr* 1976; 36:61.

35. Glinsky MJ, Smith RM, Spires H, Davis CL. Measurement of volatile fatty acid production rates in the cecum of the pony. *J Anim Sci* 1976; 42:1465.

36. Friedel D, Levine GM. Effect of short-chain fatty acids on colonic function and structure. *J Parent Enter Nutr* 1992; 16:1.

37. Ruppin H, Bar-Meir S, Soergel KH, Wood CM, Schmitt Jr MG. Absorption of short-chain fatty acids by the colon. *Gastroenterology* 1980; 78:1500.

38. Herschel DA, Argenzio RA, Southworth M, Stevens CE. Absorption of volatile fatty acid, Na, and H_2O by the colon of the dog. *Am J Vet Res* 1981; 42:1118.

39. Roediger WEW, Moore A. Effect of short chain fatty acids on sodium absorption in isolated human colon perfused through the vascular bed. *Dig Dis Sci* 1981; 26:100.

40. Balish E, Cleven D, Brown J, Yale CE. Nose, throat, and fecal flora of beagle dogs housed in "locked" or "open" environments. *Appl Environ Microbiol* 1977; 34:207.

41. Terada A, Hara H, Kato S, Kimura T, Fujimori I, Hara K, Maruyama T, Mitsuoka T. Effects of lactosucrose (4^G-β-D-galactosylsucrose) on fecal flora and fecal putrefactive products of cats. *J Vet Med Sci* 1993; 55:291.

42. Terada A, Hara H, Oishi T, Matsui S, Mitsuoka T, Nakajyo S, Fujimori I, Hara K. Effect of dietary lactosucrose on faecal flora and faecal metabolites of dogs. *Microbial Ecol Health Dis* 1992; 5:87.

43. Gibson GR, Roberfroid MB. Dietary modulation of the human colonic microbiota: Introducing the concept of prebiotics. *J Nutr* 1995; 125:1401.

44. Williams CH, Witherely SA, Buddington RK. Influence of dietary neosugar on selected bacterial groups of the human faecal microbiota. *Microbial Ecol Health Dis* 1994; 7:91.

45. Bailey JS, Blankenship LC, Cox NA. Effect of fructooligosaccharide on *Salmonella* colonization of the chicken intestine. *Poult Sci* 1991; 70:2433.

46. Rutgers HC, Batt RM, Elwood CM, Lamport A. Small intestinal bacterial overgrowth in dogs with chronic intestinal disease. *J Am Vet Med Assoc* 1995; 206:187.

47. Johnston K, Lamport A, Batt RM. An unexpected bacterial flora in the proximal small intestine of normal cats. *Vet Rec* 1993; 132:362.

48. Ramakrishna BS, Mathan VI. Colonic dysfunction in acute diarrhea: the role of luminal short chain fatty acids. *Gut* 1993; 34:1215.

49. Chapman MAS, Grahn MF, Boyle MA, Hutton M, Rogers J, Williams NS. Butyrate oxidation is impaired in the colonic mucosa of sufferers of quiescent ulcerative colitis. *Gut* 1994; 35:73.

In Vitro Fermentation as a Predictor of Fiber Utilization

Gregory A. Reinhart, PhD
Director of Strategic Research, Research and Development
The Iams Company, Lewisburg, Ohio

Gregory D. Sunvold, PhD
Reasearch and Development, The Iams Company, Lewisburg, Ohio

Dietary fiber is the fraction of the diet that is not digested by endogenous secretions of the gastrointestinal tract. It is a chemically heterogeneous substance, composed primarily of cellulose, hemicellulose, pectin, gums, mucilages, and lignin. Certain oligosaccharides are also classified as fiber because they are not degraded by mammalian enzymes. Although fiber is not required per se in the diets of dogs and cats, it performs several important roles in maintaining gastrointestinal tract health. Dependent upon its composition, dietary fiber functions to increase water-holding capacity, alter gastric emptying and intestinal transit time of food, provide bulk, impact nutrient absorption and adsorption, and maintain the structural integrity of the gastrointestinal tract mucosa.

Role of Dietary Fiber

The polysaccharides that make up fiber can be fermented to varying degrees by anaerobic bacteria in the lower small intestine and large intestine. The metabolic end-products of this fermentation include short chain fatty acids (SCFA) — acetate, butyrate, and propionate — as well as hydrogen, carbon dioxide, methane and other gases. It has been assumed that fiber fermentation is not important in dogs and cats because of the short length of their gastrointestinal tracts. However, recent research has shown that these species have very active colonic bacteria and possess moderate fermentation capabilities.[1,2] The SCFAs that are produced from the fermentation of dietary fiber are important in the maintenance of normal bowel function and may aid in recovery from intestinal disease. SCFAs are the preferred fuel source for colonocytes, which derive greater than 70 percent of their energy from luminally derived SCFAs. In the small intestine, jejunal cells utilize glutamine, glucose and SCFAs for fuel. SCFAs in the intestinal lumen also function to increase colonic blood flow, promote sodium and water absorption, prevent alteration of electrolyte transport by bile acids, and stimulate colonocyte proliferation.

Fiber sources have traditionally been classified according to degree of solubility and viscosity. While these properties allow distinctions to be made, the fermentability of a fiber provides more direct evidence of its physiological effects

Fermentation Properties

within the gastrointestinal tract. Traditionally, insoluble fibers have been classified as non-fermentable, while soluble fibers have been classified as fermentable. However, there are notable exceptions to this generalization (*Table 1*). Fibers with low fermentability produce minimal SCFAs. Fibers with very high fermentability, on the other hand, produce high amounts of SCFAs, but excessive dietary concentrations can also cause side effects such as loose stools and excess gas.

Table 1. Dietary fiber fermentation in dogs.

Fiber Type	Solubility	Fermentability
Beet pulp	Low	Moderate
Cellulose	Low	Low
Rice bran	Low	Moderate
Gum arabic	High	Moderate
Pectin	High	High
Carboxymethylcellulose	High	Low
Methylcellulose	High	Low
Cabbage fiber	Low	High
Guar gum	High	High
Locus bean gum	High	Low
Xanthan gum	High	Low

From Iams Technical Center data, 1994, Lewisburg, Ohio.

In vitro methodology has been used to study the fermentation of different fibers by canine and feline intestinal microflora. One of the first studies in dogs compared the ability of canine intestinal microflora to ferment 15 types of fiber.[3] A population of intestinal microbes was obtained by collecting freshly voided fecal samples from 3 adult English Pointers and immediately placing them under anaerobic conditions. The samples were diluted using an anaerobic dilution solution, filtered, and sealed under CO_2. Aliquots were then placed in centrifuge tubes containing a fiber source and a pre-measured volume of sterilized culture medium. The tubes were flushed with CO_2 to maintain anaerobic conditions, capped, and incubated for intervals of 6, 12, or 24 hours. Results of this study showed that citrus pectin, lactulose, and guar gum were all highly fermentable by canine fecal microflora, while Solka Floc® (a cellulose source) and oat fiber were almost non-fermentable. Beet pulp and rice bran were moderately fermented by canine microflora. The in vitro fermentation data also suggested beet pulp and rice bran would be an excellent source of SCFAs to the canine gastrointestinal tract. In contrast, cellulose would be expected to be a poor source of SCFAs for dogs (*Figure 1*). The authors concluded that the chemical composition of a fiber source dramatically affects the degree of fermentation and the end-products of fermentation that are produced. This study also demonstrated the usefulness and sensitivity of in vitro techniques in the measurement of fiber fermentation in the dog.

A similar study conducted with feline intestinal microflora using the same in vitro techniques showed that cats have minimal capability of fermenting cellulose, while certain soluble fibers such as locust bean gum, guar gum and citrus pectin were highly fermentable.[2] Some differences do exist between dogs and cats, however. Compared to dog microflora, cat microflora produces a lower proportion of butyrate from beet pulp and gum arabic (*Table 2*). The results of these in vitro studies prompted in vivo fiber fermentation investigations in both of these species.

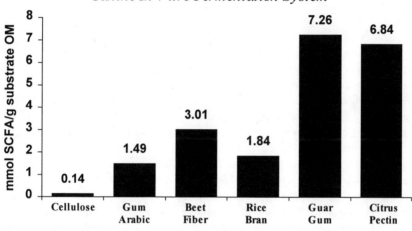

Short Chain Fatty Acid (SCFA) Production

Canine In Vitro Fermentation System

Data adapted from 3.

Figure 1.

Table 2. Fermentation characteristics of selected dietary fibers by canine and feline fecal bacteria.[a]

	CANINE			FELINE		
Fiber	OMD[b] %	SCFA Production[c]	Butyrate % of Total SCFA	OMD[b] %	SCFA Production[c]	Butyrate % of Total SCFA
Cellulose	3.0	0.20	0.0	0.9	0.07	0.0
Gum arabic	29.9	1.00	21.0	29.5	1.26	3.2
Beet pulp	31.4	2.49	21.7	33.3	1.97	5.6
Pectin	79.7	5.91	7.8	84.7	5.47	8.0
FOS[d]	84.5	5.67	5.3	86.1	4.33	9.7

[a] Data represent combined results of two dog[1,5] and two cat[5,12] in vitro fermentation experiments.
[b] Organic matter disappearance; an index of fiber fermentation.
[c] mmol/g of substrate organic matter.
[d] Fructooligosaccharides.

Several factors affect the fermentability of fiber within the gastrointestinal tracts of dogs and cats. These include the type of fiber, the amount of time that the fiber is exposed to fermentative bacteria, and the source of the bacteria. Bacterial numbers, species and fermentative activity can be altered through dietary changes. Recent research indicates that it may be possible to manipulate intestinal microorganism type and resultant fermentation products through diet. In vitro studies with dog and cat fecal microflora have shown that the diet to which an animal is adapted can significantly affect its ability to ferment dietary fiber.[4,5]

In the first study, two sources of canine fecal inocula were used. The first was collected from a group of dogs that were adapted to a diet containing a non-fermentable fiber source (cellulose). The second was from dogs adapted to a diet containing a fermentable fiber source (citrus pulp). The in vitro techniques described previously were used to collect and culture fecal microflora from the two groups of dogs. The capability of the inocula to ferment 12 different types of fiber over a period of 24 hours was examined. As previous studies had shown, the fiber types varied greatly in the degree to which they were fermented. However, the results also showed that microflora from dogs that were adapted to a diet containing a fermentable fiber source (citrus pulp) fermented dietary fiber more rapidly that did microflora from dogs adapted to a diet containing a non-fermentable fiber source (*Table 3*). These results indicate that the type of fiber in the diet influences fermentation capabilities of fecal microflora, and that a period of bacterial adaptation should be expected when introducing a diet containing a new fiber source.

Table 3. Influence of diet on fermentability of fibrous substrates by dog fecal microflora.

	CELLULOSE Incubation time (hours)			CITRUS PULP Incubation time (hours)		
	6	12	24	6	12	24
Acetate production (mmol/g OM)						
Carob bean	0.38	1.00	2.00	0.61	0.47	1.22
Citrus pulp	0.59	1.39	2.33	1.28	2.00	2.33
Pectin	0.54	1.54	4.41	1.15	3.02	2.22
Total SCFA production (mmol/g OM)						
Citrus pulp	0.81	1.88	3.31	2.08	2.72	3.42
Pectin	0.72	2.07	6.09	1.51	4.17	3.87

Data adapted from 5.

A similar study with cats involved obtaining fecal inocula from cats that were fed a diet containing no supplemental fiber, or from cats that were fed a diet containing fermentable fiber (beet pulp).[5] When results were pooled across fiber type, fecal inocula from cats that were fed a fermentable fiber had slightly higher organic matter disappearance (a measurement of fermentation) and greater production of propionate than inocula from cats fed the diet containing no supplemental fiber. The proportions of SCFA that were produced were also affected by the diet that was fed. Inocula from cats fed no supplemental fiber produced a higher ratio of acetate to propionate than inocula from cats fed beet pulp. These results show that, as in dogs, in vitro fermentation of dietary fiber increases when dietary fiber has been included in a cat's diet. This information implies that the fermentative activity of intestinal microflora can be altered with dietary fiber. Altered fermentative activity is likely due to altered enzymatic activity of intestinal bacteria and(or) changes in the composition of intestinal microflora.

Use of In Vitro Results to Predict In Vivo Effects of Dietary Fiber

It is accepted knowledge that a certain level of fiber is necessary in the diet of dogs and cats to promote normal gastrointestinal tract function and health. Recent in vivo studies have demonstrated that the type of fiber that is included in the diet is very important in maintaining health and possibly, in aiding recovery from disease. Dietary fiber, when added at approximately 7.5 percent of diet dry matter, influences fecal output, stool quality, digesta retention time, and diet digestibility to varying degrees, dependent upon fiber type.[6,7] These effects are influenced by factors such as the fiber's viscosity, water-holding capacity, and fermentability. Fiber type also affects the colonic microstructure of the intestinal mucosa.[8] Dogs that were fed either moderately fermentable (beet pulp) or highly fermentable (pectin/gum arabic mixture) fiber sources had increased colon weights, mucosal surface areas, and mucosal hypertrophy compared to dogs fed a diet containing a non-fermentable source (cellulose). The moderately fermentable fiber source (beet pulp) also minimized the incidence of cryptitis and mucus distension. Other in vivo research has studied the effects of including oligosaccharides such as fructooligosaccharide and lactosucrose in the diets of dogs and cats.[9,10,11] These novel fiber sources cause changes in the composition of intestinal bacteria which include decreasing the number of aerobic microflora, increasing the number of beneficial bacteria, and decreasing numbers of pathogenic bacteria.

Recent research has examined in vitro fermentation of dietary fiber by dog and cat fecal inoculum and has related the results of these studies to in vivo digestion and metabolism of fiber-containing diets.[1,12] This work was predicated by studies in humans and other species that have demonstrated agreement between in vitro studies of fiber utilization and in vivo results.[13,14,15] An in vivo study was conducted in which 30 adult English Pointers were fed one of six fiber-containing diets formulated using data from an in vitro fermentation experiment. Fiber was added to a complete and balanced basal diet to provide 7.5 percent supplemental total dietary fiber. Six different fiber types or blends were tested. These included beet pulp (BP), Solka Floc (SF; cellulose), citrus pulp (CP), a blend of fibers selected to minimize fermentation and maximize stool quality (SB: 75% Solka Floc, 25% gum arabic), a blend of fibers selected to maximize SCFA production (SC: 40% citrus pectin, 20% gum talha, 20% carob bean gum, 20% locust bean gum), and a blend of fibers selected to optimize both SCFA production and stool quality (CB: 80% beet pulp, 10% citrus pectin, 10% guar gum). Groups of 5 dogs were randomly assigned to each of the six dietary treatments and were ad libitum fed for an adjustment period of 12 days. This was followed by a five day period of total urine and feces collection. Nutrient intake and digestibility, energy metabolism, digesta retention time, and stool quality were determined.

Results showed that DM digestibility, fecal output, stool quality, and defecation frequency are all influenced by the fermentability of the fiber in the diet. For example, dogs fed the SC diet had a greater than 5-fold increase in fiber digestibility, which resulted in a 4.5 percentage increase in DM digestibility, compared to dogs fed the SF diet. Stool quality was also significantly affected by fiber fermentability. The production of liquid feces, diarrhea, and constipation are all undesirable. Optimal stool quality is defined as feces that are of adequate firmness to prevent diarrhea, but soft enough to prevent constipation. Fiber sources that were low in fermentability resulted in decreased defecation frequency, decreased fecal moisture content and the production of hard, dry feces. In contrast, feeding diets containing highly fermentable fiber sources caused diarrhea. Moderately fermentable fiber sources produced both excellent stool characteristics and maintained nutrient digestibility. The correlation between in vitro organic matter disappearance values and in vivo fiber digestibility values was very high in this study (R^2 = .93, P< .01). These data indicate that the in vitro techniques that were used provide a reliable and accurate method for predicting in vivo fiber fermentation characteristics in the dog (*Figure 2*).

Relationship of In Vitro Fiber Fermentation to In Vivo Fiber Digestion in Dogs

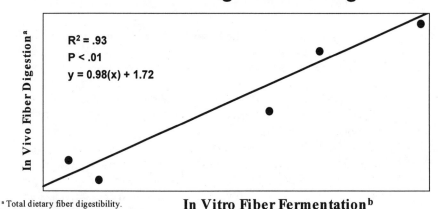

R^2 = .93
P < .01
y = 0.98(x) + 1.72

In Vivo Fiber Digestion[a]

In Vitro Fiber Fermentation[b]

[a] Total dietary fiber digestibility.
[b] Organic matter disappearance at 24 h of fermentation.

Figure 2. Data adapted from 7.

A similar in vitro fermentation experiment conducted with cat fecal microflora indicates efficient fermentation of citrus pectin, guar gum, and locust bean gum. In contrast, organic matter disappearance was less than 30 percent for cellulose, gum karaya, xanthan gum and gum arabic.[2] The results of an experiment with diets containing different sources or blends of fiber fed to cats found that feeding highly fermentable fibers to cats resulted in decreased DM, nitrogen and lipid digestibility, and production of diarrhea-like feces (*Table 4*).[12] When values for 24-hour organic matter disappearance from the in vitro study were matched with values for total dietary fiber digestibility from the in vivo study, a correlation coefficient of .93 (P < .01) was obtained. As in the dog, in vitro fermentation results were highly correlated with in vivo results (*Figure 3*).

Table 4. Dry matter, OM, total dietary fiber (TDF), N, and lipid intakes and digestibilities by cats consuming experimental diets.

Item	Diet[a]						SEM	TE[b]
	NF	BP	SF	SB	SC	CB		
Number per treatment	5	5	5	5	5	5	--	--
BW, kg	2.5	2.4	2.4	2.4	2.4	2.4	0.4	--
DM intake, g/d	38.7	43.0	44.0	50.5	34.3	48.2	6.3	0.51
OM intake, g/d	36.2	39.8	41.3	47.0	32.0	44.7	5.8	0.51
N intake, g/d	2.3	2.6	2.6	2.9	2.0	2.9	0.4	0.53
Lipid intake, g/d	9.3	10.4	10.6	12.3	8.3	12.2	1.6	0.41
TDF intake, g/d	0.7^c	4.5^d	4.9^d	5.5^d	4.1^d	5.0^d	0.7	<.01
DMD, %	88.0^c	80.4^d	81.0^d	80.3^d	61.3^e	80.8^d	1.8	<.01
OMD, %	91.6^c	83.8^d	83.5^d	83.0^d	63.7^e	83.7^d	1.8	<.01
N digestibility, %	86.7^c	83.3^c	88.4^c	86.0^c	59.0^d	83.2^c	2.1	<.01
Lipid digestibility, %	93.9^c	91.5^c	95.0^c	95.9^c	39.6^d	88.7^c	3.4	<.01
TDF digestibility, %	5.3^c	38.2^d	8.9^c	5.7^c	50.6^d	41.1^d	5.1	<.01

[a] NF=no added fiber; BP=beet pulp; SF=Solka Floc; SB=stool blend; SC=SCFA blend; CB=combination blend.
[b] Overall treatment effect P-value.
[c,d,e] Means in the same row lacking a common superscript letter differ (P<.05).
Data adapted from 13.

Relationship of In Vitro Fiber Fermentation to In Vivo Fiber Digestion in Cats

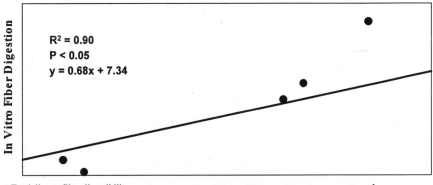

R² = 0.90
P < 0.05
y = 0.68x + 7.34

In Vitro Fiber Digestion

[a] Total dietary fiber digestibility.
[b] Organic matter disappearance at 24 h of fermentation.

In Vivo Fiber Fermentation[b]

Figure 3. Data adapted from 12.

An important difference was observed between dogs and cats with respect to their abilities to tolerate different dietary fiber sources. While fecal consistency scores were adversely affected in dogs fed highly fermentable fibers, a depression in digestibility was not observed in dogs. In contrast, digestibility coefficients were significantly decreased in cats fed diets containing highly fermentable fibers (*Table 4*). These differences may reflect the cat's inability to tolerate fibers that are highly fermentable and/or viscous. This observation also indicates the need to explore possible detrimental effects of the common practice of including viscous, highly fermentable fibers to canned cat foods as viscosity enhancers. As in the dog, diets containing moderately fermentable fiber sources resulted in optimal stool quality and nutrient digestibility in cats.

Summary

In vitro fiber evaluation has demonstrated efficacy as a method for predicting in vivo fiber fermentation responses in dogs and cats. The in vitro technique that is described allows comparisons between different fibers' degree and efficiency of fermentation, the type and amount of end products that are produced, and fermentative changes over time, under carefully controlled conditions. The fecal inoculum samples that are collected represent microflora that is present in the distal colon. While it cannot be assumed that the populations of microflora in this section of the gastrointestinal tract represent populations of microbial flora along the entire gastrointestinal tract, the samples are representative of the microbial populations that are responsible for the majority of fiber fermentation in the dog and cat. Careful handling and culturing of the inocula under anaerobic conditions further ensures the viability and consistency of the samples that are used as inocula.

In vitro studies have shown that pectin and certain bacterial gums are highly fermentable, beet pulp is moderately fermentable, and cellulose is non-fermentable by dog and cat fecal microflora. These results are well correlated with results from actual feeding studies with dogs and cats. In vitro techniques are rapid, inexpensive, non-invasive, and allow the ranking of fibers according to their degree of fermentation. In addition, data that are not obtainable through in vivo tests, such as the proportions of major SCFA that are produced and changes in fermentation patterns over time, can be collected. Information acquired through in vitro studies provides useful information to formulate diets for dogs and cats.

Clinical
Implications

Because both high and low fermentability can cause adverse effects, feeding a moderately fermentable fiber optimizes the positive effects of SCFA production without the negative effects of excess fermentation. Efficiently producing SCFAs with minimal production of intestinal gases is also important to companion animals. Both beet pulp and rice bran currently meet these criteria. In vitro methodology can be used to screen additional fiber sources which may be appropriate for inclusion in dog and cat diets.

The provision of specific bowel nutrients, including SCFAs, has been demonstrated to both protect and promote restoration of normal intestinal function in other animals. Evidence in the human suggests that chronic gastrointestinal disorders such as inflammatory bowel disease and ulcerative colitis may be related to fermentable fiber and SCFA status. It is known that malnourished animals have atrophied intestinal mucosa and reduced epithelial renewal. Intestinal disorders may be better treated with nutritional intervention that promotes mucosal growth, provides energy substrates for enterocytes and minimizes cryptitis and mucous distension. It is postulated that excessive levels of non-fermentable fiber in the diet may not provide the gut with adequate SCFAs needed for recovery, while those with moderate fermentability, or characteristics which promote the proliferation of non-pathogenic bacteria (such as fructooligosaccharides and lactosucrose) may be beneficial. Types of dietary fiber that yield a high concentration of butyrate may have beneficial effects on the large intestine, while fiber substrates that are rapidly fermented or have a high acetate production may promote small intestinal mucosal proliferation.

Because individual SCFAs (acetate, propionate, and butyrate) have different effects on the host animal, dietary fiber may also be important in its ability to provide site-specific nutrition. Continued in vitro research would provide information regarding optimal SCFA profiles and other fermentation characteristics of different fiber sources. Diets could then be formulated with blends of fiber that provide desired SCFA profiles and affect microbial populations in ways which maintain gastrointestinal tract health or which aid in the prevention or treatment of certain diseases.

References

1. Sunvold GD, Fahey GC Jr, Merchen NR, Titegemeyer EC, Bourquin LD, Bauer LL, Reinhart GA. Dietary fiber for dogs: IV. In vitro fermentation of selected fiber sources by dog fecal inoculum and in vivo digestion and metabolism of fiber-supplemented diets. *J Anim Sci* 1995; 73:1099-1109.

2. Sunvold GD, Titgemeyer EC, Bourquin LD, Fahey, GC, Reinhart GA. Fermentability of selected fibrous substrates by cat faecal microflora. *J Nutr* 1994; 2721S-2722S.

3. Sunvold, GD, Bourquin LD, Titgemeyer EC, Fahey GC Jr, Reinhart GA. Fermentability of various fibrous substrates by canine faecal microflora. *FASEB J* 1993; 7:A740.

4. Sunvold GD, Fahey GC Jr, Merchen NR, Reinhart GA. Fermentability of selected fibrous substrates by dog faecal microflora as influenced by diet. *J Nutr* 1994; 124:2719S-2720S.

5. Sunvold GD, Fahey GC Jr, Merchen NR, Reinhart GA. In vitro fermentation of selected fibrous substrates by dog and cat faecal inoculum: Influence of diet composition of substrate organic matter disappearance and short-chain fatty acid production. *J Anim Sci* 1995; 73:1110-1122.

6. Fahey GC, Merchen NR, Corbin JE, Hamilton AK, Serbe KA, Lewis SM, Hirakawa DA. Dietary fiber for dogs: I. Effects of graded levels of dietary beet pulp

on nutrient intake, digestibility, metabolizable energy and digesta mean retention time. *J Anim Sci* 1990; 68:4221-4228.

7. Fahey GC, Merchen NR, Corbin JE, Hamilton AK, Serbe KA, Hirakawa DA. Dietary fiber for dogs: II. Iso-total dietary fiber (TDF) additions of divergent fiber sources to dog diets and their effects on nutrient intake, digestibility, metabolizable energy and digesta mean retention time. *J Anim Sci* 1990; 68:4229-4235.

8. Reinhart GA, Moxley RA, Clemens ET. Source of dietary fiber and its effects on colonic microstructure, function and histopathology of Beagle dogs. *J Nutr* 1994; 124:2701S-2703S.

9. Willard MD, Simpson RB, Delles EK, Cohen ND, Fossum TW, Kolp D, Reinhart GA. Effects of dietary supplementation of fructo-oligosaccharides on small intestinal bacterial overgrowth in dogs. *Am J Vet Res* 1994; 55:654-659.

10. Terada A, Hara H, Kato S Kimura T, Fujimori I, Hara K, Maruyama T, Mitsuoka T. Effects of lactosucrose (4G-beta-D-galactosylsucrose) on fecal flora and fecal putrefactive products of cats. *J Vet Med Sci* 1993; 55:291-295.

11. Terada A, Hara H, Oishi T, Matsui S, Mitsuoka T, Nakajyo S, Fujimori I, Hara K. Effect of dietary lactosucrose on faecal flora and faecal metabolites of dogs. *Microbial Ecol Health & Dis* 1992; 5:87-92.

12. Sunvold GD, Fahey GC Jr, Merchen NR, Bourquin LD, Titgemeyer EC, Bauer LL, Reinhart GA. Dietary fiber for cats: In vitro fermentation of selected fiber sources by cat fecal inoculum and in vivo utilization of diets containing selected fiber sources and their blends. *J Anim Sci* 1995; 73:2329-2339.

13. McBurney MI, Sauer WC. Fiber and large bowel energy absorption: validation of the integrated ileostomy-fermentation model using pigs. *J Nutr* 1993; 123:721.

14. Titgemeyer, CE, Bourquin LD, Fahey GC, Garleb KA. Fermentability of various fiber sources by human fecal bacteria in vitro. *Am J Clin Nutr* 1991; 52:1418.

15. Nyman M, Asp NG, Cummings J, Wiggins H. Fermentation of dietary fibre in the intestinal tract: comparison between man and rat. *Br J Nutr* 1986; 55:487.

Dietary Fiber and Colonic Morphology

Edgar T. Clemens, PhD
Professor of Animal and Veterinary Sciences
Departments of Animal and Veterinary Sciences
University of Nebraska-Lincoln, Lincoln, Nebraska

Introduction

While in the herbiverous diet fiber plays many roles, in non-herbivorous species including humans and the domestic cat and dog, dietary fiber is synonymous with colonic function. It is assumed to be of limited nutritional value and is incorporated in the diet as a means of reducing energy intake, adding bulk, fostering bowel movement, and enhancing colonic health. The health of the bowel is of prime concern for the human population, and perhaps should be of equal concern for the domestic pet. However, fiber is a rather broad term, not limited to a single substance with specific, identifiable characteristics. Rather, fibers are a group of substances with varying qualities. Thus, not all fibers act the same within the bowel.

One might suggest that dietary fiber affects colonic health via two principle mechanisms. First the physical effects of fiber on the mucosal surface, (including the tangible, the distential, and the myo-stimulatory), and secondly, the chemical effects resulting from microbial degradation of the fibers present. This would include those components of nutritive value (short chain fatty acids) and those chemical changes influencing the colonic environment (i.e., pH, osmotic force, water movement, etc). There is, of course, the opportunity for the combined physical and chemical affects, and for these to be united in varying degrees. The source of dietary fiber(s) and their ability to be degraded within the gut define the extent of physical and/or chemical effects and would, by relationships, influence the health of the bowel. This then is the subject of this line of investigation.

Assessment of Intestinal Health

In studying the affects of fiber on colonic health, one is confronted with the question, not only as to assessing the physical and chemical consequence of fiber upon the gut, but more importantly, assessing what is a healthy gut? Is it defined via the absence of pathological occurrence, or anatomical characteristics, or physiological events. Is a thick muscular bowel showing deep prominent crypts, free of exfoliation and rapidly absorbing organic compounds the healthy bowel? Or is it a shallow crypt, covered with mucus, transporting selectively yet possessing considerably energetic potential the healthy one? The researcher accumulates the factual data, while it is the nutritionist, the clinician, and the scientist who must make the subjective assessment. And this is not an easy task.

It is within this context that I present the data, as a philosopher, a scientist not bound by the paradigm of research protocol. Not limited to making statements deemed correct or incorrect by the level of statistical inference, or judged inappropriate by the absence of experimental design. But rather data, information to incorporate within your thought, for you to decide on its validity and worth. Thus, the information on dietary fiber and colonic function in the dog is insight derived from but one group of studies. The knowledge is yet incomplete. The data on dogs has been published in refereed research journals according to proper editorial scrutiny.[1,2] Yet I reserve the right to present insight not limited by research protocol or previous publications[a].

Comparison of Dietary Fibers

Noting then that fiber directly or indirectly affects colonic health, and that the effect(s) may be derived by physical and/or chemical actions and that colonic health is assessed via anatomical characteristics, physiological events and pathological occurrence, studies were designed to compare three principle dietary fibers; i.e., cellulose, beet pulp and a pectin/gum arabic blend (*Table 1*).

TABLE 1. Nutrient analysis (%) of dry extruded canine diets formulated to contain different sources of dietary fiber.

	SOURCE OF FIBER		
	Cellulose	**Beet Pulp**	**Pectin/Arabic**
Crude protein	29.0	29.0	28.3
Nitrogen free extract	30.3	28.6	30.2
Crude fat	21.4	21.8	21.3
Total dietary fiber*	9.5	8.4	8.2
Ash	5.5	6.2	5.4
Moisture	9.0	9.2	10.5

* Diets were formulated to contain 6% supplemental fiber from the various fiber sources. The remaining fiber found in the diets was primarily cellulose and was indigenous to the ingredients used in diet formulation.

The significance of the selection of these dietary fibers is based upon their ability to be degraded within the canine large bowel. Cellulose is typically thought of as being non-degradable (non-fermentable) within the gut of the carnivorous cat and dog. And research results from the University of Illinois clearly suggest this to be true.[3] Thus cellulose possesses a physical effect (bulk, distention, tactical stimuli) but little or no chemical effect. These same researchers have also shown that a pectin/gum arabic blend is rapidly fermented by canine colonic microbes. As such, we might assume that pectin/gum arabic would quickly lose its physical effect, yet attain high chemical effects within the colon. Beet pulp appears to fit nicely as an intermediate fiber source, more slowly degraded by the colonic microbes providing a chemical response, yet not totally degraded, thus retaining some physical properties as well. Hence the selection of fibers tested; cellulose – physical effects; pectin/gum arabic – largely chemical effects; and beet pulp – intermediate (some physical and some chemical properties).

a "Facts; get the facts first and then you can distort them as much as you please." (Mark Twain)

So how then do these fibers compare, and what do they do for the colonic health of the dog or cat? Several reports clearly suggest that fiber adds weight to the bowel.[4-6] Our data would support this observation and further suggest that fermentable fibers (beet pulp and more prominently pectin/gum arabic) adds considerably more weight to the dog colon, than non-fermentable fiber (cellulose) (*Table 2*).

TABLE 2. Body weight and colonic weights of dogs fed the various fiber source.

	SOURCE OF FIBER			
	Cellulose	Beet Pulp	Pectin/Arabic	SE/LSM
Body Weight (kg)	12.5	11.2	13.2	1.23
Colonic Weight (g)	75.6	72.4	88.0	7.44
Colonic Weight/kg Body Weight	6.09[a]	6.52[b]	6.62[b]	0.11

Mean values (n=5) within a row with unlike superscripts are statistically different (P<0.05).
SE/LSM = standard error of the least square mean.

But is that weight due to cellular proliferation, tissue swelling (fluids), increased muscle mass, or alterations in the mucosal surface in terms of shallower/narrower crypts? We must also remember that dietary protein has an effect on colonic weight and structure.[7,8]

Dietary fiber and colonic morphology studies indicate a greater ratio of mucosal surface area to colonic mass [volume] in those animals receiving the fermentable fibers (i.e., beet pulp and pectin/gum arabic) relative to the non-fermentable fiber, cellulose (*Table 3*).

TABLE 3. Colonic mucosal surface-to-volume ratio, and crypt depth and width for dogs fed the various fiber source.

	SOURCE OF FIBER			
	Cellulose	Beet Pulp	Pectin/Arabic	SE/LSM
Surface:Volume (cm^{-1})	.146[a]	.156[b]	.154[b]	.054
Crypt Depth (µm)	702	718	669	28.2
Crypt Width (µm)	69	75	70	3.19

	SEGMENT OF COLON			
	Proximal	Mid	Distal	SE/LSM
Surface:Volume (cm^{-1})	.150	.151	.155	.052
Crypt Depth (µm)	758[a]	697[ab]	647[b]	29.1
Crypt Width (µm)	73	72	68	3.2

Mean values (n=15) within a row with unlike superscripts are statistically different (P<0.0).
SE/LSM = standard error of the least square mean.

Enhanced surface area is suggestive of greater absorption potential. However, the ratio components are of little particular value without a direct, or comparative, measurement of the surface area itself, since a lesser ratio, as observed for animals fed cellulose, may be the result of either less surface area, or of more mass,[9] when compared to the other fibers. While the results are not entirely clear, for the beet pulp diet at least there is evidence of greater surface area resulting from deeper and wider crypts, when compared to cellulose- and pectin/gum arabic-fed animals.

It should be noted, however, that the colon of the dog is morphologically dissimilar from the proximal to distal end. The depths of colonic crypts, and perhaps the width as well, is noticeably greater in the proximal colon than in the more distal segments.[1,10] The surface-to-volume ratio tends to increase distally.[1,10,11] The significance of the morphometric distinction undoubtedly relates to the functional differences associated with various segments of colon and it is important to note that physiological (functional) differences exist along the length of the large bowel as well.[12] Morphometric studies of the dog clearly indicate that the forepart, the proximal colon, has deeper, wider and more well defined crypts than does the more distal segments (*Table 3*), despite the fact that the surface-to-volume ratio is not markedly different. Digesta is retained, via retrograde colonic movements in the forepart of the colon and this is also the region of the bowel where greater bacterial fermentation is occurring.[13]

Subcellular events of the mucosal tissues are of similar importance when defining colonic function and health. In this respect, the DNA content (an indirect measure of cell number and density) of a given unit of colonic mucosa appears to respond to the source of dietary fiber (*Table 4*).

TABLE 4. Colonic mucosal tissue energetics and DNA content for dogs fed the various fiber source.

| | SOURCE OF FIBER | | | |
	Cellulose	Beet Pulp	Pectin/Arabic	SE/LSM
Mucosal Energetics*	.233	.206	.239	.002
Mucosal DNA**	47.4ᵃ	40.4ᵇ	38.4ᵇ	3.09
Mucosal Energy:DNA Ratio	.0047ᵃ	.0052ᵃ	.0062ᵇ	.0004

| | SEGMENT OF COLON | | | |
	Proximal	Mid	Distal	SE/LSM
Mucosal Energetics	.224	.225	.219	.021
Mucosal DNA	40.9	40.3	44.6	3.10
Mucosal Energy:DNA Ratio	.0055	.0056	.0047	.0004

*Mean energetic values expressed as $\mu mol\ O_2 g^{-1} min^{-1}$.
**Mean mucosal DNA values expressed as $\mu g/mg$ of tissue.
ᵃᵇ Values within a row with unlike superscripts are statistically different (P<0.05). SE/LSM = standard error of least square mean.

Significantly greater mucosal DNA values were recorded in those dogs fed the cellulose diet, the non-fermentable fiber, than in tissues from those fed the fermentable fibers (beet pulp or pectin/gum arabic), suggesting greater cell density or smaller cell size. Mucosal cells from dogs fed fermentable fibers trended toward higher energetic values on a constant DNA basis. This response indicates increased colonic cell metabolism in the presence of fermentable fibers.

TABLE 5. Frequency of crypt mucus distension, mucosal epithelial exfoliation, and cryptitis in dogs fed the various fiber source.

	HISTOPATHOLOGIC OBSERVATION		
	Distension	Exfoliation	Cryptitis
Cellulose	10/14 (71.4%)	1/14 (7.1%)	10/14 (71.4%)
Beet Pulp	7/15 (46.7%)	1/15 (6.7%)	3/15 (20.0%)
Pectin/Gum Arabic	8/15 (53.3%)	7/15 (46.7%)	3/15 (20.0%)

Values represent the number of segments with lesions/number of segments examined, and the percent lesions observed.

Gross lesions were not apparent in any of the dogs (*Table 5*). However, histopathological examination of the animals under investigation provided some evidence of physiological concern. Mucus distention of colonic crypts was evident in most animals, yet least prevalent for those fed the beet pulp diet (47%) and most prevalent for cellulose (71%). Such observations are, however, subjective and vary in degree of "distention" and as such are less suited for statistical comparison. Furthermore, the colon is inundated with goblet cell for the defined purpose of producing mucus.[14] Thus, mucus production may be viewed as a healthy response. One might further expect that a non-fermentable fiber with strong physical characteristics might well stimulate greater mucus production, as is seen with the cellulose diet. Thus I would place little importance on the differences observed in mucus distention, and suggest it an appropriate physiological response for physical fibers, cellulose and beet pulp diets. Of greater concern might be the mucus content of the less physical fiber, pectin/gum arabic.

Enterocyte exfoliation, that is the loss of surface cells into the luminal area, was almost nonexistent for the cellulose and for the beet pulp diets. Enterocyte exfoliation may be the result of the abrasive nature of the diet (physical effect) or of rapid cell proliferation (chemical effect). The occurrence of exfoliation for the pectin/gum arabic fed animals approached 50% and may be attributed to rapid cell turnover (remember the DNA:energetic ratio for the pectin/gum arabic colonic cells). Mucus production should reduce the abrasive effects.

Cryptitis, defined in this study as the accumulation of sloughed enterocytes and occasionally neutrophils in the crypt lumen, was observed in 71% of the tissue segments from dogs fed cellulose, and only 20% of tissue from the beet pulp or pectin/gum arabic fed animals. Cryptitis, as observed in this study, is not a gross lesion. However, there is room for interpretation.

The colonic morphology, histopathology and most certainly the mucosal cell density and energetic activity should impact the physiological components of the large bowel. And although colonic functions are much more, we tend to place physiological importance on the colon's ability to regulate fecal consistency (the extremes being diarrheas and impaction) and upon the transport of the principle electrolytes from luminal contents, sodium, and the short chain fatty acids (SCFA): acetate, propionate, and butyrate.

In vivo transport studies suggest greater SCFA absorption for those dogs fed the cellulose diet (*Table* 6) and that the proportion of acetate, propionate, and butyrate transported were similar (*Figure 1*).

TABLE 6. In vivo canine colonic electrolyte flux (mmol/hr) for dogs fed the various fiber sources.

| | SOURCE OF FIBER | | | |
	Cellulose	Beet Pulp	Pectin/Arabic	SE/LSM
Sodium	1.59	2.32	2.18	1.78
Chloride	-0.43	-1.66	-1.03	0.81
Total SCFA*	2.40	1.85	2.08	0.36
Water (ml/hr)	44.90	51.10	46.10	2.70

*Perfusion solution SCFA expressed as mmol/l contained: acetate, 31.3; propionate 29.5; and butyrate, 27.6. Positive values represent net disappearance (apparent absorption) and negative values net appearance (apparent secretion).

Net sodium absorption, on the other hand was considerably less for dogs fed cellulose. The question then arises are the fatty acids and/or sodium absorption the result of conditioning (adaptation) or need (deprivation)? Remembering that colonic organic acids may be absorbed passively down a concentration gradient and not requiring energy, or perhaps sodium, or actively thus requiring energy and most frequently sodium, one might conclude that the rapid, non-selective transport of fatty acids noted for the cellulose diet were the result of need (SCFA deprivation). This would fit well with the understanding that the dogs while on the non-fermentable cellulose diet were receiving minimal SCFA. Tissue deprivation while on the diet resulted in greater transport when offered in the perfusion solution. Using this same line of reasoning it may be concluded that the pectin/gum arabic blend selectively absorbed butyric acid due to greater need. The selectivity in transport for butyrate may be due to colonocyte preference.[16]

In Vivo Colonic Absorption of Acetate, Propionate and Butyrate in Dogs Fed the Various Fiber Source

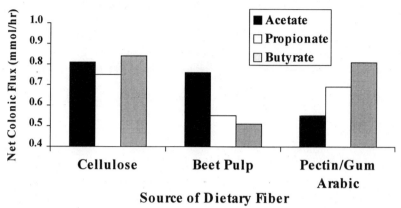

Pooled SE/ LSM = 0.134.
Figure 1.

So which is the better, healthier fiber source: (1) pectin/gum arabic with its increased colonic weight, shallow/narrow crypts, exfoliation, low cell density, high tissue energetics and active/selective transport of butyric acids; (2) cellulose with less colonic weight, reduced surface area ratio, shallow crypts, increased cryptitis, high cell density, low tissue energetics and passive/unselective and rapid fatty acid transport; or (3) beet pulp resulting in increased colonic weight and surface area ratio, deep/wide colonic crypts, modest cell density, low tissue energetics, and active/selective and moderate fatty acid absorption (*Table 7*)?

TABLE 7. Colonic response to various fiber sources.

	RESPONSE TO		
Parameter	Cellulose	Beet Pulp	Pectin/Arabic
Increased colonic weight		✔	✔
Deep, wide colonic crypts		✔	
Absence of cryptitis		✔	
Low exfoliation	✔	✔	
Moderate cell density		✔	
Mucosal tissue energetic	Low	Moderate	High
Fatty Acid Absorption			
Active/Selective		✔	✔
Rate	Rapid	Moderate	Moderate
Increased surface area ratio		✔	✔

References

1. Hallman JE, Moxley RA, Reinhart GA, Wallace EA, Clemens ET. Cellulose, beet pulp and pectin/gum arabic effects on canine colonic microstructure and histopathology. *Vet Clin Nutr* 1995; 2:137-142.

2. Hallman JE, Reinhart GA, Wallace EA, Milliken A, Clemens ET. Colonic mucosal tissue energetics and electrolyte transport in dogs fed cellulose, beet pulp or pectin/gum arabic as their primary fiber source. *Nutr Res* 1996; 16:(February Issue).

3. Sunvold GD, Fahey GC, Merchen NR. Dietary fiber for dogs: IV. In vitro fermentation of selected fiber sources by dog fecal inoculum and in vivo digestion and metabolism of diets containing selected fiber sources and their blends. *J Anim Sci* 1995; 73:1099-1109.

4. Addis T. Hypertrophy of the gastro-intestinal tract and high residue diets. *Am J Physiol* 1932; 99:417-423.

5. Rompala RE, Hoagland TA, Meister JA. Effect of dietary bulk on organ mass, fasting heat production and metabolism of the small and large intestines in sheep. *J Nutr* 1988; 118:1553-1557.

6. Burrin DG, Ferrell CL, Britton RA, Bauer M. Level of nutrition and visceral organ size and metabolic activity in sheep. *Br J Nutr* 1990; 64:439-448.

7. Dobesh GD, Clemens ET. Effect of dietary protein on porcine colonic microstructure and function. *Am J Vet Res* 1987; 48:862-865.

8. Dobesh GD, Clemens ET. Nutritional impact on the canine colonic microstructure and function. *Nutr Res* 1988; 8:625-633.

9. Hart IR, Kidder DE. The quantitative assessment of normal canine small intestinal mucosa. *Res Vet Sci* 1978; 25:157-162.

10. Hallman JE, Wallace EA, Clemens ET. Protein source and their effects upon canine colonic morphology and mucosal energetics. *Nutr Res* 1993; 13:1273-1281.

11. Zalesky AA, Rainforth LA, Clemens ET. The effects of dietary protein on the canine colonic microstructure and mucosal energetics. *Nutr Res* 1992; 12:259-264.

12. Stevens CE, Argenzio RA, Clemens ET. Microbial digestion: rumen versus large intestine. In: Ruchebusch Y, ed. *Digestive Physiology and Metabolism in Ruminants. Fifth International Symposium on Ruminant Physiology.* 1979.

13. Banta CA, Clemens ET, Krinsky MM, Sheffy BE. Sites of organic acid production and patterns of digesta movement in the gastrointestinal tract of dogs. *J Nutr* 1979; 109:1592-1600.

14. Junqueira LC, Carneiro J *Basic Histology.* Lange Medical Publications 1971.

15. Argenzio RA. Physiology of diarrhea - large intestine. *JAVMA* 1978; 173:667-672.

16. Kripke SA, Fox AD, Berman JM, Settle RG, Rombeau JL. Stimulation of intestinal mucosal growth with intracolonic infusion of short-chain fatty acids. *J Parent Enter Nutr* 1989; 13:109-116.

Physiological Response to Short Chain Fatty Acid Production in the Intestine

Monty S. Kerley, PhD
Associate Professor, Department of Animal Science
College of Agriculture, University of Missouri, Columbia, Missouri

Gregory D. Sunvold, PhD
Research and Development, The Iams Company, Lewisburg, Ohio

Introduction

Short chain fatty acids (SCFA) is a collective term that refers to acetic, propionic and butyric acids. SCFA are produced from anaerobic bacterial fermentation in the intestine. Our knowledge regarding the bacterial production and the cellular catabolism of SCFA has been derived primarily from rumen fermentation research. Research with nonruminant species has intensified as the physiological effects induced by SCFA have been discovered. Recent reviews[1-2] provide excellent discussions of SCFA research from the past to the present. SCFA production from various dietary fiber sources can be predicted by an in vitro fermentation system.[2] The known physiological responses elicited by SCFA, which are important to intestinal health of the dog and cat will be discussed in this paper.

SCFA are produced from the bacterial fermentation of fiber (polysaccharides constructed by beta glycosidic bonds) and resistant starch. The type of fiber, determined by monosaccharide composition, structure and degree of polymerization, can influence the predominant species of bacteria present, the relative proportion of the SCFA produced, production rate, and the site in the gut that SCFA production occurs. Herbivores use the SCFA as a metabolic energy source. SCFA also have a myriad of other functions in the animal. The presence of SCFA in the gut inhibit pathogenic bacterial colonization, stimulate motility and secretory responses, increase intestinal blood flow, enhance ion absorption and increase epithelial mucosal cell proliferation. Therefore, the nutritional objective in formulating the fiber component of diets is to achieve SCFA production in the various segments of the gut to maintain intestinal health. This can be achieved by providing fiber sources that are readily fermentable and which help maintain the proper intestinal microbial population.

Intestinal Pathogen Reduction

The maintenance of beneficial indigenous bacterial populations is recognized as important to prevent overgrowth of pathogenic bacteria in the intestine. The benefits provided by the indigenous bacterial population are derived from the production of SCFA as well as direct inhibition of pathogen colonization of the gut. The addition of SCFA have been demonstrated to inhibit growth of pathogenic bacteria.[3-4] The presence of *Lactobacilli*, colonized onto the ileal mucosa, was demonstrated to prevent pathogenic *E. coli* from attaching to the mucosal cells. Mechanistically, *Lactobacilli* produce a proteinaceous component which, combined with mucus components, prevent the adhesion of the K88 fimbrae to the epithelial cells in the ileum.[5]

Our laboratory has demonstrated that feeding fructooligosaccharides (FOS) to hamsters will prevent *Clostridium difficile* infection and *E. coli* infection in the piglet. We propose the mechanism that achieves this protection is a function of the concomitant increase in *Bifidobacteria* spp. populations. These studies demonstrate that indigenous bacteria control pathogen growth by several mechanisms. The inference we have made is that the most nutritionally effective fiber substrates/ combinations are those that select for beneficial bacterial species as well as promote SCFA production throughout the intestine. Other recent works provide further evidence of the mode of action of the influence of a novel fiber source, FOS, on the population of intestinal bacteria.[6-7]

Gut Motility

SCFA have been demonstrated to effect gut motility dependent upon location in the gut. The ileum and large intestine would both be expected to have sufficiently high SCFA concentrations to elicit smooth muscle effects. Administration of SCFA into the ileum of dogs increased peristaltic contractions and decreased transit time and emptying from the ileum.[8-10] The contraction stimulation is increased as SCFA chain length is decreased (acetic > propionic > butyric acids) and is concentration dependent in the ileum.[8] The effects in the ileum are not carried to the upper small intestine.

Although the stimulatory effects of SCFA in the colon have not been completely elucidated,[11] physiological and elevated SCFA concentrations appear to be inhibitory to colonic contractions. The stimulation of the ileum and lack of stimulation to the colon may prevent colo-ileal reflux. The increased dilution from the ileum stimulated by SCFA would also increase dilution from the ileum, preventing overgrowth of potentially toxic bacteria. Three hypothetical mechanisms by which SCFA stimulate intestinal contraction have been proposed:[11] (1) SCFA could elicit nervous reflexes by activating chemosensitive receptors connected to either vagal nerves or myenteric neurons, (2) regulatory peptides could be released by SCFA, exerting a motor effect; and (3) SCFA could act directly on smooth muscle tone.

While the reasons for these effects of SCFA on intestinal motility are not clear, two possible explanations exist. Increased motility of the small intestine with high amounts of SCFA would encourage emptying of small intestinal contents into the large intestine, thus preventing excessive amounts of fermentation from occurring in the ileum of the small intestine. In contrast, the lack of SCFA causing increased motility in the large intestine would enable the body to absorb and utilize SCFA as a metabolic energy source.

Instillation of SCFA into the colon of dogs increased colonic blood flow.[12] Dogs used in this experiment were denervated leading to the conclusion that neural reflexes do not appear plausible as an initiating mechanism responsible for increased blood flow. Others demonstrated that SCFA cause a relaxation of the resistance arteries at the colon.[13] This is one plausible mechanism by which SCFA can increase blood flow to the intestine. A second potential reason is that increased SCFA absorption results in increased intestinal metabolic activity which elicits increased blood flow.

The combined responses of SCFA to increase blood flow and regulate intestinal motility may act in concert to facilitate their absorption. It is probable that physiological SCFA concentrations are necessary to elicit blood flow responses.[13] Thus, the presence of SCFA in the lumen appears to facilitate SCFA absorption through altered motility and blood flow.

The presence of SCFA in the colon appear to prevent diarrhea by implementing ion (sodium) absorption and by factors surrounding SCFA production (i.e., maintenance of a beneficial indigenous microflora). The absorption of SCFA enhances sodium absorption.[14-15] Butyric acid administration to denervated colonic loops has also been shown to be necessary for sodium absorption.[15] In the absence of butyric acid, colonic mucosa changed from net absorption to net secretion of sodium. The mechanism by which SCFA cause sodium absorption was not elucidated, but SCFA were necessary for sodium removal from the colonic lumen. Prevention of osmotically induced diarrhea is achieved by maintenance of SCFA concentrations in the colon.

Factors that surround the production of SCFA by fermentation are at least as important in prevention of diarrhea as the effect of SCFA on ion absorption. The delivery of fermentable substrate to the large intestine results in bacterial growth and the subsequent production of SCFA. The SCFA are toxic to a wide range of pathogens. Therefore, diets which promote intestinal fermentation guarantee SCFA production and protection against these pathogens. The dietary substrate which promotes bacterial fermentation is also important. The fermentable substrate should help predispose the colonization of beneficial indigenous bacteria.[16] Unidentified products synthesized by *Lactobacillus* spp. have been demonstrated to inhibit *E. coli* K88ab strain G1108E and *E. coli* K88ac strain 1107 adhesion to ileal mucus.[5] Therefore, dietary fiber substrates should be selected on their ability to not only promote SCFA production but also their ability to create a niche environment promoting population growth of beneficial bacterial species.

SCFA have been shown to modulate epithelial cell proliferation.[17] The in vitro and in vivo effects of butyric acid in arresting cell proliferation, altering cell morphology and ultrastructure and altering gene expression have been summarized.[18] Butyric acid inhibited histone deacetylases, resulting in hyperacetylation of histones[18] and this has been suggested as a possible mechanism of action of butyric acid on cell proliferation. Others have demonstrated that continuous infusion of SCFA or butyrate at physiological levels increased mucosal DNA in jejenum and proximal colon epithelium.[19] Likewise, the dose-dependent stimulatory effect of SCFA on epithelial cell production rate in the jejenum and distal colon have been evaluated with the order of effectiveness being greatest for butyric acid and least for acetic acid.[20]

The proliferative activity of SCFA is important to epithelial cells in the small and large intestine. Rats infused in the proximal colon with a physiological mix of SCFA had statistically increased mucosal RNA and numerically increased mucosal weight in the ileum.[19] Thus, SCFA have proliferative effects beyond the gut regions of SCFA production that are modulated by indirect means. Research by various groups indicates that the mechanism for this may involve a relationship between SCFA and endogenous hormones. Sheep pancreatic islets released insulin from a SCFA stimulus.[21] Enteroglucagon or intestinal PYY may be the mediators for the trophic action of SCFA in species that SCFA do not stimulate insulin release.[22] SCFA have been shown to stimulate epithelial cell proliferation in the large intestine of fasted rats via the autonomic nervous system.[23] Research has demonstrated that SCFA, with butyrate having the greatest potency, are important in the proliferation and differentiation of the intestinal epithelial mucosa. Thus, SCFA are directly responsible for modulating intestinal health.

Intestinal
Cell
Metabolism

Intestinal cell proliferation in the presence of SCFA is probably due to an increased availability of an energy substrate. A well documented influence of SCFA is their ability to be metabolized by colonocytes. The preferred energy source of colonocytes in rats was as follows: butyrate > acetoacetate > glutamine > glucose.[24] Other experiments with rats, sheep and humans have confirmed the observation that SCFA are utilized as an energy source by colonocytes.[25-28] Thus, SCFA provide a luminal source of energy to intestinal cells. This information indicates a direct effect of SCFA on intestinal health. The physiological role of SCFA may be even more important during disease states. For example, studies of human patients with ulcerative colitis and others without evidence of intestinal disease revealed that impaired butyrate oxidation occurred in the individuals with ulcerative colitis.[27] These results suggest an increased demand for butyrate by intestinal cells during a specific disease state.

Intestinal
Health and
Fiber

Intestinal health is dependent upon the maintenance of beneficial indigenous bacterial populations and a functional, absorptive intestinal epithelium. The SCFA play a major physiological role in these two functions. To promote intestinal health, fiber substrates should be selected that promote SCFA production and dominance of beneficial bacterial populations.

Our laboratory conducted research with soluble oligosaccharides (xylooligosaccharides and fructooligosaccharides) that had been shown to promote *Bifidobacteria* growth.[29-30] *Bifidobacteria* have been suggested to cause decreased illness of humans and suppressed growth of pathogenic and putrefactive bacteria.[31-33] Our research identified fructooligosaccharides as being *Bifidogenic*. Xylooligosaccharides and fructooligosaccharides had differing effects on intestinal epithelial parameters (crypt depth, labelling index) dependent on gut location (cecum vs distal colon) in rodents fed an elemental diet.[34] In a similar study with a pig model, fructooligosaccharides enhanced *Bifidobacteria* populations and prevented intestinal epithelia atrophy when elemental diets were fed.[35] Our laboratory has also found that feeding fructooligosaccharides will improve nitrogen retention, prevent infection by *Clostridium difficile* and *E. coli*, and reduce odor metabolite excretion (unpublished data). Increased excretion of nitrogen through the feces can also be achieved, by feeding fermentable fiber.

The physiological functions of SCFA are numerous. These functions are responsible in large part for maintenance of intestinal health. The nutritional objective in selecting dietary fibers should be to select those which predispose the colonization of beneficial indigenous microflora and promote an SCFA production rate that improves intestinal epithelia health by stimulating cell proliferation and differentiation. Future research with dogs and cats should be directed at identifying dietary fiber substrates that achieve these objectives at locations throughout the gut. Additionally, research which confirms or refutes theories regarding the physiological impact of SCFA would further our knowledge of dog and cat nutrition.

References

1. Wrong OM. Definitions and history. In: *Physiological and Clinical Aspects of Short-Chain Fatty Acids.* (ed. JH Cummings, JL Rombeau, T Sakata). Cambridge, England: Cambridge University Press. 1995:1-14.

2. Reinhart GA. In vivo fermentation as a predictor of in vivo fiber utilization. In: *Recent Advances in Canine and Feline Nutritional Research: Proceedings of the 1996 Iams International Nutrition Symposium.* Wilmington, OH: Orange Frazer Press. 1996.

3. Van der Wal P. Salmonella control of feedstuffs by pelleting or acid treatment. *Zootechnia* 1980; Nov:28.

4. Izat AL, Tidwell NM, Thomas RA, Reiber MA, Adams MH, Colberg M, Waldroup PW. Effects of a buffered propionic acid in diets on the performance of broiler chicks and on microflora of the intestine and carcass. *Poultry Sci* 1990; 69:818.

5. Blomberg L, Henriksson A, Conway PL. Inhibition of adhesion of *Escherichia coli* K88 to piglet ileal mucus by *Lactobacillus* spp. *Appl Environ Micro* 1993; 59:34.

6. Brown D. Applications of FOS in human foods. In: *Recent Advances in Canine and Feline Nutritional Research: Proceedings of the 1996 Iams International Nutrition Symposium.* Wilmington, OH: Orange Frazer Press. 1996.

7. Willard M. Effects of dietary FOS supplementation on canine small

intestinal bacterial populations. In: *Recent Advances in Canine and Feline Nutritional Research: Proceedings of the 1996 Iams International Nutrition Symposium.* Wilmington, OH: Orange Frazer Press. 1996.

8. Kamath PS, Hoepfner MT, Phillips SF. Short-chain fatty acids stimulate motility of the canine ileum. *Am J Physiol* 1987; 253:G427.

9. Kamath PS, Phillips SF, Zinsmeister AR. Short-chain fatty acids stimulate ileal motility in humans. *Gastroent* 1988; 95:1496.

10. Fich A, Phillips SF, Hakim NS, Brown ML, Zinsmeister AR. Stimulation of ileal emptying by short-chain fatty acids. *Dig Dis Sci* 1989; 34:1516.

11. Cherbut C. Effects of short-chain fatty acids on gastrointestinal motility. In: *Physiological and Clinical Aspects of Short-Chain Fatty Acids.* Cambridge, England: Cambridge University Press. 1995:191-208.

12. Kvietys PR, Granger DN. Effect of volatile fatty acids on blood flow and oxygen uptake by the dog colon. *Gastroenterology* 1981; 80:962.

13. Mortensen FV, Nielsen H. In vivo and in vitro effects of short-chain fatty acids on intestinal blood circulation. In *Physiological and Clinical Aspects of Short-Chain Fatty Acids* (ed. J.H. Cummings, J.L. Rombeau and T. Sakata). Cambridge, England: Cambridge University Press. 1995:391-400.

14. Roediger WEW, Moore A. Effect of short-chain fatty acid on sodium absorption in isolated human colon perfused through the vascular bed. *Dig Dis Sci* 1981;26:100.

15. Roediger WEW, Rae DA. Trophic effect of short chain fatty acids on mucosal handling of ions by the dysfunctional colon. *Brit J Surg* 1982; 69:23.

16. Macfarlane GT, Gibson GR. Bacterial infections and diarrhea. In: *Human Colonic Bacteria: Role in Nutrition, Physiology, and Pathology* (ed. G.R. Gibson and G.T. Macfarlane) Boca Raton, FL: CRC Press. 1995:201-226.

17. Kruh J. Effects of sodium butyrate, a new pharmacological agent, on cells in culture. *Molecular Cell Biochem* 1992; 42:65.

18. Vidali G, Boffa LC, Bradbury EM, Allfrey VG. Butyrate suppression of histone deactylation leads to accumulation of multiacetylated forms of histone H3 and H4 and increased DNase I sensitivity of the associated DNA sequences. *Proc Natl Acad Sci. USA.* 1978; 75:2239.

19. Kripke SA, Fox DA, Berman JM, Settle RG, Rombeau JL. Stimulation of intestinal mucosal growth with intracolonic infusion of short-chain fatty acids. *J Parent Enter Nutr* 1989; 13:109.

20. Sakata T. Stimulatory effect of short-chain fatty acids on epithelial cell proliferation in the rat intestine: a possible explanation for trophic effect of fermentable fibre, gut microbes and luminal trophic factors. *Br J Nutr* 1987; 58:95.

21. Mannis JG, Boda JM. Insulin release by acetate, propionate, butyrate and glucose in lambs and adult sheep. *Sm J Physiol* 1967; 212:756.

22. Goodlad RA, Lenton W, Ghatei MA, Adrian TE, Bloom SR, Wright NA. Proliferative effects of fibre on the intestinal epithelium: Relationship to gastrin, enteroglucagon and PYY. *Gut* 1987; 28:221.

23. Sakata T, von Engelhardt W. Stimulatory effect of short chain fatty acids on the epithelial cell proliferation in rat large intestine. *Comp Biochem Physiol* 1993; 74:459.

24. Roediger WEW. Utilization of nutrients by isolated epithelial cells of the rat colon. Gastroenterology 1982; 83:424.

25. Baldwin RL, Jesse VI, Jesse BW. Developmental changes in glucose and butyrate metabolism by isolated sheep ruminal cells. *J Nutr* 1992; 122:1149.

26. Beaulieu KE, McBurney MI. Supplemental dietary fiber increases substrate oxidation in isolated rat colonocytes. *FASEB J* 1994; 8:A811(Abstr.).

27. Chapman MAS, Grahn MF, Boyle MA, Hutton M, Rogers J, Williams NS. Butyrate oxidation is impaired in the colonic mucosa of sufferers of quiescent ulcerative colitis. *Gut* 1994; 35:73.

28. Clausen MR, Mortensen PB. Kinetic studies on the metabolism of short-chain fatty acids and glucose by isolated rat colonocytes. *Gastroenterology* 1994; 106:423.

29. Mitsuoka T, Hidaka H, Eida T. Effect of fructooligosaccharides on intestinal microflora. *Die Nahrung* 1987; 31:927.

30. Okazaki M, Fujikawa S, Matumoto N. Effect of xyloogligosaccharide on the growth of bifidobacteria. *Bifidobateria Microflora* 1990; 9:77.

31. Hidaka H, Eida T, Takizawa T, Tokunaga T, Tashiro Y. Effects of fructooligosaccharides on intestinal flora and human health. *Bifidobacteria Microflora* 1986; 5:37-50.

32. Hidaka H, Tashiro Y, Eida T. Proliferation of bifidobacteria by oligosaccharides and their useful effect on human health. *Bifidobacteria Microflora* 1991; 10:65.

33. Homma N. Bifidobacteria as a resistance factor in human beings. *Bifidobacteria Microflora* 1988; 7:35.

34. Howard MD, Gordon DT, Garleb KA, Kerley MS. Dietary fructooligosacharide, xyloogilosaccharide and gum arabic have variable effects on cecal and colonic microbiota and epithelial cell proliferation in mice and rats. *J Nutr* 1995; 125:2604.

35. Howard MD, Gordon DT, Pace LW, Garleb KA, Kerley MS. Effects of dietary supplementation with fructooligosaccharides on colonic microbiota populations and epithelial cell proliferation in neonatal pigs. *J Ped Gastro Nutr* 1995; in press.

Applications of Fructooligosaccharides in Human Foods

Douglass H. Brown
Vice President and General Manager
Golden Technologies, Inc., Johnstown, Colorado

NutraFlora™ FOS is a product being introduced into the human food supply in the United States by Golden Technologies (see structure of FOS, *Figure 1*). In the early 1980's a Japanese pharmaceutical and confectionery company, Meiji Seika Kaisha, began an investigation of a group of people in Japan that seemed to have a much better level of intestinal health than the general population. Characterization of their diet showed that they consumed larger quantities of fructooligosaccharides of the type in Figure 1 than the overall Japanese population.

Development and History of Fructo-oligosaccharides (FOS) Use

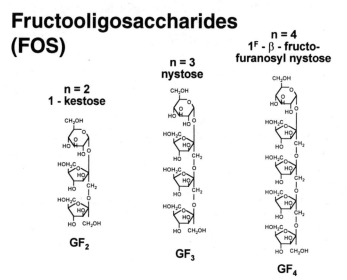

Fructooligosaccharides (FOS)

n = 2
1 - kestose
GF₂

n = 3
nystose
GF₃

n = 4
1ᶠ - β - fructo-furanosyl nystose
GF₄

Figure 1.

Meiji Seika developed a manufacturing process utilizing fermentation of sucrose with *Aspergillis niger*. A fructofuranosyl transferase enzyme ferments sucrose to the desired end product. The bonds formed between the sugar molecules are beta bonds and thus cannot be broken by mammalian digestive enzymes. Therefore, FOS is, by definition, a fiber and passes through the digestive tract into the large intestine where it is selectively utilized by beneficial bacteria, specifically *Bifidobacteria* and *Lactobacilli*.

FOS naturally occurs in banana, tomato, onion, garlic, and other common fruits, vegetables, and grains. Since the concentration of FOS in naturally-occurring sources is low, the consumption of these sources to attain a physiologically beneficial response from FOS is virtually impossible. Therefore, supplementation is necessary.

Japanese regulatory authorities have approved this product under their functional foods regulations and FOS under the trade name "neosugar." It is found in over 500 products in Japan ranging from confections to soft drinks. More research is now available on FOS and data are rapidly accumulating, showing the positive impact on gastrointestinal health, resulting from regular consumption in the human diet. Due to the widespread use of FOS in Japan and new exciting data, substantial interest in FOS has developed in the U.S. both for humans and companion animals.

The use of FOS in both human and animal markets is likely to increase for three main reasons, namely: (1) changes in the regulatory environment; (2) the human-companion animal bond; and (3) increased access to educational materials pertaining to health and nutrition of the general population.

Changes in the Regulatory Environment

Recent U.S. regulations pertaining to the use of products such as FOS are changing. Prior to 1994, the ability to market supplements and to make claims regarding potential health effects of those supplements was very restricted. Any claims could result in classification as a drug. There were only a few isolated areas dominated by drug companies like medical foods where there was any relaxation of these standards. Even independent, peer-reviewed university research was defined and viewed as drug claims.

With the passage of the Dietary Supplement Health and Education Act (DSHEA) in October, 1994, a new classification was created under the Food Drug and Cosmetic Act. The Act created a "dietary supplement" category. Key provisions of the act included:

1. Claims of ways in which dietary supplements affect the structure and function of the body may be made as long as they are truthful and not misleading. Specific claims include such things as increasing good bacteria populations, or lowering cholesterol.

2. The requirement for demonstrating safety moved to a standard where the burden of proof is on the FDA to demonstrate a dietary supplement is *not* safe.

3. Labeling standards were modified such that journal articles and other scientifically valid claims could be utilized as justification and efficacy.

In addition to U.S. regulation, Japanese regulators have moved forward with their new classification of functional foods. Some European countries also seem to be moving toward allowing more claims for foods and dietary supplements.

The relationship between people and their pets is changing. People view their pets more as a part of the family than "just" a dog or cat. They are more involved with the promotion of their companion's health and well-being in a way that is not unlike their own.

The Human-Companion Animal Bond and Nutritional Awareness

The net result of regulatory activity and shifts in the consumers' perceptions of their pets is an enhanced ability of manufacturers and marketers to communicate the efficacy of their products and dietary supplements. As a result of this improved communication, people will begin asking if those same or similar dietary supplements can be of benefit to their pets. Customers may want their animals to have the same benefits they have received from some dietary supplements. The scientific community and pet food manufacturers will need to identify those products and supplements that have merit and conduct well-designed, scientific studies to support or refute their use for companion animals.

Figure 2[1] shows the increase in *Bifidobacteria* with the ingestion of just one gram per day of NutraFlora FOS in humans. The results of FOS ingestion are dramatic and all of the other benefits flow from this change in microflora composition. Increases in *Bifidobacteria* numbers change the overall ecology of the intestine and lowers intestinal pH (*Figure 3*[2]). This results in reduced levels of enteric bacteria such as *Clostriduim perfringens* and lower levels of compounds such as indole and skatole. These putrefactive substances are known carcinogens.

Nutritional Benefits of FOS

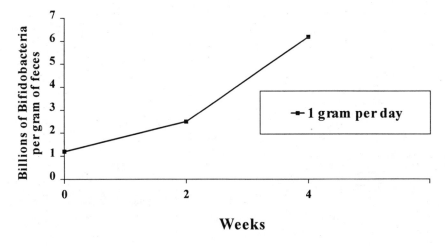

Change in Bifidobacteria with One Gram Per Day NutraFlora (in Humans)

Figure 2.

Changes in Fecal Flora with Increased Age in Humans

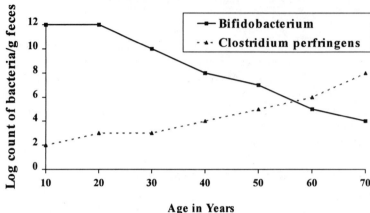

Figure 3.

FOS has positive benefits on normalization of intestinal function. Ingestion of FOS by older patients significantly improved conditions of diarrhea.[1] On the other side, improvement in water retention associated with the use of FOS has been shown to result in improvement in constipation. It has been found that diarrhea induced by antibiotic administration can be reduced in frequency and severity with the establishment of a strong population of beneficial intestinal bacteria.

The results of FOS on serum cholesterol in hyperlipidemic patients has also been evaluated. The ingestion of FOS may have a cholesterol-lowering effect in humans.[3]

Summary   New supplement introductions will have a dramatic effect on the pet food industry. It will further accelerate the segmentation and upscaling of the market. The combination of regulation, people's increasing affections for their pets, and the proliferation of "healthy" supplements will drive increasing specialization of nutrition for companion animals.

NutraFlora is a trademark of Golden Technologies, Inc.

References   1. Hidaka, et al. Effects of fructooligosaccharides on intestinal flora and human health. *Bifidobacteria Microflora* 1986; 5:37-50.

2. Mitsuoka T. Bifidobacteria and their role in human health. *J Ind Microbiol* 1990; 6:263-268.

3. Hidaka, et al. Proliferation bifidobacteria by oligosaccharides and their useful effect on human health. *Bifidobacteria Microflora* 1991; 10:65-79.

Effects of Dietary Fructooligosaccharide (FOS) Supplementation on Canine Small Intestinal Bacterial Populations

Michael D. Willard, DVM, MS, DACVIM
Texas Veterinary Medical Center, Texas A&M University,
College of Veterinary Medicine, College Station, Texas

Introduction

Bacteria inhabiting the intestinal tract have the potential to cause disease in people as well as animals. In some cases, the bacteria responsible for causing disease have various virulence factors that allow them to produce dysfunction in spite of normal host defense mechanisms. *Clostridium perfringens* has been identified as being a major cause of nosocomial, acute, and chronic large bowel diarrhea in dogs[1-3] as well as people.[4-5] *Clostridium difficile*, a major intestinal pathogen of people that is often responsible for antibiotic-associated diarrhea, has recently been implicated as a cause of canine diarrhea.[6-7] Even *Bacteroides fragilis* [8-9] has been implicated as causing diarrhea in lambs and piglets.

However, bacteria residing in the small intestine may also cause alimentary tract dysfunction simply because of their excessive numbers, rather than because they have some virulence factor(s). Canine small intestinal bacterial overgrowth (IBO) is a relatively common and clinically important cause of small intestinal disease in the dog.[10] A patient can probably be predisposed to IBO if it has any of a number of other intestinal diseases which alter host defenses (e.g., inflammatory bowel disease, partial intestinal obstruction due to tumor or stricture) and thereby allow bacteria to persist and reproduce. Recently, defects in the immune system (e.g., IgA-deficiency[11]) have been suggested to be linked to canine IBO. The current belief is that this immune defect allows bacteria that might normally be present in the alimentary tract to persist and ultimately attain inappropriately large concentrations.

Management of the Intestinal Flora

Because bacteria can cause so many important intestinal diseases, it seems reasonable to look for ways to alter or control populations of certain bacteria that reside in the gastrointestinal tract. Altering intestinal bacteria flora can probably best be done either by inhibiting selected species or genera of bacteria by using antimicrobial drugs, or by stimulating certain species or genera by altering the diet of the animal. Antibiotics are, depending upon the situation, often effective. However, they require the owners to administer them and administration of any drug for long times may be associated with side-effects. Therefore it is reasonable to look for other ways to manage intestinal bacteria populations.

Fructooligosaccharides (FOS) are naturally-occurring carbohydrates found in various foods (e.g., onions, garlic, wheat, bananas, etc) which can also be manufactured by applying microbial and/or plant enzymes to sucrose. Although FOS are not digested by mammalian pancreatic or intestinal digestive enzymes,[12-13] many intestinal bacteria can metabolize them. However, as might be expected with almost any carbohydrate source, not all bacteria can metabolize FOS. Those that can are at an advantage when FOS are present as a substrate. *In vitro* studies suggest that most *Bifidobacterium* spp and *Bacteroides* spp can utilize FOS as well as they do glucose, while most *Lactobacillus* spp and *Eubacterium* spp either do not utilize FOS or do not utilize FOS as well as they do glucose.[13] Many *Clostridium* spp are also unable to utilize FOS as well as they do glucose, especially *Clostridium perfringens*. Consequently, it comes as no surprise that *in vivo* studies in people have found that supplementing FOS in the diet is usually associated with significantly increased numbers of fecal *Bifidobacterium* spp[14] while other species of bacteria may be decreased. The increased numbers of *Bifidobacterium* spp which result from feeding FOS may have further effects on other, resident bacteria: *E. coli* and *Clostridium perfringens* have been inhibited in *in vitro* systems by the metabolites of the increased numbers of *Bifidobacterium* spp.[15]

Current Research

The effects of adding such oligosaccharides to the diet have also been studied in dogs, albeit not to the extent that they have in people. Neosugar has been fed to dogs and cats and the effects upon the fecal flora studied.[16] In general, Beagles that were fed a diet supplemented with neosugar (which is a FOS) for 7 weeks had increased numbers of *Lactobacillus* spp per gram of feces (which is contrary to what was reported in *in vitro* studies[13]). There was a tendency for *Bacteroides* to be increased and for enterics and *Staphylococcus* spp to be decreased. *Clostridium perfringens* counts tended to decrease, but this was inconsistent and erratic. Interestingly, *Bifidobacterium* spp were not found in these dogs except in one dog at one culture. In contrast, cats that ate the FOS-supplemented diet had significantly increased numbers of *Bifidobacterium* spp in their stools.[16] Both FOS[17] and lactosucrose[18] have been fed to German Shepherds and the effects studied. The latter study showed that German Shepherds fed a lactosucrose-supplemented diet had increased numbers of *Bifidobacterium* spp and decreased numbers of *Clostridium perfringens* per gram of feces. At the same time, there were decreased fecal concentrations of ammonia, phenol, and butyric acid as well as a subjective finding that the odor of the feces "decreased remarkably".

The former study[17] was performed on German Shepherds. We obtained sixteen clinically healthy, IgA-deficient German Shepherd dogs from four different litters. Each dog had asymptomatic, spontaneous small intestinal bacterial overgrowth. These dogs were randomized into two groups. Both groups were fed the same chicken-based kibble diet for three months before they were cultured for the first time. The diet was composed of 31.4% crude protein, 21.7% ether extract, and 5.77% ash. The amount of food the dogs were given was based upon their body weight. They were fed once daily and allowed to eat free choice until the next morning, when any uneaten food was discarded and fresh food was provided.

Intestinal fluid to be cultured was aspirated from a needle that was inserted into the duodenal lumen during abdominal exploratory surgery. In this manner, we were able to avoid all risk of contamination of the sample with oral contents. Next, duodenal mucosa was obtained by entering the duodenum with a gastroduodeno-scope and taking repeated mucosal samples until we had approximately 0.08-0.1 gm of mucosa. After this first culture, dogs were randomly divided into two groups, one being fed a chicken-based kibble basal diet while the other was fed the same diet but with 1% FOS supplemented at the expense of cornstarch. The FOS source contained 94.1% fructooligosaccharides, 0.5% glucose and fructose, 2.6% sucrose, and 2.8% water and was obtained from a commercial source.

After being fed either the FOS-supplemented diet or the basal diet for approximately 45 days, both groups of dogs were again cultured. We cultured and identified 83 different bacteria. Total numbers of aerobic, facultative anaerobic, and strict anaerobic bacteria were not different in the 2 groups while they were all eating diet A. However, after the dogs were divided into those eating a FOS-supplemented diet and those that were not, the dogs eating the FOS-supplemented diet had fewer aerobic/facultative anaerobic bacteria cultured from their intestinal juice and their intestinal mucosa (*Table 1*). There were no significant differences in the species of bacteria cultured from these two groups of dogs. Therefore, we concluded that the FOS in the diet affected the small intestinal bacterial populations in these dogs.

	Base-line culture		Culture after dogs were fed 2 different diets	
	Group 1 *Base diet*	*Group 2* *Base diet*	*Group 1* *Base diet*	*Group 2* *FOS diet*
Fluid	618,875; 23,900 - 63,245,000	2,171,275; 0 - 53,606,500	5,713,875[*] 24,100 - 13,461,600	1,388,250[*]; 0 - 4,945,000
Tissue	11,875; 0 - 415,000	6,250; 0 - 158,000	99,225[b]; 4,500 - 189,000	16,450[b]; 0 - 169,000

Medians with similar superscripts are different from each other at p = 0.04.
(Adapted from Willard, et al. *Amer J Vet Res* 1994; 55(5):654-659.)

Table 1. Comparison of median number/ml (and range) of aerobic/ facultative anaerobic bacteria grown from duodenal/proximal jejunal juice and the median number/gram from duodenal tissue in 2 groups of German shepherd dogs. Less than 100 bacteria/ml or /gm is denoted by "0" CFU's.[*]

These studies[16-18] document that it is possible to significantly alter the numbers of at least some species of bacteria residing in the canine intestine by changing certain dietary ingredients. However, it does not appear that all animals respond identically to similar dietary modifications. Two areas to investigate in the future are: (1) whether all dogs have essentially the same colonic bacterial flora; and (2) whether the effects of diet (or antimicrobial drugs, for that matter) on the bacteria in the intestinal lumen are the same as the effects on bacteria that live in close apposition to the intestinal mucosa. Regarding the first issue, comparison of two recent reports[16, 18] suggests that *Bifidobacterium* spp were plentiful in one group of animals but almost nonexistent in another. This difference could be due to technique or it could reflect differences in populations in different locations. We need to determine how consistent or inconsistent canine colonic bacterial populations are.

Regarding the concern about bacteria in the intestinal lumen versus those in or on the intestinal mucosa, recent data suggest that at least in some animals there are very different bacterial floras in the intestinal lumen versus the intestinal mucosa.[19] In a recent study we found marked differences in the species of bacteria cultured from the intestinal lumen versus the intestinal mucosa. The fact that the bacteria we cultured were common aerobic/facultative anaerobic bacteria that are relatively easy to grow strengthens the argument that the data are correct (i.e., that there were differences in the species of bacteria cultured in the two sites). If the bacteria had been fastidious anaerobic species, one might argue that technical problems could have been responsible for our not isolating the bacteria from one site or the other.

However, technical problems should not be a major concern with species such as *Pasturella multocida, Staphylococcus xylosus, Proteus mirabilis, Aeromonas liquefaciens,* and others. The implications of finding such a discordance in simultaneous cultures from two "adjacent" sites are noteworthy. First, we must decide if one population of bacteria is more important than another or if they are equally important. Second, we need to eventually examine dogs with small intestinal bacterial overgrowth that are symptomatic for their disease (e.g., diarrhea, weight loss) and see if they have the same dissimilarity of bacterial species in their lumen and mucosa that we found in 16 clinically normal German Shepherds. Culture of small intestinal mucosa has also been performed in humans with IBO. Different investigators have conflicting results about the correlation between bacteria cultured from intestinal fluid versus those cultured from mucosa. However, the most recent study on this technique has found it to be of diagnostic value for IBO.[20] The implication for small animal veterinary medicine is that quantitative culture of canine small intestinal mucosa might not only increase our diagnostic capabilities regarding IBO, but it may also enhance our understanding of this disease process.

1. Kruth SA, Prescott JF, Welch K, Brodsky MH. Nosocomial diarrhea associated with enterotoxigenic *Clostridium perfringens* infection in dogs. *J Am Vet Med Assoc* 1989; 195:331-334.

2. Turk J, Fales W, Miller M, Pace L, Fischer J, Johnson G, Kreeger J, Turnquist ST, Pittman L, Rottinghaus A, Gosser H. Enteric *Clostridium perfringens* infection associated with parvoviral enteritis in dogs: 74 cases (1987-1990). *J Am Vet Med Assoc* 1992; 200:991-994.

3. Twedt DC. *Clostridium perfringens* associated diarrhea in dogs. *Proc Am Coll Vet Int Med* 1993; 11:121-125.

4. Jackson SG, Yip-Chuck DA, Clark JB, Brodsky MH. Diagnostic importance of *Clostridium perfringens* enterotoxin analysis recurring enteritis among elderly, chronic care psychiatric patients. *J Clin Microbiol* 1986; 23:748-751.

5. Larson HE, Borriello SP. Infectious diarrhea due to *Clostridium perfringens*. *J Infect Dis* 1988; 157:390-391.

6. Berry AP, Levett PN. Chronic diarrhea in dogs associated with *Clostridium difficile* infection. *Vet Rec* 1986; 118:102-103.

7. Struble AL, Tang YJ, Kass PH, Gumerlock PH, Madewell BR, Silva J. Fecal shedding of *Clostridium difficile* in dogs: a period prevalence survey in a veterinary medical teaching hospital. *J Vet Diagn Invest* 1994; 6:342-347.

8. Myers LL, Firehammer BD, Shoop DS, Border MM. *Bacteroides fragilis*: a possible cause of acute diarrheal disease in newborn lambs. *Infect Immun* 1984; 44:241-244.

9. Myers LL, Shoop DS, Association of enterotoxigenic *Bacteroides fragilis* with diarrheal disease in young pigs. *Am J Vet Res* 1987; 48:774-775.

10. Rutgers HC, Batt RM, Elwood CM, Lamport A. Small intestinal bacterial overgrowth in dogs with chronic intestinal disease. *J Am Vet Med Assoc* 1995; 206:187-193.

11. Batt RM, Barnes A, Rutgers HC, Carter SD. Relative IgA deficiency and small intestinal bacterial overgrowth in German shepherd dogs. *Res Vet Sci* 1991; 50:106-111.

12. Fishbein L, Kaplan M, Gough M. Fructooligosaccharide: a review. *Vet Hum Toxicol* 1988; 30:104-107.

13. Hidaka H, Hirayama M, Tokunaga T, Eida T, The effects of undigestible fructooligosaccharides on intestinal microflora and various physiological functions on human health. In: *New developments in dietary fiber*, I. Furda et al., eds., New York: Plenum Press 1990:105-117.

14. Gibson GR, Beatty ER, Wang X, Cummings JH. Selective stimulation of bifidobacteria in the human colon by oligofructose and inulin. *Gastroenterology* 1995; 108:975-982.

15. Gibson GR, Wang X. Regulatory effects of bifidobacteria on the growth of other colonic bacteria. *J Appl Bacteriol* 1994; 77:412-420.

16. Ogata M. Use of neosugar in pets. *Proceedings of the 3rd Neosugar Conference* 1986:116.

17. Willard MD, Simpson B, Delles EK, Cohen ND, Kolp D, Fossum TW, Reinhart G. Effects of dietary supplementation of fructo-oligosaccharides on small

intestinal bacterial overgrowth in dogs. *Am J Vet Res* 1994; 55:654-659.

18. Terada A, Hara H, Oishi T, Matsui S, Mitsuoka T, Nakajyo S, Fujimori J, Hara K. Effect of dietary lactosucrose on faecal flora and faecal metabolites of dogs. *Micro Ecol Healt Diseas* 1992; 5:87-92.

19. Delles EK, Willard MD, Simpson RB, Fossum TW, Slater M, Kolp D, Lees GE, Reinhart G. Comparison of species and numbers of bacteria in concurrently cultured samples of proximal small intestinal fluid and endoscopically obtained duodenal mucosa in dogs with intestinal bacterial overgrowth. *Am J Vet Res* 1994; 55:957-964.

20. Riordan SM, Mciver CJ, Duncombe VM, Bolin TD. Bacteriologic analysis of mucosal biopsy specimens for detecting small intestinal bacterial overgrowth. *Scand J Gastroenterol* 1995; 30:681-685.

Neonatal and Reproductive Health

Canine and Feline Reproduction and Neonatal Health: A Nutritional Perspective

Allan J. Lepine, PhD
Research Nutritionist, Research and Development
The Iams Company, Lewisburg, Ohio

The desired outcome of the reproductive process in the dog and cat is the production of a healthy and vigorous litter. However, this "reproductive process" must be recognized to encompass much more than simply accomplishing pregnancy in the bitch or queen. Reproduction can be acknowledged as successfully completed only when the obligatory role of the bitch or queen is concluded following the weaning transition. It is therefore necessary to develop a more comprehensive perspective regarding reproduction and affirm that breeding, gestation, lactation, and neonatal health are all integral constituents determining its success. Accordingly, the objective of this report is to briefly review the critical aspects of this multifaceted physiological process by emphasizing the role of nutrition in optimizing reproductive outcome.

The potential impact of nutrition on reproductive outcome is clearly apparent pursuant to even a cursory review of canine and feline demographics. A total of 523,368 litters and 1,345,941 dogs were reported registered by the American Kennel Club (AKC) during the 1994 calendar year.[1] Although impossible to determine accurately, total litters and number of puppies whelped per year (i.e., purebred and crossbred) in the United States must be substantially higher than the values reported by the AKC based on a total domestic population of 51,972,600 dogs.[2] Furthermore, it is estimated that there are 3.5 million litters totaling approximately 14 million kittens born each year in the United States. These numbers are truly remarkable if viewed from a global perspective and, in conjunction with the relative paucity of data regarding the influence of nutrition on canine and feline reproductive performance and neonatal health, provide a clear directive for the pursuit of innovative nutrition research.

Establishment of innovative research directed towards optimizing reproductive performance and neonatal health requires the identification of physiological principles upon which nutrition may have a beneficial impact. One way in which this fundamental information can be obtained is through the identification of mortality patterns for the puppy and kitten. As with most mammalian species, puppy and kitten mortality figures can be indexed into specific chronological subcategories. These include losses which occur during gestation, parturition, early neonatal life (i.e., less than 2 weeks postnatally), or later neonatal life (i.e., 2 weeks postnatally to weaning).

A primary challenge in evaluating mortality patterns in the puppy and kitten is the relative lack of reliable data, especially regarding embryonic and fetal mortality. Valuable insight can be gained, however, from a brief review of prenatal mortality figures reported for other species. Embryonic and fetal mortality figures generally range from 23 - 38% in swine,[3-6] 19 - 30% in sheep,[7,8] and 16 - 42% in cattle.[9-11] Overall, the majority of reports appear to suggest that prenatal mortality figures of 20-30% are reliable with the variability in the estimate resulting primarily from breed differences and stage of gestation. Although extrapolation of data across species presents obvious interpretational difficulties, the values expressed above are likely to be relatively representative of prenatal mortality rates for the dog and cat and represent an area of potential opportunity regarding the enhancement of reproductive outcome.

Although nutritional influences on embryo and fetal survival have been observed in other species, they have not been investigated in the dog and cat. In addition, nutritional factors necessary to optimize the potential for fertilization must be considered concurrently with any evaluation of prenatal mortality. For example, several nutrients, including zinc, selenium, and vitamin E, have been identified as required for proper spermatogenesis, sperm motility, and morphology.[12-16] Nevertheless, innovative research has only recently been established in the companion animals to investigate the relationship between nutrition and reproductive potential in the male. This issue is addressed in detail by Threlfall in a subsequent manuscript in these proceedings.[17]

Nutritional effects on ovulation rate must likewise be considered as a necessary component of embryo and fetal survival. Elevated nutrient intake during the proestrus to breeding period in swine and sheep has been demonstrated to increase ovulation rate.[18] Although the mechanism(s) for this response remain equivocal at present, several hypotheses have been suggested which may independently or cooperatively regulate this increased ovulation rate. These include an increased leutinizing hormone pulse frequency resulting from a stimulation of the hypothalamic gonadotropin-releasing hormone pulse generator,[18,19] a direct effect of insulin on the ovary which decreases follicular atresia,[20] and(or) a reduced circulating estradiol concentration resulting from increased portal circulation and(or) hepatic mass thereby reducing the negative feedback of estradiol on gonadotropin secretion from the hypothalamus and anterior pituitary.[18] Interestingly, this latter hypothesis may also be responsible for the increased embryonic mortality occasionally reported following an increased intake commensurate with the time of breeding. Increased portal circulation and(or) hepatic mass may enhance the removal of progesterone from the circulation which alters the uterine environment to the detriment of embryo survival. The influence of nutrition on ovulation rate has not been investigated in the bitch or queen but merits consideration given the responses demonstrated in other species.

Following establishment of pregnancy, proper nutrition of the fetus is essential if adequate growth and development is to occur. It is the primary responsibility of the placenta to supply nutrients to and remove metabolic waste products from the growing fetus. Interestingly, growth patterns of the fetus and placenta do not parallel one another closely throughout gestation. In most species, fetal weight increases exponentially throughout gestation resulting in the majority (60 - 70%) of fetal weight accretion to occur during the last trimester. Placental weight likewise increases exponentially throughout gestation but the absolute rate of placental growth is dramatically less than that observed for the fetus.[21-23] The ability of the placenta to maintain nutrient transfer adequate to support fetal growth during late gestation must therefore relate to a mechanism other than simply increased placental mass. Indeed, angiogenesis and increased blood flow in the placenta appear to predominate during the latter stages of gestation. Regulation of this angiogenic process is unclear but mitogens have been isolated from human and ovine placenta, possibly members of the fibroblast growth factor family, which may be involved in increasing placental blood flow.[24] The potential role of maternal nutrition in regulating placental development and function in the dog and cat is unknown at present.

As stated previously, a discussion of the effect of nutrition on the overall reproductive process requires a consideration of breeding, gestation, parturition, and the neonatal period. The preceding discussion has focused on nutritional responses on breeding and gestation. In contrast, parturition is not substantially influenced by nutrition and will therefore not be emphasized here. The remainder of this review will focus on the neonate and the role of nutrition in optimizing health during this critical period.

Neonatal mortality estimates for the puppy and kitten vary considerably with most reports indicating that 15 - 40% of puppies or kittens born alive will die prior to weaning.[25-27] These mortality figures reflect a multi-factorial etiology with congenital abnormalities, disease, environmental challenges, metabolic defects, and nutritional adequacy all contributing to overall mortality. The primary nutritional consideration in this regard is maternal provision of an adequate quantity and quality of mammary secretions. Mammary secretions are essential in maintaining neonatal fluid volume, providing for passive immunity, supplying an optimal nutrient matrix, and providing other non-nutritional, bioactive substances.

Water turnover is extremely high in the neonate thereby necessitating a relatively consistent fluid intake to maintain blood volume. In fact, maintaining hydration in the neonate even takes physiological priority over the provision of metabolic fuels. This is an often overlooked, but extremely consequential function of mammary secretions.

The essentiality of mammary secretions in the establishment of passive immunity reflects the placental structure in both the bitch and queen. Placental transfer of maternal antibodies is inversely related to the number of placental layers across which the antibodies must traverse to reach the fetus (*Table 1*).

Table 1. Placental Type By Species

Placental Type	Tissue Layers	Species
Epitheliochorial	6	Ruminants, Swine, Horse
Syndesmochorial	5	Ruminants
Endothelialchorial	4	Dog, Cat
Hemochorial	3	Human, Monkey
Hemoendothelial	2	Rabbit, Rat, Guinea Pig

Most domestic species (e.g., swine, ruminants, horses) have either syndesmochorial or epitheliochorial placentas consisting of either 5 or 6 layers, respectively, essentially preventing placental antibody transfer. In contrast, the hemochorial placenta (3 tissue layers) in the human and the hemoendothelial placenta (2 tissue layers) in the rat, rabbit, and guinea pig allows passive immunity to be obtained almost exclusively *in utero*. The dog and cat have a endothelialchorial placenta (4 tissue layers) which allows approximately 10 - 20% of the passive immunity to be acquired by the fetus *in utero*. This underscores the importance of the provision of colostral antibodies to the puppy and kitten in the immediate neonatal period. Furthermore, these antibodies must be provided within the initial 24 - 48 hours after birth since the ability of the neonatal intestine to absorb intact proteins is dramatically reduced after this period. This rapid gut closure appears to be hormonally mediated, possibly via increased circulating insulin following nutrient intake.[28]

The essential nature of mammary secretion acquisition by the neonate is also obvious based on the nutrient matrix of this food source. It is perfectly matched to the ontogeny of the digestive enzymes and nutrient transporters within the neonatal gastrointestinal tract and is therefore ideally suited to support neonatal growth. Digestive development and its relationship to nutritional considerations has been evaluated in several species, especially the neonatal pig.[29-33] Intestinal ontogeny, however, has only recently received research attention in the dog and cat. Furthermore, ontological considerations of the gastrointestinal system must be viewed in conjunction with the constantly changing nutrient matrix of the mammary secretions. The important research directives of neonatal intestinal ontogeny and changing milk composition throughout lactation are reviewed in detail by Buddington[34] and Lonnerdal,[35] respectively, elsewhere in these proceedings.

Apart from the nutrients provided by the mammary secretions, a host of non-nutritional factors have been identified as normal components of milk. More than 45 enzymes (*Table 2*)[36] and a number of hormones and growth factors (*Table 3*)[37] have been identified to date in bovine milk, one of the most widely studied mammary secretions. Although it is possible that some of these non-nutritional factors are simply byproducts of milk synthesis and secretion, it is likely that many are biologically active compounds that are involved in growth and development of the nursing neonate. We are only beginning to evaluate the non-nutritional components of dog and cat milk in an effort to understand their role in gastrointestinal and systemic growth of the neonate. The reader is referred to the manuscript authored by White[38] for a review of research efforts directed towards growth factors in dog and cat milk, with special emphasis on the insulin-like growth factors (IGFs) and the IGF binding proteins.

Table 2. Enzymes in Bovine Milk

Amine Oxidase	Alanine AT	Leucine Aminopeptidase
Catalase	Aspartate AT	Lipoprotein Lipase
Dihydrolipoamide DH	α-Amylase	Lysozyme
Glucose-6-phosphate DH	β-Fucosidase	Glucosaminidase
Glutathione Peroxidase	β-Amylase	Plasmin
Isocitrate DH	β-Glucosidase	Ribonuclease
L-Iditol DH	Acid Phosphatase	γ-Glutamyltransferase
Lactate DH	Alkaline Phosphatase	Lactose Synthase
Lactoperoxidase	Arylesterase	UDP Galactosyltransferase
Malate DH	Arylsulfatase	DNA Polymerase
Malic Enzyme	ATPase	Pyrophosphorylase
NADH DH	Carboxylesterase	Rhodanase
Phosphoglucuronate DH	Cholinesterase	Aldolase
Sulfhydryl Oxidase	5'- Nucleotidase	Carbonic Anhydrase
Superoxide Dismutase	G6-Phosphatase	G6P Isomerase
Xanthine Oxidase	Pyrophosphatase	Acetyl-CoA Carboxylase

Adapted from[36]

DH = Dehydrogenase
AT = Aminotransferase

Table 3. Hormones and Growth Factors in Bovine Milk

Hormones

Corticosterone	Thyrotropin-Releasing Hormone
Estradiol	Growth Hormone
Estriol	Prolactin
Estrone	Bombesin
Progesterone	Gastrin
Vitamin D	Insulin
Thyroxine (T3 & T4)	Gastrin
Gonadotropin-Releasing Hormone	Gastrin-Releasing Hormone
Somatostatin	Neurotensin

Growth Factors

Insulin-like growth factor-I	Transforming Growth Factor-α
Insulin-like growth factor-II	Transforming Growth Factor-β
IGF Binding Proteins	Nerve Growth Factor
Epidermal Growth factors	

Adapted from[37]

In conclusion, it is apparent that optimization of the reproductive process necessitates consideration of nutritional influences on breeding, gestation, lactation, and neonatal health. Also obvious is the lack of data regarding these influences for the dog and cat relative to that available for other species. Commitment to innovative research directed to the enhancement of reproduction and neonatal health in the dog and cat is clearly demonstrated by the manuscripts contained within these proceedings.

References

1. 1994 Registration Statistics. *AKC Gazette* April 1995; 37-42.
2. Euromonitor, *The Pet Food Industry* February 1995.
3. Hafez ESE. Nutrition in relation to reproduction in sows. *J Agric Sci* (Cambridge) 1960; 54:170-186.

4. Heap FC, Lodge GA, Lamming GE. The influence of plane of nutrition in early pregnancy on the survival and early development of embryos in the sow. *J Reprod Fertil* 1967; 13:269-277.

5. King JWB, Young GB. Maternal influence in litter size in pigs. *J Agric Sci* 1957; 48:457-463.

6. Knight JW, Bazer FW, Wallace HW. Effect of progesterone induced increase in uterine secretory activity in development of the porcine conceptus. *J Anim Sci* 1974; 38:743-746.

7. Edey TN. Prenatal mortality in sheep: a review. *Anim Breed Abstr* 1969; 37:173-190.

8. Quinlivan TD, Martin CA, Taylor WB, Cairney IM. Estimates of pre- and perinatal mortality in the New Zealand Romney Marsh ewe. *J Reprod Fertil* 1966; 11:379-390.

9. Ayalon N. A review of embryonic mortality in cattle. *J Reprod Fertil* 1978; 54:483-493.

10. Diskin MG, Sreenan JM. Fertilization and embryonic mortality rates in beef heifers after artificial insemination. *J Reprod Fertil* 1980; 59:463-468.

11. Maurer RR, Chenault JR. Fertilization failure and embryonic mortality in parous and nonparous beef cattle. *J Anim Sci* 1983; 56:1186-1189.

12. Ashizawa K, Ozowa K, Okauchi K. Comparative studies of elemental composition of ejaculated fowl, bull, rat, dog and boar spermatozoa by electron probe x-ray microanalysis. *Comp Biochem Physiol* 1987; 88A:269-272.

13. Blesbois E, Mauger I. Zinc content of fowl seminal plasma and its effects on spermatozoa after storage at 4°C. *Br Poult Sci* 1989; 30:677-686.

14. Clapper DL, Davis JA, Lamothe PJ, Patton C, Epel D. Involvement of zinc in regulation of pH, motility, and acrosome reactions in sea urchin sperm. *J Cell Biol* 1985; 100:1817-1824.

15. Marin-Guzman J, Mahan DC, Jones LS, Pate JL. Efficacy of dietary selenium and vitamin E on semen quality of boars. *J Anim Sci* 1988; 66(1):142.

16. Marin-Guzman J, Mahan DC, Whitmoyer RE. Effect of selenium and vitamin E on the ultrastructure of boar spermatozoa. *J Anim Sci* 1988; 66(1):327.

17. Threlfall, WR. Influence of diet on sperm quality and quantity. *Recent Advances in Canine and Feline Nutritional Research: Proceedings of the 1996 Iams International Nutrition Symposium.* Wilmington: Orange Frazer Press; 1996.

18. Ashworth CH. Nutritional factors related to embryonic mortality. In: Zavy and Geisert (Eds), *Embryonic Mortality in Domestic Species*. Boca Raton: CRC Press Inc. 1994; 179-194.

19. Flowers B, Martin MJ, Cantley TC, Day BN. Endocrine changes associated with a dietary-induced increase in ovulation rate (flushing) in gilts. *J Anim Sci* 1989; 67:771-778.

20. May JV, Schomberg DW. Granulosa cell differentiation in vitro. Effect of insulin on growth and functional integrity. *Biol Reprod* 1981; 25:421-431.

21. Ibsen HL. Prenatal growth in guinea-pigs with special reference to environmental factors affecting weight at birth. *J Exp Zool* 1928; 51:51-57.

22. Reynolds LP, Millaway DS, Kirsch JD, Infeld JE, Redmer DA. Growth and in vitro metabolism of placental tissues of cows from day 100 to day 250 of gesta-

tion. *J Reprod Fertil* 1990; 83:213-218.

23. Warwick BL. Prenatal growth of swine. *J Morphol Physiol* 1928; 46:59-63.

24. Reynolds LP, Redmer DA. Utero-placental vascular development and placental function. *J Anim Sci* 1995; 1839-1851.

25. Hoskins JD. Puppy and kitten losses. In: J.D. Hoskins (Ed.), *Veterinary Pediatrics. Dogs and Cats From Birth to Six Months*. Philadelphia: W.B. Saunders Co. 1995; 51-55.

26. Lawler DF, Monti KL. Morbidity and mortality in neonatal kittens. *Am J Vet Res* 1984; 45:1455-1459.

27. Norsworthy GD. Kitten mortality complex. *Feline Prac* 1979; 9:57-60.

28. Donovan SM, Odle J. Growth factors in milk as mediators of infant development. *Annu Rev Nutr* 1994; 14:147-167.

29. Buddington RK. Intestinal transport during ontogeny of vertebrates. *Am J Physiol* 1992; 32:R503-R509.

30. Kelly D, Smyth JA, McCracken KJ. Digestive development of the early-weaned pig. 1. Effect of continuous nutrient supply on the development of the digestive tract and on changes in digestive enzyme activity during the first week post-weaning. *Br J Nutr* 1991; 65:169-180.

31. Kelly D, Smyth JA, McCracken KJ. Digestive development of the early-weaned pig. 2. Effect of level of food intake on digestive enzyme activity during the immediate post-weaning period. *Br J Nutr* 1991; 65:181-188.

32. Pierzynowski SG, Westrom BR, Svendsen J, Karlsson BW. Development of exocrine pancreas function in chronically cannulated pigs during 1-13 weeks of postnatal life. *J Ped Gast Nutr* 1990; 10:206-212.

33. Puchal AA, Buddington RK. Postnatal development of monosaccharide transport in the pig intestine. *Am J Physiol* 1992; 262:G895-G902.

34. Buddington RK. Structure and functions of the dog and cat intestine. *Recent Advances in Canine and Feline Nutritional Research: Proceedings of the 1996 Iams International Nutrition Symposium*. Wilmington: Orange Frazer Press; 1996.

35. Lönnerdal B. Lactation in the dog and cat. *Recent Advances in Canine and Feline Nutritional Research: Proceedings of the 1996 Iams International Nutrition Symposium*. Wilmington: Orange Frazer Press; 1996.

36. Swaisgood HE. Enzymes indigenous to bovine milk. In: R.G. Jensen (Ed.), *Handbook of Milk Composition*. New York: Academic Press. 1995; 472-476.

37. Campana WM, Baumrucker CR. Hormones and growth factors in bovine milk. In: R.G. Jensen (Ed.), *Handbook of Milk Composition*. New York: Academic Press. 1995; 476-494.

38. White ME. The role of growth factors in canine and feline milk. *Recent Advances in Canine and Feline Nutritional Research: Proceedings of the 1996 Iams International Nutrition Symposium*. Wilmington: Orange Frazer Press; 1996.

Structure and Functions
of the Dog and Cat Intestine

Randal K. Buddington, PhD
Associate Professor, Department of Biological Sciences
Mississippi State University, Mississippi State, Mississippi

Introduction

A central issue in nutrition research is the influence of diet on growth and development. This issue is particularly evident for the developing vertebrate intestine as it is faced with qualitative and quantitative changes in dietary inputs that impose different functional demands. Perhaps the most dramatic are those at birth when mammals shift from obtaining nutrients via the placenta to complete dependence on the intestine for processing milk and other external foods. Changes in functional demands occur again at weaning, when mammals shift from milk to the adult diet, which tends to be harder to digest and more variable in composition. Overlying the age-related changes in diet composition, are the needs of growing animals to eat and process larger amounts of food to meet increasing requirements for energy and nutrients.

Although diets for dogs and cats have been commercially available for over 130 years,[1] there is surprisingly little known about basic digestive system functions, changes during the life history, and the relations with diet. Furthermore, most of what is known is from studies that use the dog for examining motility, surgical procedures and outcomes, development of lipid digestion, and secretory mechanisms. Much less is known for the cat. The limited information shows that the intestinal digestive physiology of dogs and cats is similar to that described for other monogastric mammals.

Comparative studies have revealed a close relationship between intestinal characteristics, the evolutionary diet, and requirements for energy and nutrients. Cats originate from a family comprised only of strict carnivores (felidae) whereas dogs and several other canids are omnivorous. There are also species-specific differences in requirements, such as the higher requirements of cats for protein and essential amino acids than dogs and the ability of cats to live on a diet devoid of carbohydrate.[2,3] Cats also differ from dogs in being hypersensitive to deficiencies in the amino acids arginine and taurine.

The present paper examines what is known about structure-function relations of the dog and cat intestine. The objective was to provide insights and an introduction to the field, not produce an exhaustive review of the literature. It considers how intestinal characteristics reflect patterns of gene expression that are related to each species evolutionary diet. The emphasis is on events that occur at the brush-border membrane (BBM), which is responsible for the final stages of hydrolysis and subsequent absorption of dietary components. Additional information is included about basic intestinal structure and the resident microflora. The processes associated with lumenal digestion of the complex polymers that constitute most feedstuffs have been previously described and are known to be similar to those of other mammals.[4]

<table>
<tr><td>Intestinal
Structure</td><td>Characteristics of the adult intestine. Similar to other carnivores, total length of the small intestines of dogs and cats, when normalized to body length or weight, is shorter than that of omnivorous and herbivorous mammals.[5] Comparisons of intestinal structure-function relations reveal additional differences between dogs and rats.[6] Similar to all other mammals, the intestines of dogs and cats can be separated into three regions, though there are no distinct demarcations at gross or histologic levels. A short duodenum extends from the pyloric sphincter for about 10% of the length of small intestine. This region receives regulated amounts of digesta from the stomach as well as digestive secretions from the pancreas and gall bladder. The remainder of the small intestine is roughly divided equally between jejunum and the terminal ileal section, which ends at the ileocolonic junction. The small intestine of dogs decreases in diameter from proximal to distal, with a similar decline in thickness of the mucosa.[7] However, mucosal and BBM protein and DNA content per mg intestine remain constant throughout the length, suggesting the changes are caused by fewer cells, not changes in the protein and DNA content of individual cells.</td></tr>
</table>

The large intestine of both species is relatively short and simple, and a small cecum is present at the ileocolonic junction. Correspondingly, the contribution of volatile fatty acids (i.e., short chain fatty acids) from colonic microbial fermentation to body metabolic requirements of dogs (7%) is lower than that of most rodents, pigs, and hindgut fermenters, but is comparable to that of humans.[8] Data are not available for the cat, but based on size of the cecum and large intestine, values may be similar to those of dogs and humans.

Among the different species of mammals the gastrointestinal tract (GIT) is the most variable organ system in terms of anatomical structure, corresponding with the wide diversity of feeding habits. Basic intestinal histology and ultrastructure are comparable across species. The intestine consists of four distinct tissue layers (*Figure 1A*). The inner-most layer, or mucosa is organized into finger-like villi that project into the lumen of the intestine (*Figure 1B*). The simple columnar epithelial layer that covers the villi and lines the interposed crypts is directly exposed to digesta. Epithelial stem cells are present in the crypts and are considered to be the only epithelial cell type capable of proliferation. Some of the daughter cells resulting from stem cell proliferation migrate deeper into the crypts where they differentiate into enterochromaffin and crypt cells with endocrine and secretory functions, respectively. The remaining daughter cells migrate up the villi where they are more exposed to digesta. The majority of these cells differentiate into columnar absorptive cells (enterocytes), with the remainder becoming mucous secreting goblet cells (*Figure 1B*).

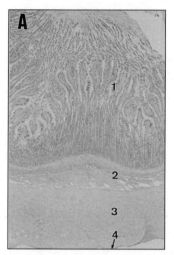

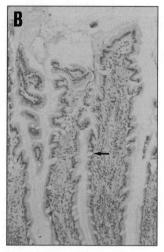

Figure 1A. Photomicrographs of adult dog intestinal structure. The four tissue layers are indicated (1: mucosa, 2: submucosa, 3: muscularis externa, 4: serosa).

Figure 1B. A higher magnification of villi, with a goblet cell indicated by the arrow. Hematoxylin and eosin; magnifications are 40 x in Figure 1A and 200 x in Figure 1B.

The apical membrane of the enterocyte is often called the brush border due to the presence of numerous projections (microvilli), which effectively increase the surface area available for hydrolysis and absorption. When considered together, the villi and microvilli amplify the surface area of a smooth bore cylinder up to 500-fold. Villus atrophy and reduction of intestinal surface area can be a cause of malabsorption in dogs.[9] This is a common consequence of diarrhea and needs to be considered when feeding recovering animals.

The epithelial layer of the mucosa overlies a basal lamina. In addition to providing support, the basal lamina serves as an attachment site for the epithelial cells and is thought to provide signals that induce enterocyte differentiation. Beneath the basal lamina is the cellular, loose connective tissue of the lamina propria. Blood vessels and lacteals course through this layer and collect nutrients absorbed and released by the enterocytes. Lymphocytes are numerous in the lamina propria, though they are also present in the mucosal epithelium. They represent an arm of the enteric immune system and are thought to play a critical role in recognizing, destroying, and signalling the presence of foreign antigens that traverse the epithelial boundary. Different types of T and B lymphocytes, associated with cell and humoral mediated immunity, respectively, can be detected. A fine layer of smooth muscle cells, the muscularis mucosa, is present beneath the lamina propria and extends into the villi. Contraction of the muscle cells causes villus movement, reducing stagnation of digesta at the epithelial layer and thereby improving absorption.

The submucosa is the second tissue layer and consists largely of connective tissue penetrated by blood and lymphatic vessels. The muscularis externa is the third tissue layer and surrounds the submucosa. It is composed of an inner circular layer and an outer longitudinal layer of smooth muscle. The muscularis externa is involved in segmental and peristaltic contractions, which are coordinated by a well-developed nerve plexus. The muscularis externa and submucosa together represent nearly 50% of wall thickness in adult dogs (*Figure 1A*), which is markedly thicker than in pigs and other omnivores and herbivores. The muscle layers are not well developed at birth, but are evident by three weeks of age, corresponding with when dogs begin to sample solid food items.

The serosa is the outer most intestinal tissue layer and consists of a thin layer of connective tissue covered by a simple, squamous epithelium (the peritoneum).

Prenatal development. Gestation lengths for both cats and dogs are 63 days, which is intermediate in length when compared to other mammals. During this time the intestine undergoes three phases of development; organogenesis, differentiation, and growth and maturation. Although the relations between prenatal development of intestinal structure and functions has yet to be defined for dogs and cats, a recent synthesis of data for several mammalian species indicate the intestine develops and acquires functions earlier in species with long gestations.[10] If dogs and cats follow this trend, villi lined by differentiated enterocytes with microvilli and capable of glucose transport should appear at about 50% of gestation (fetal days 30-35). These events would be preceded first by formation of the intestine from endoderm surrounded by mesenchyme, followed by restriction of cell proliferation to presumptive crypts.

Postnatal development. The two organ systems that experience the most dramatic changes in functional demands at birth are the GIT and lungs. With the transition to the external environment these systems assume full responsibility for providing nutrients and gas exchange. In other species, the first swallows of milk trigger surges in intestinal motor activity, oxygen extraction, and secretion of hormones associated with digestion and metabolism.[10] Species vary, however, in perinatal changes of intestinal structure. The intestines of dogs and pigs increase in weight by up to two-fold during the first 24 h after birth.[11,12] The most dramatic growth in pigs occurs during the first 6 h of suckling, mainly due to an increase in mucosal tissue, and coincides with higher protein content.[12] Similar data are not available for dogs. The rapid growth can be attributed to a combination of: (1) pinocytosis of colostral immunoglobulins; (2) enterocyte proliferation; and (3) synthesis of protein by existing enterocytes. Interestingly, even though cats, like dogs, acquire the majority of passive immunity postnatally,[13] the intestines of cats grow little during the first week after birth.[14] The reasons for the discrepancies between cats and dogs during the perinatal period and the consequences are not understood.

Throughout suckling, intestinal dimensions of cats grow slower than expected from dimensional analysis.[14] Specifically, if older cats are simply larger versions of newborn kittens, then slopes of logarithmic plots for intestinal length, area, mass, and mucosal mass relative to body weight would be 0.33, 0.67, 1.0, and 1.0, respectively. However, between postnatal days 1 and 35 the slopes for cats were 0.23, 0.54, 0.62, and 0.52 (all significantly lower than expected). The lower growth was attributed to the virtual lack of growth during the first week after birth. As a result, intestinal mass represented 5.6% of body weight at birth, but was 3% at 21 days (*Table 1*). After day 35, intestinal growth exceeded predicted rates. Even so, at 60 days, the percentage of body weight represented by the intestine (4.6%) had not recovered to that at birth. Unlike the small intestine, growth of the cat colon throughout the first 60 days matched predicted rates, even during the first week after birth. The reasons for the different growth rates of the two intestinal regions have not been explained.

Table 1. Body weights and intestinal characteristics of beagles and shorthaired cats at various stages of postnatal development.

	Beagle[a]					
Age	0 h	24 h	3 wk	6 wk	9 wk	Adult
n	4	5	11	10	17	7
Body Weight (kg)	0.316	0.301	1.19	2.12	3.89	11.5
Intestinal Length (cm)	77	93	145	183	238	294
Intestinal Weight (g)	7.8	13.3	58	119	182	237
Intestinal Area (cm^2)	54	83	306	465	747	1005

	Cat[b]				
Age	1 d	1 wk	3 wk	6 wk	9 wk
n	5	5	6	6	4
Body Weight (kg)	0.131	0.189	0.369	0.542	0.956
Intestinal Length (cm)	50	54	67	76	116
Intestinal Weight (g)	7.3	8.5	12.8	17.6	44.4
Intestinal Area (cm^2)	62	57	94	124	282

[a] Buddington, unpublished data.
[b] From 14.

After the rapid perinatal increase, the dog small intestine continues to grow (*Table 1*). However, when normalized to body weight, there are declines in length, surface area, and weight during suckling.[a] Furthermore, the percentage of intestinal weight represented by mucosa declines due to proportionally greater increases of the underlying tissues. There are few data for intestinal growth throughout the life history of dogs, but preliminary studies indicate the pattern of postnatal development is similar to that of cats, except for the perinatal period.[a]

Digestive Functions of the Intestinal Mucosa   The enterocytes exposed to the lumen of the intestine are polarized cells with two distinct membrane domains. Attached to or embedded in the apical membrane are numerous enzymes for the final stages of hydrolysis and transporters for uptake of the resulting nutrients. Nutrients exit the enterocytes through another set of transporters present in the other membrane domain (basolateral) and are collected by the blood vessels and lacteals in the lamina propria of the mucosa. Although much more is known about digestive functions of the apical membrane, regulation of basolateral membrane processes play an important role in delivery of nutrients to the organism. This section considers the apical functions, the developmental aspects, and the relations with diet.

Brush-border hydrolysis. After the complex polymers present in feedstuffs are broken down to smaller subunits by digestive secretions, the final stages of hydrolysis occur at the brush border membrane by the actions of a variety of disaccharidases and peptidases. The monosaccharides and amino acids that are released are then absorbed.

Although the natural diet of both cats and dogs is low in carbohydrate, both species have sucrase, maltase, isomaltase, but activities are about 80-90% lower than those of omnivores, such as pigs, humans, and rodents. Cats differ from dogs in lacking trehalase, which is characteristic of other felids.[15] Similar to other species, activities of the disaccharidases are higher in the proximal intestine whereas peptidase activity is distributed more distally.[7,16]

Brush-border absorption. Although there are few detailed studies in dogs and cats, water soluble nutrients are probably absorbed by the same carrier-mediated mechanisms that have been described for other species in numerous reviews. The aldohexoses glucose and galactose are absorbed by active transport and kinetic studies have revealed the possible presence of more than one Na-dependent aldohexose transporter in cats,[14,17] as well as in pigs and other species.[18] The different aldohexose transporters are separated based on rates of transport and substrate affinity, and have separate spatial and temporal patterns of distribution in the intestine.

Even though fructose, a ketohexose, is not present in the natural diet of either species, the intestine of each is able to absorb fructose.[14, 19] Since rates of accumulation exceed those for a marker for passive permeation, a carrier-mediated

---

[a] Buddington, unpublished data

66

process is involved. The most likely candidate is GLUT-5, an energy independent, facilitative diffusion carrier.

What sets dogs and cats apart from each other and other species are the relative proportions of the various sugar transporters. Notable are the higher densities of sugar transporters in apical membranes of omnivorous species, which coincide with higher rates of uptake.

Rates of amino acid uptake by dog and cat intestine exceed those for glucose and other monosaccharides;[14,20,21] the exception is an earlier study of dogs.[22] Several different types of amino acid transporters have been described. The transporters tend to have broad ranges of substrate specificity, and many of them can handle a variety of amino acids. Although rates of uptake may be less for amino acids from other classes, the presence of multiple uptake mechanisms reduces the possibility of amino acid deficiencies because of defects in a single transporter. This may explain why cystinuria in dogs is probably related more to renal dysfunction rather than to defects in intestinal transport.[22]

Corresponding with the hyperessential requirement of cats for arginine, rates of uptake for basic amino acids are higher than those for other types of amino acids.[14] Interestingly, even though cats have a high requirement for taurine, active transport processes are present only during early development, with only passive influx evident in adults.[23,24] Thê speculation is that since the diet of adult cats is sufficiently high in taurine, active transport is dispensable.

For both species, the distribution of amino acid and sugar transporters along the length of the small intestine is matched to that of the hydrolases, being higher proximally for sugar transporters, and more distally for amino acid transporters.[7,14,21,25] These regional patterns are consistent with those described for other mammals. Since rates of passive sugar influx through the apical membrane do not vary along the length of small intestine of dogs,[7] regional differences can be attributed to varying densities of transporters.

Water soluble vitamins are absorbed by carrier-mediated processes in other species. Vitamin B_{12} (cobalamin) absorption by dogs is similar to that of other species and involves receptor-mediated endocytosis of cobalamin complexed with intrinsic factor.[26] There is very little other information for vitamin uptake by dogs and cats.

Digestion of lipid involves a complex sequence of events and there have been few studies of apical absorption by the dog and cat intestine. Rates of absorption of labelled fatty acids by dog intestine are known to be related to acyl chain length and degree of saturation,[27] and are mediated by the presence of intracellular fatty acid binding proteins.[28] Additionally, whereas some fatty acids exit the enterocytes and directly enter the circulation of dogs (e.g., caproic acid), others enter the lymphatic system (oleic and stearic).

Finally, passive influx has been proposed as an important mechanism for intestinal uptake of water soluble nutrients.[29] However, sugar and amino acid concentrations measured in the intestinal contents of mammals, including dogs, are generally less than 10 mM.[30] This is not high enough to open paracellular channels or drive significant amounts across the apical membrane. Furthermore, the dog intestine is less permeable than that of other species,[31] with that of the cat apparently even less permeable.[32] Therefore, carrier-mediated processes are critical for absorption of dietary components.

Age-related changes. In other species the intestine is not quiescent during gestation and is known to actively process amniotic fluid swallowed by fetuses. The various nutrients and numerous biologically active molecules present in amniotic fluid play a critical role in growth and development of the intestine itself and the entire organism.[10,33] This has been shown in other species by two approaches. First, preventing access of the amniotic fluid to the intestine by esophageal ligation retards growth and maturation. Second, adding nutrients and growth factors to amniotic fluid or directly into the intestine accelerates development. The importance of fetal swallowing appears to be directly related to length of gestation, being greater in species born at more advanced stages of development, such as sheep, less so in rats and mice, and intermediate in rabbits. If this relationship holds, it can be expected that fetal swallowing and intestinal processing of amniotic fluids will be important for normal prenatal development of dogs and cats.

The intestines of neonates must be capable of processing and absorbing sufficient amounts of food to meet their high weight specific requirements for nutrients and energy. Corresponding with this, digestive functions necessary for processing milk develop prenatally and at birth the activities of brush border hydrolase and nutrient transporters are higher than at any other time of development.[34,35] The proximal to distal patterns of hydrolase and transporter distribution are also established before birth in dogs, cats, and other species.[14,21,a]

After birth and onset of suckling there are gradual declines in rates of uptake for most nutrients by dog and cat intestine,[14,21] due presumably to lower densities of transporters per unit intestine. The greater proportional decline in transporters for galactose relative to glucose in cats coincides with a decrease in dietary galactose as milk intake declines. The extreme case is the earlier described loss of Na^+-dependent, concentrative taurine uptake. However, throughout postnatal development rates of amino acid uptake by dog and cat intestine are higher compared to those of omnivorous and herbivorous mammals.

Not all digestive functions develop prenatally to the same degree. Notable is the age-related reciprocal relationship between lactase and the α-glycosidases (maltase, sucrase, trehalase). In both dogs and cats lactase is the predominant disaccharidase present during suckling, but as weaning approaches activity declines and is supplanted by the α-glycosidases.[15,36] It is interesting that the various α-glycosidases are present at birth in dogs and cats, though at low levels. This

---

[a] Buddington, unpublished data

contrasts with the delayed appearance until at or shortly before weaning in altricial rodents and many other species and probably reflects the relatively advanced state of intestinal development in neonatal dogs and cats. Since substrates for the α-glycosidases are lacking in the natural diet, the early appearance is probably not an adaptation to allow dogs and cats to utilize alternative carbohydrates.

Not all rates of transport decline after birth. Notable is the delayed onset of active bile acid uptake in the mammals studied to date. During suckling bile acids are absorbed exclusively by passive influx in dogs[37] and other species.[35] Active transport appears at weaning, but only in the distal ileum of dogs and cats,[38,39] with the onset evident in other species by the presence of both mRNA and transporters.[40] The reason for the paradoxical absence of active bile acid transport during suckling, despite high dietary fat intake, has yet to be explained.

One of the more dramatic age-related changes in mucosal functions is the decline in macromolecular uptake. Dogs and cats acquire the majority of passive immunity postnatally during the first 24 h after birth.[13] This requires receptor-mediated endocytosis of immunoglobulins present in colostrum by the apical membrane, transfer to the basolateral membrane, and release allowing the immuno-globulins to enter the systemic circulation. Polyvinyl pyrrolidone uptake by enterocytes, which is representative of nonselective macromolecular uptake, persists for 10-14 days in cats.[41] Although the loss coincides with changes in enterocyte characteristics (decreased vacuolization), the relationship with acquisition of passive immunity is not clear. If information for other species is relevant to dogs and cats, the loss of macromolecular uptake and/or passive immunity transfer is not due to the appearance of a new enterocyte population but instead is caused by a reprogram-ming of the functions of existing enterocytes.

Two other life history events have relevance to the relationship between intestinal functions and companion animal nutrition. First, during pregnancy and lactation requirements for energy and nutrients increase dramatically. In other species, the increased dietary intake is matched by the production of more intestinal tissue. It is less clear whether the numbers of the associated hydrolases and trans-porter increase in proportion (a non-specific adaptation) or, alternatively, there is a proportionally greater increase in a subset of the functional proteins (a specific increase). Such information may provide valuable insights about the specific needs of bitches and queens. Second, it is recognized that the senescent animal's needs for nutrients and energy differ from those of younger stages. If mucosal digestive functions are lower in senescent dogs and cats, as found in other species,[42] it will be necessary to determine if all functions decline in parallel and understand the mechanisms responsible for the declines.

Signals and mechanisms. Studies with adult dogs have shown that increases in lumenal osmolarity are sufficient to stimulate jejunal absorption of electrolytes and water,[43] and physical stimulation of the mucosa causes hyperemia.[44] The regulatory pathways include hormones and neural signals.[45,46]

It has proven much harder to identify the signals causing age-related changes in mucosal digestive functions. They can originate from external sources, such as the diet. Bitch milk contains numerous biologically active substances that can encourage growth and development of the intestine,[47,48] and trigger postnatal surges in endocrine activity.[49] Alternatively, the changes can be genetically programmed with the signals originating from internal sources, such as the enterocytes themselves, or from central control sites, such as the adenohypophysis.[35] In light of evidence for both sources, it is likely that age-related changes in the mucosal functions of dogs and cats are the result of dietary inputs interacting with genetic determinants. This has been shown in rats by the well known interaction between early weaning, increased glucocorticoid levels, and precocial intestinal maturation. The normal age-related changes of rat mucosal functions are not prevented when weaning is delayed, but they are of lower magnitude.[50]

Functional Capacities and Intestinal Adaptation

Of critical importance to organisms are the total capacities of the intestine to hydrolyze and absorb dietary constituents. Capacities are the product of activity or rates per unit tissue times the total amount of tissue, and can be used as predictors of limits of dietary loads. For example, kittens and puppies can tolerate 100 and 36 g of lactose per kg body weight each day.[16] Because of the age-related decline, total lactase activity in the jejunum of mature cats and dogs is sufficient to hydrolyze only 2 and 3 g/kg body weight per day, respectively. When dietary loads of lactose exceed these functional capacities, diarrhea or other signs of GIT distress are manifested. Coinciding with this, cats can tolerate up to 20% of the dry diet as lactose before signs of GIT distress.[51] It needs to be noted that despite declining specific activity, in many cases the capacities of adult animals to hydrolyze lactose is not less than that of sucklings because of a much larger intestine. However, because adult animals can eat larger volumes of food, dietary loads can exceed limited capacities.

The vertebrate intestine can compensate for qualitative and quantitative changes in dietary inputs by adapting intestinal structure and functions. These adaptive responses occur over three time scales. During a species evolution, intestinal characteristics adapt to match the natural diet.[5] Similarly, during the life history of mammals the intestine changes to match the shift from milk to an adult diet that is different in composition. This is exemplified by the above descriptions of changes in activities of lactase and α-glycosidase activities during development of dogs and cats. Finally, changes in diet composition can elicit rapid and reversible changes in intestinal characteristic. However, the magnitude of adaptive responses is related to the evolutionary diet. Omnivorous species, such as rats and mice, show the greatest range of dietary modulation. In contrast, cats and species from other families with only carnivorous representatives have either lost or never developed the ability to adaptively modulate brush border hydrolase activities[16,51] or rates of sugar transport[52] to match changes in levels or types of dietary carbohydrates. Apparently cats are provided with enough disaccharidase activity and sugar transport to handle a limited dietary intake of novel carbohydrates, such as sucrose. Adaptive modulation of dog mucosal functions has been reported for the distal small intestine.[20] It is likely the proximal intestine would also be responsive to diet. Therefore, dogs, like mink, which come from a family with some omnivorous representatives have some capacity to adapt digestive functions to match shifts in diet composition.

The abilities of neonates to adaptively regulate digestive functions has been examined in other species.[53,a] Corresponding with the relative nutritional constancy of milk, sucklings are like carnivores in having little if any ability to alter mucosal digestive functions to match changes in diet composition. As a consequence, it can be predicted that the most effective early weaning transition diets for dogs and cats should mimic milk composition and not include novel feedstuffs in excess of the limited digestive capacities.

Numerous enteric pathogens can cause diarrhea and mucosal enteritis in dogs and cats. Notable is *Rotavirus* which reduces villus height, hence surface area, and causes disturbances in dynamics of the enterocyte population.[54] There is a need to develop a better understanding of the impact on associated digestive functions, the recovery process, and how certain dietary components might accelerate recovery and reduce the risk of secondary infections.

Impact of Enteric Pathogens

The GIT provides a variety of different habitats that collectively harbor over 400 species and strains of bacteria. The highest densities are found in the large intestine of monogastric mammals, but bacteria can be isolated from all regions of the GIT, including the stomach. The percentage of aerotolerant bacteria decline distally, and in the colon over 99% of the bacteria are anaerobes. Even though there is variation between individuals in species composition, each host species has a unique microflora. This is evident from comparisons of bacterial groups present in the stools of dogs and cats.[55,56,57]

Intestinal Microflora

At birth the GIT of dogs is sterile, but within 24 h bacterial densities are comparable to those of adults.[b] Although densities remain stable during postnatal development, there are changes in the relative proportions of different bacterial groups. Initially, aerotolerant forms dominate in the large intestine, but within the first days after birth they are largely replaced by anaerobic forms. During suckling *Bifidobacteria, Lactobacilli,* and *Clostridia* are commonly isolated from the stools of various species, but they too are gradually supplanted by groups, such as the *Bacteroides*. The age-related changes, particularly those at the time of weaning, can be attributed to changes in dietary components. Milk is known to contain numerous factors that encourage the proliferation of *Bifidobacteria*. After weaning, when milk is no longer available, densities of *Bifidobacteria* decline. There are other factors that can influence the developing microflora. For example, bile acids are known to differentially affect various species of bacteria and are used in some selective media for that very reason. It is possible the absence of active uptake and

[a] Buddington, unpublished data
[b] Jackson and Buddington, unpublished data.

lower enterohepatic recycling of bile acids during suckling may be an adaptive mechanism that allows bile acids to enter the colon and thereby encourage the growth of tolerant groups, such as the *Bifidobacteria*. Coinciding with this, the *Bacteroides*, which are bile acid sensitive, do not increase in abundance until after weaning when active bile acid uptake is established and would reduce colonic bile acid concentrations. Also to be considered are the competitive and synergistic relationships that exist between different bacterial groups.

Disturbances of the large intestine's microbial ecology have been reported to have widespread influences in dogs.[58] This highlights the interesting, but as yet poorly understood, interactions between diet, digestive functions, the resident microflora, and health. These interactions may be more pronounced during early development when the microflora is unstable and adult digestive functions have not been acquired. They may also be involved in some of the problems associated with senescent animals that suffer from declining digestive functions.

Volatile fatty acids (VFA) produced by bacterial fermentation represent the principal anion in the large intestine. They are rapidly absorbed,[59] provide a metabolic fuel for the host, and appear to play a role in secretion and absorption by colonocytes. VFA's and other bacterial metabolites are known to inhibit the growth of pathogenic and putrefactive bacteria.[60]

Bacteria have been reported to influence structure and functions of the dog small intestinal mucosa,[61] with the specific influences differing between aerobic and anaerobic forms. Small intestinal bacterial overgrowth (SIBO) in dogs can be caused by pancreatic dysfunction.[62] It is characterized by densities exceeding 10^5 bacteria per ml or g contents and may be a commonly overlooked cause of GIT distress.[63] Interestingly, bacterial densities in the proximal small intestine of normal cats exceed those characteristic of SIBO in dogs.[64] The higher densities of bacteria in normal cats and dogs with SIBO are associated with lower disaccharidase activities and may have a detrimental impact on nutrient availability.[65,66]

Even though the microflora of adult animals is considered to be stable, changes in diet can cause shifts in the relative proportions and metabolic activities of the various bacterial groups.[67] Feeding dogs and cats specific substrates has been shown to selectively encourage the proliferation of groups perceived as beneficial,[45,46] with the concept of prebiotics introduced for adding substances that encourage growth of beneficial bacteria to diets of humans.[68] These findings are encouraging in that they indicate it should be possible to formulate special diets that improve health of the host and may accelerate recovery of the intestinal microflora after GIT distress and reduce risk of secondary infections.

Summary and Perspectives   For over 130 years, formulated feeds have been available for companion animals and there have been numerous studies about energy and nutrient requirements. Much less effort has been devoted to understanding the intestinal physiology of dogs and cats, despite the obviously important role in nutrition. What is known shows that mucosal structure and digestive functions of dogs and cats are similar to those described for other mammals. However, intestinal structure and the proportions of the different functional proteins present in the BBM are species specific and are related to the evolutionary diet. Therefore, a better understanding of intestinal functions during the life history will enhance efforts to formulate feeds that are matched to digestive capabilities and provide optimal nutrition. There is also a need to identify dietary components that promote better health of the intestine and the resident microflora.

Adaptive modulation of digestive functions is critical for animals that are faced with changes in dietary inputs. This is particularly true for pets when owners switch between the numerous formulated feeds now available. Information about the capacities for adaptation is needed to determine the limits of dietary changes that can be tolerated. Previous studies suggest the range of tolerance will be much less for cats compared to dogs.

In addition to digestive functions, the intestine and associated organs represent the largest endocrine organ in the body, and several endocrine cell types have been identified in the intestines of dogs[69] and cats.[70] Hormones originating from the GIT of other species are critical for regulating digestive processes and whole body metabolism. Furthermore, the mucosa acts as a barrier between the organism and an external environment (the lumen) containing high densities of bacteria and other microorganisms, many of which are pathogenic. The intestine represents the first line of defense against invasion and includes as many immune-associated cells as the rest of the body combined. To date, there is virtually nothing known about the impact of nutrition on the endocrine and immune functions of the dog and cat intestine. Of related interest is how the enteric immune, endocrine, nervous, and digestive functions interact, particularly the "crosstalk" between enteric functions leading to diarrhea when certain pathogenic organisms invade the intestine.[71]

Acknowledgements

Dr. Sharon Black (College of Veterinary Medicine, Mississippi State University) kindly provided the photomicrographs of the adult dog intestine and assisted in the description of intestinal histology. Preliminary data for the developing dog intestine were made possible by the cooperation of Dr. Karyl Buddington, Mr. Mike Bassett and coworkers who provided care for the experimental animals, and Mr. Mike Bishop, Mr. Ken Jackson, Mr. J.C. Cuadra, Ms. Katie Brand, and other individuals who conducted the studies.

References

1. Case LP, Carey DP, Hirakawa DA. *Canine and feline nutrition*. St. Louis: Mosby, 1995:455.
2. National Research Council. *Nutrient requirements of dogs*. Washington DC: National Academy Press, 1985:79.

3. National Research Council. *Nutrient requirements of cats.* Washington DC: National Academy Press, 1986:78.

4. Batt RM. The molecular basis of malabsorption. *J Small Anim Pract* 1980; 21:555-569.

5. Stevens CE. *Comparative physiology of the digestive system.* New York: Cambridge University Press, 1988:300.

6. Robinson JWL, Menge H, Sepulveda SV, Mirkovitch V. Functional and structural characteristics of the jejunum and ileum in the dog and in the rat. *Digestion* 1977; 15:188-199.

7. Laganiere S, Berteloot A, Maestracci D. Digestive and absorptive functions along dog small intestine: comparative distributions in relation to biochemical and morphological parameters. *Comp Biochem Physiol* 1984; 79A:463-472.

8. Rechkemmer, G, Rönnau K, von Engelhardt W. Fermentation of polysaccharides and absorption of short chain fatty acids in the mammalian hindgut. *Comp Biochem Physiol* 1988; 90A:563-568.

9. Hart JR, Kidder DE. The quantitative assessment of mucosa in canine small intestinal malabsorption. *Res Vet Sci* 1978; 25:163-167.

10. Buddington RK. Nutrition and ontogenetic development of the intestine. *Can J Physiol Pharmacol* 1980; 72:251-259.

11. Heird WC, Schwarz SM, Hansen IH. Colostrum induced enteric mucosal growth in beagle puppies. *Pediatr Res* 1984; 18:512-515.

12. Zhang H, Malo C, Buddington RK. Intestinal growth and brush-border digestive functions of pigs during the first 24 hours of suckling. *J Pediatr Gastroenterol Nutr* 1996; in press.

13. Patt JA. Factors affecting the duration of intestinal permeability to macromolecules in newborn animals. *Biol Rev* 1977; 52:411-429.

14. Buddington RK, Diamond JM. Ontogenetic development of nutrient transporters in cat intestine. *Am J Physiol* 1992; 263:G605-G616.

15. Hore P, Hesser M. Studies on disaccharidase activities of the small intestine of the domestic cat and other carnivorous mammals. *Comp Biochem Physiol* 1968; 24:717-725.

16. Kienzle E. Carbohydrate metabolism of the cat. 4, Activity of maltase, isomaltase, sucrase, and lactase in the gastointestinal tract in relation to age and diet. *J Anim Physiol Anim Nutr* 1993; 70:89-96.

17. Wolffram S, Eggenberger E, Scharrer E. Kinetics of D-glucose transport across the intestinal brush-border membrane of the cat. *Comp Biochem Physiol* 1989; 94A:111-115.

18 Buddington RK, Malo C. Intestinal brush-border membrane enzyme activities and transport functions during prenatal development of pigs. *J Pediatr Gastroenterol Nutr* 1995; in press.

19. Varkoni T, Vittman T, Varro V. Fructose transport in isolated dog small intestine. *Fiziol Zh SSSR Sechenova* 1982; 68:1269-1273.

20. Stelzner M, Fonkalsrud EW, Buddington RK, Phillips JD, Diamond JM. Adaptive changes in ileal mucosal nutrient transport following colectomy and endorectal ileal pull-through with ileal reservoir. *Arch Surg* 1990; 125:586-590.

21. Buddington RK. Nutrient transport by canine intestine during postnatal

development. *FASEB J* 1996; in press (abstract).

22. Tsan M-F, Jones TC, Wilson TH. Canine cystinuria: intestinal and renal amino acid transport. *Am J Vet Res* 1972; 33:2463-2468.

23. Anon. Age associated loss of carrier-mediated intestinal taurine transport in cats. *Nutr Rev* 1993; 51:22-23.

24. Wolffram S, Hagemann C, Scharrer E. Regression of high-affinity carrier-mediated intestinal transport of taurine in adult cats. *Am J Physiol* 1991; 261:R1089-R1095.

25. Levinson RA, Englert Jr E. Small intestinal absorption of simple sugars and water in the cat. *Experientia* 1970; 26:262-263.

26. Marcoullis G, Rothenberg SP. Intrinsic factor mediated intestinal absorption of cobalamin in the dog. *Am J Physiol* 1981; 241:G294-G299.

27. Ohki M. Basic studies on digestion and absorption in the small intestine 7. Experimental studies on ^{14}C labelled fatty acid absorption in dog small intestine. *Nihon Univ J Med* 1980; 22:231-248.

28. Theodore C, Cerf M. The enterocytic phase of triglyceride absorption. *Gastroenterol Clin Biol* 1977; 1:369-376.

29. Pappenheimer JR. Paracellular intestinal absorption of glucose, creatinine and mannitol in normal animals: relations to body size. *Am J Physiol* 1990; 263:G290-G299.

30. Ferraris RP, Yasharpour SY, Lloyd KCK, Mirzayan R, Diamond JM. Luminal glucose concentrations in the gut under normal conditions. *Am J Physiol* 1990; 259:G822-G837.

31. Jezyk N, Rubas W, Grass GM. Permeability characteristics of various intestinal regions of rabbit, dog, and monkey. *Pharm Res* 1992; 9:1580-1586.

32. Hawkins EC, Meric SM, Washabau RJ, Feldman EC, Turrel JM. Digestion of bentiromide and absorptoin of xylose in healthy cats and absorption of xylose in cats with infiltrative intestinal disease. *Am J Vet Res* 1986; 47:567-569.

33. Sangild PT, Silver M, Schmidt M, Fowden AL. The perinatal pig in pediatric gastroenterology. In: *Swine in Biomedical Research* (M.E. Tumbleson, ed.) 1996; in press.

34. Buddington RK. Intestinal nutrient transport during ontogeny of vertebrates. *Am J Physiol* 1992; 263:R503-R509.

35. Buddington RK, Diamond JM. Ontogenetic development of intestinal nutrient transporters. *Annu Rev Physiol* 1989; 51:601-619.

36. Galand G. Brush border membrane sucrase-isomaltase, maltase-glucoamylase and trehalase in mammals. Comparative development, effects of glucocorticoids, molecular mechanisms, and phylogenetic implications. *Comp Biochem Physiol* 1989; 94B:1-11.

37. Lester R, Smallwood RA, Little JM, Brown AS, Piasecki CJ, Jackson BT. Fetal bile salt metabolism: the intestinal absorption of bile salt. *J Clin Invest* 1977; 59:1009-1016.

38. Wolffram S, Greenacher B, Scharrer E. Intestinal transport of taurocholae in the cat. *J Vet Med Ser* 1993; A40:178-184.

39. Fujii T, Yanagisawa J, Nakayama F. Absorption of bile acids in dog as determined by portal blood sampling: Evidence for colonic absorption of bile acid

conjugates. *Digestion* 1988; 41:207-214.

40. Kramer WF, Girbig U, Gutjahr S, Kowalewski K, Jouvenal G, üller D, Tripier, Wess G. Intestinal bile acid absorption. Na⁺-dependent bile acid transport activity in rabbit small intestine correlates with the coexpression of an integral, 93 kDa and a peripheral 14 kDa bile acid-binding membrane protein along the duodenum-ileum axis. *J Biol Chem* 1993; 1268:18035-18046.

41. Clarke RM, Hardy RN. Structural changes in the small intestine associated with the uptake of polyvinyl pyrrolidone by the young ferret, rabbit, guinea pig, cat, and chicken. *J Physiol* 1970; 209:669-687.

42. Ferraris RP, Vinnakota RR. Regulation of intestinal nutrient transport is impaired in aged mice. *J Nutr* 1993; 123:502-511.

43. Bastidas JA, Orandle MS, Zinner MJ, Yeo CJ. Small-bowel origin of the signal for meal-induced jejunal absorption. *Surgery* 1990; 108:376-383.

44. Biber B, Jodal M, Lundgren O, Svanvik J. Intestinal vasodilation after mechanical stimulation of the jejunal mucosa. *Experientia* 1970; 26:263-264.

45. Gingerich RL, Gilbert WR, Comens PG, Gavins III PR. Identification and characterization of insulin receptors in basolateral membranes of dog intestinal mucosa. *Diabetes* 1987; 36:1124-1129.

46. Sjovall H, Redfors S, Jodal M, Lundgren O. The mode of action of the sympathetic fibers on intestinal fluid transport: Evidence for the existence of a glucose stimulated secretory nervous pathway in the intestinal wall. *Acta Physiol Scand* 1983; 119:39-48.

47. Yamashiro Y, Sato M, Shimizu T, Oguchi S, Maruyama K, Kitamura S. Possible biological growth factors in breast milk and postnatal development of the gastrointestinal tract. *Acta Paediatr Jpn* 1989; 31:417-423.

48. Lonnerdal B. Lacation in the dog and cat. *Advances in Canine and Feline Nutritional Research: Proceedings of the 1996 Iams International Nutrition Symposium.* Wilmington OH: Orange Frazer Press. 1996.

49. Berseth CL. Breast milk is essential for natural postnatal surges of plasma gastrin and bombesin. *Pediatr Res* 1991; 29:100A.

50. Toloza E, Diamond JM. Ontogenetic development of nutrient transporters in rat intestine. *Am J Physiol* 1992; 263:G593-G604.

51. Morris JG, Trudell J, Pencovic T. Carbohydrate digestion by the domestic cat (*Felis catus*). *Br J Nutr* 1977; 37:365-373.

52. Buddington RK, Chen JW, Diamond JM. Dietary regulation of intestinal brush-border sugar and amino acid transport in carnivores. *Am J Physiol* 1991; 261:R793-R801.

53. Vega YM, Puchal AA, Buddington RK. Intestinal amino acid and monosaccharide transport in suckling pigs fed milk replacers with different sources of carbohydrate. *J Nutr* 1992; 122:2430-2439.

54. Johnson CA, Snider TG, Fulton RW, Cho D. Inoculation of neonatal gnotobiotic dogs with a canine rotavirus. *Am J Vet Res* 1983; 44:1687-1693.

55. Terada A, Hara H, Oishi T, Matsui S, Mitsuoka T, Nakajyo S, Fujimori I, Hara K. Effect of dietary lactosucrose on faecal flora and faecal metabolites of dogs. *Microbial Ecol Health Dis* 1992; 5:87-92.

56. Terada A, Hara H, Kato S, Kimura T, Fujimori I, Hara K, Maruyama T, Mitsuoka T. Effect of lactosucrose (4^G-β-D-galactosylsucrose) on fecal flora and fecal putrefactive products of cats. *J Vet Med Sci* 1993; 55:291-295.

57. Davis CP, Cleven D, Balish E, Yale CE. Bacterial association in the gastrointestinal tract of beagle dogs. *Appl Environ Microbiol* 1977; 34:194-206.

58. Buttin P, Sergheraert R. The ecology of the dog large intestine, digestive intolerance, and dietary dermatitis. *Rec Med Vet. l"Ecole d'Alfort* 1993; 169:885-893.

59. Stevens CE. Physiological implications of microbial digestion in the large intestine of mammals: relation to dietary factors. *Am J Clin Nutr* 1978; 31:S161-S168.

60. Gibson GR, Wang MBX. Inhibitory effects of bifidobacteria on other colonic bacteria. *J Appl Bacteriol* 1994; 77:412-420.

61. Batt RM, McLean L. Comparison of the biochemical changes in the jejunal mucosa of dogs with aerobic and anaerobic bacterial overgrowth. *Gastroenterol* 1987; 93:986-993.

62. Westermarck E, Myllys V, Aho M. Effect of treatment on the jejunal and colonic bacterial flora of dogs. *Pancreas* 1993; 8:559-562.

63. Westermarck E, Siltanen R, Maïjala R. Small intestinal bacterial overgrowth in seven dogs with gastointestinal signs. *Acta Vet Scand* 1993; 34:311-314.

64. Johnston K, Lamport L, Batt RM. An unexpected bacterial flora in the proximal small intestine of normal cats. *Vet Rec* 1993; 132:362-363.

65. Batt RM, Needham JR, Carter MW. Bacterial overgrowth associated with a naturally occurring enteropathy in the German shepherd dog. *Res Vet Sci* 1983; 35:42-46.

66. Johnston K, Lamport A, Batt RM. An unexpected bacterial flora in the proximal small intestine of normal cats. *Vet Rec* 1993; 312:362-363.

67. Perman JA. Gastrointestinal flora: developmental aspects and effects of nutrients. In: *Human Gastrointestinal Development* (E. Lebenthal, ed.), New York: Raven Press, 1989:777-786.

68. Gibson GR, Roberfroid MB. Dietary modulation of the human colonic microbiota: introducing the concept of prebiotics. *J Nutr* 125:1401-1412.

69. Tange A. Distribution of peptide containing endocrine cell and neurons in the gastrointestinal tract of the dog: immunohistochemical studies using antisera to somatostatin, substance P, vasoactive intestinal polypeptide, methionine enkephalin, and neurotensin. *Biomed Res* 1983; 4:9-24.

70. Kitamura N, Yamada J, Yamashita T, Yanaihara N. Endocrine cells in the gastrointestinal tract of the cat. *Biomed Res* 1982; 3:612-622.

71. Nilsson O, Cassuto J, Larsson P-A, Jodal M, Lidberg P, Ahlman H, Dahlstrom A, Lundgren O. 5 hydroxytryptamine and cholera secretion: A histochemical and physiological study in cats. *Gut* 1983; 24:542-548.

Lactation in the Dog and Cat

Bo Lönnerdal, PhD
Professor of Nutrition and Internal Medicine
Department of Nutrition
University of California, Davis, California

It is well recognized that the optimum food for the neonate is its own *Introduction* mother's milk. It is widely believed that the amounts of nutrients provided by the mother's milk are close to the requirements of its offspring. Studies in several species have shown that homeostatic mechanisms which attempt to regulate the nutrient composition of the milk are present in the mother, and that the nutritional quality of the milk is maintained even in nutritionally compromised situations. Thus, in most situations, the milk is likely to supply adequate quantities of most, if not all, nutrients. On the other side of the spectrum, it is evolutionary and ecologically unlikely that the milk of any species would apply excessive amounts of any nutrient. Therefore, the nutrient composition of milk from any species fed a "normal" diet is likely to represent the concentrations of nutrients that are required but not in excessive amounts.

Dogs and cats are today two of the most popular family pets in the United States. In most cases, puppies and kittens are nursed and raised by their mothers, but there are many situations in which dog and cat milk replacers are needed. However, to date many of these replacers have not been able to provide adequate nutrition to the newborns, resulting in diarrhea, metabolic imbalances, and increased mortality.[1] Most replacers have a composition based on old compositional data and it is highly likely that they may be improved, provided more detailed information on the composition of dog and cat milk can be obtained.

The physiological effects of a species' own milk on its offspring are not limited to the absolute amounts of nutrients provided. It has been shown in several species, particularly in human infants, that mother's milk provides many bioactive components.[2] In particular, a multitude of proteins have been shown to be active in the infant, ranging from providing immunity (immunoglobulins), aiding in lipid digestion (bile salt-stimulated lipase), facilitating the absorption of other nutrients (lactoferrin/iron, folate-binding protein, etc.), enhancing gut maturation (growth factors) and degrading bacteria (lysozyme). Thus, it is important not only to characterize the nutrient composition of milk but also to define the important protein constituents of the milk, before a thorough understanding of the provision of nutrients from the diet (milk) and its utilization by the infant can be obtained.

The energy content of dog milk increases during the first 40 days of lactation and then decreases during days 41-50, possibly because of weaning of the puppy and involution of the gland.[3] In early lactation, milk contains about 550 kcal ME/L, while it contains around 800 kcal/L in mid-lactation. In our study, the major constituent of dog milk was found to be protein, with a concentration of 43 g/L during the first 10 days of lactation, which later increased to 50-60 g/L (*Figure 1*). Another study of beagle milk composition showed somewhat higher protein levels at ~ 70-75 g/L in mid-lactation.[4] Different methods were used for protein quantitation in the two studies and it is possible that the colorimetric method underestimated milk protein concentration as non-protein nitrogen constitutes about 4.4 % of total nitrogen.[4] The protein components of dog milk have generally not been well characterized, although there is some information on the characteristics of one casein subunit and one whey protein.[5] Recently, the bile salt-stimulated lipase[6] and lysozyme[7] in dog milk have been characterized.

Carbohydrate, of which most is lactose, provides about 42-48 g/L, with no pronounced variation throughout the lactation period. The concentration of fat is relatively low in early lactation at 2.4%, increases to 4.5-5.2% during mid-lactation, and decreases to about 2.6% in late lactation. The subsequent study by Oftedal[4] showed higher lipid concentrations at ~ 9-10% in mid-lactation. It should be cautioned, however, that the extent to which the gland was emptied of milk has a pronounced effect on milk fat content. In a study of lactating women, in which serial milk samples were collected during one nursing event, milk fat increased from ~ 0.5% in foremilk to ~ 10% in hindmilk.[8] Thus, it is quite likely that less milk was collected from the lactating dogs in our study than in the one by Oftedal.[4] It has not been determined to what extent the nursing puppies can "empty" the gland, but our studies in women have shown that infants frequently leave relatively substantial volumes of milk in the breast.[9] Thus, too vigorous collection of milk by pumping or manual expression may be unphysiological and not truly represent the composition of milk as consumed by the puppy. Some of the difference in lipid concentrations found may have been due to differences between the methods of analysis used in the two studies.[4] The patterns seen for carbohydrate and lipids are similar to those of most species, while the increase in protein concentration is the opposite of what is known for milk from other species, like human and cow milk.[10, 11] The solids content of the milk was about 23% and the energy content was about 1400-1500 kcal GE/L.[4]

The concentration of calcium in dog milk is high; in early lactation it is around 1400 mg/L and then increases to 1600-1900 mg/L by late lactation.[3] Calcium concentrations closely follow those of protein (Figure 1), which is not too surprising considering that casein, which binds Ca^{2+} to phosphorylated serine, threonine, and colloidal calcium phosphate groups within the casein micelle,[12] is the major protein class in dog milk.[5] The concentration of magnesium is similar to that of other species at roughly 60 mg/L and it is not found to vary with stage of lactation. This lack of change is most likely related to the fact that the major part of magnesium in milk is associated to low molecular weight complexes and not bound to protein.[13]

COMPOSITION OF DOG MILK DURING LACTATION

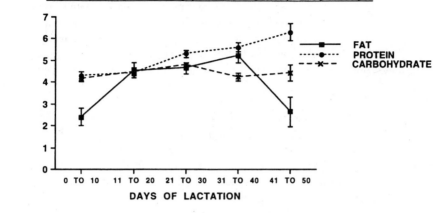

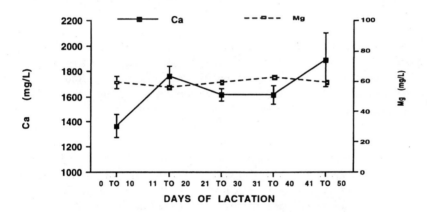

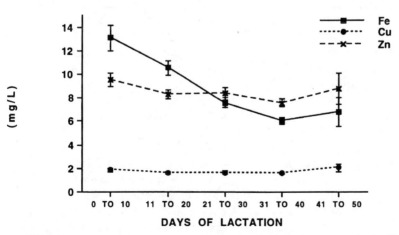

Figure 1. Developmental changes in nutrient concentrations during lactation in the dog (beagle). Adapted from 3.

The concentration of iron in dog milk decreased significantly during lactation (*Figure 1*), from about 13mg/L in early milk to 6 mg/L in late lactation.[3] Milk copper concentrations remain relatively stable throughout lactation at about 1.7 mg/L. The concentration of zinc decreases from an initial level of about 9-10 mg/L to 7-8 mg/L over the course of lactation. There are no changes in milk manganese concentrations throughout lactation; values remain stable at 140-160 µg/L.

The concentration of iron in dog milk (~ 10 mg/L) was found to be considerably higher than that of human milk (0.2 - 0.5 mg/L)[14] or milk from dairy animals (0.2 - 0.3 mg/L).[15] However, it was found to be similar to the iron concentration of rat milk.[16] The decrease in milk iron in the dog is similar to what has been observed in several species.[15] It is noteworthy that the iron concentration in dog milk is about 10 times higher than that of serum.[3] This suggests that iron is actively taken up by the mammary gland and that the mechanism for iron accrual may be different from that in species with iron concentrations considerably lower than in serum, like the human.

It is not known whether the high iron content of dog milk is well absorbed by the puppy. It has been shown, however, that the dog, like many other species, is born with large stores of liver iron.[17] This observation, together with the finding that liver iron is rapidly mobilized during the early neonatal period, suggests that the young puppy has a high iron requirement.

In contrast to other species, the concentration of copper in dog milk does not decrease during lactation.[15] Milk copper concentrations (~ 1.7 mg/L) are higher than in human milk (0.2 - 0.4 mg/L) and milk from dairy animals (0.1 - 0.3 mg/L), but considerably lower than in rat milk (~ 12 mg/L), which is very high in copper.[16,17] The finding that liver copper concentration does not decrease in the growing puppy[17] suggests that dog milk copper is highly bioavailable.

The concentration of zinc in dog milk was influenced by the stage of lactation, with the highest values in early lactation. This pattern is similar to what has been observed in most species.[15] Milk zinc concentration in the dog (~ 9 mg/L) is similar to that of some species, like the rat (~ 10 mg/L), but higher than that reported for most other species (~ 1 mg/L).[15,16] In dogs, the "toxic milk" syndrome, which affects puppies between 3 and 14 days of age, may be treated with zinc supplements, suggesting that the disorder may be due, in part, to inadequate zinc intake.[18] Thus, the importance of milk zinc to the growing puppy is evident.

It is apparent that even if we have some knowledge about the nutrient content of dog milk and how it varies during lactation, more information is needed to better understand nutrition of the puppy. For example, the only detailed study to date on dog milk focused on the beagle. Are there differences among breeds? One limited study on four different breeds suggests that there are only minor differences in milk composition among breeds.[19] What are the protein, carbohydrate and lipid constituents in dog milk? What ligands bind minerals and trace elements in dog milk and how do they affect absorption? What quantities of fat and water soluble vitamins are provided from dog milk? Such knowledge will improve our understanding of early nutrition in the dog and aid in the design of dog milk replacers.

Milk Intake
of Puppies

Milk intake of beagle puppies was determined by using the deuterium oxide dilution method and was found to be ~ 160-175 g/day.[4] The bitches were found to have daily milk yields of ~ 900-1100 g/day. Another study on beagles indicated much lower milk volumes;[20] however, these dogs were fed semi-purified diets that did not appear to support normal growth.[4] Larger size dogs produce higher volumes of milk. For example, the German Shepherd appears to produce ~ 1700 g/day at peak lactation, while smaller breeds produce less.[21] In early lactation, the German Shepherd was found to produce ~ 915 g/day, while the Dachshund produced 102-184 g/day. However, there are few systematic studies exploring both the influence of maternal size and litter size on milk production. The effect of partial weaning on milk consumption should also be carefully considered. Puppies will initiate feeding on semisolid foods soon after the appearance of teeth (days 21-35 postpartum) and milk alone has been estimated to support normal growth up to 4 weeks of age.[4] Once weaning has started, milk intake will decline to variable extent.

Energy
Requirements
of Puppies

Attempts have been made to estimate the energy and nutrient requirements of puppies from data on milk composition. The Subcommittee on Dog Nutrition of the National Research Council has estimated the metabolizable energy requirement of 3-6 week old puppies to be 274 kcal/$kg^{0.75}$.[22] In the study by Oftedal,[4] puppies consumed only 244 kcal/$kg^{0.75}$ gross energy, which corresponds to 219 kcal/$kg^{0.75}$ metabolizable energy. The author concluded that the estimates of energy requirement of young puppies by the National Research Council appear to be too high.

Composition
of Cat Milk

The energy content of cat milk increases during lactation, from about 850 kcal ME/L in early lactation to about 1550 kcal ME/L in mid-lactation. The protein concentration has been shown to steadily increase throughout lactation,[23] starting at ~ 40 g/L in early milk to ~ 60-70 g/L in mature milk (*Figure 2*). A recent study, however, shows that colostrum (day 1 of lactation) is high in protein ~ 83 g/L, but that it rapidly declines and by day 2 is only about half this value.[24] Since the previous study had not analyzed any colostrum samples, the initially high values were not detected. It is possible that the high protein concentration in samples from the first day of lactation is due to high levels of immunoglobulins, as the whey protein/casein ratio was found to be higher than later in lactation.[24] In most species, immunoglobulin concentrations are high in colostrum.[15] It is believed that the cat has a requirement for protein which is higher than that of most mammalian species, particularly when considering its relative growth rate.

COMPOSITION OF CAT MILK DURING LACTATION

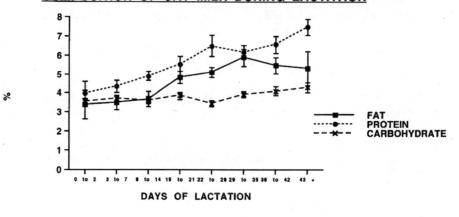

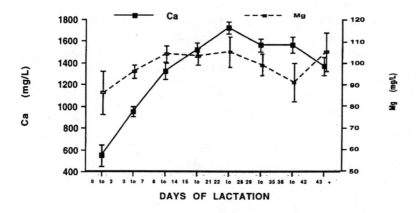

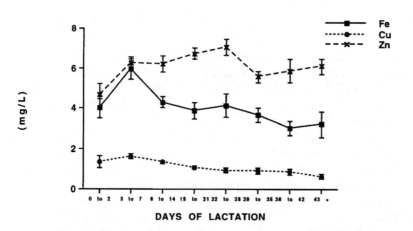

Figure 2. Developmental changes in nutrient concentrations during lactation in the cat. Adapted from 23.

It has been shown that the activity of urea cycle enzymes in cat liver are nonadaptive.[25] Thus, it may be predicted that the protein content of cat milk should be high relative to most species. At mid-lactation, cat milk protein provides about 28% of the total energy, which is considerably higher than the maintenance requirement of adult cats, which has been calculated to 12%.[26] Most of the proteins in cat milk have not been isolated and characterized in detail, but our recent study shows two major types of casein subunits (MW 25-35 kD) and four major whey proteins with MWs of 14, 21, 42 and 78 kD.[24,27] Among the whey proteins are also the bile salt-stimulated lipase[28] and lysozyme,[7] but they are likely low in absolute concentration. The carbohydrate concentration in cat milk is more stable at ~40g/L, even if a more recent study shows an increase in carbohydrate during early lactation; colostrum had a lactose concentration of ~30g/L.[24] The lipid content of cat milk was found to increase from ~3.5% in early lactation up to ~6% at 5 weeks of lactation, and then decline somewhat. In our recent study, care was taken to obtain a more complete expression and the lipid concentration was found to be higher (see above). Colostrum was found to have a lipid content of ~9.3%, by day 2 it was only 5.3%, and it then gradually increased to 9-12%.[24] The patterns for protein, carbohydrate and lipid concentrations in milk are similar in the cat and the dog, although the carbohydrate concentration is somewhat lower and the lipid content somewhat higher in cat milk as compared to dog milk.

The concentration of calcium in cat milk increases dramatically during lactation,[23] with values of ~600 mg/L in early lactation to ~500-1700 mg/L in mid- to late lactation (*Figure 2*). In our recent study, even higher calcium concentrations (~2000 mg/L) were found after 1 week of lactation. Since the increase in phosphate concentration during lactation is much less pronounced, the Ca/P ratio changes from ~0.4 in early lactation to ~1.2 in later lactation.[24] This may reflect a develop- mental shift to more active bone growth during late infancy. The concentration of magnesium in cat milk does not undergo any pronounced change during lactation; levels range from 90 to 100 mg/L. It is notable that cat milk is about 50-75% higher in magnesium than in dog milk, while the calcium concentration is similar in the two species.

The concentration of iron in cat milk has been found to initially increase from ~4 mg/L (day 0-2) to ~6 mg/L (days 3-7), and then gradually decline to ~3-4 mg/L (*Figure 2*). Our recent study shows lower milk iron values, starting at about 2 mg/L, increasing to about 4 mg/L and then declining to 2-3 mg/L.[24] It is not yet known whether this is due to methodological differences between the studies, or if maternal intake of iron changes and affects milk iron concentration. A small increase in milk copper is also seen during early lactation in the cat, and values then decrease slowly. The concentration of zinc in cat milk increases steadily from colostrum (~5 mg/L) to day 22-28 of lactation (7 mg/L), and then decreases to ~6 mg/L.

Milk iron concentration is considerably higher (2-3 fold) in the dog than in the cat which may suggest a higher iron requirement in the newborn puppy. The somewhat unusual initial increase in milk iron in the cat may reflect increased synthesis of an iron-binding protein, possibly lactoferrin,[27] after a few days of lactation. It is possible that this protein can carry more iron into the milk, or that mechanisms for iron accrual by the mammary gland become more active a few days post partum. The concentration of copper is similar in cat milk and dog milk. Milk zinc concentration also increases during lactation in the cat, suggesting that either synthesis of zinc-binding ligands in milk is increased or that the export of zinc into milk becomes more effective after a few days of lactation. Cat milk is somewhat lower in zinc concentration than dog milk (5-7 mg/L vs 8-10 mg/L).

Concluding Remarks

It is apparent that nursing puppies and kittens generally have normal growth and development. However, in situations when their own mothers' milk can not be consumed, outcome is less than satisfactory. Although we now have some basic knowledge of the composition of dog and cat milk, further knowledge of the nutritionally and physiologically important components of milk and how they interact with each other, and with the newborn animal, is needed. With such information, more accurate estimates of nutrient requirements of puppies and kittens can be established.

References

1. Remillard RJ, Pickett JP, Thatcher CD, Davenport DJ. Comparison of kittens fed queen's milk with those fed milk replacers. *Am J Vet Res* 1993; 54:901-907.

2. Lonnerdal B. Biochemistry and physiological function of human milk proteins. *Am J Clin Nutr* 1985; 42:1299-1317.

3. Lonnerdal B, Keen CL, Hurley LS, Fisher GL. Developmental changes in the composition of beagle dog milk. *Am J Vet Res* 1981; 42:662-666.

4. Oftedal O. Lactation in the dog: milk composition and intake by puppies. *J Nutr* 1984; 114:803-812.

5. Nagasawa T, Kiyosawa I, Kato R, Kuwahara K. Isolation of canine-casein and major whey protein component A and their amino acid composition. *J Dairy Sci* 1972; 55:1550-1556.

6. Iverson SJ, Kirk CL, Hamosh M, Newsome J. Milk lipid digestion in the neonatal dog - the combined actions of gastric and bile salt stimulated lipases. *Biochim Biophys Acta* 1991; 1083:109-119.

7. Halliday JA, Bell K, Shaw DC. Feline and canine milk lysozymes. *Comp Biochem Physiol* B 1993; 106:859-865.

8. Forsum E, Lonnerdal B. Variation in the contents of nutrients of breast milk during one feeding. *Nutr Rep Int* 1979; 19:815-820.

9. Dewey KG, Lonnerdal B. Infant self-regulation of breast milk intake. *Acta Paediatr Scand* 1986; 75:893-898.

10. Lonnerdal B, Forsum E, Hambraeus L. A longitudinal study of the protein, nitrogen, and lactose contents of human milk from Swedish well-nourished mothers. *Am J Clin Nutr* 1976; 29:1127-1133.

11. Jenness R, Sloan RE. The composition of milk from various species—a review. *Dairy Sci Abstr* 1970; 32:599-614.

12. McGann TCA, Pyne GT. The colloidal phosphate of milk. III. The nature of its association with casein. *J Dairy Res* 1960; 27:403-409.

13. Lonnerdal B, Yuen M, Glazier C, Litov RE. Magnesium bioavailability from human milk, cow milk and infant formula in suckling rat pups. *Am J Clin Nutr* 1993; 58:392-397.

14. Siimes MA, Vuori, E, Kuitunen, P. Breast milk iron - a declining concentration during the course of lactation. *Acta Paediatr Scand* 1979; 68:29-31.

15. Lonnerdal B, Keen CL, Hurley LS. Iron, copper, zinc and manganese in milk. *Annu Rev Nutr* 1981; 1:149-174.

16. Keen CL, Lonnerdal B, Clegg M, et al. Developmental changes in composition of rat milk: Trace elements, minerals, protein, carbohydrate and fat. *J Nutr* 1981; 111:226-236.

17. Keen CL, Lonnerdal B, Fisher GL. Age-related variations in hepatic iron, copper, zinc, and selenium concentrations in Beagles. *Am J Vet Res* 1981; 42:1884-1887.

18. Mosier JE. The puppy from birth to six weeks. *Vet Clin North Am* 1978; 8:79-100.

19. Mundt HC, Thomée A, Meyer H. Zur Energie- und Eiweissversorgung von Saugwelpen über die Muttermilch. *Kleintier-Praxis* 1981; 26:353-360.

20. Romsos DR, Palmer HJ, Muiruri KL, Bennink MR. Influence of a low carbohydrate diet on performance of pregnant and lactating dogs. *J Nutr* 1981; 111:678-689.

21. Rüsse I. Die Laktation der Hündin. Zentralbl. *Veterinaehrmed.* 1961; 8:252-281.

22. National Research Council. *Nutrient Requirements of Dogs.* Washington DC: National Academy of Sciences. 1974.

23. Keen CL, Lonnerdal B, Clegg MS, Hurley LS, Morris J, Rogers QR, Rucker RB. Developmental changes in composition of cats' milk: trace elements, minerals, protein, carbohydrate and fat. *J Nutr* 1982; 112:1763-1769.

24. Adkins Y, Zicker SC, Lepine A, Lonnerdal B. Protein and nutrient composition of cat milk throughout lactation. *FASEB J* 1995; 9:A1019.

25. Rogers QR, Morris JG, Freedland RA. Lack of hepatic enzymatic adaptation to low and high levels of dietary protein in the adult cat. *Enzyme* 1977; 22:348-356.

26. Burger IH, Blaza SE, Kendall PT. The protein requirement of adult cats. *Proc Nutr Soc* 1981; 41:361A.

27. Adkins Y, Lonnerdal B, Lepine A. Isolation and characterization of cat milk proteins. *FASEB J* 1996; in press.

28. Wang C, Martindale ME, King MM, Tang J. Bile-salt-activated lipase: effect on kitten growth rate. Am J Clin Nutr 1989; 49: 457-463.

The Role of Growth Factors in Canine and Feline Milk

Michael E. White, PhD
Associate Professor, Department of Animal Science
University of Minnesota, St. Paul, Minnesota

Marcia R. Hathaway, PhD[a]; William R. Dayton, PhD[a]; Allan J. Lepine, PhD [b]
[a] University of Minnesota, St. Paul, Minnesota
[b] Research and Development, The Iams Company, Lewisburg, Ohio

Introduction

Colostrum and milk contain many different biologically active agents including immunoglobulins, allergins, opiates, enzymes,[1-3] hormones and growth factors.[4] Many of these factors are both transported from the maternal circulation into mammary secretions as well as synthesized by the mammary gland itself. The functions of many of these agents in the milk is currently unknown. They may be necessary factors for the maintenance and regulation of the mammary gland. In addition, these agents may be sequestered into the milk in order to affect growth and differentiation in the tissues of the suckling young (*Figure 1*).

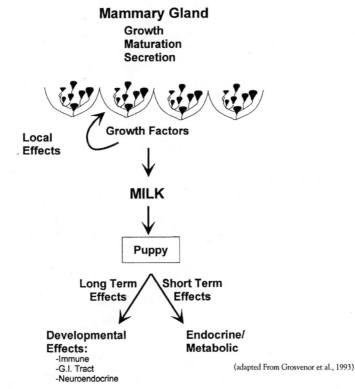

Figure 1.
Potential role of growth factors in milk on the mammary gland itself as well as possible short and long term effects on the neonate.[4]

(adapted From Grosvenor et al., 1993)

Insulin-like growth factors (IGF-1 and -2) and their binding proteins (IGFBPs) are very important growth factors found in mammary secretions. The investigation of growth factors in milk such as the IGFs and IGFBPs is accelerating.[4] These biologically active molecules are found in relatively high concentrations in the milk and colostrum at levels equal to or exceeding those found in the maternal circulation. This indicates that the mammary gland has the capability to synthesize these factors and/or transport them from the blood, concentrating some in the mammary secretions. It has been shown that some of these factors appear to survive in the gastrointestinal (GI) tract of the neonate and have the potential to have local effects on the growth of cells in the GI tract. In addition, they can be absorbed into the neonatal circulation where they may possibly exert systemic effects on the young animal.

IGFs and
IGFBPs

Growth factors and hormones play a crucial role in the growth, development and health of animals. Insulin like growth factors (IGF-1 and IGF-2) are proteins (M_r = 7500) that are present in relatively high concentrations in the blood and biological fluids of most animals. They are structurally similar to proinsulin and have potent metabolic, growth and differentiation-promoting effects on tissues and cells. Consequently, they are believed to play a significant role in regulating tissue and cellular growth. IGF-1 and IGF-2 are noncovalently bound to specific binding proteins that dramatically affect their biological activity. In mammalian species there are 6 specific IGFBPs (IGFBP-1 through -6) which regulate the half-life and biological activity of the IGFs and appear to be crucial components of the IGF growth-regulatory system.[5] Western Ligand Blots of non-reduced human, bovine, ovine and porcine sera reveal a pattern of different molecular weight IGFBPs consisting of a 43 and 39 kDa doublet which is IGFBP-3, a 34 kDa band which is IGFBP-2, a 28 kDa and a 24 kDa band which may represent IGFBP-1, glycosylated IGFBP-5 and non-glycosylated IGFBP-4 or combinations of these IGFBPs. Initially, the liver was thought to be the source of both IGFs and IGFBPs. More recently, however, many cell types[6-13] have been shown to synthesize both IGFs and IGFBPs. Even within the same tissue, different cell types produce IGFs and/or different types of IGFBPs. Because these factors are produced within most tissues, it is believed that the IGFs possess the ability to regulate tissue growth at the local autocrine/paracrine level as well as at the systemic level (*Figure 2*).

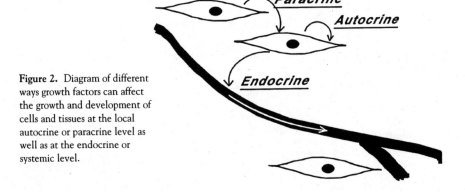

Figure 2. Diagram of different ways growth factors can affect the growth and development of cells and tissues at the local autocrine or paracrine level as well as at the endocrine or systemic level.

The IGFBPs have profound effects on the biological activity of the IGFs at the cellular and tissue level. When added to cells in culture, IGFBPs can either potentiate or antagonize the growth-promoting activity of IGFs, depending upon such factors as the specific binding protein, binding protein concentration, pre-incubation conditions and the cell type.[14-22] Thus, IGFBPs produced by specific tissues may act locally in an autocrine or paracrine manner to provide tissue-specific regulation of IGF-1 and IGF-2 activity.

As with all protein hormones and growth factors, the IGFs exert their growth-promoting activity on tissues and cells by interacting with specific cell surface receptors. The IGFs have two cell surface receptors. The type-1 IGF receptor binds IGF-1 with the highest affinity, IGF-2 with slightly less affinity and weakly binds insulin. Whereas the type-2 IGF receptor (which has also been identified as the mannose-6 phosphate receptor), has a higher affinity for IGF-2, with somewhat less affinity for IGF-1 and no affinity for insulin. The type-1 IGF receptor and the insulin receptor are very similar in structure. They are both composed of two alpha subunits (extracellular) and two beta subunits (transmembranous). Because of the structural similarity of the IGFs with insulin and the structural similarity of their receptors, the IGFs can weakly bind to the insulin receptor and insulin can weakly interact with the type-1 IGF receptor. It has also been reported that hybrid insulin/IGF-1 receptors exist. These receptors contain alpha or beta subunits from the insulin receptor or from the IGF type-1 receptor.[23-28] The biological significance of these receptor hybrids is currently unknown. It has been shown that the growth-promoting actions of the IGFs is through the type-1 IGF receptor.[29] When one considers that there are 2 IGFs (IGF-1 and -2) which can bind to three (or four) different receptors (IGF type-1, IGF type-2, insulin receptors and hybrids) and the interaction between the IGFs with their receptors is regulated by six different IGFBPs, the complexity of this growth-regulatory system becomes apparent. However, it is this very complexity that may provide the fine regulation necessary to control these highly potent growth factors which have been shown to have crucial roles in regulating body and tissue growth as well as reproduction, lactation and development. Additionally, since these potent growth factors and their binding proteins are found in colostrum and milk, they may play important roles in the growth and development of the mammary gland and the neonate.

Growth Factors in Milk

Growth factors and hormones present in colostrum and milk may play a crucial role in the development and health of young animals by affecting GI tract development as well as whole body growth[30] (*Figure 1*). IGF-1 and -2 are present in relatively high levels in mammary secretions of many species[4] and can stimulate gut development as well as cell proliferation which may be crucial for proper puppy nutrition and growth. In the very young animal, these growth factors also can be transferred from the gut to the general circulation where they may affect tissue development elsewhere in the body. Mammary secretions have also been reported to contain significant levels of IGF Binding Proteins (IGFBPs) which are responsible for modulating the biological activity of the IGFs on cells and tissues.

Although IGFs and IGFBPs in mammary secretions may be critically important to the development of the gut in newborn puppies, essentially nothing is known about the types and levels of different growth factors in canine colostrum, milk or blood.

IGFs in Canine Milk

We have recently conducted a study with the objective of determining the concentration of IGF-1 in canine mammary secretions and maternal and puppy serum.[31] In this study we used seven gestating Beagles which were fed common nutritionally complete and adequate gestation/lactation diets. Milk samples were collected 12 hr post partum and on days 3, 7, 21, 28, 35, and 42 after IV oxytocin injection. Two puppies per litter were identified at whelping for the collection of blood samples corresponding to the days of milk collection. Maternal blood samples were obtained on days 1, 7, and 49. Milk and blood samples were subjected to glycylglycine, acid ethanol extraction and acid gel filtration to determine the appropriate extraction method to measure IGF-1 in these samples. Acid ethanol extraction was determined to be the most appropriate method for removing IGF binding protein interference for the IGF-1 radioimmunoassay (RIA). Sera pools and individual milk samples were acid ethanol extracted and analyzed using a validated IGF-1 RIA.

Analysis of IGF-1 in mammary secretions revealed that colostrum contained 40 to 58 ng/ml IGF-1 (Figure 3) which was nearly double the IGF found in maternal serum at whelping (Figure 4).

Canine Milk IGF-1

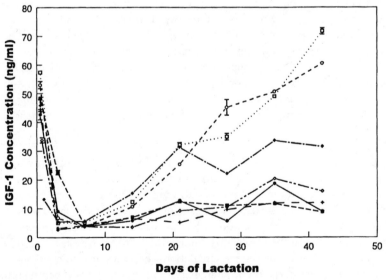

Figure 3. IGF-1 levels in the colostrum and milk of bitches during lactation. Mammary secretions were collected from 7 bitches, 12 hr post-partum and on days 3, 7, 14, 21, 28, 35 and 42 of lactation. Colostrum and milk samples were extracted with acid-ethanol. Individual samples were assayed in the IGF-1 RIA.[30]

Maternal Serum IGF-1

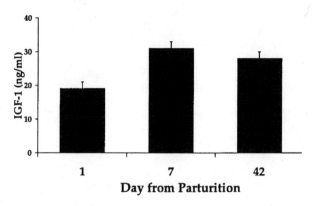

Figure 4. IGF-1 levels in the sera of bitches during lactation. Blood samples were collected from 7 bitches on day 1, 7 and 42 of lactation. The sera samples were extracted with acid-ethanol and pooled (n=7) by day. The IGF-1 levels were determined using the IGF-1 RIA.[30]

The IGF level in mammary secretions dropped 5 to 10 fold by day 3. For 4 of the bitches, milk IGF-1 remained low (~10 ng/ml) throughout lactation whereas the remaining 3 bitches showed increasing milk IGF-1 levels that ranged between 30 and 70 ng/ml by day 42 of lactation. The relatively high IGF-1 levels found in colostrum may be biologically important for newborn puppy survival and/or gut maturation as has been suggested in other species.[30] The high milk IGF-1 levels observed during late lactation in 3 bitches suggest that dogs may exhibit different milk IGF-1 patterns than those reported from other species.[32-33] To our knowledge, these data are the first to report IGF-1 levels in the mammary secretions of dogs.

IGF-1 and IGFBPs in Canine Serum

In this study, we also measured serum IGF-1 levels and the IGFBP banding pattern in canine serum. At whelping, maternal sera IGF-1 levels were approximately 20 ng/ml and increased over 40% to 30 ng/ml by day 7 of lactation and remained near that level at 42 days of lactation (*Figure 4*) . Puppy sera IGF-1 levels were approximately 40 ng/ml 12 hr post whelping and fluctuated around that level throughout lactation (*Figure 5*). In addition to measuring IGF-1, we also measured IGFBP-3 levels in puppy serum. Puppy sera IGFBP-3 concentrations were low at birth and gradually increased to 42 days of age. Maternal IGFBP-3 levels were very low at whelping and gradually reappeared as lactation progressed. This low IGFBP-3 (43 and 39-kDa IGFBP) concentrations in bitch sera at whelping may suggests the presence of a pregnancy-associated IGFBP-3-specific protease that has been reported for other species.[34-38]

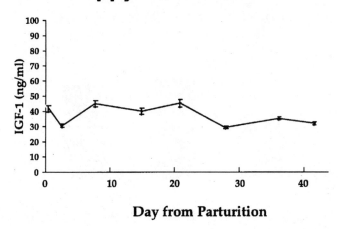

Puppy Serum IGF-1

IGF-1 (ng/ml) vs **Day from Parturition**

Figure 5. IGF-1 levels in the sera of male and female puppies. Blood samples were collected from 2 puppies/litter for a total of 7 litters, 12 hr post-partum and on days 3, 7, 14, 21, 28, 35 and 42 of lactation. The sera samples were pooled by collection day (n=7) and by gender and extracted with acid-ethanol. The IGF-1 levels were determined using the IGF-1 RIA. IGF-1 levels were not different for the male and female puppies. Consequently the values for males and females were averaged together for the same time point.[30]

Comparison of Canine IGFBPs with Other Species

We have performed experiments comparing IGFBP banding patterns among different species. As indicated previously, Western Ligand Blots of non-reduced human, bovine, ovine, feline and porcine sera reveal a pattern of different apparent molecular weight IGFBPs consisting of a 43 and 39 kDa doublet which is IGFBP-3, a 34 kDa band which is IGFBP-2, a 28 kDa and a 24 kDa band which may represent IGFBP-1, glycosylated IGFBP-5 and non-glycosylated IGFBP-4 or combinations of these IGFBPs. However, when canine sera is compared with sera from other mammals including cats, canine sera appears to contain IGFBPs with apparent molecular weights of 43, 39, 37, 28 and 24-kDa. The striking difference is the lack of the 34 kDa IGFBP-2 in canine serum and the presence of a novel 37 kDa molecular weight IGFBP. This novel 37 kDa IGFBP is not seen in the serum of other species studied including other carnivores such as the cat. Therefore, we initiated a project with the goal of identifying and characterizing this novel 37 kDa IGFBP observed in canine serum.

As indicated above, the IGFBPs play a crucial role in regulating IGF action. The ability of the different IGFBPs to bind IGFs and inhibit or enhance IGF action is due to various structural components of these molecules. IGFBP-1 through -6 are encoded by different genes and are all very different molecules having unique biological roles. However, all six different IGFBPs possess structural similarities including 18 conserved cysteine residues in their peptide sequence and the placement of these cysteines within the protein is also highly conserved. These cysteines are responsible for forming disulfide cross bridges that cause the IGFBPs to fold in a specific way that is necessary for IGF binding. Thus the number and placement of these 18 cysteines in all six IGFBPs appears to be of fundamental importance for the proper functioning of the IGFBPs. Any alteration in the number or placement of these cysteines would result in an altered molecular conformation of the IGFBP and would likely alter its functional properties.

Although the novel 37 kDa canine IGFBP does not match up with any of the known IGFBPs in sera from other species with respect to size, it is likely that this 37 kDa canine IGFBP is a different molecular form of one of the known IGFBPs (IGFBP-1 through -6). We have utilized a number of commercially available antibodies against some of the known IGFBPs to perform identification experiments. The 37 kDa canine IGFBP reacted with an anti-IGFBP-2 antibody indicating that it is a canine analog of IGFBP-2. However, the large difference in apparent molecular size indicates that this is a unique molecular form of IGFBP-2. Three reasonable hypotheses that could explain the different molecular form of the 37 kDa canine IGFBP are: (1) the existence of covalently attached carbohydrate chains to the protein making it a larger molecular weight; (2) a difference in the secondary structure (folding) of the protein; this could involve the disulfide bonds formed by the 18 conserved cysteines found in all IGFBPs that holds the protein in a specific conformation; or (3) a larger peptide with more amino acids.

We have performed experiments investigating these three hypotheses and the results indicate that exposure of the 37 kDa canine IGFBP to N- and O-glycanases (which should digest carbohydrate chains from the protein) does not change the molecular size of this IGFBP. However, when the disulfide bonds formed by the conserved cysteines are chemically broken which changes the protein conformation from a folded functional form to an unfolded form, the 37 kDa canine IGFBP drops to a molecular weight similar to that of reduced IGFBP-2 from other species. These data suggest that the 37 kDa canine IGFBP-2 has a similar peptide chain length to IGFBP-2 from other species and is not glycosylated. These data indicate that canine IGFBP-2 represents a unique molecular form of IGFBP-2 with a different molecular conformation due to changes in the placement or disulfide bonding pattern of the cysteines, resulting in a larger apparent molecular size. This difference in molecular form could result in a very different shape of the molecule potentially affecting its ability to bind IGF and regulate its action. Since IGFBPs are also highly conserved between different species,[39] such a structural difference would indicate that this IGFBP is not similar with IGFBP-2 of other species studied. This could represent a fundamental difference between dogs and other species with respect to IGFBP-IGF interaction and function.

Growth factors and hormones play a crucial role in the growth, development and health of animals and the insulin like growth factors and their binding proteins are believed to play a significant role in regulating tissue and cellular growth. It has been shown that some of these factors appear to survive in the GI tract of the neonate and have the potential to have local affects on the growth of cells in the GI tract as well as be absorbed into the neonatal circulation, possibly exerting systemic effects on the young animal. We have demonstrated that these factors are found in relatively high concentrations in both the mammary secretions and the blood of dogs. Additionally, we have identified and characterized a novel form of IGFBP-2 in canine serum that may be unique to the dog. Since the IGFs and IGFBPs have profound effects on metabolism, growth and development, further investigation and characterization of these factors in the dog as well as study of their function in canine nutrition, growth and development is needed.

References

1. West DW. The origin, transport and function of hormones and growth factors in milk. *Exp Clin Endocrinol* 1989; 145-156.

2. Britton JR, Kastin AJ. Biologically active polypeptides in milk. *Am J Med Sci* 1991; 301:124-132.

3. Koldovsky O, Thornburg W. Hormones in milk. *J Pediatr Gastroenterol Nutr* 1987; 6:172-196.

4. Grosvenor CE, Picciano MF, Baumrucker CR. Hormones and growth factors in milk. *Endocr Rev* 1993; 14:710-728.

5. Jones JI, Clemmons DR. Insulin like growth factors and their binding proteins: Biological actions. *Endocrine Reviews* 1995; 16:3-34.

6. Scott CD, Martin JL, Baxter RC. Production of insulin-like growth factor I and its binding protein by adult rat hepatocytes in primary culture. *Endocrinology* 1985; 116:1094-1101.

7. McCusker RH, Clemmons DR. Insulin-like growth factor binding protein secretion by muscle cells: Effect of cellular differentiation and proliferation. *J Cell Physiol* 1988; 137:505-512.

8. Schmid C, Ernst M, Zapf J, Froesch ER. Release of insulin-like growth factor carrier proteins by osteoblasts: Stimulation by estradiol and growth hormone. *Biochem Biophys Res Commun* 1989; 160:788-794.

9. McCusker RH, Camacho-Hübner C, Clemmons DR. Identification of the types of insulin-like growth factor-binding proteins that are secreted by muscle cells *in vitro. J Biol Chem* 1989; 264:7795-7800.

10. Conover CA, Liu F, Powell D, Rosenfeld RG, Hintz RL. Insulin-like growth factor binding proteins from cultured human fibroblasts. Characterization and hormonal regulation. *J Clin Invest* 1989; 83:852-859.

11. Yang YW-H, Brown AL, Orlowski CC, Graham DE, Tseng LY-H, Romanus JA, Rechler MM. Identification of rat cell lines that preferentially express insulin-like growth factor binding proteins rIGFBP-1, 2, or 3. *Mol Endocrinol* 1990; 4:29-38.

12. Martin JL, Willetts KE, Baxter RC. Purification and properties of a novel insulin-like growth factor-II binding protein from transformed human fibroblasts. *J Biol Chem* 1990; 265:4124-4130.

13. Ernst CW, McCusker RH, White ME. Gene expression and secretion of insulin-like growth factor-binding proteins during myoblast differentiation. *Endocrinology* 1992; 130:607-615.

14. Clemmons DR. Insulin-like growth factor binding proteins: Roles in regulating IGF physiology. *J Dev Physiol* 1991; 15:105-110.

15. Binoux M, Roghani M, Hossenlopp P, Hardouin S, Gourmelen M. Molecular forms of human IGF binding proteins: Physiological implications. *Acta Endocrinol (Copenh)* 124 Suppl. 1991; 2:41-47.

16. Baxter RC. Insulin-like growth factor (IGF) binding proteins: The role of serum IGFBPs in regulating IGF availability. *Acta Paediatr Scand* 80 Suppl. 1991; 372:107-114.

17. Reeve JG, Morgan J, Schwander J, Bleehen NM. Role for membrane and secreted insulin-like growth factor-binding protein-2 in the regulation of insulin-like growth factor action in lung tumors. *Cancer Res* 1993; 53:4680-4685.

18. Oh Y, Müller HL, Lamson G, Rosenfeld RG. Insulin-like growth factor (IGF)-independent action of IGF-binding protein-3 in Hs578T human breast cancer cells. Cell surface binding and growth inhibition. *J Biol Chem* 1993; 268:14964-14971.

19. Frost RA, Mazella J, Tseng L. Insulin-like growth factor binding protein-1 inhibits the mitogenic effect of insulin-like growth factors and progestins in human endometrial stromal cells. *Biol Reprod* 1993; 49:104-111.

20. Figueroa JA, Sharma J, Jackson JG, McDermott MJ, Hilsenbeck SG, Yee D. Recombinant insulin-like growth factor binding protein-1 inhibits IGF-I, serum, and estrogen-dependent growth of MCF-7 human breast cancer cells. *J Cell Physiol* 1993; 157:229-236.

21. Conover CA, Kiefer MC. Regulation and biological effect of endogenous insulin-like growth factor binding protein-5 in human osteoblastic cells. *J Clin Endocrinol Metab* 1993; 76:1153-1159.

22. Clemmons DR, Jones JI, Busby WH, Wright G. Role of insulin-like growth factor binding proteins in modifying IGF actions. *Ann NY Acad Sci* 1993; 692:10-21.

23. Kasuya J, Paz IB, Maddux BA, Goldfine ID, Hefta SA, Fujita-Yamaguchi Y. Characterization of human placental insulin-like growth factor-I/insulin hybrid receptors by protein microsequencing and purification. *Biochemistry* 1993; 32:13531-13536.

24. Schäffer L, Kjeldsen T, Andersen AS, Wiberg FC, Larsen UD, Cara JF, Mirmira RG, Nakagawa SH, Tager HS. Interactions of a hybrid insulin/insulin-like growth factor-I analog with chimeric insulin/type I insulin-like growth factor receptors. *J Biol Chem* 1993; 268:3044-3047.

25. Treadway JL, Morrison BD, Soos MA, Siddle K, Olefsky J, Ullrich A, McClain DA, Pessin JE. Transdominant inhibition of tyrosine kinase activity in mutant insulin/insulin-like growth factor I hybrid receptors. *Proc Natl Acad Sci USA* 1991; 88:214-218.

26. Treadway JL, Morrison BD, Goldfine ID, Pessin JE. Assembly of insulin/insulin-like growth factor-1 hybrid receptors *in vitro*. *J Biol Chem* 1989; 264:21450-21453.

27. Soos MA, Siddle K. Immunological relationships between receptors for insulin and insulin-like growth factor I. Evidence for structural heterogeneity of insulin-like growth factor I receptors involving hybrids with insulin receptors. *Biochem J* 1989; 263:553-563.

28. Moxham CP, Duronio V, Jacobs S. Insulin-like growth factor I receptor-subunit heterogeneity. Evidence for hybrid tetramers composed of insulin-like

growth factor I and insulin receptor heterodimers. *J Biol Chem* 1989; 264:13238-13244.

29. Ewton DZ, Falen SL, Florini JR. The type II insulin-like growth factor (IGF) receptor has low affinity for IGF-I analogs: pleiotypic actions of IGFs on myoblasts are apparently mediated by the type I receptor. *Endocrinology* 1987; 120:115-123.

30. Burrin DG, Shulman RJ, Reeds PJ, Davis TA, Gravitt KR. Porcine colostrum and milk stimulate visceral organ and skeletal muscle protein synthesis in neonatal piglets. *J Nutr* 1992; 122:1205-1213.

31. White ME, Hathaway MR, Dayton WR, Henderson T, Lepine A. IGF-1 levels in mammary secretions and serum of dogs. *J Vet Int Med* 1995; 9:186(Abstract).

32. Vega JR, Gibson CA, Skaar TC, Hadsell DL, Baumrucker CR. Insulin-like growth factor (IGF)-I and -II and IGF binding proteins in serum and mammary secretions during the dry period and early lactation in dairy cows. *J Anim Sci* 1991; 69:2538-2547.

33. Campbell PG, Baumrucker CR. Insulin-like growth factor-I and its association with binding proteins in bovine milk. *J Endocrinol* 1989; 120:21-29.

34. Fowlkes JL, Suzuki K, Nagase H, Thrailkill KM. Proteolysis of insulin-like growth factor binding protein-3 during rat pregnancy: A role for matrix metalloproteinases. *Endocrinology* 1994; 135:2810-2813.

35. Nonoshita LD, Wathen NC, Dsupin BA, Chard T, Giudice LC. Insulin-like growth factors (IGFs), IGF-binding proteins (IGFBPs), and proteolyzed IGFBP-3 in embryonic cavities in early human pregnancy: Their potential relevance to maternal-embryonic and fetal interactions. *J Clin Endocrinol Metab* 1994; 79:1249-1255.

36. Davenport ML, Pucilowska J, Clemmons DR, Lundblad R, Spencer JA, Underwood LE. Tissue-specific expression of insulin-like growth factor binding protein-3 protease activity during rat pregnancy. *Endocrinology* 1992; 130:2505-2512.

37. Suikkari A-M, Baxter RC. Insulin-like growth factor-binding protein-3 is functionally normal in pregnancy serum. *J Clin Endocrinol Metab* 1992; 74:177-183.

38. Gargosky SE, Nanto-Salonen K, Tapanainen P, Rosenfeld RG. Pregnancy in growth hormone-deficient rats: Assessment of insulin-like growth factors (IGFs), IGF-binding proteins (IGFBPs) and IGFBP protease activity. *J Endocrinol* 1993; 136:479-489.

39. James PL, Jones SB, Busby WH, Jr., Clemmons DR, Rotwein P. A highly conserved insulin-like growth factor-binding protein (IGFBP-5) is expressed during myoblast differentiation. *J Biol Chem* 1993; 268:22305-22312.

The Influence of Diet on Sperm Quality and Quantity

Walter R. Threlfall, DVM, MS, PhD
Diplomate and President, The American College of Theriogenologists
The Ohio State University, Columbus, Ohio

Allan J. Lepine, PhD; John R. Burr, DVM
Research and Development, The Iams Company, Lewisburg, Ohio

Introduction

The reproductive system is a "luxury" body system and nutritional deficiencies or inadequacies are most likely to affect only this system or affect it prior to other systems. Body systems other than the reproductive system are paramount to the survival of the animal and, therefore, when nutritional stresses such as deficiencies occur, the reproductive system may reduce or eliminate activity in order for the body to conserve existing nutrients. This review focuses primarily on those dietary substances known to influence male reproduction. Most texts reporting on the effects of various nutrients on reproduction exclude the male and focus solely on the bitch prior to, during, and immediately after gestation. Although solitary deficiencies of dietary substances "under practical conditions" probably rarely occur, it is important to appreciate the significance of each nutrient on male reproduction.

Determination of the adequacy of a diet is accomplished by either requiring the product be formulated so that essential nutrient levels fall within the ranges as set in the Association of American Feed Control Officials (AAFCO) Nutrient Profiles, or by requiring a food manufacturer to conduct animal feeding trials in accordance with the AAFCO protocols.[1] The AAFCO Nutrient Profiles for dog foods has recommendations relating to nutrient requirements for growth and reproduction. However, this information is primarily based upon the female, not the male. The following is a summarization of the effects of nutrients on male reproduction and is for a large part from other species since this information is lacking for the male dog.

Vitamin A

Vitamin A and β-carotene are required for optimal reproductive efficiency.[2] The mechanism of action appears most likely to be through failure of release of gonadotropic releasing hormones. Specific activities induced by the retinoids include mitosis and cell differentiation, RNA and protein synthesis, protein glycosylation, steroid synthesis, and protein and steroid sulfation.[3] Retinoid binding proteins have been identified in the testis, proximal and distal epididymis, vas deferens, seminal vesicle and prostate. A deficiency of vitamin A or its precursors can result in testicular degeneration.[4] It is believed that vitamin A has its action through retinol or retinoic acid which binds to the cell and alters the gene expression in the nucleus.[5] However, in certain species, testicular degeneration is apparently due to a deficiency of retinol since retinoic acid supplementation did not prevent the degeneration. It has also been reported that a decrease in testosterone and luteinizing hormone have occurred in animals with a vitamin A deficiency, possibly resulting from a change of lipids within the testis or a direct effect on the pituitary, respectively.[6]

A vitamin A deficiency in the rat is reflected in the form of a reduction in testicular size, spermatogenesis, and testicular steroidogenesis.[3] A vitamin A surplus in the diet of the rat has been reported to cause testicular degeneration and lipid accumulation in the tubules and in the Leydig cells.[7] Since younger animals experiencing a vitamin A deficiency do not mature normally, separation of cause, either due to abnormal body maturation or directly due to the deficiency on the testicular germinal epithelium spermatogenesis, as well as delayed puberty and reduced libido[8] has not been possible.

Vitamin E

Vitamin E has been shown to be responsible for germinal epithelium degeneration when a deficiency in the diet of the rat exists.[9] A deficiency can also cause an inhibition of spermatogenesis in rats which is not reversible by later vitamin E supplementation.[10] Vitamin E deficiency in rats has not been associated with alterations in luteinizing hormone, follicle stimulating hormone, testosterone or inhibin.[11] A deficiency does, however, cause testicular degeneration. Supplemental vitamin E did not influence semen quality or fertility in bulls where rations contained recommended quantities.[12] Large doses of vitamins A, D, E, and C have reportedly affected semen quality in bulls.[13]

In addition to the antioxidant properties of vitamin E and selenium, they may also influence reproduction through their effect on the production of prostaglandins. Vitamin E is reportedly capable of controlling phospholipase A_2 cleavage of arachidonic acid from membrane phospholipids.[14] Arachidonic acid is a precursor for prostaglandin synthesis.

A deficiency of dietary α-tocopherol with or without vitamin E supplementation in rats resulted in a decrease in testicular weight within 16 weeks.[4] The loss was due to a decrease in phospholipid content. In cows, vitamin E and selenium supplementation has been associated with enhanced sperm transport possibly by increased uterine and oviductal contractions.[15]

Vitamin C

Ascorbic acid may function as an antioxidant, as an inhibitor of steriogenesis in the adrenal gland, and as a cofactor in steroidogenesis. Ascorbic acid may be involved in normal sperm production and has been demonstrated to be of value in treating infertility in heavily used bulls and in young bulls.[16] Animals having experienced infection, injury or malnutrition which has resulted in infertility may respond to ascorbic acid supplementation.[16]

High concentrations of ascorbic acid are normally found in the pituitary of cattle[17] and have been reportedly present in other endocrine glands associated with reproduction.[18] It is possible, however, to have ascorbic acid concentrations in the ejaculate of bulls higher than normal and in association with signs of subfertility.[17]

Pyridoxine is involved in the release of pituitary gonadotropins or with a reduction in gonadal binding sites.[19] Deficiencies of this hormone may, therefore, result in a reduction in fertility due to action(s) at these sites.

Vitamin B

Chromium apparently has its most important actions in relation to carbohydrate metabolism by potentiating the activity of insulin.[20] It has also been reported that chromium is important in maintaining the structural integrity of nucleic acids.[21] Since spermatozoa contain high concentrations of nucleic acids, a deficiency of chromium may have a detrimental influence through the deterioration of structural integrity. It has been reported that male rats raised on a diet low in chromium have decreased sperm numbers and fertility at 8 months of age.[22] The reduction in cell numbers as well as fertility were not present at 4 months of age. By 8 months of feeding the restricted diet, sperm production was one half of those fed a supplemented diet. The deficiency was apparently related to age and duration of low dietary chromium rather than any other factor.

Chromium

Calcium has an affect on lactation, skeletal growth, and intracellular processes mediated through calcium binding proteins.[23] Examples of these functions include nucleotide metabolism, protein phosphorylation, secretory functions, contraction of muscles, microtubule assembly, metabolism of glycogen, and calcium flux. Steroid synthesis is calcium dependent within the testes[24] and maximal testosterone production by Leydig cells in vitro is also calcium dependent.[25] The release of luteinizing hormone involves a calcium dependent mechanism since none is released if calcium is absent.

Calcium

There are in excess of 200 proteins and enzymes which contain zinc.[26] Zinc may be involved in steroidogenic enzyme activation and act through the gonadotropic hormones of the pituitary or by combining with ligands within the gonads or prostate. Zinc is stimulated to enter into the prostate by testosterone.[27] Deficiencies of zinc have been shown to cause tubular epithelium atrophy in the buck and rat and cause a reduction of zinc in the testes, epididymis and prostate.[28,29] Testicular degeneration has also been reported in animals fed diets deficient in zinc.[30] Zinc deficiencies have been related to reduced testicular weight, abnormal testicular morphology, morphologically abnormal sperm, reduced numbers of sperm in the

Zinc

ejaculate, and reduced motility.[31] Zinc deficiency resulted in a reduction of spermatogenesis and a change in testicular fatty acids and lipids.[4] Zinc is found in highest concentrations in the tail of the sperm cell and is involved in membrane stability, mechanical properties of the sperm tail, and with sperm motility.[32] Sperm motility is influenced by zinc through its action on ATP and regulation of phospholipid energy reserves.[33] Although zinc is essential for normal spermatogenesis,[27] increased concentrations of zinc above normal have been associated with a reduction in fertility.[32] Retarded testicular growth in bull calves has been corrected by zinc supplementation without permanent damage.[34] Vitamin A uptake by sperm and by the seminiferous tubules is enhanced by the presence of zinc.[35]

Zinc is essential for testosterone production with deficiencies creating a reduction in pituitary gonadotropin release[29] as well as directly affecting the testis.[36] Zinc may further influence testosterone production by affecting gonadotropin receptors or luteinizing and follicle stimulating hormone activity.[37] Reduced dietary intake of zinc has resulted in less binding of androgens and reduced production of dihydrotestosterone.[38] There has also been a reported reduction in testosterone[39] while luteinizing hormone and follicle stimulating hormones are elevated.[40]

Molybdenum   Molybdenum is involved in several enzyme systems such as xanthine oxidase and aldehyde oxidase. Molybdenum also has the capability to stabilize steroid hormone receptor sites thus preventing binding.[41] High dietary molybdenum fed to bulls resulted in complete lack of libido and degeneration of seminiferous tubules and interstitial tissue.[42]

Manganese   A manganese deficiency can have a detrimental affect on mucopolysaccharide synthesis, hydrolases, kinases, decarboxylases, transferase, redox processes, tissue respiration, bone formation, growth, blood formation, endocrine organ function and steroid production.[26] Many of these afffects can obviously influence reproduction directly or indirectly.

Iodine   Iodine deficiency can result in secondary hypothyroidism and thus affect reproduction. A deficiency can result in a reduction in pituitary release of gonadotropins and a reduction in libido and semen quality.[43,44]

Cobalt   The importance of cobalt appears to be through its involvement in cobalamin. Anemia can result from deficiencies and this may lead to infertility. Other actions are yet to be defined.

Selenium   Selenium has been demonstrated to be tightly bound to the sperm cell. Selenium has also been reported to be an essential component of the enzyme glutathione peroxidase which protects most tissues from oxidative damage. This enzyme has been found to be present in the ejaculate of the dog,[45] ram,[45] goat,[45] bull,[46] and man.[45] The function of the cellular binding and the enzyme presence are unknown. Selenium also acts to stabilize the outer mitochondrial membrane. Selenium is concentrated in the sperm midpiece[47] and enhances sperm motility.[48,49] The first change to occur in rat sperm following a selenium deficiency is abnormal development of the sperm midpiece.[50] As the deficiency continues, abnormalities include mitochondrial sheath disorganization. This is then followed by reduced motility, decreased sperm production and testicular size.[50] A selenium deficiency results in an inhibition of spermatogenesis in rats.[10] Selenium incorporation into rat sperm appears to occur during late meiosis and increases rapidly during early spermiogenesis.[51]

Studies indicate that when rats are fed diets deficient in selenium, the concentration of selenium within the testis is comparable to control animals fed supplemented diets.[52] When the pituitary was removed the concentration of testicular selenium decreased but returned to normal when equine chorionic gonadotropin was administered. This finding may aid in explaining the relatively long feeding trials necessary with selenium deficient diets to produce a reduced testicular concentration and an effect on fertility. The testis is the preferred site of supply in the animal on a selenium deficient diet.[52] Bulls that were moderately selenium deficient had semen evaluations performed before and after selenium supplementation.[53] The semen quality was not affected by selenium supplementation.[53]

Cadmium and Mercury

Cadmium and mercury are detrimental to sperm motility even in very low concentrations.[54] Selenium has the capability to alleviate the harmful effects of these substances on sperm.[55] The spermicidal effects of cadmium may be due to glyceraldehyde phosphate dehydrogenase inactivation which interferes with the production of energy rich ATP.[54] Mercury is spermicidal by the formation of mercury albuminates with the sperm protein.[56] The protection provided by the selenium may be due to binding with the cadmium and mercury and thus inactivating their potential detrimental effects. Zinc to some extent has the capability to prevent some of the toxic effects of cadmium.[57] Intratesticular injections of cadmium cause an increase in the concentration of cholesterol and a decrease in concentrations of triglycerides. It is not known if sperm produced under these conditions are capable of fertilization.

Inherited Disorders

There exist several inherited nutrition abnormalities which can result in reproductive as well as other body system problems. These are of concern to the breeder and the veterinarian not only because of their direct affect on the animal, but also because of their influence on future generations produced by the animal carrying the genetic anomally. Malabsorption of vitamin B_{12} occurs in Giant Schnauzers; copper storage abnormalities in Doberman Pinschers,[58] Bedlington

Terriers, West Highland Terriers, and Cocker Spaniels;[59] zinc malabsorption in Siberian Huskies, Alaskan Malamutes, Great Danes and Doberman Pinschers;[60-62] hyperlipidemia in Miniature Schnauzers;[63] and abnormal purine metabolism in Dalmatians[64] exist as inherited nutrition disorders.

Fatty Acids

Linoleate and Arachidonate. When males were fed diets deficient in essential fatty acids for 2 years, extensive degeneration of the testes resulted. The majority of mammals have the capability to convert linoleate to arachidonate in the liver. This permits the fulfilling of their essential fatty acid requirements. The conversion may occur by either denaturation of 18:2 to form 18:3 followed by elongation to 20:3 or elongation of linoleate to 20:2 which is then desaturated at the Δ^5 position to form arachidonate. Since cats cannot convert linoleate to arachidonate in the liver, diets deficient in arachidonate fed to male cats should cause testicular degeneration.[65] However, when males were fed linoleate but not arachidonate, the testicular concentrations of arachidonate were higher than in animals receiving neither. This was an indication of the testes ability to convert linoleate to arachidonate. Testicular degeneration was not evident in animals fed linoleate. Either linoleate or arachidonate can provide the essential fatty acid requirements of most mammals. However, linolenate when supplemented to essential fatty acid deficient rats was not capable of preventing degeneration.[66]

Furthermore, animals fed a diet deficient in essential fatty acids have been demonstrated to be less fertile than control animals.[67] Prolonged feeding of the deficient diet resulted in lower concentrations of fatty acid within the testis. Although essential fatty acids may not be essential at the testicular level, there must be some fat in the diet since rabbits fed a fat free diet for 14 weeks demonstrated a seminiferous tubule degeneration.[68] Sperm never progressed past the secondary spermatocyte stage of development.

Male rats maintained on essential fatty acid deficient diets demonstrated signs of testicular degeneration and became sterile.[69] Lipids within the testis have been reported to increase in men with lowered spermatogenesis and reduced sperm in the ejaculate.[70] The major accumulation of lipids occurred in the Sertoli cells. In addition, there was an increase in interstitial cholesterol and lipids. Since the testis contains numerous fatty acids and lipids, it is apparent that there is a purpose for their presence. The quantity of lipids present is related to the functional capability of the testis. A testis which is producing normal quantities of sperm cells has a lower concentration of lipids. When spermatogenesis is impaired, the concentration of lipids increases, especially in the Sertoli cells. If there is a decreased steroid production capacity, there is an increase in lipids in the interstitial cells.

An additional report indicated that rams with lowered fertility had increased concentrations of cholesterol, lipids, and phospholipids within the testis.[71] There has also been a proposed relationship between the value of treatments for infertility and their effect on the lipid content of the testis. Treatments which are inadequate result in lipid accumulation, whereas treatments which are adequate will decrease lipid concentrations to normal. There is also an elevation in esterified cholesterol during spermatogenic reduction and a return to normal concentrations once normal fertility is regained. Therefore, it has been concluded that the lower the concentration of lipids within the testis, the higher the fertility. However, it has been reported that although the fertilization percentages as well as sperm morphology and motility percentages from normal rams and ones with elevated testicular lipid content was equal, a difference between the two groups was found as higher embryo loss rates in ewes bred by rams with elevated lipids in the testis.[71]

The lipid concentration of the mature sperm in the bull and boar is approximately 12%[72,73] and is approximately 14% in the stallion.[74] Sperm within the testis and epididymis has the capability to synthesize lipids from glucose but this capability decreases rapidly once the cell is ejaculated.[75] Mature sperm can utilize acetate in the production of certain lipids.

Vitamin E deficiencies, in addition to having the capability of inducing testicular degeneration and sterility directly, also have the capability of decreasing the concentration of certain testicular lipids.[76] It has been suggested that the brain and the testis of rats and possibly other species are capable of saturated fatty acid production and are, therefore, independent of the fatty acid make up of the diet.[77]

Protein

Protein is required for optimal reproductive efficiency. The mechanism of action appears to be at the level of the hypothalamus by interfering with release of gonadotropic releasing hormones. Reduced protein in the feed has also been shown to be responsible for reduced sperm production. However, a reduction of protein in the diet of cattle also caused a reduction in feed intake which caused a reduction in energy as well.[78] Whenever a diet is deficient in energy or protein the animal may enter into a negative energy balance depending on the extent of the deficiency.

Severe restriction in energy or protein will delay puberty and sperm production capabilities after puberty in rams[79] and bulls.[80] The testicular size was smaller than in animals receiving adequate nutrition and the size remained smaller following availability of a adequate diet. Sperm production in mature bulls fed inadequately was less than half of that produced by controls.[81] Feeding protein-free diets resulted in retarded spermatogenesis in rats.[82] These animals had lipid deposition near the basement membrane in the area of the Sertoli cells and the spermatogonia.

Research was recently conducted in the male canine to evaluate the effect of a high quality protein source (animal-based protein; 30% of the diet) versus a low quality protein source (plant-based protein) fed at the AAFCO minimum requirement for reproduction (22% of the diet) on ejaculate volume, sperm concentration, motility and morphology.[a] Ejaculate volume, concentration and motility were not affected while there was a trend for an increased number of distal protoplasmic

---

[a] Threlfall et al.; unpublished results

droplets (*Figure* 1) with the low quality protein diet. These diets were not isocaloric which may also have contributed to the observed sperm abnormality (see energy discussion below).

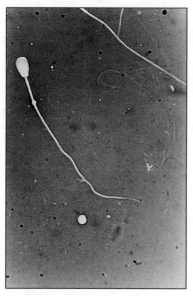

Figure 1. Sperm with distal protoplasmic droplet

Energy

Adequate energy concentration is required for optimal reproductive efficiency. A failure in release of gonadotropin releasing hormone appears to be the mechanism by which inadequate energy affects reproduction.[83] Although the pituitary production of luteinizing hormone in rams was not influenced by under-feeding, the pituitary of bulls was smaller and luteinizing hormone production was reduced.[84] The anterior pituitary has been demonstrated to be the mechanism by which under nutrition has its effect but may be in part due to direct effects upon the testis.[85] Underfed rams do not exhibit a decrease in luteinizing hormone stimulated testosterone production.[86]

Young male rats fed starvation diets to the point of a 50% reduction in body weight did not lose testicular weight but did not have the normal increase.[87] There was atrophy in both Leydig cells and germinal epithelium with lipid accumulation in the area where the Sertoli cells had been.

A reduction in feed intake prior to puberty in rams slowed preputial breakdown and increased age at puberty.[79] Diets which resulted in weight loss caused a reduction in daily sperm output.[84] Furthermore, rams which lost weight had a reduction in testosterone production.[88] Undernutrition has also been reported to be responsible for reduced testosterone production and a noticeable reduction in fructose and citric acid was present in the seminal vesicles of bulls.[89] Although reduction in energy and/or protein can greatly influence testicular size, testosterone concentrations, sperm production and luteinizing hormone production, the male continues to have adequate sperm and libido for natural service.[90]

After having rams on a restricted energy and protein ration for 3 months, testosterone production was approximately 10% of control fed rams.[85] Also in underfed rams, the diameter of seminiferous tubules, epididymal sperm content and seminal vesicle vesicular gland weight were reduced.[85] Undernutrition has been reported to cause testicular degeneration in guinea pigs and rabbits[91] and in pigeons.[92] In the human, decreased sperm production and decreased libido following malnutrition have been reported.[93] There was also a decease in sperm concentration and motility in the male canine.[94] The influence of undernutrition in rats and mice includes a reduction in size of seminal vesicles and prostates.[95] The administration of human chorionic gonadotropin to animals underfed reversed the effects of diet to some degree.[96] Undernutrition may also cause a reduction in germinal epithelium activity directly.[85] Testosterone production and spermatogenesis were affected more by energy deficiencies than by protein deficiencies in the ram.[97]

Bulls maintained on a 60% of recommended total digestible nutrient diet from 2 months to 46 months of age resulted in an eight month delay in the production of "appreciable" sperm.[98] During the last 12 months of the project the group was fed a ration containing 100% of the recommended total digestible nutrients without a significant improvement in sperm quantity. This deficient diet also resulted in a lower ejaculate volume and a longer period of time for sperm reserves to be replenished. When mature bulls were placed on a 60% total digestible nutrient diet there was no significant effect on sperm production. It has been reported that bulls raised on a medium energy diet had higher sperm reserves than bulls raised on a high energy diet.[99] This study did not substantiate previous finding that the testes weight would be greater for bulls on a high energy diet.[100] The reason for reduced sperm reserves for high energy diet animals may be related to increased scrotal heat causing a reduction in production, an increase in rate of passage, or an increased rate of resorption.

The feeding of high concentrate diets to bulls was responsible for a reduction in epididymal sperm reserves compared to that present in bulls fed total roughage.[100] High energy diets were compared to medium energy diets in regard to effects on scrotal circumference, testes weights, epididymal sperm reserves, and survival traits in bulls.[100] Semen quality was inferior in bulls fed a high energy diet in regard to motility. There was also an increased occurrence of sperm with crater defects in the head. Hereford bulls were more susceptible to the detrimental effects of the high energy diet compared to Angus bulls. Since other available literature[101,102] is in disagreement with the aforementioned research, it is possible that the age of the bulls at the time of exposure or the length of exposure to the high energy diet may account for the differences reported.

Reduced body weight due to a reduction in protein and energy results in a reduction in sperm output in the ram and buck.[103-105] The reduction in nutrients affected not only testicular size but also the functional capability of the testes. Adequate nutrition markedly increased the diameter of the seminiferous tubule, the seminiferous tubule percentage of the testis, and the percentage of seminiferous epithelium lined tubules.

In addition, body mass does not necessarily need to change in order to increase sperm production. "Flushing" rams similar to ewes has increased sperm output before body condition changes occurred.[106] Reduction in nutrients is probably reflected through the effects on the hypothalamus and pituitary rather than at another site.[107] The gonadotropin releasing hormone pulse frequency is influenced by nutrition.

Opioidergic pathways do not appear to be the pathway through which reduced nutrients affect male reproduction.[108] Undernutrition has been demonstrated to cause an increase in neuropeptide Y which inhibits gonadotropin releasing hormone.[109] This substance would be active entirely within the hypothalamus. Other methods of influencing fertility independent of gonadotropin releasing hormone have been proposed.[110] The substantiation for other mechanisms include experiments where rams have been immunized against gonadotropin releasing hormone and increased nutrition was able to increase testicular size.[111]

Another possibility is that growth hormone and insulin-like growth factor I may act directly on the testes to affect sperm production.[112] However, in undernutrition studies involving immunization against growth hormone and insulin-like growth factor I, concentrations were observed to decrease while testicular size increased once the diet was supplemented.[113] Although it is not apparent whether energy or protein was responsible for the increase in testicular size, reports in rams indicate it was energy.[104] It is certain that both dietary energy and protein are closely related. Although it was reported that there existed a relationship between energy and canine reproduction, no mention was made as to those effects on the male.[114]

As indicated in the preceding literature review, there exists minimal information regarding the effect of diet on canine male fertility. The literature which is available is directed toward the bitch. It is therefore necessary to continue innovative research, using the knowledge gained through the investigation of reproduction in other species as summarized above, in an effort to elucidate nutritional truths which will enhance and improve the reproductive efficiency of the male canine.

References

    1. Dzanis DA. *The Association of American Feed Control Officials Dog and Cat Food Nutrient Profiles: Substantiation of Nutritional Adequacy of Complete and Balanced Pet Foods in the United States.* American Institute of Nutrition. 1994:2535S.

    2. Dunn TG, Moss GE. Effects of nutrient deficiencies and excesses on reproductive efficiency of livestock. *J Anim Sci* 1992; 70:1580.

3. Ganguly J, Rao MRS, Murthy SK, Sarada K. Systemic mode of action of vitamin A. *Vitam Horm* 1980; 38:1.

4. Bieri JG, Prival EL. Effect of deficiencies of alpha tocopherol, retinol and zinc on the lipid composition of rat testes. *J Nutr* 1966; 89:55.

5. Chytil F, Ong DE. Cellular retinoid binding proteins. In: *The Retinoids*. Vol 2, Academic Press, New York NY, 1984:89.

6. Gambal D. Effect of hormones on the testicular lipids of vitamin A deficient rats. *J Nutr* 1966; 89:203.

7. Biswas NM, Deb C. Testicular degeneration in rats during hypervitaminosos A. *Endokrinologie* 1965; 49:64.

8. Erdman RA, Shaver RD, Vandersall JH. Dietary choline for the lactating cow: possible effects on milk fat synthesis. *J Dairy Sci* 1984; 67:410.

9. Scott ML. Vitamin E. In: *Handbook of Lipid Research* Vol 2. New York: Plenum Press. 1978:133.

10. Wu SH, Oldfield JE, Whanger PD, Weswig PH. Effect of selenium, vitamin E, and antioxidants on testicular function in rats. *Biol Reprod* 1973; 8:625.

11. Cooper DR, Kling OR, Carpenter MP. Effect of vitamin E deficiency on serum concentration of follicle stimulating hormone and testosterone during testicular maturation and degeneration. *Endocrinology* 1987; 120:83.

12. Salisbury GW. A controlled experiment in feeding wheat germ oil as a supplement to the normal ration of bulls used for artificial insemination. *J Dairy Sci* 1944; 27:551.

13. Kozicki LR, Silva G, Barnabe RC. Effects of Vitamins A, D³, E and C on the characteristics of bull semen. *Zentralbl Veterinaermed* 1981; 28:538.

14. Pappu AS, Fatterpaker P, Sreenivasan A. Role of vitamin E in cellular processes. *World Rev Nutr Diet* 1978; 31:190.

15. Sergerson EC, Libby DW. Ova fertilization and sperm number per fertilized ovum for selenium and vitamin E treated Charolais cattle. *Therio* 1982; 17:333.

16. Phillips PH, Lardy HA, Heizer EE, Rupel IW. Sperm stimulation in the bull through the subcutaneous administration of ascorbic acid. *J Dairy Sci* 1940; 23:873.

17. Phillips PH, Stare FJ. The distribution of a reducing substance (vitamin C) in the tissues of fluorine fed cows. *J Biol Chem* 1934; 104:351.

18. Levine M, Morita K. Ascorbic acid in endocrine systems. *Vitam Horm* 1985; 42:1.

19. Wooten E, Nelson MM, Simpson ME, Evans HM. Effect of pyridoxine deficiency on the gonadotrophic content of the anterior pituitary in the rat. *Endocrin* 1955; 56:59.

20. Anderson RA, Mertz M. *Trends Biochem Sci* 1977; 2:277.

21. Hermann H, Speck LB. *Science* 1954; 119:221.

22. Anderson RA, Polansky MM. Dietary chromium deficiency effect on sperm count and fertility in rats. *Biological Trace Element Research* 1981; 3:1-5.

23. Dickson I. New approaches to vitamin D. *Nature* 1987; 325:18.

24. Podestra EJ, Milani A, Steffen H, Neher R. Steroidogenic action of calcium ions in isolated adrenocrotical cells. *Biochem J* 1980; 186:391.

25. Lin T. Mechanism of action of gonadotropin releasing hormone stimulated bv steroidogenesis. I. The stimulatory effect is calcium dependent and not mediated by cyclic nucleotides. *J Androl* 1984; 5:193.

26. Hurley WL, Doane RM. Recent developments in the roles of vitamins and minerals in reproduction. *J Dairy Sci* 1989; 72:784.

27. Apagar J. Zinc and reproduction. *Ann Rev Nutr* 1985; 5:43.

28. Miller WJ, Pitts WJ, Clifton CM, Schmittle SC. Experimentally produced zinc deficiency in the goat. *J Dairy Sci* 1964; 47:556.

29. Millar MJ, Fischer MI, Elcoate PV, Mawson CA. The effects of dietary zinc deficiency on the reproductive system of male rats. *Can J Biochem Physiol* 1958; 36:557.

30. Hafiez AA, El Kirdassy ZHM, El Malkh NM, El Zayat EMI. Role of zinc in regulating testicular function. Part 3. Histopathological changes induced by dietary zinc deficiency in testes of male albino rats. *Nahrung* 1990; 34:65.

31. Apagar J. Zinc and reproduction: an update. *J Nutr Biochem* 1992; 3:266.

32. Swarup D, Sekhon H. Correlation of vitamin A and zinc concentration of seminal plasma to fertility of bovine semen. *Nutr Rep Int* 1976; 13:37.

33. Hidiroglou M, Knipfel JE. Zinc in mammalian sperm: a review. *J Dairy Sci* 1984; 67:1147.

34. Miller JK, Swanson EW. Experimental zinc deficiency and recovery of calves. *J Nutr* 1966; 76:467.

35. Swarup D, Sekhon H. Incorporation of labeled retinol in bovine spermatozoa. III. Effect of zinc, fructose, and pH on the incorporation. *Nutr Rep Int* 1975; 12:255.

36. Leathem JH. Nutrition. In: *The Testis. Vol. 3, Influencing Factors.* New York: Academic Press, 1970:193.

37. Root AW, Duckett G, Sweetland M, Reiter EO. Effects of zinc deficiency upon pituitary function in sexually mature and immature male rats. *J Nutr* 1979; 109:958.

38. Chung KW, Kim SY, Chan WY, Rennert OM. Androgen receptors in ventral prostate glands of zinc deficient rats. *Life Sci* 1986; 38:351.

39. Hafiez AA, El Kirdassy ZHM, Mansour MMS, Sharada HM, El Zayat EMI. Role of zinc in regulating testicular function. Part 1. Effect of dietary zinc deficiency on serum levels of gonadotropins, prolactin and testosterone in male albino rats. *Nahrung* 1989; 33:935.

40. Mansour MMS, Hafiez AA, El Kirdassy ZHM, El Malkh NM, Halawa FA, El Zayat P EMI. Role of zinc in regulating testicular function. Part 2. Effect of dietary zinc deficiency on gonadotropins, prolactin and testosterone levels as well as 3b-hydroxysteroid dehydrogenase activity in testes of male albino rats. *Nahrung* 1989; 33:941.

41. Dahmer MK, Housley PR, Pratt WB. Effects of molybdate and endogenous inhibitors on steroid receptor inactivation, transformation, and translocation. *Ann Rev Physiol* 1984; 46:67.

42. Thomas JW, Moss S. The effect of orally administered molybdenum on growth, spermatogenesis and testes histology of young dairy bulls. *J Dairy Sci* 1951; 34:929.

43. Hignett SL. Factors Influencing herd fertility in cattle. *Vet Rec* 1950; 62:652.

44. Maqsood M. Thyroid function in relation to reproduction of mammals and

birds. *Biol Rev Camb Philos Soc* 1952; 27:281.

45. Li TK. The glutathione and thiol content of mammalian spermatozoa and seminal plasma. *Biol Reprod* 1975; 12:641.

46. Smith DG, Senger PL, McCutchan JF, Landa CA. Selenium and glutathione peroxidase distribution in bovine semen and selenium retention by the tissues of the reproductive tract in the bull. *Biol Reprod* 1979; 20:377.

47. Brown DG, Burk RF. Selenium retention in tissues and sperm of rats fed a torula yeast diet. *J Nutr* 1973; 103:102.

48. Julien WE, Murray FA. Effect of selenium and selenium with vitamin E on in vitro motility of bovine spermatozoa. *Proc Amer Soc Anim Sci*, 69th Annual Meeting, University of Wisconsin, Madison, 1977:174 (abstr).

49. Pratt W. A study of the effect of in vitro supplementation of sodium selenite on the metabolism of bovine sperm. MS Thesis, Ohio State University, Columbus, Ohio. 1978.

50. Wallace E, Calvin HI, Cooper GW. Progressive defects observed in mouse sperm during the course of three generations of selenium deficiency. *Gamete Res* 1983; 4:377.

51. Calvin HI, Grosshans K, Musicant-Shikora SR, Turner SI. A developmental study of rat sperm and testis selenoproteins. *J Reprod Fert* 1987; 81:1.

52. Behne D, Hoffer T, von Berswordt-Wallrabe R, Elger W. Selenium in the testis of the rat: studies on its regulation and its importance for the organism. *Amer Inst Nutr* 1982; 1682.

53. Segerson EC, Johnson BH. Selenium/vitamin E and reproductive function in angus bulls. *J Anim Sci* 1979; 48(Suppl 1):336 (Abstr).

54. White IG. The toxicity of heavy metals to mammalian spermatozoa. *Aust J Exp Biol* 1955; 33:359.

55. Kar AB, Das RP, Mukerji B. Prevention of cadmium induced changes in the gonads of rats by zinc and selenium: a study in antagonism between metals in the biological system. *Proc Natl Inst Sci India, Part B Biol Sci* 1960; 26:40.

56. Baker JR. The spermicidal powers of chemical contraceptives. *J Hyg* 1931; 31:189.

57. Johnson AD, VanDemark NL, Gomes WR Butler WR, Hodgen GD. Effect of antispermatogenic and hormone treatments on testicular cholesterol. *Federation Proc* 1967; 26:645.

58. Fyfe JC, Jexyk PF, Giger U, et al. Inherited selective malabsorption of vitamin B12 in giant schnauzers. *J Am Anim Hosp Assoc* 1989; 25:533.

59. Thornburg LP, Polley D, Dimmitt R. The diagnosis and treatment of copper toxicosis in dogs. *Can Pract* 1984; 11:36.

60. Codner EC, Thatcher CD. The role of nutrition in the management of dermatoses. *Semin Vet Med Surg Sm Anim* 1990; 5:167.

61. Fadok VA. Zinc responsive dermatosis in a great dane: a case report. *J Am Anim Hosp Assoc* 1982; 18:409.

62. Brown RG, Hoag GN, Smart ME, et al. Alaskan malamute chondrodysplasia. V. Decreased gut zinc absorption. *Growth* 1978; 42:1.

63. Ford RB. Idiopathic hyperchylomicronemia in miniature schnauzers. *J Sm Anim Pract* 1993; 34:488.

64. Kuster G, Shorter RG, Dawson B. Uric acid metabolism in dalmatians and other dogs. *Arch Int Med* 1972; 129:492.

65. MacDonald ML, Rogers QR, Morris JG, Cupps PT. Effects of linoleate and arachidonate deficiencies on reproduction and spermatogenesis in the cat. *J Nutr* 1984; 114:719.

66. Leat WMF, Clarke NGE, Harrison FA. Testicular lipids of rats given an EFA deficient diet supplemented with linoleate or linolenate. *Proc Nutr Soc* 1982; 41:159.

67. Berti F, Fumagalli R. Rapporto tra composizione in acidi grassi del testicolo e fertilita nel ratto. *Atti Accad Med Lombarda* 1965; 20:447.

68. Ahluwalia B, Pincus G, Holman RT. Essential fatty acid deficiency and its effects upon reproductive organs of male rabbits. *J Nutr* 1967; 92:205.

69. Evans HM, Lepkovsky S, Murphy EA. Vital need of the body for certain unsaturated fatty acids. VI. Male sterility on fat free diets. *J Biol Chem* 1934; 106:445.

70. Long ME, Engle ET. Cytocyhemistry of the human tesis. *Ann NY Acad Sci* 1952; 55:619.

71. Judy JK. Differences in the level of fertility among rams when measured by fertility and fecundity of ewes and methods for predicting this trait. PhD Dissertation, Ohio State University, 1968.

72. Komerek RJ, Pickett BW, Lanz RN, Jensen RG. Lipid composition of bovine spermatozoa and seminal plasma. *J Dairy Sci* 1964; 47:531.

73. Komerek RJ, Pickett BW, Gibson EW, Jensen RG. Lipids of porcine spermatozoa, seminal plasma and gel. *J Reprod Fertility* 1965; 9:131.

74. Komarek RJ, Pickett BW, Gibson EW, Lanz RN. Composition of lipids in stallion semen. *J Reprod Fertility* 1965; 10:337.

75. Scott TW, Boglmayr JK, Setchell BP. Lipid composition and metabolism in testicular and ejaculated ram spermatozoa. *Biochem J* 1967; 102:456.

76. Bieri JG, Andrews EL. Fatty acids in rat testes as affected by vitamin E. *Biochem Biophys Res Commun* 1964; 17:115.

77. Whorton AR, Coniglio JG. Fatty acid synthesis in testes of fat deficient and fat supplemented rats. *J Nutr* 1977; 107:79.

78. Wiltbank JN, Warwick EJ, Davis RE, Cook AC, Reynolds WL, Hazen MW. Influence of total feed and protein intake on reproductive performance in the beef female through second calving. *Tech Bull 1314*. Washington, DC: USDA; 1965.

79. Pretorius PS, Marincowitz G. Postnatal penis development, testes descent and puberty in merino ram lambs on different planes of nutrition. *S Afr J Agric Sci* 1968; 11:319.

80. Bratton RW, Musgrave SD, Dunn HO, Foote RH. Causes and prevention of reproductive failures in dairy cattle. II. Influence of underfeeding and overfeeding from birth to 80 weeks of age on growth, sexual development, and semen production of holstein bulls. *Bull No 940*. Cornell Univ Agric Exp Sta, Ithaca, NY, 1959.

81. VanDemark NL, Mauger RE. Effect of energy intake on reproductive performance of dairy bulls. II. Semen production and replenshiment. *J Dairy Sci* 1964; 47:798.

82. Horn EH. Nutritional and hormonal influences upon reproductive matura-

tion, organ weights and histochemistry of the immature male rat. *Endocrinology* 1955; 57:399.

83. Terqui M, Chupin D, Gauthier D, Perez N, Pelot J, Mauleon P. Influence of management and nutrition on postpartum endocrine function and ovarian activity in cows. In: *Factors Influencing Fertility in the Postpartum Cow*. Vol 20. The Hague, Netherlands: Martinus Nijhoff Publishers, 1982:408.

84. Alkass JO, Bryant MJ, Walton JS. Some effects of level of feeding and body condition score upon sperm production and gonadotrophin concentrations in rams. *Anim Prod* 1982; 34:265.

85. Setchell BP, Waites GMH, Lindner HR. Effect of undernutrition on testicular blood fow and metabolism and the output of testosterone in the ram. *J Reprod Fert* 1965; 9:149.

86. Martin GB, Tjondronegoro S and Blackberry MA. Effects of nutrition on testicular size and the concentrations of gonadotrophins, testosterone and inhibin in plasma of mature male sheep. *J Repro and Fert* 1994; 101:121.

87. Lynch KM, Scott WW. Lipid distribution in the sertoli cell and leydig cell of the rat testis as related to experimental alterations of the pituitary gonad system. *Endocrinology* 1951; 49:8.

88. Setchell BP, Waites GMH, Lindner HR. Effect of undernutrition on testicular blood flow and metabolism and the output of testosterone in the ram. *J Reprod Fertil* 1965; 9:149.

89. Mann T, Rowson LEA, Short RV, Skinner JD. The relationship between nutrition and adrogenic activity in pubescent twin calves, and the effect of orchitis. *J Endocrinol* 1967; 38:455.

90. Parker GV, Thwaites CJ. The effects of undernutrition on libido and semen quality in adult merino rams. *Aust J Agric Res* 1972; 23:109.

91. Simonowitsch J (1896). Ueber pathologisch anatomische veranderungen der joden bei vollstandigem und unvollstandigem hungern der thiere und auffutterung nach dem hungern. Dissertation. St. Petersburg Abstracts in Muhlmann, M (1899). Russische Literatur uber die Pathologie des Hungers. *Zbl allg Path path Anat* 10:160 and in *Jber Fortschr Anat Entwickl gesch* 3:735 (1897).

92. Grandis V. La spermatogenese durant l inanition. *Arch ital Biol* 1889; 12:215.

93. Miles WR. The sex expression of men living on a lowered nutritional level. *J Nerv Dis* 1919; 49:208.

94. Poiarkov E. L influence du jeune sur le travail des glandes sexuelles du chien. *CR Soc Biol Paris* 1913; 1:141.

95. Moore CR, Samuels LT. The action of testis hormone in correcting changes induced in the rat prostate and seminal vesicles by vitamin B deficiency or partial inanition. *Amer J Physiol* 1931; 96:278.

96. Mason KE, Wolfe JM. The physiological activity of the hypophyses of rats under various experimental conditons. *Anat Rec* 1930; 45:232.

97. Davis JR, Morris RN. Effect of glucose on incorporation of L-lysine-U-C14 into testicular proteins. *Amer J Physiol* 1963; 205:833.

98. VanDemark NL, Fritz GR, Mauger RE. Effect of energy intake on reproduc-tive performance of dairy bulls. II. Semen production and replenishment. *J Dairy Sci* 1964; 47:898.

99. Coulter GH, Bailey DRC. Epididymal sperm reserves in 12 month old angus and hereford bulls: effects of bull strain plus dietary energy. *Anim Repro Sci* 1988; 16:169.

100. Coulter GH, Kozub GC. Testicular development, epididymal sperm reserves and seminal quality in two year old hereford and angus bulls: effects of two levels of dietary energy. *J Anim Sci* 1984; 59:432.

101. Breuer DJ. Effects of 140 day feed test on some fertility parameters in beef bulls. PhD Dissertation. University of Missouri, Columbia, 1980.

102. Pruitt RJ. Effect of energy intake on the sexual development of yearling beef bulls. PhD Dissertation. Kansas State University, Manhattan, 1983.

103. Cameron AWN, Murphy PM, Oldham CM. Nutrition of rams and output of spermatozoa. *Proc Austral Soc Anim Prod* 1988; 17:162.

104. Murray PJ, Rowe JB, Pethick DW, Adams NR. The effect of nutrition on testicular growth in the merino ram. 1990; 41:185.

105. Hiroe K, Tomizuka T. Effects of nutrition on the characteristics of goat semen. *Bulletin of Natl Inst of Anim Indust* 1965; 8:17.

106. Clark RT. Studies of reproduction in sheep. I. The ovulation rate of the ewe as affected by the plane of nutrition. *Anat Rec* 1934; 60:125.

107. Parr RA, Tilbrook AJ. The influence of nutrition on circulating levels of testosterone in rams and testosterone treated wethers. *Proc Aust Soc Anim Prod* 1990; 18:328.

108. Miller DW, Lane RIF, Boukhliq R, Hotzel M, Martin GB. Nutrition and the opioidergic control of LH secretion in the ram. *Proc of the Endo Soc Aust* 1992; 35:59.

109. Morley JE. Neuropeptide regulation of appetite and weight. *Endo Rev* 1987; 8:256.

110. Martin GB, Walkden Brown SW, Boukhliq R, Tjondronegoro S, Miller DW, Fisher JS, Hotzel MJ, Restall BJ, Adams NR. Non-photoperiodic inputs into seasonal breeding in male ruminants. In: *Perspectives in Comparative Endocrinology*. Ottawa: National Research Council of Canada, 1994:574.

111. Hotzel MJ, Martin GB, Markey CM. Effect of nutrition on testicular function of rams immunised against GnRH. *Proc Endocrine Soc of Aust* 1993; 36:102.

112. Spiteri-Grech J, Nieschlag E. The role of growth hormone and insulin-like growth factor I in the regulation of male reproductive function. *Hormone Res* 1992; 38(Supp 1):22.

113. Martin GB, Walkden Brown SW. Nutritional influences on reproduction in mature male sheep and goats. *J Repro & Fert* 1995; 49:437.

114. Moser E. Feeding to optimize canine reproductive efficiency. *Problems in Vet Med* 1992; 4:545.

Renal Health

Dietary Protein and the Kidney

Daniel P. Carey, DVM
Director, Technical Communications
Research and Development, The Iams Company, Lewisburg, Ohio

Few topics in veterinary clinical nutrition have been as widely discussed, uniformly accepted, and frequently applied as dietary protein modifications and the canine kidney. For years, veterinary students in North America have learned that chronic renal failure is often progressive and that some of the signs of uremia are due to metabolic waste from protein catabolism. The link between protein and progression was not proven but suspected and promoted by some lecturers. Concurrently, some veterinary medical foods, espoused as appropriate for the disease, seemingly validated the connection between the progression of the renal damage and dietary protein. The resulting confusion has led 42% of practicing North American veterinarians to believe that dietary protein was actually involved in the etiology of chronic renal failure.[1]

This misunderstanding is slowly changing as new, scientifically sound studies are conducted and published. Current reports are building upon the groundwork laid over the past 20 years of investigations and rely not only upon developments in veterinary medicine but also nutritional science and pet food processing.

Introduction

Chronic renal failure is characterized as irreversible and progressive with clinical signs developing as the regulatory and excretory functions of the kidney decrease. Numerous causes have been identified including trauma, infection, immunological disease, neoplasia, renal ischemia, genetic anomalies and toxins.[2] In most cases, the initiating factor(s) are no longer present when clinical signs are first noticed. This is the result of significant compensation by the remaining viable nephrons while the inciting cause is removed. With time, however, most cases progress. Progression involves the gradual decline in glomerular filtration rate (GFR), accumulation of metabolic by-products, increased histopathogical changes, and development or worsening of clinical signs. Although $^3/_4$ to $^{15}/_{16}$ of the renal mass must be loss before progression occurs,[3] individual variation exists with some dogs or cats not showing progression even in the face of large losses of renal mass.[4] The pathogenesis of progression is not clear. Indeed, the absence of a consistent rate of progression makes it difficult to study. Several hypotheses have been suggested with the current emphasis placed on hyperfiltration.[5] While this mechanism explains the changes seen in the rat model,[6,7,8] several studies in dogs do not show the same results.[9,10,11]

Chronic Renal Failure and Progression

Rat studies have shown that dietary changes which limit hyperfiltration and intrarenal hypertension also slow the progression of the disease.[7] Because the adverse affects may be linked to the adaptive changes necessary for compensation, it is possible that the dietary manipulations actually slow the adaptation. Although much attention has been given to protein, other factors such as sodium, lipid, and energy intake have also been studied.[12,13] Indeed, the effects attributed to protein intake in some early studies appears to be due to reduced caloric intake rather than protein.[12]

High protein intakes increase the renal blood flow in all species studied, including the dog.[8,9,14] This effect is noted in both healthy animals and those with compromised kidney function. Restricting protein intake in rats slows the progression of experimental chronic renal disease.[7,8] The same slowing of the progression of renal disease is also seen in Fischer 344 rats genetically predisposed to chronic renal disease as they age.[15,16]

The rat model is convenient and has led to numerous methods and findings, but there are key differences between rats and dogs that make direct extrapolation of rat results invalid. Many of the rat models used have spontaneous renal disease associated with aging.[15,17] The rat also continues to grow throughout its life while the dog reaches a mature size early and then maintains that size; this might explain part of the longevity effects of caloric restriction in rats.

Dog Studies   The relationship between protein intake and progression seen in rats has not been found in the dog. Contrary to the rat findings, increased protein levels have not been shown to be related to the progression of renal disease in dogs with experimental or natural renal disease.[9,10,11,18] Dogs do experience renal hyperfiltration and hypertension, but moderate (16%) protein restriction did not prevent its development.[19] Further, a direct relationship between protein intake and GFR has been shown in the dog.[20] The same relationship exists for renal plasma flow.[20]

Diets containing either 19, 27 or 56% protein were fed to dogs with 75% reduction in renal mass for a period of four years.[9] Dogs on the highest protein intake had higher GFR and renal plasma flow than dogs fed the lowest protein diet, but significant morphological or functional deterioration was not noted in either group. In contrast to the rat studies, increased protein intake was not associated with elevated BUN or with clinical signs of kidney disease. Although the diets used in this study had more variables than just protein level and the dogs were not azotemic, the fact remains that there was no detectable deleterious effect of consuming 56% protein over a four-year period with a 75% reduction in renal mass.

Similar results were obtained in a more recent study in which diets containing 16.1, 24.5 and 50% protein were fed to dogs with $^{7}/_{8}$ to $^{15}/_{16}$ renal mass reduction.[10] The study concluded after 92 days with no relationship found between dietary protein and renal disease progression. However, the more azotemic dogs had more severe clinical signs on the higher protein foods.

The effects of dietary protein on the renal compensation following renal mass reduction were studied with two diets differing only in protein content: 15 and 31%.[21] Since increased GFR and compensatory renal growth are deemed desirable following renal mass loss, the diets were compared in dogs with 7/8 nephrectomy. The 31% protein group showed significantly greater GFR and renal growth than did dogs consuming 15% protein. Microscopic renal lesions were indistinguishable between groups and proteinuria was not increased or progressive in the 31% group. These findings are potentially critical to the maximal recovery of patients with acute renal disease: inappropriate protein restriction may limit the kidney's compensatory response to injury.

Inherent in all of these protein restriction studies is the concern that reduced protein intake may result in subtle effects of protein malnutrition: impaired immunological response, reduced hemoglobin production and anemia, decreased plasma protein levels and muscle wasting.

Confusion Versus Controversy

With the evidence failing to support a role of dietary protein restriction, where is the confusion arising that leads 42% of veterinarians to believe that protein is not only important in the progression of renal disease but also in the etiology? While there is controversy among investigators regarding the level of protein to feed uremic patients and regarding the value of vitamin D_3, there is not disagreement regarding the absence of a protein effect on progression. The confusion may be related to: (1) inaccurate use of terms relating to renal failure; (2) lack of clear distinction between renal disease progression and management of the uremic patient; and (3) extrapolation of rat data to the dog.[17] Veterinary medical foods intended for use in dogs with renal failure and the marketing of those foods has regularly placed the protein-restriction hypothesis in front of practitioners. Some lecturers still speak of managing renal patients with specific low protein diets to slow the progression of the disease. Furthermore, veterinarians and consumers are cautioned that "old" dogs need to be on reduced protein intakes to either prevent the onset of kidney disease or to slow the progression of what might be undetectable renal insufficiency. Neither concept has a basis in fact.

With some of the myths of the past addressed, attention can be turned to the future. Innovative studies into the roles of common nutrients on renal function will reveal clinically important results. Beneficial effects of protein, phosphorus restriction and dietary lipids have all been shown.[17,20-23] These studies and those currently underway will help to more clearly define the role that diet can play in managing renal health in dogs and cats.

In the meantime, some general guidelines for the nutritional management of canine patients are:

- Feed a level of protein appropriate for the dog's activity and balanced to the remainder of the diet.
- There is no scientific basis for reducing dietary protein due to age.

- Dietary protein is not involved in the progression of canine renal disease.

- Dogs with renal failure and uremia must be managed on an individual basis to control the azotemia while maintaining nitrogen balance.

References

1. Survey conducted Novemeber, 1990.

2. Case LP, Carey DP, Hirakawa DA. Chronic kidney disease. In: *Canine and feline nutrition*. St. Louis: Mosby. 1995:389-400.

3. Churchill J, Polzin D, Osborne CA, et al. The influence of dietary protein intake on progression of chronic renal failure in dogs. *Semin Vet Med Surg Sm Anim* 1992; 7:244-250.

4. Brown SA. Dietary protein restriction: some unanswered questions. *Semin Vet Med Surg Sm Anim* 1992; 7:237-243.

5. Gonin-Jmaa D, Senior DF. The hyperfiltration theory: progression of chronic renal failure and the effects of diet in dogs. *J Amer Vet Med Assoc* 1995; 207:1411-1415.

6. Shimamura T, Morrison AB. A progressive glomerulosclerosis occurring in five-sixths nephrectomized rats. *Am J Pathol* 1975; 79:95-106.

7. Hostetter TH, Olson JL, Rennek HG. Hyperfiltration in remnant nephrons: a potentially adverse response to renal ablation. *Am J Physiol* 1981; 241:F85-F92.

8. Brenner BM, Meyer TW, Hostetter TH. Dietary protein intake and the progressive nature of kidney disease: the role of hemodynamically mediated glomerular injury in the pathogenesis of progressive sclerosis, renal ablation and intrinsic renal disease. *N Engl J Med* 1982; 307:652-659.

9. Bovee KC, Kronfeld DS, Ramberg C, Goldschmidt M. Long-term measurement of renal function in partially nephrectomized dogs fed 56, 27 or 19% protein *Invest Urol* 1979; 16:378-384.

10. Finco DR, Crowell WA, Barsanti JA. Effects of three diets on dogs with induced chronic renal failure. *Am J Vet Res* 1985; 46:646-652.

11. Polzin DJ, Leininger JR, Osborne CA, et al. Development of renal lesions in dogs after 11/12 reduction in renal mass. Lab Invest 1988; 58:172-183.

12. Tapp DC, Kobayoshu S, Fernandes S. Protein restriction or calorie restriction? A critical assessment of the influence of selective calorie restriction on the progression of experimental renal disease. *Semin Nephrol* 1989; 9:343-353.

13. Keane WF, Kasiske BL, O'Donnell MP. Hyperlipidemia and the progression of renal disease. *Am J Clin Nutr* 1987; 47:157-160.

14. Bourgoigne JJ, Gavellas G, Martinex E, et al. Glomerular function and morphology after renal mass reduction in dogs. *Lab Clin Med* 1987; 109:380-388.

15. Maeda H, Gleiser CA, Masoro EJ, et al. Nutritional influences on aging of Fischer 344 rats. II, Pathology. *J Geront* 1985; 40:671-688.

16. Masoro EJ, Iwaski K, Gleiser CA, et al. Dietary modulations of the progression of nephropathy in aging rats: an evaluation of the importance of protein. *Am J Clin Nutr* 1989; 49:1217-1227.

17. Bovee KC. Influence of dietary protein on renal function in dogs. *J Nutr* 1991; 121:S128-S139.

18. Robertson JL, Goldschmidt M, Kronfeld DS, et al. Long term renal responses to high dietary protein in dogs with 75% nephrectomy. *Kidney Int* 1986; 29:511-519.

19. Brown SA, Finco DR, Crowell WA, Navar LG. Dietary protein intake and the glomerular adaptation to partical nephrectomy in dogs. *J Nutr* 1991; 121:S125-S127.

20. Bovee KC, Kronfeld DS. Reduction of renal hemodynamics in uremic dogs fed reduced protein diets. *J Amer Anim Hosp Assoc* 1981; 17:277-285.

21. White JV, Finco DR, Crowell WA, Brown SA, Hirakawa DA. Effect of dietary protein on functional, morphologic and histologic changes of the kidney during compensatory renal growth in dogs. *Am J Vet Res* 1991; 52:1357-1365.

22. Finco DR, Brown SA, Crowell WA, et al. Effects of dietary phosphorus and protein in dogs with chronic renal failaure. *Am J Vet Res* 1992; 53:2264-2271.

23. Brown SA. Role of dietary lipids in renal disease in dogs. *ACVIM Proc* 1992.

Effects of Dietary Protein and Phosphorus on the Kidneys of Dogs

Delmar R. Finco, DVM, PhD, DACVIM
Scott A. Brown, VMD, PhD, DACVIM
Wayne A. Crowell, DVM, PhD
Department of Physiology and Pharmacology
College of Veterinary Medicine
The University of Georgia, Athens, Georgia

Effects Of Phosphorus (P) And Protein In Young Dogs With Azotemia

Background

Reduction of renal mass in mammals is followed by marked functional and structural changes in remaining nephrons.[1-4] Functionally, single nephron glomerular filtration rate (SNGFR) increases and tubular functions are enhanced. Structurally, hypertrophy of many renal cell types occurs. Changes that follow reduction of renal mass traditionally were presumed to be beneficial because they imparted increased functional capacity on each of the residual nephrons.

More recent studies in rodents indicated that reduction of renal mass was followed by structural and functional deterioration of residual nephrons that was attributed to the process of hypertrophy.[5-7] In rats these adverse renal effects could be ameliorated by dietary restriction of protein or phosphorus (P). These findings led to the hypothesis that after an initial reduction in renal mass, renal damage becomes a self-perpetuating phenomenon, which may be ameliorated by certain dietary manipulations.[7-10]

Effects of certain diets on dogs with renal failure also have been examined but results have not been consistent.[11-13] Inconsistencies may be related to two factors. First, studies differed in the degree of renal dysfunction that existed; some studies were done on dogs without azotemia whereas other studies were done on dogs with azotemia. Secondly, each study compared commercially available foods which differed not only in protein and P content, but in the quantitiy of several other components as well. We are aware of two studies[14,15] in which variation in dietary composition was restricted to protein or P concentration.

Experimental Methods

In our study, 4 experimental dry diets were manufactured to our specifications. Diets were formulated to be 16% protein, 0.4% P (diet 1); 16% protein, 1.4% phosphorus (diet 2); 32% protein, 0.4% phosphorus (diet 3); and 32% protein, 1.4% phosphorus (diet 4). Ingredients commonly used to formulate commercial dog foods were used as a basis for all diets, and casein provided the additional protein present in diets 3 and 4. Diets 2 and 4 had levels of P increased to 1.4% by addition of dicalcium phosphate. Diets were formulated to be isocaloric and to have a calcium: P ratio of 1.2 to 1. Diets were analyzed for composition.

Table 1. Composition of diets expressed on a dry matter basis.

Component	Diet 1	Diet 2	Diet 3	Diet 4
Protein	16.7	17.0	31.6	32.0
Fat	11.9	10.8	12.9	12.2
Fiber	1.82	1.78	1.65	1.80
Ash	3.16	7.64	3.55	7.80
Sodium	0.33	0.35	0.33	0.29
Potassium	0.48	0.48	0.38	0.39
Magnesium	0.13	0.15	0.10	0.09
Calcium	0.57	1.91	0.60	1.92
Phosphorus	0.44	1.50	0.49	1.46

Major ingredients in the diets included corn, poultry, soybean meal, and beef fat. (From 14.)

Young adult mongrel dogs (25 males, 23 females) were studied. Dogs had renal mass reduced 15/16 by surgery, and were maintained for 3 months on diet 1 to assure the same dietary effects on hypertrophy and glomerular filtration rate (GFR). Based on 3-month GFR data, dogs were separated into groups of 12 with equal mean GFR per group. For 24 months thereafter, group 1 remained on diet 1, while groups 2, 3, and 4 received diets 2, 3, and 4 respectively. Each dog was fed a weighed amount of food once daily based on body weight, using the formula: weight $(kg)^{0.75}$ x 132 = Calories provided[16], and food intake was measured. Gradual introduction of diets 3 and 4 over a 4 week period circumvented the development of diet-related uremia; dogs in groups 3 and 4 developed metabolic acidosis, and were treated with potassium citrate.

Dogs were observed daily for clinical abnormalities. At 1 month intervals body weight, PCV, and plasma chemical analyses were performed. At 4 month intervals GFR, urine culture, urine protein/creatinine (P/C) ratio, and blood pressure measurements[17] were made. At the conclusion of the study, PTH concentration was determined on plasma obtained from each dog just prior to group assignment, 2 months later, at the midpoint of the period of survival, and 1 month prior to the study end.[18] Timed (48 or 72 hr) collections of urine were made for measurement of urinary protein at intervals during the study.

During the study dogs that developed uremia were humanely euthanized if they failed to respond to fluid therapy. After 24 months, kidneys were evaluated histologically and by mineral analysis. For histologic evaluation a semiquantitative method was used to judge fibrosis, inflammatory infiltrate, and tubular changes (atrophy, collecting duct hyperplasia, other) from slides stained with H&E. Glomerular lesions and mesangial cellularity and matrix accumulation were evaluated in sections stained with PAS.

All data were analyzed statistically to determine diet effects. Values of P≤ 0.05 were considered statistically significant.

Major nonrenal clinical abnormalities were not observed in dogs during the study. Dogs that developed signs of uremia (anorexia, depression, vomiting) lost body weight prior to development of uremia. For all survivors, body weight at 24 months was 96.2% ± 2.3 of initial weight. For groups 1 through 4 body weight of survivors was 97.7% ± 0.58, 104.4% ± 0.67, 99.5% ± 0.6, and 94.8% ± 0.9 at 24 months.

Results

<u>Survival</u> — Of the 12 dogs in each group, 8, 3, 7, and 5 survived to 24 months in groups 1 through 4 respectively. Survival related to dietary P and protein level was: 0.4% P - 15 dogs (groups 1, 3); 1.4% P diet - 8 dogs (groups 2, 4); 16% protein - 11 dogs (groups 1, 2); 32% protein - 12 dogs (groups 3,4). Chi-square analysis of survival indicated that dietary P concentration significantly affected survival, but that dietary protein concentration did not affect survival. (*Figure 1*)

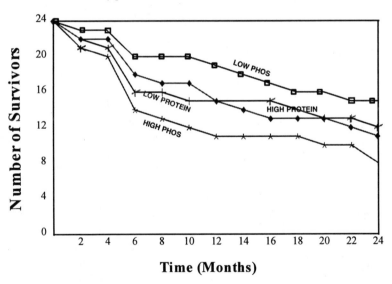

Figure 1. Diet effects on mortality. Dietary phosphorus significantly affected mortality, but dietary protein intake did not affect mortality. (From 14.)

<u>Changes in renal function with time</u> — Data for GFR levels were normalized by transforming values on each dog to a percent of the initial (3 months post-nephrectomy) GFR. Transformed data were analyzed by regression analysis for effects of P and protein, since interaction between the 2 variables was absent. A 2 phase model best fit the data, characterized by a period of relatively stable function, followed by a decline in function. The time period of stable GFR was significantly longer with 0.4% P diets (12.67 ± 2.04 months) than with 1.4% P diets (7.50 ± 2.04 months), but the subsequent rate of decline was not significantly affected by dietary P concentration (*Figure 2*).

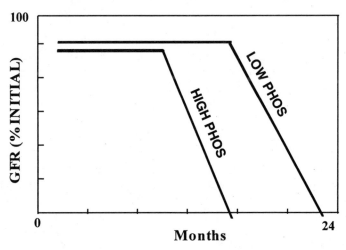

Figure 2. Regression analysis model of effects of dietary P on glomerular filtration rate. While dietary phosphorus affected GFR, dietary protein levels (not shown) had no effect (From 14.)

Dietary protein concentration did not have a significant effect on either the period of time of stability (16% = 9.50 ± 2.04 months; 32% = 10.67 ± 2.04 months) or on the subsequent rate of decline.

<u>Blood chemical values</u> — Comparison of monthly blood chemical values for effects of P and protein indicated several differences between groups. As expected, 1.4% P diets caused a significantly higher plasma P and lower calcium than 0.4% P diets. The 32% protein diets caused a significantly higher BUN and chloride, but a significantly lower creatinine and anion gap than the 16% protein diets. Time-related changes also occurred for some blood components. Plasma BUN, creatinine, P, and anion gap increased with time. Values for PCV and plasma calcium, chloride, and total CO_2 decreased significantly with time.

<u>Urinary excretion of protein</u> — In 48 or 72 hour collections, the quantity of urinary protein was not significantly affected by dietary concentration of P or protein. Evaluation of data from urine P/C ratios determined on all groups at 4-month intervals revealed no interaction between dietary protein and P effects. When analyzed for effects of dietary protein, P, and for time, a significant increase in proteinuria occurred with time, but no significant effect of diet existed (*Figure 3*).

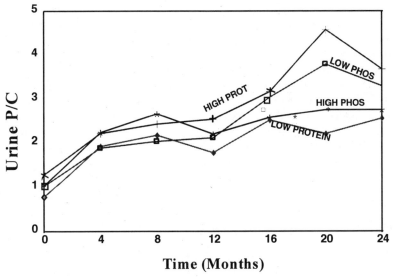

Figure 3. Effects of diet on urine protein/creatinine ratios at 4-month intervals during feeding trials. proteinuria increased with time but there were no diet effects. (From 14.)

<u>Plasma concentration of PTH</u> — Both time and diet had significant effects on plasma PTH concentrations. In all groups plasma PTH concentrations increased with time. However, the 0.4% P diets transiently prevented an increase in PTH concentrations (2 months) prior to the subsequent increases. The 1.4% P diets induced progressive increases in PTH concentrations. The 32% protein diets caused a significant increase in PTH concentrations presumably via their effects on P homeostasis which was reflected in increased urinary P excretion. As a consequence of both P and protein effects, the PTH values for group 4 were significantly greater than for the other groups (*Figure 4*).

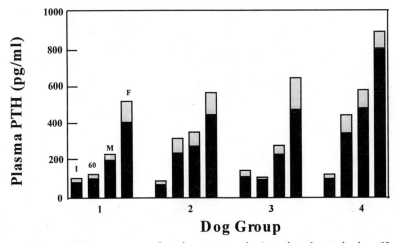

Figure 4. Plasma PTH concentrations from dogs receiving the 4 test diets. I=initial values; 60=after diets given 60 days; M=midpoint of survival period; F=prior to euthanasia. Black =mean, grey=SE.

An important finding from PTH studies was the lack of efficacy of even the low P diets in preventing renal secondary hyperparathryoidism.

Morphologic studies of the kidneys — Diet was not a significant factor in the degree of mineralization, fibrosis, cellular infiltration, or tubular lesions. Mesangial cellularity was significantly greater in group 1 than other groups, and significantly less in group 2 than in other groups. Mesangial matrix accumulation was significantly greater in group 1 than in other groups. The fate of the animal (survivor vs. mortality) significantly affected renal mineralization and fibrosis. Regardless of diet, survivors had significantly less mineralization and fibrosis.

Mineral concentration of kidneys — Renal cortical concentrations of calcium, P, magnesium, and potassium were significantly increased in kidneys removed at necropsy, compared to kidneys removed during nephrectomy. However, kidneys collected at necropsy did not differ in concentration of any mineral except potassium, which was significantly less in group 4. When kidney mineral values from 24-month survivors were compared with values from dogs euthanatized because of uremia, calcium, P, and magnesium concentrations were significantly higher in dogs with uremia (*Figure 5*).

Kidney Calcium

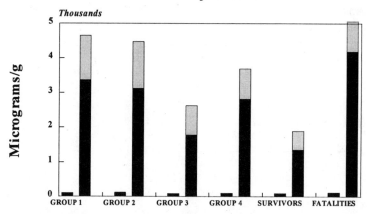

Figure5. Concentration of calcium in renal cortical tissues. Pre values were obtained from kidneys at the time of nephrectomy. Post values were from kidneys obtained at necropsy. Notice that calcium concentration increased markedly (ore vs post) regardless of diet. Calcium concentration was lower in survivors than in fatalities. Black=mean, clear=SE.

Summary   These results indicated that P restriction was an important factor in management of dogs with renal failure, affecting progression of renal dysfunction and mortality. However, dietary restriction of protein did not affect mortality, rate of progression of uremia, or development of renal lesions.

Since these results on protein are contrary to the unsubstantiated but widely held belief that protein is harmful to the dog's kidneys, we posed another question. Do the kidneys of old dogs respond differently to protein than those of young dogs? Our next major study was designed to answer this question.

Effects Of Dietary Protein On Kidneys Of Geriatric Dogs

In human beings, GFR and other indices of renal function undergo a gradual decline after the 4th decade of life, presumably unrelated to specific renal diseases.[19] The pathogenesis of this decline is poorly understood, albeit renal lesions are more commonly found at autopsy of geriatric patients, compared with younger patients.[20] Studies of GFR in geriatric dogs have not been reported. Furthermore, studies have not been performed to establish whether aging puts geriatric dogs at risk for renal damage from dietary components. We performed the studies subsequently described to determine whether GFR declined with aging, and to examine effects of certain dietary components on aging dogs.[21]

Background

Dogs — Thirty-one purebred dogs (17 Cocker Spaniels, 11 Miniature Schnauzers, and 3 Doberman Pinschers) were studied. Twenty-eight females and 3 males were represented. The Cockers and Schnauzers were obtained from a breeding kennel. The Dobermans previously were used for food palatability trials. Birthdates of all dogs were known; dogs were between 7 and 8 years old when the study was initiated.

Experimental Methods

Experimental diets — Diets A and B were formulated from commercially available ingredients to meet the nutritional requirements of adult dogs. Diet A contained 18% protein, compared with 34% protein for diet B. Diets were formulated to have an equal caloric density (carbohydrates replacing protein in diet A), and to have equal mineral composition. Diets were analyzed for composition and tested for digestibility (*Table 2*).

Experimental design — Initially, dogs were evaluated for health status by performing physical examination, CBC, serum biochemical analyses, urinalysis, and bacteriologic culture of urine. Then uninephrectomy was performed (month -2), and excised tissue was used as subsequently described.

All dogs were fed diet A for 2 months after uninephrectomy. Then GFR was measured to determine baseline values while all dogs were on the same diet. Immediately after baseline GFR determinations (month 0), dogs were divided into 2 groups on the basis of breed. Group A (2 Dobermans, 9 Cockers, 5 Schnauzers) continued receiving diet A while group B (1 Doberman, 8 Cockers, 6 Schnauzers) were fed diet B for the subsequent 48 months. Dogs were fed an amount of food designed to maintain an ideal weight; food intake was measured daily.

Each dog was observed daily for clinical signs of abnormality and body weight was determined monthly. At 3-month intervals after month 0, CBC and serum biochemical analyses were made. At 6-month intervals after month 0, GFR was measured and urine was procured for urinalysis, U P/C, and bacterial culture. Dogs alive at month 48 had renal response to an acute protein ingestion studied.

Morphologic studies — Formalin-fixed kidney removed at time of nephrectomy (-2 months) and terminally (48 months) from each dog were processed for histologic examination. Paraffin-imbedded sections were stained with H&E for evaluation of fibrosis, cell infiltration, and renal pelvic lesions. A PAS stain of plastic-imbedded tissue was used for evaluation of glomeruli. Sections were graded semiquantitatively (0=normal, 1=mild, 2= moderate, and 3=severe).

Kidney mineral analysis — Frozen kidney was used for dry weight determinations and for analysis for mineral content using plasma emission spectroscopy.

Statistical analyses — Serial measurements over time were analyzed for diet effects, time effects, and interactions, using ANOVA for repeated measures. Within diet groups, effects of time were determined by regression analyses. Unpaired observations were analyzed, using one-way ANOVA, and paired observations on the same dog were tested using a paired t-test. For all comparisons, significance of P <0.05 was used.

Table 2. Analysis of diets fed to dogs of group A (diet A) and group B (diet B).

	% of Dry Weight	
Component	Diet A	Diet B
Protein	18.10 ± 0.06	34.60 ± 0.76
Fat	20.01 ± 0.61	20.81 ± 0.78
Fiber	2.21 ± 0.56	1.73 ± 0.14
Ash	6.34 ± 0.36	6.27 ± 0.35
Calcium	1.59 ± 0.09	1.55 ± 0.05
Phosphorus	0.89 ± 0.03	0.93 ± 0.03
Sodium	0.62 ± 0.19	0.59 ± 0.16
Potassium	0.92 ± 0.20	0.93 ± 0.03
Magnesium	0.10 ± 0.01	0.08 ± 0.01
Chloride	0.94 ± 0.19	0.84 ± 0.13

Mean ± SEM of 4 productions. Dietary components were chicken, chicken byproducts, meat meal, dried whole egg, chicken fat, ground corn, brewers rice, beet pulp, bone meal, vitamins and minerals. Gross energy was 4919 ± 2.5 kc/kg for diet A; 5257 kc/kg ± 87.5 for diet B. Moisture was 7.49% ± 0.54 for diet A and 6.40% ± 0.33 for diet B. Protein digestibility in 12 clinically normal adult dogs was 79.1% and 87.4% for diets A and B respectively; metabolizing energy was 4,157 kc/kg and 4,572 kc/kg, resepectively. Protein digestibility in 4 dogs in the study was 76.7% and 81.2% for diets A and B; metabolizable energy was 3,891 kc/kg and 3,848 kc/kg, respectively. From 21.

Clinical course — All dogs entering the feeding trials were free of physical abnormalities that warranted exclusion from the experiment. Results from hematologic, blood biochemical, and urine studies were normal. Histologic evaluation of H&E-stained sections of kidney removed by nephrectomy (month -2) revealed no major abnormalities in any of the dogs.

During subsequent study, medical and surgical diseases that developed were treated by use of standard veterinary procedures. Major abnormalities caused death or led to euthanasia of 8 dogs (*Table 3*).

Table 3. Major diseases of group-A and group-B dogs during 48 months of study.

Diet	Disease	Outcome
A	Renal amyloidosis	Euthanasia month 39
A	Osteogenic sarcoma	Euthanasia month 15
A	Parathyroid hyperplasia, pyometra, renal anyloidosis	Euthanasia month 47
A	Obstructive jaundice, systemic thromboembolism	Died month 28
A	Mammary adenocarcinoma	Euthanasia month 6
A	Cervical vertebra stabilization month 22, gastric torsion month 38	Died month 38
B	Renal amyloidosis	Euthanasia month 5
B	Organophosphate toxicosis	Died month 3
A	Cervical vertebra stabilization month 23	Completed study
A	Mammary adenocarcinoma	Completed study
A	Lower urinary tract infection	Completed study
A	Leukocytosis months 39-43	Completed study
A	Pyometra, ovariohysterectomy month 35	Completed study
A	Pyometra, inguinal hernia surgery month 38	Completed study
A	Organophosphate toxicity month 3	Completed study
A	Pyometra, Ovario-hysterectomy month 28	Completed study
B	Sudden decrease in GFR month 18	Completed study
B	Leukocytosis months 36-39	Completed study
B	Multiple mammary tumors	Completed study
B	Pyometra, ovario-hysterectomy month 38	Completed study
B	Pyometra, ovario-hysterectomy month 35	Completed study
B	Pyometra, month 48	Completed study
B	Inguinal hernia repair, month 35	Completed study

From 21.

Other dogs had major abnormalities, but completed the experiment. At 48 months, 10 of 16 dogs from group A and 13 of 15 dogs from group B had survived. Data from dogs that did not survive the 48-month trial were excluded from analysis. At termination of the study, renal pelves of all dogs were culture-negative for bacteria.

Food intake and body weight changes — The mean ± SEM of monthly body weight determinations was 10.97 ± 0.25 kg for group A and 11.52 ± 0.28 kg for group B. When each dog's mean weight for 48 months was compared with the mean weight for each of its 4 years of study, body weight of both groups increased significantly with time, but diet did not significantly affect year-to-year weight changes.

For the 48 months, mean weekly food intake was significantly higher in group A (133.85 ± 3.68 g/kg) than in group B dogs (122.85 ± 2.72 g/kg). Food intake decreased significantly and progressively in both groups between year 1 and year 4 of feeding. Overall, protein intake was 3.46 g/kg/day for group A and 6.07 g/kg/day for group B. Based on digestibility studies digestible protein intake was 2.74 g/kg/day for group A and 5.31 g/kg/day for group B dogs.

Three-month interval observations — Hematologic and blood biochemical measurements made on dogs indicated only minor effects of diet or time. Serum alkaline phosphatase activity and serum phosphorus concentration were significantly higher, and alanine transaminase activity was significantly lower in group A dogs, compared with group B dogs. Values for BUN approached but did not reach significance for diet effects.

Six-month interval studies — At month 0, the GFR of dogs assigned to group A (3.25 ± 0.23 ml/min/kg of body weight) was not significantly different from the GFR of dogs assigned to group B (3.12 ± 0.16 ml/min/kg of body weight). During the subsequent 48 months, significant effects on GFR of diet or diet-time interaction were not detected (*Figure* 6). Although GFR was significantly different between times, regression analysis revealed no significant change in GFR with time within either group of dogs.

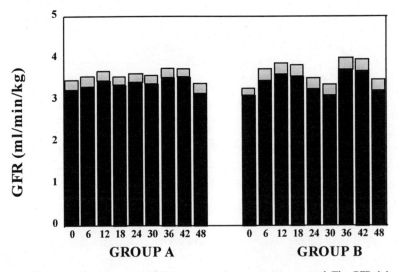

Figure 6. Glomerular filtration rate (GFR) in geriatric dogs over a 4-year period. The GFR did not decrease over 4 years, whether diets of 18% protein or 34% protein were fed. (From 21.)

Urine P/C values were not significantly different between groups A and B at month 0 (0.30 $\pm$ 0.06 vs 0.24 $\pm$ 0.06, respectively). During the ensuing 48 months, the U P/C were not significantly affected by diet, but did vary significantly with time. However, diet-time interactions were not significant and regression analysis did not reveal a progressive increase in time in either group of dogs.

48-month physiologic studies — Casein administration caused only a minor change in GFR in group B, and caused no increase in GFR in group A dogs. After casein administration, urinary protein excretion increased in group B but values did not reach significance in group A. The renal plasma flow (RPF) did not change significantly in either group after casein administration.

Morphologic studies — Right kidney weight of group A dogs at month 48 was 125.5 $\pm$ 0.035% of the weight of the left kidney removed during nephrectomy. Right kidney weight of group B dogs was 152.0 $\pm$ 0.063% of the weight of the left kidney removed during nephrectomy. Kidney weights for both groups increased significantly between uninephrectomy and necropsy, and kidney weight of group B dogs increased significantly more than group A dogs.

Glomerular area increased significantly between -2 and 48 months in both groups, but diet did not influence the change. At month -2, area was 17,700 $\pm$ 700 μm^2 and 16,600 $\pm$ 900 μm^2 in groups A and B respectively; at month 48, area was 28,000 $\pm$ 2,900 μm^2 and 27,900 $\pm$ 2,000 μm^2 in groups A and B, respectively.

For mesangial matrix, group B dogs had a higher score ratio (48 mo/-2 mo) than did group A dogs, and values nearly reached statistical significance. Comparison of subgroups of dogs on the basis of presence or absence of major medical diseases, presence or absence of pyometra, and UP/C of <1.0 to UP/C > 1.0 indicated that month 48 to month -2 matrix ratios were not significantly related to major medical diseases or pyometra, but were significantly correlated with degree of proteinuria.

A significant increase in fibrosis (interstitial and periglomerular); cell infiltration (cortical and medullary); and lesions of the renal pelvis occurred between months -2 and 48. A significant effect of diet was not detected for fibrosis, cell infiltrate, and pelvic lesions. A significant diet-time interaction was observed for cellularity but not for fibrosis or pelvic lesions. On the scale of 0 to 3, the abnormalities were minor in magnitude (*Figure 7*).

Kidney mineral analyses — Renal cortical mineral concentrations were not significantly different between groups A and B, either for kidneys obtained at month -2 or for kidneys obtained at month 48. Within group A, kidneys obtained at month 48 had a significantly higher concentration of potassium, but significantly lower concentrations of magnesium and sodium than did kidneys obtained at month -2. Within group B, kidneys obtained at month 48 had a significantly higher concentration of potassium, but significantly lower concentrations of calcium, magnesium, and phosphorus than did kidneys obtained at month -2.

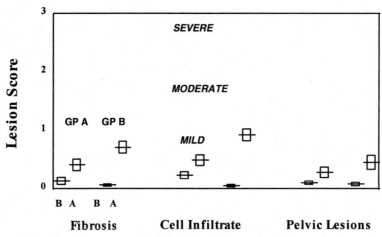

Figure 7. Renal lesions in geriatric dogs before (B) and 4 years after (A) uninephrectomy. Gp A dogs received an 18% protein diet, while Gp B dogs received a 34% protein diet. Notice that mild lesions developed over 4 years in both groups. (From 21.)

Summary   These studies demonstrated that old dogs did not have a decrease in GFR during the 4 years between 7-8 and 11-12 years of age. Furthermore, even old dogs compromised by loss of 50% of renal mass had no significant evidence of renal damage from a high protein diet given for 4 years. Acute protein loading was not associated with a marked increase in GFR or renal plasma flow as occurs in young dogs, suggesting that old dogs may not experience the glomerular hypertension that young dogs do upon protein ingestion.

Feeding of a P-replete diet to these dogs was not associated with renal mineralization over a period of 4 years, despite 50% reduction of renal mass. These results do not support the recommendation that dietary P should be restricted as a formulation feature of maintenance diets.

Role of Renal Secondary Hyperparathyroidism in Progression of Renal Failure

Background   Although even old dogs with 50% reduction of renal mass do not require P restriction, our previous study demonstrated that P restriction did benefit dogs with azotemia. The level of P restriction imposed on dogs in our study was inadequate to prevent renal secondary hyperparathyroidism, and neither renal lesions nor renal mineralization were attenuated by P restriction. Among questions yet to be answered are: What are the mechanisms involved in the benefits of P restriction? Is PTH a uremic toxin? Would further P restriction have been of benefit to the dogs?

Hyperparathyroidism often develops secondary to chronic renal failure. Development of renal secondary hyperparathyroidism (RSH) has been attributed to a decrease in plasma ionized calcium (Ca^{++}) related to impaired urinary excretion of inorganic phosphate and subsequent hyperphosphatemia. A significant role for P in development of RSH was proved in dogs by demonstrating that RSH was prevented if dietary P intake was reduced in proportion to reduction of renal mass.[22]

More recent studies indicated that the active form of vitamin D (calcitriol) also influences parathyroid gland function during renal failure. Calcitriol suppresses parathyroid hormone (PTH) production independent of plasma Ca^{++} concentration.[23]

The development of RSH was considered beneficial during initial stages of renal failure because of the phosphaturic effect of PTH. However, adverse effects of RSH also occur. In human beings with renal failure, RSH contributes to renal osteodystrophy, which is a major clinical problem in patients whose lifespan is prolonged by dialysis.[24] Evidence indicates that PTH may adversely affect many tissues and organ functions other than bone. For example, glucose intolerance reported to occur in dogs with induced chronic renal failure could be prevented by thyroparathyroidectomy.[25] Several in vitro studies also have indicated an adverse effect of PTH on cells.[26-30] Such findings have led to the hypothesis that PTH is a "uremic toxin".[31]

In dogs with renal failure, renal osteodystrophy usually is subclinical, presumably because life is not extended by dialysis procedures. However, if soft tissue damage occurs because of increased plasma PTH concentration, suppression or depletion of plasma PTH would have clinical application. Some clinical studies suggested a benefit from PTH suppression on progression of renal failure in dogs,[32] but controlled conditions of study are difficult to maintain on clinical patients. We performed the following study to determine effects of PTH depletion on dogs with induced renal failure.

Dogs — Twelve young adult mixed breed male dogs (15 to 22.5 kg body weight) were studied. Dogs had normal results from clinical examination, complete blood count, serum chemical profile, urinalysis, U P/C, and negative results from microfilaria examination and urine culture for bacteria.

Experimental design — Six dogs were parathyroidectomized (PTX). After 6 months, the parathyroidectomized dogs (PTX) and 6 non-parathyroidectomized (intact) dogs underwent 15/16 reduction of renal mass. Reduction of renal mass was designated as zero time. Dogs were maintained for the subsequent 33 weeks, and studied at intervals during this period.

Dogs were observed daily for clinical abnormalities. Blood Ca^{++} and pH were measured biweekly for 6 weeks, and once weekly subsequently. Serum total calcium (Ca), creatinine, and P were measured weekly. The GFR, urinalysis, U P/C, BUN, and serum concentrations of total CO_2, Na^+, and K^+ were determined at weeks 1, 4, 8, 14, and 32. Plasma for PTH assay and serum for thyroxin determination were obtained biweekly. Body weight was measured monthly. After 32 weeks, glucose and P tolerance tests were performed. The study was ended at 33 weeks.

<u>Diets</u> — PTX dogs received dietary supplementation with $CaCO_3$ for the duration of the study. Intact dogs received dietary supplementation with $CaCO_3$ beginning 18 days after surgical reduction of renal mass. Calcium supplementation was performed by mixing 2.0 gm/kg of body weight of $CaCO_3$ with dry dog food and water.

A 16% protein, 1.2% Ca, 0.9% P experimental dry dog food (supplemented with $CaCO_3$) was fed for the first 60 days following reduction of renal mass. Thereafter, a 24% protein, 1.8% Ca, 1.1% P commercially available diet (supplemented with $CaCO_3$) was fed.

<u>Management of dogs</u> — Calcitriol was administered orally to PTX dogs to maintain eucalcemia. Dosage of calcitriol was tailored to dogs individually, using biweekly or weekly Ca^{++} values to guide in making dose adjustments. Doses varied from 0 to 0.25 µg/dog/day. Initial determinations indicated that PTX dogs had lower plasma T_4 concentrations than intact dogs. Consequently, L-thyroxin (0 to 1.0 mg/day/dog was administered to PTX dogs to attain a euthyroid state.

Serum TCO_2 values were maintained at greater than 15 mM/L by administering potassium citrate orally; TCO_2 measurements were performed in addition to those routinely scheduled, in order to make dose adjustments.

<u>Tolerance tests</u> — Both glucose and P tolerance tests were done to determine if PTX had effects on either test.

<u>Tissue studies</u> — Zero-time and 33-week formalin-fixed kidneys were processed and stained with H&E for microscopic evaluation. Glomerular lesions (periglomerular sclerosis, mesangial matrix accumulation, mesangial cellularity) tubulointerstitial fibrosis, inflammatory infiltrate, tubular changes, and glomerular lesions were evaluated.

One-gram samples of remnant kidney cortex, aorta, brain grey matter, heart muscle, lung, and skeletal muscle were collected during necropsy and stored at -10 C until analyzed for minerals by plasma emission spectroscopy.

<u>Statistical methods</u> — Variables measured initially and terminally were examined by 1-way ANOVA. Variables measured at intervals during the study were compared for effects of time and parathyroid state (intact vs PTX) with multiple comparison ANOVA. Regression analysis was used to determine relationships between 2 variables. A significance level of <0.05 was used for comparisons.

Results

<u>Clinical course</u> — Two parathyroid-intact dogs developed uremia and were euthanatized within 18 days of reduction of renal mass. Data from these dogs were excluded from analyses. The remaining 10 dogs survived the 33 weeks of study, and were clinically normal during this time. Slight weight gain occurred in both groups during the study. Two PTX dogs had positive urine and kidney cultures for bacteria at necropsy.

Blood chemical changes — No significant difference existed between PTX and intact groups for BUN, creatinine, Na^+, K^+, and T_4. Total Ca values were significantly higher in intact dogs (12.41 mg/dl $\pm$ 0.09) than in PTX dogs (12.02 mg/dl $\pm$ 0.13). Ionized Ca values were significantly higher in intact dogs (1.36 mM/L $\pm$ 0.01) than in PTX dogs (1.31 mM/l $\pm$ 0.01). Ionized Ca values were more variable in PTX dogs than in intact dogs (*Figure* 8). Serum P concentration was significantly greater in the intact group initially, but values were similar in both groups after $CaCO_3$ supplementation of intact dogs was begun. Plasma PTH concentrations were undetectible in PTX dogs, but increased above normal in intact dogs.

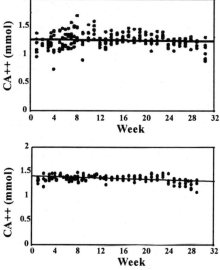

Figure 8. Ionized Calcium concentrations in parathyroidectomized dogs supplemented with calcitriol (upper panel) and in parathyroid-intact dogs (lower panel). All dogs had induced renal failure at time 0 of the 33-week study.

GFR, U P/C — Differences between groups in GFR were not detected. Urine P/C measurements done in association with GFR measurements revealed no significant difference between intact and PTX dogs.

Glucose tolerance tests — No significant difference existed between intact and PTX dogs in glucose tolerance, nor in serum insulin concentrations. Calcitriol administration had no effect on glucose tolerance. Basal and maximum insulin secretion was less in dogs in this study, compared to clinically normal non-azotemic dogs.[33]

Phosphate tolerance test — The fractional excretion of P increased following P loading in both intact and PTX dogs. Neither fractional excretion of P nor 5-hour excretion of P was remarkably different between intact and PTX dogs.

Renal histology — Comparison of renal tissue obtained during nephrectomy with renal tissue obtained at necropsy indicated a significant difference in presence and severity of lesions. There was no significant difference between intact and PTX dogs in any category of histology examined.

Tissue mineral concentrations — Mineral concentrations of aorta, brain, heart, lung, and skeletal muscle tissues harvested at necropsy were not significantly different between intact and PTX dogs. Comparison of renal cortex obtained by nephrectomy at zero time with necropsy tissue obtained at 33 weeks indicated an increase in renal cortical Ca with time, but no protective effect from PTX. One PTX dog with declining GFR values had a renal Ca concentration of 3,766 mg/kg wet wt renal cortex, compared to a mean of 341 for other PTX dogs, and 236 for intact dogs. In this PTX dog, the Ca concentration of all other tissues except brain was greater than for all other dogs studied, indicating generalized soft tissue calcification.

Summary   This study demonstrated that both PTX dogs and parathyroid-intact dogs responded in a similar fashion to induced renal failure. This finding suggests that beneficial effects of dietary P restriction in dogs with renal failure that were previously identified were not related to PTH. Failure to demonstrate glucose intolerance in dogs with renal failure casts doubt on previous reports of its occurrence, other than as a terminal event immediately prior to death from uremia. Use of calcitriol to alter PTH levels in dogs is not warranted based on results of this study.

Role of Plasma Ca^{++} X Phosphorus Product in Progression of Renal Failure

Background   Previous studies have documented that restriction of dietary P intake is beneficial in dogs with azotemia associated with reduced renal mass. However, this benefit was not mediated via PTH. A considerable body of evidence supports the hypothesis that tissue damage during uremia is due to soft tissue mineralization secondary to hyperphosphatemia.[34] According to this theory, the P X Ca^{++} product, when exceeded, results in precipitation of both minerals. Dogs with advanced renal failure develop hyperphosphatemia; hypocalcemia also may occur with further progression of disease. In both circumstances, an increased P X Ca^{++} product occurs.

We hypothesized that abnormalities in mineral balance related to P X Ca^{++} products could explain beneficial effects of P restriction in dogs with renal failure. We analyzed data from a recent study to test this hypothesis.

Experimental Design   Young adult dogs of both sexes had renal mass reduced surgically, and some dogs underwent PTX during the surgical episode. Dogs were divided into 2 groups of 12 with the same baseline GFR level. Dogs were maintained on the same diet (24% protein, 0.9% P) but PTX dogs had calcium carbonate added to avoid clinical signs of hypocalcemia. Food intake of each dog was monitored daily. Dogs were maintained for 2 years with evaluations conducted at intervals during that time.

Blood chemical and body weight determinations were done monthly and GFR and urine P/C ratios were done every 4 months. Dogs that developed signs of uremia were treated with parenteral fluids, but euthanatized if improvement did not occur in 48 hours. After 24 months all survivors' tissues were processed for histologic examination and for mineral analysis.

Results

Mortality rate was lower in PTX dogs than in parathyroid-intact (PI) dogs, with the difference occurring during the 2nd year of study. Glomerular filtration rate was better preserved in PTX dogs than in PI dogs.

To test the hypothesis that $Ca^{++} \times P$ was an important determinanant in progression of renal failure, the $Ca^{++} \times P$ product was calculated for each dog over time, and data were analyzed by survival vs mortality and by PTX vs PI. The values for $Ca^{++} \times P$ clearly separated survivors from mortalities, regardless of PTX vs PI status.

Summary

The results of this study suggested that the beneficial effects of P restriction were related to plasma $P \times Ca^{++}$ product.

A Perspective: Diet Effects on the Kidneys of Dogs and Implications in Dietary Recommendations

Our findings refute some of the older "truths" that were the product of speculation rather than research.

At present, there are no convincing data to warrant restriction of dietary protein intake at any life stage based on concern that protein contributes to renal damage. Although several "geriatric diets" for dogs are protein-restricted, there does not appear to be any scientific basis for the restriction. Use of low-protein diets for dogs with renal failure is indicated when the level of azotemia is consistent with impending clinical signs (depression, vomiting, anorexia, weight loss) but no benefit on progression of renal disease seems to be derived before that time.

Our studies indicate that restriction of P is unneeded with 50% loss of renal mass, but restriction is beneficial to dogs with azotemia that have 90% plus loss of renal mass. Further research will be required to determine the point between 50% and 90% when P restriction should be implemented. Unfortunately at present none of the commercial "kidney" diets available are sufficiently reduced in P to maintain normal P balance in dogs with moderate renal failure. Use of intestinal P-binding agents has been recommended but no studies have been done to determine an appropriate dose. A diet markedly restricted in P without undue protein restriction is needed for management of dogs with chronic renal failure.

References

1. White JV, Finco DR, Crowell WA, et al. Effect of dietary protein on functional, morphologic, and histologic changes of the kidney during compensatory renal growth in dogs. *Am J Vet Res* 1991; 52:1357-1365.

2. Nowinski WW, Gross RJ (ed). *Compensatory renal hypertrophy*. New York: Academic Press, 1969.

3. Brown SA, Finco D, Crowell WA, et al. Single-nephron adaptations to partial renal ablation in the dog. *Am J Physiol* 1990; 258:F495-F503.

4. Wesson LG. Compensatory growth and other growth responses of the kidney. *Nephron* 1989; 51:149-184.

5. Shimamura T, Morrison AB. A progressive glomerulosclerosis occurring in partial five-sixths nephrectomized rats. *Am J Path* 1975; 79:95-106.

6. Deen WM, Maddox DA, Robertson CR, et al. Dynamics of glomerular ultrafiltration in the rat. VII. Response to reduced renal mass. *Am J Physiol* 1974; 227:556-562.

7. Hostetter TH, Olson JL, Rennke HG, et al. Hyperfiltration in remnant nephrons: a potentially adverse response to renal ablation. *Am J Physiol* 1981; 241:F85-F92.

8. Gimeney L, Walker WG, Tew WP, et al. Prevention of phosphate-induced progression of uremia in rats by 3 phosphocitric acid. *Kidney Int* 1982; 22:36-41.

9. Lumlertgul D, Burke TJ, Gillum DM, et al. Phosphate depletion arrests progression of chronic renal failure independent of protein intake. *Kidney Int* 1986; 29:658-666.

10. Dworkin LD, Feiner HE. Glomerular injury in uninephrectomized spontaneously hypertensive rats. A consequence of glomerular capillary hypertension. *J Clin Invest* 1986; 77:797-809.

11. Bovee KC, Kronfeld DS, Ramberg C, et al. Long-term measurement of renal function in partially nephrectomized dogs fed 56, 27, or 19% protein. *Invest Urol* 1979; 16:378-384.

12. Polzin DJ, Osborne CA, Hayden DW, et al. Influence of reduced protein diets on morbidity, mortality, and renal function in dogs with induced chronic renal failure. *Am J Vet Res* 1984; 45:506-517.

13. Finco DR, Crowell WA, Barsanti JA. Effects of three diets on dogs with induced chronic renal failure. *Am J Vet Res* 1985; 46:646-653.

14. Finco DR, Brown SA, Crowell WA, et al. Effects of dietary phosphorus and protein in dogs with chronic renal failure. *Am J Vet Res* 1992, 53:157-163.

15. Polzin DJ, Osborne CA, O'Brien TD, Hostetter TH. Effects of protein intake on progression of canine chronic renal failure (CRF). *Proc 11th Ann Vet Med Forum*, 1993:938.

16. Kendall PT, Blaza SE, Smith PM. Comparative digestible energy requirements of adult beagles and domestic cats for body weight maintenance. *J Nutr* 1983; 113:1946-1955.

17. Coulter DB, Keith JC: Blood pressure obtained by measurement in conscious dogs. *J Am Vet Med Assoc* 1984; 184:1375-1378.

18. Torrence D, Nachreiner R. Human-parathromone assay for use in dogs: validation, sample handling studies, and parathyroid function testing. *Am J Vet Res* 1989; 50:646-653.

19. Smith HW. *The Kidney: Structure and Function in Health and Disease.* Oxford Press, New York, 1951.

20. Brown WW, Davis BB, Spry LA, et al. Aging and the kidney. *Arch Int Med* 1986; 146:1790-1796.

21. Finco DR, Brown SA, Crowell WA, et al. Effects of aging and dietary protein intake on uninephrectromized geriatric dogs. *Am J Vet Res* 1994; 55:1282-1290.

22. Slatopolsky E, et al. On the pathogenesis of hyperparathyroidism in chronic experimental renal insufficiency in the dog. *J Clin Invest* 1971; 50:492.

22. Slatopolsky E, Berkoben M, Kelber J, et al. Effects of calcitriol and non-calcemic vitamin D analogs on secondary hyperparathyroidism. *Kidney Int* 1992; 42:S-43-S49.

23. Sherrard D, Hercz G, Pei Y, et al. The spectrum of bone disease in end-stage renal failure-An evolving disorder. *Kidney Int* 1993; 43:436-442.

24. Akmal M, Massry S, Goldstein A, et al. Role of parathryoid hormone in glucose intolerance of chronic renal failure. *J Clin Invest* 1985; 75:1037-1044.

25. Bogin E, Massry S Harary. Effects of parathyroid hormone on rat heart cells. *J Clin Invest* 1981; 67:1215-1227.

26. Meytes D, Bogin E, Ma A, et al. Effects of parathyroid hormone on erythro-poiesis. *J Clin Invest* 1981; 67:1263-1269.

27. Perna A, Fadda G, Zhou X, et al. Mechanisms of impaired insulin secretion following chronic excess of parathyroid hormone. *Am J Physiol* 1990; 259:F 210-F216.

28. Smogorewski M, Piskorska G, Borum P, et al. Chronic renal failure, parathyroid hormone and fatty acid oxidation in skeletal muscle. *Kidney Int* 1988; 33:555-560.

29. Alexiewicz J, Klinger M, Pitts T, et al. Parathyroid hormone inhibits B-cell proliferation; Implications in chronic renal failure. *J Am Soc Nephrol* 1990; 1:236-244.

30. Massry S. Parathyroid hormone: a uremic toxin. In: Ringoir S, Van Holder R, Massry S, eds. *Uremic toxins,* New York: Plenum Press, 1986:1-19.

31. Nagode L, Chew D, Steinmeyer C, et al. Low doses of oral calcitriol retard progression of naturally occurring renal disease in the dog. In: Norman A, Bouillon R, Thomasset M, et al, eds. *Vitamin D- gene regulation, structure-function analysis and clinical application.* New York: de Gruyter, 1991:879-880.

32. Moore GE, Hoenig M. Effects of orally administered prednisone on glucose tolerance and insulin secretion in clinically normal dogs. *Am J Vet Res* 1993; 54:126-129.

33. Lau K. Phosphate excess and progressive renal failure: The precipitation-calcification hypothesis. *Kidney Int* 1989; 36:918-937.

Prevention of Acute Renal Failure:
The Effects of Dietary Protein Conditioning on Gentamicin-induced Nephrotoxicosis in Dogs [1,2]

Gregory F. Grauer, DVM, MS, DACVIM
Professor, Department of Clinical Sciences
College of Veterinary Medicine and Biomedical Sciences
Colorado State University, Fort Collins, Colorado

Introduction

Acute renal failure (ARF) is frequently caused by an ischemic or toxic insult to the kidneys.[3] In general, this injury damages tubular epithelial cells causing impaired regulation of water and solute balance. Specifically, nephrotoxicants interfere with essential tubular cell functions and cause cellular injury and death; renal ischemia causes cellular hypoxia and nutrient insufficiency, which leads to ATP depletion and cellular swelling and death. Most importantly, renal vasoconstriction occurs secondary to toxic or ischemic tubular epithelial injury and further exacerbates tubular damage and decreased function.

Renal failure associated with ischemic insults is frequently iatrogenic (e.g., hypovolemia and/or hypotension associated with anesthesia).[4,5] Likewise, renal failure that is toxicant-induced is frequently associated with therapeutic agents (e.g., gentamicin, nonsteroidal anti-inflammatory drugs, amphotericin B, and cis-platinum.)[4,5] Gentamicin-induced nephrotoxicity and renal failure is not only a well established model in dogs but is also a common problem in pet dogs due to the widespread use of this antibiotic for serious gram-negative infections with concurrent volume depletion, fever and/or sepsis.[6] In dogs, renal failure induced by gentamicin is often irreversible and dogs that do recover adequate renal function do so only after prolonged and expensive intensive care.[6] Two recent retrospective studies have documented the poor prognosis associated with ARF in dogs. In a study of hospital acquired ARF, the survival rate was 38%,[4] whereas in another study of all types of ARF, the survival rate was 24%.[5] (Even in human beings, toxicant and ischemic induced acute renal failure is associated with a survival rate of only 40%–50% despite the widespread availability of dialysis.[7]) Prevention is truly the best therapy for eitherl ischemic or toxicant-induced renal failure.

Several risk factors have been identified that predispose dogs and human beings to gentamicin-induced renal failure.[6,8] These factors may also predispose dogs and cats to other types of toxicant-induced renal failure, as well as renal failure induced by ischemia. In particular, pre-existing renal disease or renal insufficiency, advanced age, dehydration, decreased cardiac output, sepsis, fever, liver disease, electrolyte abnormalities, and concurrent use of potentially nephrotoxic drugs have been identified as risk factors for the development of ARF. Dehydration, decreased cardiac output, electrolyte abnormalities, and use of concurrent drugs are risk factors the clinician can usually control, however many risk factors cannot be controlled.

Recent evidence in rats indicates that the quantity of protein fed prior to renal ischemia or administration of a nephrotoxicant may significantly affect the renal damage and dysfunction associated with the insult.[9-12] In some instances, low dietary protein has been shown to be beneficial. Rats conditioned to 0 or 5% dietary protein for a period of 6 to 28 days prior to ischemia induced by renal pedicle clamping had significantly improved postischemia survival, compared with rats conditioned to 20 or 60% dietary protein.[9] Similarly, rats conditioned to 0 or 5% dietary protein prior to IV administration of uranyl nitrate had improved survival, compared with rats conditioned to 20 or 60% dietary protein.[10] However in the same study, rats conditioned to 60% protein maintained the highest creatinine clearance and urine volume after infusion of uranyl nitrate.[10]

In other studies, high dietary protein conditioning not only improved renal function but survival as well. In a model of acute renal failure induced by IV administration of mercuric chloride, rats conditioned to 60% dietary protein had 100% survival and normal renalfunction within 4 days, compared with rats conditioned to 20% dietary protein that had severe renal dysfunction and 100% mortality.[11] Additionally, in rats treated daily with 150 mg of gentamicin/kg for 6 days, 60% dietary protein conditioning resulted in less uptake of gentamicin by the kidneys, compared with 5 or 20% dietary protein conditioning.[12] In the same study, rats conditioned to 60% dietary protein and subsequently fed 5% dietary protein coincident with gentamicin administration, had significant improvement in renal function and survival, compared with rats conditioned to 5 or 20% dietary protein.[12]

On the basis of these results, the quantity of protein fed prior to a renal insult appears to be a controllable risk factor for nephrotoxicosis and renal ischemia in rats. If dietary protein conditioning can be shown to have renal protective effects in the well established canine model of gentamicin-induced nephrotoxicosis, it may have important clinical implications. In instances where exposure to nephrotoxicants is being considered (eg, chemotherapy, analgesics,radiographic contrast agents, and certain antimicrobial agents), it may be possible to delay treatment for a period while the patient is conditioned to a specific dietary protein level and thereby, attenuate kidney damage. The purpose of the study reported here was to assess the effects of dietary protein conditioning on gentamicin-induced nephrotoxicosis in the dog.

Objectives

1) To determine the effects of dietary protein conditioning (low=9.4%, medium=13.7%, and high=27.3%) on renal function (creatinine clearance and urinary electrolyte and protein excretion), enzymuria (gamma-glutamyltransferase [GGT], and N-acetyl-ß-D-glucosaminidase[NAG]), renal histology, and serum and

renal cortical gentamicin concentrations in dogs with gentamicin induced nephrotoxicosis.

2) To determine the effect of dietary protein conditioning on gentamicin pharmacokinetics.

Eighteen, 6 month old, male beagles with normal renal function (see renal function tests listed below) were randomly divided into 3 groups (n = 6). Each group was fed a diet that was similar except for protein content (27.3% = high protein, 13.7% = medium protein, 9.4% = low protein; *Table 1*) for 21 days.

	Diet 1 (9.4% Protein)	Diet 2 (13.7% Protein)	Diet 3 (27.3% Protein)
Protein (kjeldahl)	9	13	26
Carbohydrate (calculated)	65	62	51
Fat (acid hydrolysis)	19	16	14
Moisture (forced draft oven)	3.9	5.3	4.6
Fiber (crude)	1.2	0.8	1.6
Ash	2.7	3.3	4.2
Calcium	0.65	0.71	0.69
Phosphorus	0.38	0.33	0.41
Potassium	0.18	0.29	0.67
Sodium	0.24	0.21	0.26
Calories/100 g	467	444	434

*Prepared by Mark Morris Associates

After the conditioning period, gentamicin was administered at 10mg/kg IM every 8 hours for 8 days (the first dose on days 1 and 7 was administered IV to facilitate pharmacokinetic determinations) and each group was continued on its respective diet. Endogenous creatinine clearance (ml/min/kg), 24-hour urinary excretion of protein (mg/kg/24h) and enzymes (NAG, GGT, IU/kg/24h), and fractional clearance of sodium and potassium (%) were determined after the dietary protein conditioning (designated day 0) and on days 2, 4, 6, and 8 during gentamicin administration. Additionally, trough serum gentamicin concentrations (blood samples were obtained just prior to the next dose of gentamicin and measured in µg/ml) were determined on days 2, 4, 6, and 8 during gentamicin administration. At the end of the study, renal histology was graded using a continuous ranking scale based on severity of proximal tubular necrosis and renal cortical gentamicin concentrations (µg/g) were measured.

Data were first described by parametric methods to determine mean and standard deviation for each of the groups on each day of the study. Bartlett's test of homogeneity of variances was applied to data with large standard deviations.

Because of heterogeneous variances, data were analyzed by a non-parametric equivalent of a two-way analysis of variance procedure (Friedman test). Data were ranked, then analyzed for group and time effects using a two-way analysis of variance procedure on the ranked data. Differences between variable means by day were analyzed by a Waller-Duncan K ratio test. Differences between groups on each day were analyzed by Tukey's test for multiple comparisons of means. The renal cortical gentamicin concentrations and the renal histologic scores were analyzed by use of a one-way non-parametric ANOVA (Kruskal-Wallis test). Data were described as mean ± SD except where indicated. Comparison of the k_{el} between days 1 and 7 within a group were performed using a Wilcoxon signed rank test. Values were considered significantly different at the $P < 0.05$ level.

Results   Physical examination and renal function testing results were normal for all dogs prior to dietary conditioning. Body weight and quantity of food consumed did not differ between groups during the conditioning period. After the dietary conditioning period (prior to gentamicin administration), dogs fed high protein had higher creatinine clearance compared with dogs fed low protein (*Figures 1-8*). The pharmacokinetic data on day 1 best fit a two compartment open model for all dogs. Dogs fed high protein had increased volume of distribution and clearance of gentamicin and decreased mean residence time compared with dogs fed medium and low protein (*Table 2*).

Table 2. Pharmacokinetic data (mean ± SD) from day 1 and elimination rate constants from days 1 and 7.

	V_d (L/kg)	MRT (min)	Cl_{gent} (ml/min/kg)	k_{el} (Day 1) (1/hr)	k_{el} (Day 7) (1/hr)
27.3% Protein	4.31(0.46)	74.8(15.1)	4.72(0.91)	5.76(0.31)	4.83(0.51)
13.7% Protein	3.78(0.38)*	97.3(13.9)	3.22(0.37)*	5.41(0.40)	2.75(1.65)*
9.4% Protein	3.67(0.30)*	95.4(11.9)	3.30(0.38)*	5.18(0.60)	2.32(2.12)*

* = significantly different from the 27.3% protein group. V_d = volume of distribution, MRT = mean residence time, Cl_{gent} = clearance of gentamicin, k_{el} = apparent elimination rate constant.

During the course of gentamicin administration, nephrotoxicity was exhibited in most dogs by decreased creatinine clearance, increased urinary excretion of protein, NAG, GGT, sodium,and potassium, and increased serum trough gentamicin concentrations, however there were significant differences between groups. (*Figures 1–8.*)

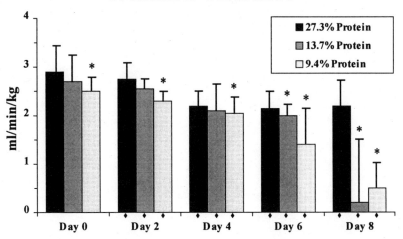

Figure 1. Endogenous creatinine clearance for dogs fed 9.4, 13.7, and 27.3% protein over 8 days of gentamicin administration. * Indicates significantly different values from the 27.3% protein group on that day. Arrowheads indicate significant difference from day-0 values. The light shaded bars indicate median and the line error bars indicate the upper range and maximal value. (From Grauer et al.[1]; reproduced with permission from AJVR.)

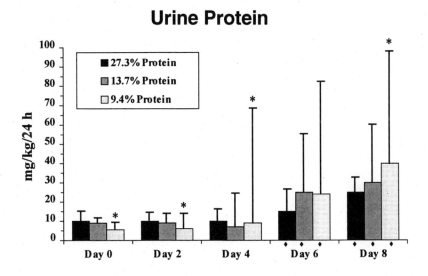

Figure 2. Urinary excretion of protein for dogs fed 9.4, 13.7, and 27.3% protein over 8 days of gentamicin administration. * Indicates significantly different values from the 27.3% protein groupon that day. Arrowheads indicate significant difference from day-0 values. See Figure 1 for key. (From Grauer et al.[1]; reproduced with permission from AJVR.)

Serum Creatinine

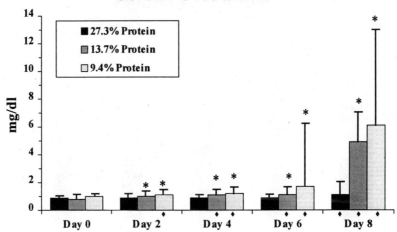

Figure 3. Serum creatinine concentration for dogs fed 9.4, 13.7, and 27.3% protein over 8 days of gentamicin administration. * Indicates significantly different values from the 27.3% protein group on that day. Arrowheads indicate significant difference from day-0 values. See Figure 1 for key. (From Grauer et al [1]; reproduced with permission from AJVR.)

Urine NAG

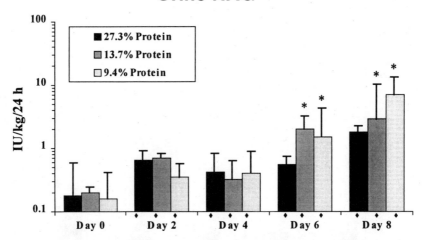

Figure 4. Urinary excretion of N-acetyl-ß-D-glucosaminidase (NAG) for dogs fed 9.4, 13.7, and 27.3% protein over 8 days of gentamicin administration. * Indicates significantly different values from the 27.3% protein group on that day. Arrowheads indicate significant difference from day-0 values. Notice the logarithmic scale. See Figure 1 for key. (From Grauer et al.[1]; reproduced with permission from AJVR.)

Urine GGT

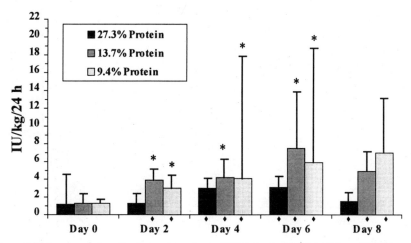

Figure 5. Urinary excretion of γ-glutamyl transferase (GGT) for dogs fed 9.4, 13.7, and 27.3% protein over 8 days of gentamicin administration. * Indicates significantly different values from the 27.3% protein group on that day. Arrowheads indicate significant difference from day-0 values. See Figure 1 for key. (From Grauer et al.[1]; reproduced with permission from AJVR.)

Fractional Clearance of Na

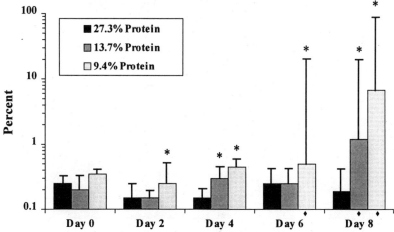

Figure 6. Fractional clearance of sodium for dogs fed 9.4, 13.7, and 27.3% protein over 8 days of gentamicin administration. * Indicates significantly different values from the 27.3% protein group on that day. Arrowheads indicate significant difference from day-0 values. Notice the logarithmic scale. See Figure 1 for key. (From Grauer et al[1]; reproduced with permission from AJVR.)

Fractional Clearance of K

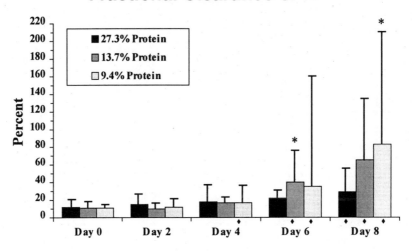

Figure 7. Fractional clearance of potassium for dogs fed 9.4, 13.7, and 27.3% protein over 8 days of gentamicin administration. * Indicates significantly different values from the 27.3% protein group on that day. Arrowheads indicate significant difference from day-0 values. See Figure 1 for key. (From Grauer et al[1]; reproduced with permisiion from AJVR.)

Trough Serum Gentamicin

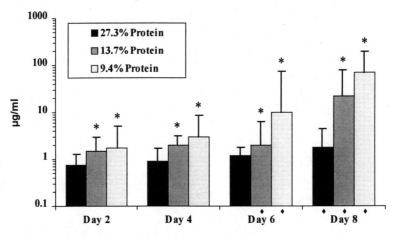

Figure 8. Trough serum gentamicin concentration in dogs fed 9.4, 13.7, and 27.3% protein over 8 days of gentamicin administration. * Indicates significantly different values from the 27.3% protein group on that day. Arrowheads indicate significant difference from day-2 values. Notice the logarithmic scale. See Figure 1 for key.(Freom Grauer et al[1]; reproducedwith permission from AJVR.)

In general, dogs fed high protein had fewer and less severe renal functional abnormalities than did dogs fed medium and low protein. The following significant differences existed between groups after 8 days of gentamicin administration. Dogs fed high protein had lower serum creatinine concentrations and higher creatinine clearances compared with dogs fed medium and low protein. Dogs fed high protein also had lower fractional clearance of sodium and potassium and lower serum trough gentamicin concentrations compared to dogs fed medium and low protein. Conversely, dogs fed low protein had increased urinary excretion of protein and NAG compared to dogs fed medium and high protein. No difference was observed in the gentamicin elimination rate constant between days 1 and 7 for dogs fed high protein, however in dogs fed medium and low protein, the apparent elimination rate constant was lower on day 7 compared to day 1. Dogs fed medium and low protein became depressed and lost their appetites on days 7 and 8, whereas those dogs fed high protein ate well and were bright and alert throughout the study. Finally, proximal tubular necrosis was more severe in dogs fed medium protein compared with dogs fed high protein, however there were no differences in renal cortical gentamicin concentrations between groups (*Table 3*).

Table 3. Renal histology scores and renal cortical gentamicin concentrations.

	Tubular necrosis (mean rank score, 1 = best, 18 = worst)	Mean cortical gentamicin concentration (µg/g)
27.3% Protein	5.4 (3.7)†	1001 (251)
13.7% Protein	12.0 (3.7)*	821 (243)
9.4% Protein	11.1 (5.9)	913 (321)

† = Mean (SD); * = Significantly different from the 27.3% protein group.

Discussion

Dogs fed high protein prior to and during gentamicin administration had reduced nephrotoxicity and faster gentamicin clearance with a larger volume of distribution compared with dogs fed medium or low protein. In addition, in dogs fed high protein, renal elimination of gentamicin was preserved through 7 days of treatment, whereas in dogs fed medium or low protein, elimination of gentamicin decreased over the treatment period. Although dogs fed high protein fared considerably better than their medium and low protein counterparts, clearly all dogs in the high protein group exhibited some renal injury from the gentamicin. It is possible that continued administration of gentamicin to the high protein dogs would have resulted in nephrotoxicity similar to that observed in the medium and low protein dogs. Nonetheless, feeding high protein prior to and during gentamicin administration delayed the onset of nephrotoxicity and improved the therapeutic index of gentamicin.

In contrast to results of this study, other investigators observed renal protective effects associated with low dietary protein[13] and low dietary protein conditioning.[10,12] Specifically, rats fed 5% protein during gentamicin administration had less nephrotoxicosis than did rats fed 18% protein.[13] Additionally, rats conditioned to 5% dietary protein prior to administration of uranyl sitrate or gentamicin had improved survival, compared with rats conditioned to 20 or 60% dietary protein.[10,12] It is interesting to note, however, in two of the aforementioned studies, rats conditioned to high dietary protein but switched to low dietary protein at the time of the renal insult had less nephrotoxicosis than did rats maintained on high- or low-protein diets before and after the renal insult.[10,12]

Difference in results between this study and previous studies of gentamicin and uranyl nitrate-induced nephrotoxicosis in rats may be explained by the animal model or the type and dosage of toxicant. Rats and dogs may respond differently to dietary protein. Furthermore, uranyl nitrate causes peracute renal failure compared with the delayed nephrotoxicosis caused by gentamicin. The dosage of gentamicin used in the rat studies (120 mg/kg/d[13] and 150 mg/kg/d[12]) was higher than the 30 mg/kg/d dosage used in this study and, therefore, the renal damage in the rat studies may have been more extensive and/or rapid in onset. Once azotemia develops, high dietary protein is thought to be detrimental[10,12] and may have accounted for some of the adverse effects observed in previous studies. In the present study, dogs fed high protein did not become azotemic; however it is possible that continued intake of the high protein diet, in the face of azotemia, would have worsened their condition.

Based on the present study, the amount of dietary protein fed to dogs prior to and during nephrotoxicant exposure can have an effect on nephrotoxicity as well as nephrotoxicant pharmacokinetics. The observed differences in nephrotoxicity and pharmacokinetics between dogs fed high protein and dogs fed medium and low protein were likely caused in part by dietary induced changes in glomerular filtration rate (GFR). Decreased endogenous creatinine clearance, an indicator of GFR, was observed in dogs fed low protein at the end of the dietary conditioning period. Decreased creatinine clearance was also observed in similar studies when rats were conditioned to low dietary protein.[12] Conversely, increases in renal blood flow and GFR have been observed in normal dogs subsequent to high protein ingestion.[14] In as much as gentamicin is dependent upon GFR for elimination[15] and reabsorption of gentamicin is inversely proportional to GFR,[16] the decreased GFR associated with low dietary protein may have resulted in decreased filtration and elimination of gentamicin. Serum trough concentrations of gentamicin were significantly greater in dogs fed low protein compared with dogs fed high protein as early as the second day of gentamicin administration. There was no difference in renal cortical gentamicin concentrations between groups, however previous studies have also failed to demonstrate a correlation between renal cortical aminoglycoside concentrations and nephrotoxicosis.[17-19]

The results of this study are truly exciting. Many factors that increase the risk of ARF are uncontrollable. This study has identified a risk factor (dietary protein level) for acute renal failure that is controllable. In many cases where potentially nephrotoxic therapy is being considered (e.g., chemotherapy, analgesics, radiographic contrast agents, and certain antimicrobial agents) or potential renal hypoperfusion/hypotension may exist (elective anesthetic procedures), it may be possible to delay the procedure or therapy for a period while the patient is conditioned to a specific level of dietary protein. In those cases where dietary protein conditioning is not possible prior to the procedure or drug administration, knowledge of the current level of dietary protein will allow the clinician to more accurately assess the risk:benefit ratio for the patient.

We hope to build on these previous results by assessing the protective effects of dietary n-3 fatty acid supplementation as well as specific thromboxane synthetase inhibition in conjunction with high dietary protein in dogs treated with high dose gentamicin. Thromboxane A_2 is a prostanoid derived from the action of cyclooxygenase on arachidonic acid (AA). It is produced by a number of cells including platelets, glomerular epithelial and mesangial cells and tubular cells within the renal medulla.[20] Thromboxane A_2 is a potent inducer of platelet aggregation and is a chemotactic factor that attracts neutrophils[21] which release enzymes and oxygen radicals that can damage cell membranes.[22] In addition, thromboxane is a powerful vasoconstrictor and causes mesangial cell contraction[23] which may result in decreased GFR.[24] When thromboxane B_2, the stable metabolite of thromboxane A_2, is infused into the renal arteries of normal dogs, severe decreases in renal blood flow and GFR occur and result in decreased urine production and electrolyte excretion.[25]

Future Studies

Thromboxane A_2 has been shown to play an important role in a variety of renal diseases including glomerulonephritis, lupus nephritis, ureteral obstruction, renal allograft rejection, diabetic nephropathy, and ARF. Increased production of thromboxane secondary to an ischemic or toxic insult is thought to be a major cause of the renal vasoconstriction that is associated with ARF.[26,28] Vasoconstriction adversely affects renal function by decreasing GFR and contributes to renal damage by decreasing delivery of oxygen and nutrients to tubular cells. Specifically, in models of ARF in rats, including those induced by cyclosporin,[26] glycerol,[27] gentamicin,[28] endotoxin,[29] adriamycin,[30] and ischemia,[31] urinary excretion of thromboxane is increased. In these models, treatment with thromboxane synthetase inhibitors not only decreased urinary thromboxane B_2 excretion but attenuated renal damage as evidenced by preserved renal blood flow and GFR, decreased proteinuria, decreased enzymuria, and decreased tubular necrosis.[26-31]

We have previously examined the effects of a specific thromboxane synthetase inhibitor, methyl-2(3pyridyl)-1-indoleoctanoic acid (CGS 12970)[32] in dogs. In healthy beagles, a 97% reduction of whole blood generation of thromboxane B_2 occurred 2 hours after a single oral dose of CGS 12970.[33] Twice daily administration of CGS 12970 for 8 days resulted in an 80% reduction of thromboxane generation.[33] Additionally, oral CGS 12970 significantly decreased AA-induced whole blood platelet aggregation and ATP secretion in healthy beagles.[34] Following a single dose, platelet aggregation was maximally inhibited at 1 hour, remained negligible through 12 hours, and returned to normal by 96 hours.[34] No adverse effects were observed in healthy dogs treated with CGS 12970.[33,34]

We have also assessed the effects of thromboxane synthetase inhibition in dogs with experimentally induced immune complex glomerulonephritis. When treatment was initiated at the time of glomerular injury, damage was less severe as evidenced by renal histology (decreased glomerular cell proliferation, epithelial crescent formation, neutrophil infiltration, and fibrin deposition in glomeruli) and renal function (decreased renal excretion of protein).[35,36] When CGSHz 12970 was used to treat established experimentally induced glomerulonephritis (treatment started 30 days after initiation of glomerulonephritis) or naturally occurring glomerulonephritis, urinary excretion of protein was significantly decreased.[37,38] Urinary excretion of thromboxane B_2 was increased in each of these models of canine glomerulonephritis and treatment with CGS 12970 attenuated this increase in urinary thromboxane B_2 excretion. Finally, treatment with CGS 12970 caused no adverse effects in dogs with glomerulonephritis.[35,38]

Alternatively, it is well established that dietary supplementation with n-3 fatty acids can significantly reduce thromboxane A_2 synthesis in stimulated platelets[39] and glomerular cells.[40,41] The mechanism for such an effect includes the partial substitution of eicosapentaenoic acid (EPA) and docosahexaenoic acid (DHA) for AA in membrane phospholipid and a resulting lessened quantitative release of AA (via phospholipase A_2) and therefore a lessened availability for cyclooxygenase mediated conversion to thromboxane A_2.[42,43] In addition, EPA and DHA can significantly inhibit cyclooxygenase activity.[44] A modest amount of EPA is converted viad cyclooxygenase to form thromboxane A3 which has little or no vasoconstrictive potential.[45] In contrast, under physiologic conditions, AA and EPA appear to be comparable substrates for the formation of vasodilatory prostacyclins (PGI) and their respective products, PGI_2 and PGI_3 are of similar biologic potency.[45,46] Recently, EPA was observed to exert important effects on renal function in normal human beings[47] and was shown to favorably influence renal function and prostanoid production in rats and human beings with renal transplants that are treated with cyclosporine.[48-50] Importantly, EPA and DHA supplementation has also been shown to protect dogs from ischemic ARF.[51] Control dogs had decreased GFR and increased urinary excretion of thromboxane B_2 in response to renal ischemia, whereas dogs supplemented with EPA and DHA maintained normal GFR and had no increase in urinary excretion of thromboxane B_2.[51]

Based on results from the above studies, thromboxane appears to be involved in the pathogenesis of several different renal disease processes in several species. Additionally, thromboxane synthetase inhibition and dietary supplementation with n-3 fatty acids have been used successfully to prevent ARF in rats and dogs. It is our hypothesis that:

1) Specific thromboxane synthetase inhibition (CGS 12970) and high dietary protein will have additive protective effects on renal function and morphol-

ogy in dogs treated with gentamicin. The effects of high dietary protein on GFR are thought to be mediated via a variety of vasodilatory substances (glucagon, growth hormone, endothelium derived relaxing factor/nitric oxide, prostaglandins, and dopamine), not decreased production of thromboxane.[52] By combining a thromboxane synthetase inhibitor with high dietary protein, we expect to observe additive effects on renal blood flow and GFR and therefore greater attenuation of gentamicin-induced nephrotoxicity compared with dogs treated with high dietary protein only.

2) High dietary protein supplemented with n3 fatty acids will have additive protective effects on renal function and morphology in dogs treated with gentamicin. Similar to specific thromboxane synthetase inhibition, we expect n-3 fatty acid supplementation will decrease production of thromboxane A_2. However, n-3 fatty acid supplementation will likely affect the production of several eicosanoids in addition to thromboxane and therefore may have a greater effect on renal function compared with thromboxane synthetase inhibition alone. For example, production of the vasodilatory prostaglandins E_3 and I_3 is expected to occur with n-3 fatty acid supplementation. Additionally, n-3 fatty acid supplementation is expected to increase production of endothelium derived relaxing factor/nitric oxide and decrease production of leukotrienes and oxygen free radicals.

3) Dietary supplementation with n-3 fatty acids or administration of CGS 12970 to dogs treated with gentamicin will not affect initial gentamicin pharmacokinetics. In normal kidneys, generation of thromboxane is minimal, and therefore at the start of gentamicin administration we do not expect either of the above treatments to affect renal blood flow, GFR, or gentamicin pharmacokinetics. However, as nephrotoxicity occurs, thromboxane production increases and contributes to decreased renal function. At this point, n-3 fatty acid supplementation and thromboxane synthetase inhibition will likely serve to improve renal blood flow, GFR, and gentamicin elimination.

References

1. Grauer GF, Behrend EN, Greco DS, et al. Effects of dietary protein conditioning on gentamicin-induced nephrotoxicosis in healthy male dogs. *Am J Vet Res* 1994; 55:90-97.

2. Behrend EN, Grauer GF, Greco DS, et al. Effects of dietary protein conditioning on gentamicin pharmacokinetics in dogs. *J Vet Pharmacol Therap* 1994; 17:259-264.

3. Grauer GF. Toxic-antinduced acute renal failure. In, *Current Veterinary Therapy Small Animal Practice* . Kirk RW (ed), WB Saunders Co, Philadelphia, 1989, pp126-130.

4. Behrend EN, Grauer GF, Mani I, et al. Hospital acquired acute renal failure: A study of potential risk factors and prognostic indicators in 29 cases (1983-1992). *J Am Vet Med Assoc* 1996; 208: 537-541.

5. Vaden SL, Levine JF, Correa MT, et al. Retrospective analysis of 106 dogs with acute renal failure. (abstr) *J Vet Int Med* 1995; 9:209.

6. Brown SA, Barsanti JA, Crowell WA. Gentamicin-associated acute renal failure in the dog. *J Vet Med Assoc* 1985; 186:686-690.

7. Lieberthal W, Levinsky NG. Treatment of acute tubular necrosis. *Seminars in Nephrology* 1990; 110:571-583.

8. Meyer RD. Risk factors and comparisons of clinical nephrotoxicity of aminoglycosides. *Am J Med* 1986; 80:119-125.

9. Andrews PM, Bates SB. Dietary protein prior to renal ischemia dramatically affects post-ischemic kidney function. *Kidney Int* 1986; 30:299-303.

10. Andrews PM, Bates SB. Effects of dietary protein on uranyl-nitrate-induced acute renal failure. *Nephron* 1987; 45:296-301.

11. Andrews PM, Chung EM. High dietary protein regimes provide significant protection from mercury nephrotoxicity in rats. *Toxicol Appl Pharmacol* 1990; 105:288-304.

12. Andrews PM, Bates SB. Dietary protein as a risk factor in gentamicin nephrotoxicity. *RenalFailure* 1987-88; 10:153-159.

13. Whiting PH, Power DA, Petersen J, et al. The effect of dietary protein restriction on high dose gentamicin nephrotoxicity in rats. *Br J Exp Pathol* 1988; 69:35-41.

14. Brown SA, Finco DR. Characterization of the renal response to protein ingestion in dogs with experimentally induced renal failure. *Am J Vet Res* 1992; 53:569-573.

15. Brown SA, Riviere JE. Comparative pharmacokinetics of aminoglycoside antibiotics. *J Vet Pharmacol Therap* 1991; 14:1-35.

16. Verpooten GA, Pattyn VM, Giuliano RA, DeBroe ME. The effect of proteinuria and hyperfiltration on the renal cortical uptake of gentamicin in rats (abstr), *Kidney Int* 1987; 31:377.

17. de Rougemont D, Oeschger A, Konrad L, et al. Gentamicin induced acute renal failure in the rat: Effect of dehydration, DOCA-saline and furosemide. *Nephron* 1981; 29:176-184.

18. Savin V, Karniski L, Cuppage F, et al. Effect of gentamicin on isolated glomeruli and proximal tubules of the rabbit. *Lab Invest* 1985; 52:93-102.

19. Whelton A, Stout RL, Bendush B, et al. Hyperalimentation reduces cortical uptake of aminoglycosides but increases aminoglycoside nephrotoxicity. (abstr) *Kidney Int* 1979; 16:778.

20. Petrulis AS, Aikawa M, Dunn MJ. Prostaglandin and thromboxane synthesis by rat glomerular epithelial cells. *Kidney Int* 1981; 20:469-474.

21. Boot JR, Dawson W, Kitchen EA. The chemotactic activity of thromboxane B_2 : A possible role in inflammation. *J Physiol* 1976; 257:47-48.

22. Hawkins D. Neutrophilic leukocytes in immunologic reactions: Evidence for the selective release of lysosomal constituents. *J Immunol* 1972; 108:310-317.

23. Mene P, Dunn MJ. Contractile effects of TxA_2 and endoperoxide analogues on cultured rat glomerular mesangial cells. *Am J Physiol* 1986; 251:F1029-F1035."

24. Baylis C. Effects of administered thromboxane on the intact, normal rat kidney. *Renal Physiol Basel* 1987; 10:110-121.

25. Gerber JG, Ellis E, Hollifield J, et al. Effect of prostaglandin endoperoxide analogue on canine renal function, hemodynamics and renin release. *Eur J Pharmacol* 1979; 53:239-246.

26. Grieve EM, Hawksworth GM, Simpson JG, et al. Effect of thromboxane synthetase inhibition and angiotensin converting enzyme inhibition on acute cyclosporin A nephrotoxicity. *Biochem Pharmacol* 1990; 40:2323-2329.

27. Papanikolaou N, Hatziantoniou C, Bariety J. Selective inhibition of thromboxane synthesis partially protected while inhibition of angiotensin II formation did not protect rats against acute renal failure induced with glycerol. *Prostaglandins Leukotrienes and Medicine* 1986; 21:29-35.

28. Papanikolaou N, Peros G, Morphake P, et al. Does gentamicin induce acute renal failure by increasing renal TXA$_2$ synthesis in rats? *Prostaglandins, Leukotrienes, Essential Fatty Acids* 1992; 45:131-136.

29. Badr KF, Kelley VE, Rennke HG, et al. Roles for thromboxane A$_2$ and leukotrienes in endotoxininduced acute renal failure. *Kidney Int* 1986; 30:474-480.

30. Remuzzi G, Imberti L, Rossini M, et al. Increased glomerular thromboxane synthesis as a possible cause of proteinuria in experimental nephrosis. *J Clin Invest* 1985; 75:94-101.

31. Masamura H, Kunitada S, Irie K, et al. A thromboxane A$_2$ synthetase inhibitor, DP-1904, prevents rat renal injury. *Eur J Pharmacol* 1991; 193:321-327.

32. Ambler J, Butler KD, Ku EC, et al. CGS 12970: a novel, long acting thromboxanesynthetase inhibitor. *Br J Pharmac* 1985; 86:497-504.

33. Longhofer SL, Johnson HC, Culham CA, et al. Effects of a specific thromboxane synthetase inhibitor on thromboxane generation and excretion in normal dogs. *Am J Vet Res*; 1990; 51:1746-1750.

34. Grauer GF, Rose BJ, Toolan L, et al. Comparison of the effects of low-dose aspirin and specific thromboxane synthetase inhibition on whole blood platelet aggregation and ATP secretion in healthy dogs. *Am J Vet Res* 1992; 53:1631-1635.

35. Grauer GF, Culham CA, Dubielzig RR, et al. Effects of a specific thromboxane synthetase inhibitor on development of experimental D. *immitis* immune complex glomerulonephritisin the dog. *J Vet Int Med* 1988; 2:192-200.

36. Longhofer SL, Frisbie DD, Johnson HC, et al. Effects of a thromboxane synthetase inhibitor on immune complex glomerulonephritis. *Am J Vet Res* 1991; 52:480-487.

37. Grauer GF, Frisbie DD, Longhofer SL, et al. Effects of a thromboxane synthetase inhibitor on established immune complex glomerulonephritis in dogs. *Am J Vet Res* 1992; 53:808-813.

38. Grauer GF, Frisbie DD, Snyder PS, et al. Treatment of membranoproliferative glomerulonephritis and nephrotic syndrome in a dog with a thromboxane synthetase inhibitor. *J Vet Int Med* 1992; 6:77-81.

39. Herold PM, Kinsella JE. Fish oil consumption and decreased risk of cardiovascular disease:a comparison of findings from animal and human feeding trials. *Am J Clin Nutr* 1986; 43:566-598.

40. Scharschmidt LA, Gibbons NB, McGarry L, et al. Effects of dietary fish oil on renal insufficiency in rats with subtotal nephrectomy. *Kidney Int* 1987; 32:700-709.

41. Barcelli UO, Beach DC, Pollack VE. The influence of n-6 and n-3 fatty acids on kidney phospholipid composition and on eicosanoid production in aging rats. *Lipids* 1988; 23:309-312.

42. Dyerberg J, Bang HO. Haemostatic function and platelet polyunsaturated fatty acids in Eskimos. *Lancet* 1979; ii:433-435.

43. Weaver BJ, Holub BJ. Health effects and metabolism of dietary eicosapentaenoic acid. *ProgFood Nutr Sci* 1988; 12:111-150.

44. Corey EJ, Shih C, Cashman JR. Docosahexaenoic acid is a strong inhibitor of prostaglandin but not leukotriene biosynthesis. *Proc Natl Acad Sci USA* 1983; 80:3581-3584.

45. Needleman P, Raz A, Minkes MS, et al. Triene prostaglandins: prostacyclin and thromboxane biosynthesis and unique biological properties. *Proc Natl Acad Sci USA* 1979; 76:944-948.

46. Bunting S, Gryglewski R, Moncada S, Vane JR. Arterial walls generate from prostaglandin endoperoxides a substance (prostaglndin X) which relaxes strips of mesenteric and coeliacarteries and inhibits platelet aggregation. *Prostaglandins* 1976; 12:293-311.

47. Dusing R, Struck A, Gobel BO, et al. Effects of n-3 fatty acids on renal function and renal prostaglandin E metabolism. *Kidney Int* 1990; 38:315-319.

48. Coffman TM, Yohay D, Carr DR, et al. Effect of dietary fish oil supplementation on eicosanoid production by rat renal allograft. *Transplantation* 1988; 45:470-474.

49. Elzinga L, Kelley VE, Houghton DC, Bennett WM. Modification of experimental nephrotoxicity with fish oil as the vehicle of cyclosporin. *Transplantation* 1987; 43:271-275.

50. Homan an der Heide JJ, Bilo HJG, Tegzess AM, Donker AJM. The effects of dietary supplementation with fish oil on renal function in cyclosporin-treated renal transplant recipients. *Transplantation* 1990; 49:523-527.

51. Neumayer HH, Heinrich M, Schmissas M, et al. Amelioration of ischemic acute renal failure by dietary fish oil administration in conscious dogs. *J Am Soc Nephrol* 1992; 3:1312-1320.

52. Tolins JP, Raij L. Effects of amino acid infusion on renal hemodynamics: Role of endothelium-derived relaxing factor. *Hypertension* 1991; 17:1045-1051.

53. Weber PC. The modification of the arachidonic acid cascade by n-3 fatty acids. *Adv Prostaglandin Thromboxane Leukotriene Res* 1990; 20:232-240.

Fatty Acid Supplementation and Chronic Renal Disease

Scott A. Brown, VMD, PhD, DACVIM
Delmar R. Finco, DVM, PhD, DACVIM
Department of Physiology & Pharmacology
College of Veterinary Medicine
University of Georgia, Athens, Georgia

Introduction

End-stage renal disease is a common cause of death in dogs and cats. Unfortunately, dogs and cats with spontaneous renal disease frequently exhibit a temporal pattern of renal function that is characterized by progressive decrements of GFR.[1,2] This has at least two important consequences for a dog or cat with renal disease. First, the disease is inherently unstable and frequent re-evaluations and adjustments in therapy are required. In addition, because of the tremendous cost and technical difficulty associated with therapy for end-stage uremia (i.e., dialytic therapy or renal transplantation), efforts designed to slow the rate of progression of renal disease are particularly important in veterinary medicine. A variety of factors appear to be responsible for the progressive nature of renal injury in animals, including those directly or indirectly related to dietary lipid intake. In particular, emphasis has been placed upon possible roles for (A) the triad of glomerular hyperfiltration, hypertension, and hypertrophy and (B) systemic hypertension.[3-8] Other factors that may contribute to progressive renal injury and be affected by dietary fatty acid composition include hyperlipidemia, lipid peroxidation, and platelet-induced renal injury.[3-8]

Glomerular Hyperfiltration, Hypertension, and Hypertrophy and Progressive Renal Injury

The causes of progression of renal disease in dogs and cats are, in general, poorly understood. In animals, it has been proposed that one or more factors associated with renal disease cause a perpetuation of renal injury.[3] These factors may occur as a result of a disruption of homeostasis or may be a consequence of the adaptive renal response to injury. Following surgical reduction of renal mass in rats, remaining (remnant) nephrons are initially normal. However, over the ensuing months, remnant glomeruli develop lesions and are ultimately destroyed. As more and more nephrons are destroyed, renal function declines over time. As investigators studied this model of progressive renal disease, it became apparent that important adaptive changes were observed following reduction of renal mass. The surviving, or remnant, glomeruli became larger, exhibited an increase in glomerular capillary pressure, and an increase in filtration rate. These changes are referred to as glomerular hypertrophy, glomerular hypertension, and glomerular hyperfiltration, respectively. Brenner and colleagues[3] proposed that these changes in nephron structure and function are maladaptive, causing renal injury (*Figure 1*).

Hemodynamic "Maladaptations":
Theory of Progressive Renal Injury

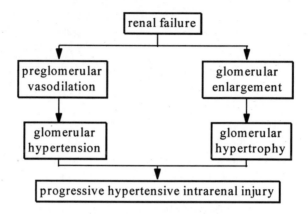

Figure 1. The hemodynamic theory of progressive renal injury.

Many investigators and clinicians have extrapolated results from studies in inbred strains of rats to the clinical management of dogs and cats. Unfortunately, these extrapolations may be invalid. In fact, results in the Munich-Wistar rat strain may not even apply to other inbred strains of rats, such as the Wistar-Kyoto strain. Thus, it is likely that a genetically heterogeneous set of animals from a different species (pet dogs and cats) will respond in a somewhat different manner to a disease process. Recently, several studies have addressed these issues in dogs and cats. In particular, studies have shown that, in both dogs and cats with renal insufficiency, glomerular hypertension (*Figure 2*) and hypertrophy are observed in dogs and cats with renal insufficiency.[9-10]

Glomerular Hypertension:
Dogs with Renal Insufficiency

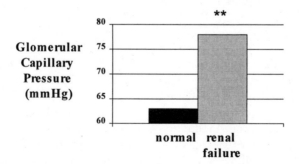

Figure 2. Glomerular hypertension was present in dogs with induced chronic renal insufficiency.

Since these changes in remnant nephron structure and function are apparently an inherent property of nephrons following substantial renal injury in rats, dogs, and cats, this hypothesis may apply to nonrodent species as well.

Recently, in an experimental model of diabetic nephropathy, therapy designed to lower the extent of glomerular hypertension and hypertrophy was shown to be renoprotective.[11] As with remnant nephrons following surgical reduction of renal mass, this model of diabetes is characterized by glomerular hyperfiltration, glomerular hypertension, and glomerular hypertrophy. The chronic administration of an angiotensin converting enzyme (ACE) inhibitor limited glomerular capillary hypertension and hypertrophy. This response to an ACE inhibitor was associated with a limitation of the degree of mesangial expansion and glomerulosclerosis, markers of diabetic nephropathy.[12] Because of similarities in adaptive changes in diabetes and remnant kidney, two models of renal disease, it is tempting to speculate that the favorable response to lowering glomerular pressure in diabetic dogs would also be observed in nondiabetic dogs with renal disease. If so, efforts to lower glomerular hypertension and hypertrophy might prove beneficial in these animals.

Dietary Fatty Acids Supplementation and Glomerular Hypertension

The type of dietary fatty acid ingested by affected animals appears to be critical.[13-15] Fatty acids are generally categorized on the basis of number and location of carbon-carbon double bonds. Dietary fatty acids that contain no double bonds, such as palmitic acid, are referred to as saturated fatty acids. Animal fats, which contain predominantly saturated fatty acids, are often incorporated into feline diets because of availability and palatability. In contrast, plant sources of fat contain high proportions of the polyunsaturated fatty acid, linoleic acid. Linoleic acid is referred to as an omega-6 polyunsaturated fatty acid (ω-6 PUFA) because the first carbon-carbon double bond occurs at the sixth carbon from the methyl group. In most mammals, including people and dogs, linoleic is readily converted to arachidonic acid, the immediate precursor of eicosanoids (prostaglandins and thromboxanes). However, in cats the conversion of linoleic to arachidonic acid is limited and both are essential dietary fatty acids in this species.[16-18] An alternative source of PUFA is menhaden oil derived from fish feeding on plankton. These oils are rich in eicosapentaenoic acid and docosahexaenoic acid, which are omega 3 PUFA (ω-3 PUFA).

Thus substantially different chemical forms of fatty acids are obtained when pet foods are supplemented with lipids obtained from animal fat, plant oil, or menhaden oil. These dietary fatty acids may affect renal function through effects on renal eicosanoid metabolism. Eicosanoids are compounds derived from PUFA within cell membranes and include prostaglandins, prostacyclin, and thromboxanes.[19-20] The usual precursor for eicosanoids is arachidonic acid. In dogs, people and rats, arachidonic acid is derived from the PUFA linoleic acid, which comprises 50-80% of plant oils. However, cats have limited hepatic Δ-6 desaturase activity and thus cannot effectively convert linoleic to arachidonic acid and both are considered essential dietary fatty acids in cats.[16-18] It should be noted, however, that the activity of this enzyme in the feline kidney and the intrarenal capacity to convert linoleic to arachidonic acid have not been studied.

The principal eicosanoids (*Figure 3*) derived from the ω-6 polyunsaturated fatty acid, arachidonic acid, include prostaglandin E2 (PGE2), prostacyclin (PGI2), and thromboxane A2 (TxA2).

Renal Eicosanoids: ω–6 Precursor

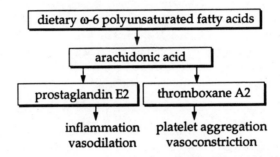

Figure 3. Eicosanoids derived from ω-6 fatty acids are of the 2-series and tend to be pro-inflammatory and enhance platelet aggregation. Some are vasoconstrictive while others are vasodilatory.

The vasodilatory eicosanoids, PGE2 and PGI2, increase renal blood flow and glomerular filtration rate (GFR).[19,20] In contrast, renal blood flow and GFR are decreased by TxA2 through renal vasoconstrictor effects. Both thromboxanes and PGI2 alter platelet function: thromboxanes enhance and PGI2 inhibits platelet aggregation.

Menhaden oil contains ω-3 PUFA which compete with arachidonic acid in the production of eicosanoids. Consequently, animals fed menhaden oil have a diminution of the 2-series of eicosanoids normally derived from arachidonic acid. Importantly, the eicosanoid derivatives of ω-3 polyunsaturated fatty acids (*Figure 4*) are less potent than the usual arachidonic acid derivatives.[4,13-15,19] In particular, thromboxanes derived from ω-3 PUFA have little vasoconstrictive or platelet aggregating effect. Unlike ω-6 and ω-3 PUFA, the saturated fatty acids present in animal fat do not serve as precursors for eicosanoid production.

Proponents of this unifying theory of the hemodynamic causes of progressive nature of renal disease have proposed a link between production of the 2-series of prostaglandins and thromboxanes and progressive renal disease. This theory is based upon renal micropuncture studies suggesting that glomerular hyperfiltration, glomerular hypertension, and glomerular hypertrophy are dependent upon vasodilatory renal prostanoids.[3] Manipulations that alter renal production of eicosanoids, such as dietary supplementation with menhaden oil which serves as a precursor to production of the 3-series of prostaglandins and thromboxanes, alter the course of chronic renal disease in laboratory animals.[13-15]

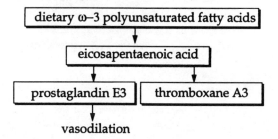

Figure 4. Eicosanoids derived from ω-3 fatty acids are of the 3-series and are less potent, non-inflammatory, vasodilatory, and inhibit platelet aggregation.

Studies in our laboratory have shown that a low fat diet supplemented with fish oil that is rich in ω-3 polyunsaturated fatty acids will preserve renal function of dogs with induced renal failure when compared to supplementation with safflower oil a rich source of ω-6 polyunsaturated fatty acids or the highly saturated fat-source, beef tallow (*Figure 5*).

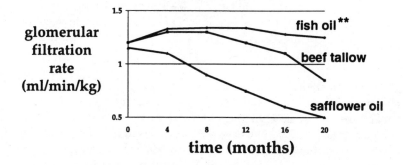

Figure 5. Changes in glomerular filtration rate over time in dogs fed a low fat diet enriched with beef tallow, menhaden oil, or safflower oil.

<table>
<tr><td>Systemic
Hypertension
and Progressive
Renal Injury</td><td>Frequently, dogs and cats with chronic renal failure exhibit elevations of systemic arterial pressure.[21-24] Systemic hypertension can lead to renal injury in rats.[25] The mechanism of renal injury in systemic hypertension appears to involve both direct effects of blood pressure elevation and an indirect effect due to transmission of high pressures to the glomerular capillary bed. In particular, cats and dogs with renal disease are susceptible to hypertensive renal injury whenever blood pressure becomes even transiently elevated. Recent studies in our laboratory have shown that blood pressure in dogs and cats is much more variable than generally realized. Further, dogs (and presumably cats) with renal insufficiency have dilated preglomerular vessels that allow even transient elevations of systemic arterial pressure to be transmitted directly to the susceptible glomerular capillary bed.[26] Thus, transient elevations of arterial pressure pose a particular risk in animals with renal disease.</td></tr>
</table>

<table>
<tr><td>Dietary
Fatty Acids
Supplementation
and Systemic
Hypertension</td><td>Recent studies in people with renal disease indicated that dietary supplementation with ω-3 polyunsaturated fatty acids may lower systemic arterial pressure.[27] This may prove to be an effective therapy in dogs and cats with renal failure and systemic hypertension. Any antihypertensive therapy, such as dietary fatty acid modification, designed to normalize systemic arterial pressure should be monitored with successive measurements of blood pressure.</td></tr>
</table>

<table>
<tr><td>Dietary Fatty
Acids and
Hyperlipidemia</td><td>Abnormalities of lipid metabolism in renal disease have been characterized in human beings[5] and dogs[28,29] and generally include elevated serum levels of total cholesterol, lower density lipoproteins, and triglycerides. Support for an adverse effect of diets enriched with saturated fatty acids was derived from experiments in which rats were fed high calorie diets containing saturated fatty acids to induce hyperlipidemia, which led to glomerulosclerosis and progressive renal injury.[5] Lipids (triglycerides, cholesterol, and/or some classes of lipoproteins) stimulate glomerular mesangial cell proliferation and production of excess mesangial matrix, a process referred to as glomerulosclerosis.[5] Uremic renal failure has also been causally linked to hyperlipidemia in guinea pigs[30] and rats.[31-33] While diets rich in saturated fatty acids raise serum cholesterol and triglyceride concentrations in laboratory animals with renal failure; enhancing diets with PUFA lowers plasma lipid concentrations.[13,30-32]</td></tr>
</table>

Preliminary studies in our laboratory have established that cats and dogs with induced renal dysfunction exhibit hypercholesterolemia (e.g., mean serum cholesterol concentration of 215 ± 18 mg/dl in cats with renal dysfunction vs 105 ± 15 mg/dl in normal cats, $P<0.05$). We have recently observed that the hyperlipidemia in dogs with induced chronic renal failure can be modified by changes in dietary fatty acid composition. Specifically, animals fed a diet enriched with PUFA (safflower oil or menhaden oil) exhibited an amelioration of the hyperlipidemia observed in dogs fed a diet containing predominantly saturated fatty acids. Similar results have been observed in preliminary studies in cats. Previous studies in our laboratory have established an association between hyperlipidemia and renal failure in dogs.[29] Loss of renal function in dogs with experimental renal disease was directly related to plasma triglyceride (r^2=0.49, P=0.012) and total cholesterol (r^2=0.48, P=0.013) concentrations. The long-term effects of hyperlipidemia on renal function in dogs and cats and the effects of dietary manipulations on plasma cholesterol concentration remain to be established.

A role for a platelet-induced coagulopathy in progressive renal disease was suggested in studies of rodents with experimental renal failure.[6] Investigators have reported that selective thromboxane synthase inhibition can preserve renal structure and/or function in dogs.[33] While they have a variety of effects, selective thromboxane synthase antagonists are inhibitors of platelet function which likely contributes to their protective effect in the kidney. Another such anti-platelet therapy is ingestion of a diet enriched with menhaden oil (ω-3 PUFA). Compared to the usual pro-aggregatory eicosanoid (TxA2), thromboxanes derived from ω-3 PUFA only weakly facilitate platelet aggregation. Although dietary fatty acid deficiency may alter canine and feline platelet function,[34] the ultimate role of platelets in progressive renal disease in cats are poorly understood.

Dietary Fatty Acids and Platelets

Carbon-carbon double bonds of unsaturated fatty acids within cell membranes are subject to attack by electrophilic oxygen molecules. Free radical derivatives of oxygen and PUFA generate a self-propagating chain reaction. Such oxidation, referred to as lipid peroxidation, damages cell membrane structure and may play an important role in renal injury. Supplementation of diets with PUFA (e.g., diets enriched with plant or menhaden oils) provides additional substrate for lipid peroxidation and may encourage progressive renal disease.

Dietary Fatty Acids and Lipid Peroxidation

Preliminary evidence from recent studies in our laboratory suggest that, compared to dogs fed menhaden oil enriched diet, a safflower oil enriched contributes to progressive renal disease.[28] However, the ω-6:ω-3 ratios of the diets in this study were 0.2:1 and 50:1. The key issue will be to define the appropriate ratio for diets with dogs with renal failure. Current studies are underway to define the ideal ω-6:ω-3 ratio for dogs with renal failure.

Renal Disease and Dietary Fats

1. Polzin DJ, Osborne CA. Update: Conservative medical management of chronic renal failure. In Kirk RW (ed): *Current Veterinary Therapy* IX. Philadelphia: WB Saunders, 1986:1167-1173.

2. DiBartola SP, Rutgers HC, Zack PM, et al. Clinicopathological findings associated with chronic renal disease in cats: 74 cases. *J Am Vet Med Assoc* 1987; 190:1196-1202.

3. Brenner BM, Meyer TW, Hostetter TH. Dietary protein intake and the

References

progressive nature of renal disease. *N Engl J Med* 1982; 307:652-659.

4. Barcelli U, Pollak V. Is there a role for polyunsaturated fatty acids in the prevention of renal disease and renal failure. *Nephron* 1985; 41:209-212.

5. Moorhead JF, Chan MK, Varghese Z. The role of abnormalities of lipid metabolism in the progression of renal disease. In: *The Progressive Nature of Renal Disease.* Mitch WE, ed. New York: Churchill Livingstone, 1986:133-148.

6. Purkerson ME, Hoffsten PE, Klahr S. Pathogenesis of the glomerulopathy associated with renal infarction in rats. *Kidney Int* 1976; 9:407-417.

7. Fries JWU, Sandstrom DJ, Meyer TW, Rennke HG. Glomerular hypertrophy and epithelial cell injury modulate progressive glomerulosclerosis in the rat. *Lab Invest* 1989; 60:205-218.

8. Nath KA, Croatt AJ, Hostetter TH. Oxygen consumption and oxidant stress in surviving nephrons. *Am J Physiol* 1990; 258:F1354-F1362.

9. Brown SA, Finco DR, Crowell WA, Choat DC, Navar LG. Single nephron adaptations to partial renal ablation in the dog. *Am J Physiol 258 (Renal, Fluid, Electrolyte Physiol 27)* 1990:F495-F503.

10. Brown SA, Brown CA. Single-nephron adaptations to partial renal ablation in cats. *Am J Physiol (Regulatory Integrative Comp Physiol 38)* 1995; 269:R1002-R1008.

11. Brown SA, Walton C, Crawford P, Bakris G. Long-term effects of antihypertensive regimens on renal hemodynamics and proteinuria in diabetic dogs. *Kidney Int* 1993; 43:1210-1218.

12. Gaber L, Walton C, Brown S, et al. Effects of antihypertensive agents on the morphologic progression of diabetic nephropathy in dogs. *Kidney Int* 1994; 46:161-169.

13. Barcelli UO, Weiss M, Pollak VE. Effects of dietary prostaglandin precursor on the progression of experimentally induced chronic renal failure. *J Lab Clin Med* 1982; 100:786-797.

14. Scharschmidt LA, Gibbons NB, McGarry L, et al. Effects of dietary fish oil on renal insufficiency in rats with subtotal nephrectomy. *Kidney Int* 1987; 32:700-709.

15. Miller M, Holthofer H, Sinha A, et al. A fish oil diet is protective against accelerated nephrotoxic serum nephritis. *Kidney Int* 1988; 33:322(A).

16. *Nutrient Requirements of Cats.* Washington DC: National Research Council, National Academy Press, 1986.

17. MacDonald ML, Anderson BC, Rogers QR, Buffington CA, Morris JG. Essential fatty acid requirements if cats: Pathology of essential fatty acid deficiency. *Am J Vet Res* 1984; 45:1310-1317.

18. MacDonald ML, Rogers QL, Morris JG, Cupps PT. Effects of linoleate and arachidonate deficiencies on reproduction and spermatogenesis in the cat. *J Nutr* 1984; 114:719-725.

19. Patrono C, Dunn MJ. The clinical significance of inhibition of renal prostaglandin synthesis, *Kidney Int* 1987; 32:1-15.

20. Brown S. Effects of nonsteroidal anti-inflammatory agents on canine renal function. *Current Veterinary Therapy X*, Philadelphia: WB Saunders, 1989:1158-1161.

21. Cowgill LD, Kallet AJ. Recognition and management of hypertension in the dog. In: R. W. Kirk, ed. *Current Veterinary Therapy VIII.* Philadelphia PA: W.B. Saunders, Co. 1983:1025-1028.

22. Morgan RV. Systemic hypertension in four cats: Ocular and medical findings. *Am Anim Hosp Assoc* 1986; 22:615.

23. Ross LA. Hypertensive diseases In: S. Ettinger, ed. *Textbook of Veterinary Internal Medicine.* Philadelphia PA: W.B. Saunders, 1989:2047-2056.

24. Littman MP. Spontaneous systemic hypertension in 24 cats. *J Vet Int Med* 1994; 8:79-86.

25. Bidani A, Mitchell K, Schwartz MM, et al. Absence of glomerular injury or nephron loss in a normotensive rat remnant kidney model. *Kidney Int* 1990; 38:28-38.

26. Brown S, Finco D, Navar L. Impaired renal autoregulatory ability in dogs with reduced renal mass. *J Am Soc Nephr* 1995; 5:1768-1774.

27. Radack K, Huster G. The effects of low doses of n-3 fatty acid supplementation on blood pressure in hypertensive subjects: a randomized controlled trial. *Arch Int Med* 1991; 151:1173-1180.

28. Brown S, Finco D, Barsanti J, Crowell W. Effects of dietary lipids on chronic renal disease in the dog and cat. Morris Animal Foundation 1989-1996.

29. Brown S, Crowell WA, Barsanti JA, White JV, Finco DR. Beneficial effects of dietary mineral restriction in dogs with 15/16 nephrectomy. *J Am Soc Nephr* 1991; 1:1169-1179.

31. Heifets M, Morrissey JJ, Purkerson ML, et al. Effect of dietary lipids on renal function in rats with subtotal nephrectomy. *Kidney Int* 1987; 32:335-341.

32. Barcelli UO, Pollack VE. Is there a role for polyunsaurated fatty acids in the prevention of renal disease and renal failure? *Nephron* 1985; 41:209-2312.

33. Keane WF, Kasiske BL, O'Donnell MP. Hyperlipidemia and the progression of renal disease. *Am J Clin Nutr* 1988; 47:157-160.

30. French SW, Yamanaka W, Ostred R. Dietary induced glomerulosclerosis in the guinea pig. *Arch Path* 1967; 83:204-210.

33. Longhofer SL, Frisbie DD, Johnson HC, Culham CA, Cooley AJ, Schultz KT, Grauer GF. Effects of thromboxane synthetase inhibition on immune complex glomerulonephritis. *Am J Vet Res* 1991; 52:480-487.

34. MacDonald ML, Rogers QR, Morris JG. Effects of dietary arachidonate deficiency on the aggregation of cat platelets. *Comp Biochem Physiol* 1984; 78:123.

Nutrition of the Physically Stressed Dog

Overview of the History of Sled Dogs, the Iditarod Race, and Sled Dog Research in Alaska

Gregory A. Reinhart, PhD
Director of Strategic Research, Research and Development
The Iams Company, Lewisburg, Ohio

Susan M. Bolser
Research and Development, The Iams Company, Lewisburg, Ohio

"Endurance, Fidelity, Intelligence" These words, emblazoned on a statue in New York City's Central Park to honor one of the greatest sled dogs of all time, epitomize the ultimate canine athlete - the sled dog. Certainly these are the preeminent performance dogs whose sport demands power, strength, agility, and stamina. They must be in peak physical condition to withstand the physiological and psychological challenges of prolonged, exhaustive exercise under the most extreme temperatures.

History of Sled Dogs

The bond between these special dogs and man has an ancient, colorful history. Legends abound in the northern and polar regions that detail how the harsh climate and rough terrain forged man and dog together, relying on each other for mutual survival. Ancient rock paintings found in central Siberia are the first evidence that dogs and sleds were used approximately 4,000 years ago.[1] People of the Samoyed, Koryak and Chukchis tribes were nomadic hunters and perfected the use of dog teams for transportation and hauling.

Although scientists and anthropologists can only speculate on when humans first inhabited North America, it is generally accepted that the first men to venture into the continent arrived via the Bering land bridge, a narrow strip of land across the Bering Sea that joined Asia and North America. Early ancestors of the Eskimo people[a] were rugged individuals who ventured across this gateway into the unknown to establish their hold in the cold and barren, yet spectacular lands that would later become Alaska. Eskimo tribes also forged their way to inhabit areas of Greenland. Use of sled dogs was the way of life for the people of these lands.

European explorers first encountered the Eskimos, their dogs, and their unusual mode of transportation during the mid-18th century. Although the idea of using dogs in harness was totally foreign, the concept and obvious success of the

---

[a] It is believed that the term Eskimo is an adaptation of the word "Askimew" from the Montagnais Indian language and literally means "snowshoe netters". In 1977 the term "Inuit" was selected by the Eskimos as the official designation for all Eskimo people. The term encompasses the entirety of their ethnic group which includes various polar and northern tribes. Any references to Eskimo or Inuit are interchangeable.[1]

dogs was fascinating to them. Exploration teams tried using sled teams, with varying degrees of success, to convey their Arctic expeditions.

Early Canine Nutritionist

Sir Leopold McClintock of Great Britain is considered one of the first Europeans to successfully utilize sled dog teams. In 1857, while heading a search party to locate the lost expedition of another Arctic explorer, McClintock kept copious notes about his observations of the dogs and their diet.[1] McClintock recognized the importance of proper nourishment for the dogs and experimented with several types of foods. He observed the variation in the dogs' energy levels when fed beef and suet versus a diet of seal, seabirds, and fish. He watched their eating habits and noted the importance of spreading the food over a large area of snow to ensure that all members of the dog team, even the weakest, received proper amounts of food.

Sled Dogs in Alaska and the World

The lands of future Alaska remained relatively untouched and uninhabited, except by Eskimo tribes and occasional adventurers until gold was discovered in the late 1800's. Fortune seekers from the United States and other parts of the world converged in the frozen Klondike and Canadian territories surrounding the Yukon River. Mining camps and boom towns sprang up overnight to fill the housing, food, and clothing needs of thousands of prospectors as they streamed into the wilderness in search of their fortunes.

The towns of Nome and Iditarod would later become famous for sled dog racing, but each started out as gold mining camps. Located on the banks of the Bering Sea on the southern end of Seward Peninsula, Nome was the site of a major gold strike in 1889. By the year 1900, more than 18,000 gold seekers converged on the small town. Over the next seven years, prospectors had exhausted the gold resources and Nome was returned to its original inhabitants, mostly comprised of Inuit peoples. Soon after that time in 1908, miners founded a camp near the ancient hunting grounds of the Athabascan Indians who called the place "Haiditarod, or "the distant place". Miners convinced the Alaska Roads Commission to forge a trail which would connect the coastal towns of Seward and Knik to the interior mining camps of Alaska, including their town called Iditarod.[2] Mail, supplies, and gold from the mines was transported across the Iditarod Trail via dog sled until the trail was abandoned in the 1950's. Today the once thriving gold camp of Iditarod is now only a ghost town.

Dog teams were the accepted mode of transport for the prospectors and homesteaders during the 19th century. The very lives of these physically untested men and women relied on the strength and stamina of their dogs to provide reliable transportation across the frozen and desolate northern tundra.

While the gold fields of Alaska were still being mined at the beginning of the new century, other adventurers were also recognizing the value of using sled dogs. In 1909 Robert Peary succeeded in reaching the North Pole and two years later, Roald Amundsen conquered the South Pole. Both feats, and the incalculable number of attempts that went before them, drew upon the strength and endurance of sled dog teams to lead these expeditions. Over the next 90 years, dog teams also served research stations in the Antarctic, and guided U.S. Army rescue efforts into the frozen wilderness and battlefields during World Ward II.

There is actually no official breed that defines a "sled dog" since the term collectively encompasses a range of breeds and cross-breeds. But the common trait that distinguishes these magnificent dogs is their desire for and love of running. These dogs run and pull from instinct. Teams have been known to uproot small trees and snap heavy ropes in their eagerness to hit the trail. In fact, one team of ten dogs was reported to have dragged the pickup truck they were tied to prior to a race while the truck was in gear and the parking brake in place.[2]

Sled dogs are trained to pull as a team and to obey commands. They are physically suited to mushing and work as hard as any athlete on earth. The sled dog has a natural coat of thick fur and a bush tail to cover and protect the nose when the animal sleeps. They are comfortable at -20 degrees F and tend to be too hot when the temperature rises above 40 degrees F. They have thick footpads to withstand crusty ice and snow. Their deep chest, narrow waist, and strong legs are perfect for continuous, efficient trotting.

Because of their thick coat, it is important that the dogs do not get too hot. Particularly the darker haired breeds are susceptible to overheating because the coat will absorb radiation from the sun, causing the body temperature to rise. These animals have been selected, through years of specific breeding, to pull sleds in cold temperatures.

Siberian Husky - Considered by many to be the consummate racing dog, these are the fastest of the sled dogs. They are extremely intelligent dogs and endearing human companions. This breed originates from the harsh lands of Siberia where they were bred and raised by the Chukchis people as endurance sled dogs. Research has shown that the Chukchis maintained the purity of their dogs through the 19th century and that these dogs were the sole and direct ancestors of the breed known today as the Siberian Husky.[3] These dogs are small to medium in size. Females generally weigh between 23 and 51 pounds (10-23 kg), while males can range from 45 to 62 pounds (20-28 kg).

Samoyed - Origins of these dogs, that are usually all white in color, are traced to the Samoyed people, a nomadic tribe native to the Russian Arctic. The Samoyed is generally considered the first publicly recognized sled dog. Size ranges from 19 to 24 inches in height (48-60 cm). He is considered a good trotter with a quick and energetic pace.

Alaskan Malamute - The Malamutes acquired their name from their original companions, the nomadic Mahlemut Indians of northwest Alaska. One of the larger sled dog breeds, the Malamute ranges from 23 to 25 inches (58-64 cm) in height and from 72 to 86 pounds (33-39 kg). Because they have a heavy coat, combined with their large size, Malamutes are generally considered more suited to pulling heavy loads rather than to sprint or long distance racing.

Alaskan Husky - The term Alaskan Husky is generally applied to northern-type dogs that were bred by villagers for specific traits. These dogs have become what are considered the best marathon runners in the world. The word Husky, or Huski, is a derivative of an Eskimo term meaning "eater of raw flesh". It is not uncommon to have wolf strains in these dogs that are selected and bred for their speed, power, endurance, and resistance to the harshest climates.

Greenlander - Considered to be the toughest of sled dogs, the Greenlanders were originally companions to the Eskimos that migrated to Greenland. A medium size dog, 21 to 24 inches in height (55-60 cm), they maintain strong hunting instincts and require strong discipline.

Eskimo Dog (Canadian Eskimo Dog) - These dogs are powerfully built and recognized as being more suitable for hauling loads than for speed racing. They are big boned and males often weigh upwards to 100 pounds. Referred to as "Qimmiq" by the Inuit people of Greenland, the breed has been in continuous use for about 2,000 years.[4]

The Ideal Racing Sled Dog - Although kennel clubs may not recognize the pedigrees of sled dogs, mushers are expert at tracing the lineage of their dogs, always in search of the perfect racers. Sled dog racing in the 1970's tended to favor larger dogs, but in recent years the preference has shifted to the small to medium size dog, with no more than 50 pounds generally considered ideal. Other important characteristics include tough feet, a good attitude, a good appetite, not prone to nervousness or stress, good body conformation with a heavy chest and shoulders, muscular haunches, and of course, speed and endurance.

Sled Dog Racing   It is likely that as soon as there were sled dog teams, there were also sled dog races. Whether Eskimo, miner, or trapper, mushers were sure to claim bragging rights that their dogs were the fastest and smartest.

The first recorded sled dog race started in Nome, Alaska as an offshoot of dog races organized by the town's children looking for winter recreation. The boys and girls challenged each other to a weekly event, racing their dogs over a seven mile course. After observing these races, prominent Nome citizen Albert Fink proposed the idea of holding a longer distance race for adults to challenge the true strength and endurance of their dogs. From his enthusiasm, the Nome Kennel Club was formed and the All Alaska Sweepstakes was conceived.[1]

The first organized race was held on a 408 mile course in April 1908. The All Alaska Sweepstakes was run annually until 1917 (it was resumed some years later) and winners included some of the greatest mushers of all time. Legendary musher Leonhard Seppala won the Sweepstakes in 1915, 1916, and 1917. A Norwegian who is credited with introducing the Siberian husky to Alaska, Seppala[5] is also famous for his role in inspiring what would later become known as The Last Great Race on Earth: The Iditarod.

Today's sled dog races are classified as either sprints, mid-distance, or long distance. In a sprint race the dogs will run 15 to 20 mph for distances of 3 to 30 miles. The pace of the long distance race is slower, between 7 and 12 mph, but the distances covered range anywhere from 300 to 1,500 miles. Mid-distances races are run continuously between 100 to 300 miles. Sprint race courses are normally set in and around villages or towns, whereas the mid- and long-distance races are situated on courses that lead the team through wilderness terrain.[5]

The sport is becoming increasingly popular in many parts of the world,[6] including Europe, Alaska, and several of the lower 48 states. Some of the more well-known races include the Copper Basin 300, Yukon Quest, Kusko 300, and Beargrease. More than a hundred organized sled dog races are now run each year in Alaska alone. The Alpirod has been the biggest sled dog race in Europe, although its future at this time is in question. The Alpirod is run through France, Switzerland, Austria, and Italy on a 757 kilometer course.

Probably the most famous sled dog race is the Iditarod, also referred to as "The Last Great Race on Earth". Beginning in Anchorage and ending in Nome this race celebrates the art of dog sled racing and the unique bond between dog and musher, relying on each other to survive against nature. The Iditarod race was actually started to commemorate and preserve Alaskan heritage, but its route and more recognized purpose is to honor a race to save human lives.
Origins of The Iditarod Race

In late January 1925, an outbreak of diphtheria threatened to take the lives of 1,700 people in Nome, most of them Eskimos who were highly susceptible to the deadly disease. But the serum necessary to halt an epidemic was a thousand miles away in Anchorage. Severe weather prohibited transport of the serum by plane. Sled dog teams were the only way the people of Nome could be saved.

A relay of dog teams was set up starting in Nenana, where the serum arrived by train from Anchorage. The first musher in the 20-man relay was seasoned dog puncher Wild Bill Shannon who headed out of Nenana at 10:00 pm on January 27, 1925 to temperatures recorded at -50 degrees F.[5] About that same time, Leonhard Seppala, answering a personal plea by the Governor of Alaska, drove a team east out of Nome to meet the relay team halfway.

Seppala dropped several dogs at a way station in Bluff, including lead dog Balto, so the dogs could rest and prepare to rejoin the final team on the return trip back to Nome. Seppala's most trusted dog, Togo, continued with him and the remaining team, traveling eastward through blizzard conditions to meet the serum relay team that was moving westward.

Seppala picked up the serum from a relay musher crossing the frozen Norton Sound near the town of Unalakleet. Seppala then passed the cargo on and musher Gunnar Kaasen made the final drive from Bluff to Nome. On February 2 at 5:30 am Kaasen and the team, led by Balto (who would years later be memorialized in the statue that stands in New York City's Central Park) arrived in Nome in time to rescue the town's men, women, and children from certain death. The 20 mushers and their teams who transported the life-saving serum in just 5 days, 7 hours over 674 miles would later be honored annually by the running of the Iditarod race.

The Iditarod Today

Although the story of the Nome "race for life" is inspiring and justly represents the spirit of the Iditarod, this great race actually was conceived by veteran mushers who were concerned with the decline of mushing skills and the erosion of the sled dog breeds. The advent of planes, snowmobiles, and ATVs were replacing the traditional use of dog teams, not only in rural Alaska, but in all arctic regions of the world.[7,8]

Led by veteran musher, Joe Redington Sr., and Alaska historian, Dorothy Page, concerned Alaskans set about organizing the Iditarod race in order to rekindle interest in dog mushing and call attention to the heroes, legends and spirit of Alaska's past. In 1967, 100 miles of the Iditarod Trail was reopened and the first race was held. Over the next few years race organizers extended the race along the wilderness trail to the long-abandoned gold rush town of Iditarod, nearly 600 miles from Anchorage. Shortly after that, the U.S. Army cleared much of the historic trail as a winter exercise, opening the door to the 1,049 mile Iditarod race to Nome that was first run in 1973.

Although the official distance of the Iditarod is 1,049 miles, this measurement is symbolic rather than actual. The chosen race length is: 1,000 miles (because it is at least that long) plus 49 miles (because Alaska is the 49th state admitted to the U.S.). The actual race distances are 1,158 miles by the northern route and 1,163 miles by the southern route.[5] The northerly route is run during even-numbered years, the southerly route during odd-numbered years.

The Iditarod Race course is extremely challenging, not only in its distance, but also in its terrain. Weather can be severe during its March run and the course traverses mountains, frozen lakes, rivers, scrub ground, and of course, snow. Weather conditions often cover up trail markers, leaving dog and musher to forge their way, often relying on the lead dog's instincts alone.

IDITAROD CHECKPOINTS AND DISTANCES (Northern Route)		
	Interval (miles)	Total Miles
Anchorage to Eagle River	20	20
Eagle River to Wasilla	29	49
Wasilla to Knik	14	62
Knik to Rabbit Lake	52	114
Rabbit Lake to Skwentna	34	148
Skwentna to Finger Lake	45	193
Finger Lake to Rainy Pass	30	223
Rainy Pass to Rohn	48	271
Rohn to Nikolai	93	364
Nikolai to McGrath	48	412
McGrath to Takotna	23	435
Takotna to Ophir	38	473
Ophir to Cripple	60	533
Cripple to Sulatna Crossing	45	578
Sulatna Crossing to Ruby	75	653
Ruby to Galena	52	705
Galena to Nulato	52	757
Nulato to Kaltag	42	799
Kaltag to Unalakleet	90	889
Unalakleet to Shaktoolik	40	929
Shaktoolik to Koyuk	58	987
Koyuk to Elim	48	1,035
Elim to Golovin	28	1,063
Golovin to White Mountain	18	1,081
White Mountain to Safety	55	1,136
Safety to Nome	22	1,158

Adapted from 7 and 9.

Iditarod Mission Statement: "To promote, sponsor and sustain the world premier sled dog race along the Iditarod Trail, which incorporates traditional wilderness mushing skills, mandates the humane treatment of dogs, reflects the human wonder and challenge of Alaska's wilderness, contributes to the historic, social, economic and cultural fabric of Alaska, and preserves the historic contribution and contemporary practice of dog mushing."[7]

The Iditarod and Sled Dog Research

Because of the unique nature of sled dogs, the musher is continually challenged to meet their special nutritional needs. Proper nutrition must prepare them for a harsh, unforgiving environment, and can be the key to sustained exertional output.

The Iditarod is the ultimate nutritional test for the canine. These dogs average over 100 miles per day with energy expenditures in excess of 11,000 calories.[10] A situation that may not surface as a problem in a "normal" companion animal will manifest itself as a glaring deficiency in this high performance animal.

Scientists have found the sled dog to be a unique model for studying the nutritional requirements of companion animals. The researchers interested in this field of study, however, are faced with unusual challenges of their own.

Many of the research studies conducted in Alaska during the past 4 to 5 years have relied on the use of motor homes to serve as mobile research units for the research teams. A standard motor home, equipped with sleeping and dining facilities for 6 to 8 adults, is normally used. In addition to the 4 to 8 research team members, test equipment, supplies, and provisions must be transported in the mobile unit. In order to properly equip the team, hundreds of pounds of instruments, supplies, and equipment must be air freighted into Alaska. Sensitive test instruments require special packing and handling. Sometimes it is necessary to locate certain items locally, such as gas canisters which may not be taken onto airplanes, although this type of equipment is often difficult to find and secure.

After the research team has outfitted the motor home, they will head out to meet the musher and dogs at remote locations. It is important to note that although the motor homes are equipped as best as possible, they are still best suited to their original design — leisure vehicles for traveling and camping in warm weather conditions. Even sport utility vehicles and trucks find the roads in Alaska extremely difficult to traverse since the frigid temperatures, snow, and ice make it hard to properly maintain. Mountain ranges must often be traversed under less than ideal conditions. Moose are also a threat to the mobile research team when traveling the remote highways in Alaska. Most encounters between a moose, which can weigh up to 1,500 pounds, and a motor vehicle result in serious human injury.

Once reaching the designated checkpoints, the researchers will wait for the musher to arrive, which can mean round the clock vigils for 24 to 36 hours. When the dog team arrives, blood and urine samples must be taken quickly so the musher can rest the dogs as soon as possible. When temperatures fall below -25 degrees F, which is not unusual, blood may freeze in the needles as samples are drawn. Hemolysis can also occur due to improper collection and storage of serum and plasma. Sampling is further hindered by reduced mobility of the fingers because gloves must be worn at all times to prevent frostbite.

High winds and sub-zero temperatures will often cause mechanical failures in the motor home's heating and electrical systems, as well as malfunctions in electric generators and electronic scales. Not only does this pose hazardous and uncomfortable conditions for the research team, but sample preparation is at increased risk since plasma and whole blood can freeze even while housed inside the motor home. Reduced daylight hours during the winter months further hinder efficiency and progress of the research study.

Even as the musher and dogs are challenged, researchers must continually find ways to meet the demands of each new research study. The scientist who is familiar with working in a controlled laboratory setting must set aside all regular procedures because they simply will not work in the Alaskan research environment. Even the most experienced scientist cannot fully anticipate, either personally or professionally, the situations that will be faced or imagine the innovative means that must be found to meet the challenge. In desolate surroundings, the researcher must stretch the imagination, relying on the creativity and resourcefulness of the team, as well as the generosity and spirit of the Alaskan people to complete the task at hand.

In spite of the difficulties and risks associated with conducting these studies, researchers dedicated to studying sled dog nutrition also experience rich rewards, including the breathtaking beauty of the Alaskan landscape. But most valuable is the opportunity to interact with the indomitable personalities of the mushers, their dogs, and the Alaskan people.

In addition to the nutritional advances pioneered in the sled dog research field, the advancement of humane practices and use of dogs has been greatly advanced in recent years because of organized sled dog races. Race officials go to great lengths to ensure that the highest safety standards are embraced by all participants. A dedicated team of veterinarians are on hand for the duration of the race and have tremendous authority to make decisions that will ensure dog safety. Race veterinarians can mandate a rest period or order that a dog be dropped from the race for health reasons.

Benefits of Sled Dog Research

Copper Basin 300 officials allowed scientific studies to be conducted during the 1993 and 1994 races. These studies resulted in data that have determined dietary caloric intake and energy expenditure, water turnover rates, as well as hematological and biochemical profile changes that occur during an actual event.[10] During the 1995 Iditarod, research studies were undertaken to collect data on sled dog cardiology and further define biochemical profile changes that occur over this long distance event.

Both the races and training exercises have become proving grounds for research teams who strive to develop diets that provide optimum nutrition for the performance dog. The new nutritional truths which have been tested and proven with the racing sled dog in some of the harshest physical conditions will benefit the performance of all racing and sporting dogs, as well as the nutritional well-being of all companion animals.

The Iams Company acknowledges and greatly appreciates musher Rick Swenson for his cooperative research efforts. His unselfish dedication to the health and betterment of sled dogs has directly benefited not only performance dogs, but all companion animals as well.

Acknowledgment

MILESTONES IN IDITAROD HISTORY

1967	First short race (100 miles) along the Iditarod Trail is held
1973	Dick Wilmarth wins the first 1,049 mile Iditarod race in 20 days, 49 minutes, 41 seconds. 34 teams are entered in the race.
1977	Rick Swenson wins his first title. The northern route is created to be run in even-numbered years.
1978	Dick Mackey beats Rick Swenson in a controversial one-second lead finish, the closest in Iditarod history.
1985	Libby Riddles becomes the first woman Iditarod champion.
1990	Susan Butcher wins her fourth Iditarod.
1991	Rick Swenson becomes the only 5-time Iditarod champion.
1992	The largest number of teams in race history enters the Iditarod.
1995	Doug Swingley wins the Iditarod in record time of 9 days, 2 hours, and 42 seconds. 48 teams are entered in the race.

Adapted from 7 and 9

References

1. Cellura D. *Travelers of the Cold: Sled Dogs of the Far North*. Anchorage AK: Alaska Northwest Books; 1990.

2. Riddles L, Jones T. *Race Across Alaska*. Harrisburg PA: Stackpole Books; 1988.

3. American Kennel Club. *Complete Dog Book, 17th Ed*. New York: Macmillan Publishing Co. 1985:341-345.

4. Slater K. Finding a home for the huskies. *Mushing* Jan/Feb 1995:23.

5. Heacox K. *Iditarod Sprit*; Portland OR: Graphic Arts Center Publishing Company; 1991.

6. Siino B. A mutual trust. *Dog Fancy* Jan 1994:30.

7. *Iditarod Official 1992 Race Program and Trail Guide*. Wasilla AK: Iditarod Runner. 1992:4

8. Cowan N, Wolf M. The Iditarod: setting a new course. *Mushing* Jan/Feb 1995:19.

9. For the record. *Mushing* May/June 1995; 31.

10. Hinchcliff K. Energy expenditure and water turnover in Alaskan sled dogs during running. *Recent Advances in Canine and Feline Nutritional Research: Proceedings of the 1996 Iams International Nutrition Symposium*. Wilmington OH: Orange Frazer Press. 1996.

The Effect of Diet on Sled Dog Performance, Oxidative Capacity, Skeletal Muscle Microstructure, and Muscle Glycogen Metabolism

Arleigh J. Reynolds, DVM, PhD
Assistant Professor, Clinical Nutrition
Department and Section of Clinical Sciences
New York State College of Veterinary Medicine
Cornell University, Ithaca, New York

C. Richard Taylor, PhD, MD(Hon.)[a]; Hans Hoppeler, MD[b]; Ewald Wiebel, MD, DSc[b];
Peter Weyand, PhD[a]; Thomas Roberts, PhD[a]; Gregory Reinhart, PhD[c]
[a]CFS, Harvard University, Bedford, Massachusetts
[b]Department of Anatomy, University of Bern, Bern, Switzerland
[c]Research and Development, The Iams Company, Lewisburg, Ohio

Since the dawn of athletic competition, athletes and their trainers have sought means of optimizing their performance through nutritional modifications. The writings of Pythagoras and Plato suggest that the diet of the ancient Olympic athlete was significantly higher in protein, and significantly more expensive than that of the general populace.

The Role of Protein for the Athlete

In the late nineteenth century, a researcher named Lebig claimed that protein was the most important fuel for muscular work. He theorized that carbohydrate and fat were not available for energy generation in the muscle but were instead burned in the lungs to prevent "oxygen poisoning." Near the turn of the century, Lebig's views were disputed by Fick and Wislicenus.

These scientists observed that the increase in urea excretion measured from men participating in a climbing expedition could support less than half of the energy required to perform the task. They concluded that fuels other than protein must be available for energy generation within skeletal muscle.

Still there is mounting evidence that exercise does increase an athlete's protein requirement. This increased need for protein is a reflection of both an increased rate of protein synthesis and an increased rate of protein catabolism. Athletes in training experience an increase in plasma volume and red blood cell mass.
Capillary density, mitochondrial volume, and muscle fiber volume also increase with training, as does the mass and activity of nearly all enzymes which

Protein Requirements for the Canine Athlete

catalyze energy generating reactions. The increase in protein catabolism associated with exercise is due to a small but significant increase in the oxidation of amino acids for energy. During prolonged bouts of steady state exercise, amino acid oxidation comprises between 5 and 15% of the energy generated. Amino acid oxidation proceeds at a greater rate as glycogen stores diminish and gluconeogenesis becomes the predominant pathway for the maintenance of blood glucose.

In a recent study we compared the metabolic responses to training in dogs fed diets deriving 16, 24, 32, and 40% of their calories from protein. We found that dogs fed 40% of their calories as protein maintained a larger plasma volume and red blood cell mass during strenuous training than dogs fed diets containing less than 40% of their calories as protein (*Figure 1*).

Plasma Volume

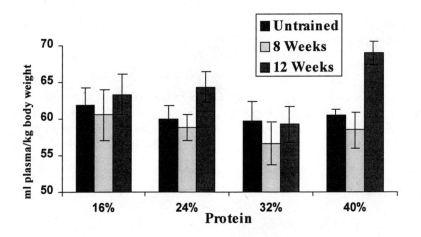

Figure 1. Dogs fed 40% of calories as protein had greater plasma volume than other groups.

None of the dogs eating only 16% of their calories as protein made it through the training and racing season without at least one injury serious enough to remove them from training for at least one week. There were two such injuries in the group fed 24% of their calories as protein, and no injuries were observed in the groups eating 32 and 40% of their calories as protein (*Figure 2*). Insuring adequate protein intake thus enhances blood volume and may help prevent injury during training.

While protein requirements increase with training, the intake of non protein calories must also increase. An important nutritional goal for the athlete is to supply adequate calories in fat and carbohydrate so that the protein fed is used mostly for tissue protein synthesis and not for energy. Today we know that protein is actually one of the least desirable muscle fuels. Protein cannot be stored like fat or carbohydrate, and all protein in the body has a function. These functions can be impaired if body stores of protein are drained in support of muscular work.

Injuries Decreased
as Protein Calories Increased

Injuries/Group	*Protein in Diet*
• No injuries	32% and 40%
• 2 injuries	24%
• At least one injury in every dog.	16%

Figure 2.

Muscle Specific Energy Sources: Fat vs. Carbohydrate

Just how the energy requirement should be partitioned between carbohydrate and fat has been a point of considerable debate for the past 25-30 years. In the late 1960's Bergstrom and his colleagues demonstrated that high carbohydrate diets in conjunction with endurance training led to a two-fold increase in the muscle glycogen concentration of human athletes. They also showed that at exercise intensities similar to those encountered during a marathon race, endurance was highly correlated with pre-exercise muscle glycogen concentration. In other words, by eating a high carbohydrate diet during training, human athletes could store more carbohydrate (glycogen) in their muscle and run for a longer period of time at a marathon race pace. This concept known as "carbohydrate loading" has become a popular and successful strategy for human distance runners.

In the early 1970's, Kronfeld observed that a dog team on a high carbohydrate diet exhibited poor endurance and a stiff gait while racing. When he switched these dogs to a high protein, high fat diet their gait and performance improved. He suggested that carbohydrate loading in dogs may lead to an increase in lactic acid production during exercise and thus the stiff gait observed by the musher.

Unfortunately, Kronfeld never got the opportunity to test this hypothesis. (It is difficult to convince a musher to let you recreate a disease in his dogs just to find the cause when whatever you have done seems to have solved the problem!) In further work he showed that working dogs have no absolute carbohydrate requirement, although they seem to be slightly less prone to diarrhea when their diet contains at least a small amount of this nutrient. His studies on sled dogs led him to the conclusion that fat is the preferred fuel for endurance in the racing sled dog.

Why, one might ask, does human endurance depend on carbohydrate metabolism, while canine endurance relies on fat metabolism? The answer is complex and involves species differences in locomotion, cardiovascular physiology, and energy metabolism. We decided to look at the metabolism side of the question first.

We began by looking at the influences of diet and training on fat and carbohydrate metabolism in a group of sixteen Alaskan Huskies. We fed half of the dogs a high fat diet (15% carbohydrate, 25% protein, 60% fat on an energy basis) and half of them a high carbohydrate diet (60% carbohydrate, 25% protein, 15% fat on an energy basis) during a six month experimental trial. The dogs were fed to maintain body weight and given one month to acclimate to the diets.

After diet acclimatization, they performed a standard "aerobic" and a standard "anaerobic test" on a high speed variable slope treadmill. The aerobic test was designed to mimic the type of work dogs on the Iditarod Trail or Yukon Quest might perform. It consisted of a one hour run at 9 mph on a flat treadmill. The anaerobic test was intended to simulate the type of exercise a dog might experience while running up Cordova hill during the last few minutes of the Fur Rendezvous. It consisted of running 15 mph on a 10 degree slope for three minutes.

After this initial testing in the untrained state, the dogs entered a two month aerobic training program where they built up to running 15 mph for 7 to 10 miles at a time on four occasions per week. This level of training was continued for one month and then the dogs repeated the standard aerobic test. Next, they entered an anaerobic training period where they ran intervals on a sloped treadmill three days a week. After one month on this program the dogs repeated the standard anaerobic test. Blood and muscle samples were collected before and after each of the training periods.

During the first aerobic test, (*Figure 3*) neither dietary group relied very heavily on muscle glycogen as a muscle fuel. This was demonstrated by only a small decrease in the concentration of this carbohydrate store between pre and post exercise measurements. One would expect that a low intensity bout of exercise might rely more heavily on fat metabolism for energy generation. This expectation was supported by the elevated levels of free fatty acids (FFA) (*Figure 4*) measured in the post exercise blood samples of both diet groups (FFA are the principal product of fat metabolism used for energy by muscle). The size of the increase in FFA concentration was, however, quite different between diets. The dogs on the high fat diet were able to achieve significantly higher circulating levels of FFA during the aerobic test than those on the high carbohydrate diet.

One of the major determinants of the rate of FFA utilization in working muscle is the concentration of FFA in the blood stream. By giving rise to elevated plasma levels of FFA, the high fat diet promoted FFA utilization during exercise. Before the dogs were ever trained, their diet had a significant influence on how they responded to exercise.

AEROBIC TESTS
Muscle Glycogen Concentrations
(Mean ± SE) in mmoles Glucose/kg Muscle Wet Weight

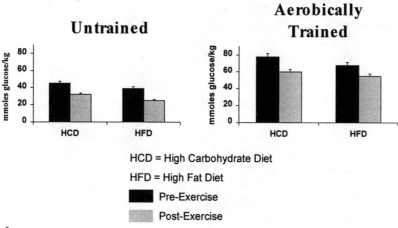

Figure 3.

AEROBIC TESTS
Serum Free Fatty Acid (FFA) Concentrations
(Mean ± SE) in mmoles/l

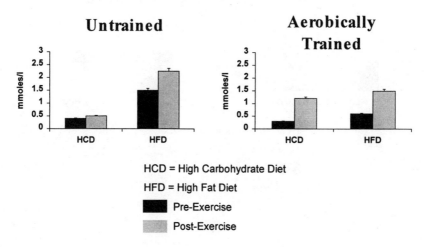

Figure 4.

Many people who work dogs feed them as well as they can during the training and racing seasons and then switch to less expensive diets during the off season. A better strategy might be to begin the dogs on a high fat ration one month before the onset of a training program, or better yet, feed them a high quality ration year round. This program would "prime their metabolic pump" so they should be better prepared to provide fuel for their muscles when conditioning resumes. One word of caution: those not accustomed to feeding sedentary dogs high fat diets need to closely monitor weight and food intake to avoid weight gain.

The superiority of the high fat diet was still evident after two months of aerobic training. The high fat fed dogs had greater pre and post exercise FFA levels than their high carbohydrate fed counterparts. The high fat diet was also associated with a significantly higher post exercise triglyceride concentration after training.

Although triglycerides are not a significant source of fuel during exercise, they are the most important source of FFA for replenishment of intramuscular triglycerides during recovery (*Figure 5*). Other studies in the rat, the dog, and man have shown that intramuscular triglycerides are a very important source of FFA during the first 1-2 hours of exercise. Thus, by changing the caloric distribution in favor of feeding fats, the most important fuel for exercise and the most important substrate for replacement of intramuscular lipid were both made more available.

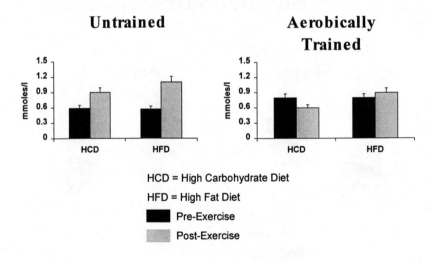

Figure 5.

The limited availability of carbohydrate fuels imposes one of the limits of exercise duration at relatively high (<70% VO_2 max) exercise intensities. An average fit working dog has approximately 50 times more potential energy available in its fat depots than in its stores of muscle glycogen. It is therefore not surprising that one of the main adaptations accompanying training is an increased reliance on fat metabolism at nearly all submaximal (below VO_2 max) exercise intensities. This increase in fat utilization spares some glycogen and thus prolongs the onset of glycogen depletion.

Effects of Diet on VO$_2$ Max, Mitochondrial Volume, and Maximal Rate of Fat Oxidation

This increased reliance on fat for fuel is demonstrated by a decreased respiratory quotient (RQ) for given absolute submaximal exercise intensity (i.e., speed and incline). The respiratory quotient is the number of moles of CO_2 produced divided by the number of moles of oxygen consumed during a bout of steady state exercise. When carbohydrates are burned the amount of CO_2 produced is nearly equal to the amount of O_2 consumed resulting in a respiratory quotient of 1.0. Fat oxidation produces relatively less CO_2 and consumes relatively more O_2 resulting in an RQ less than 1.0 and as low as 0.7. Thus by measuring the RQ, an investigator can determine the relative amounts of carbohydrates and fats burned during a bout of exercise.

Several of the mechanisms by which training increases fat utilization during exercise have been defined. Several workers have measured training associated increases in the activities of the rate determining enzymes of the fat oxidation pathways. Training is also associated with an increase in VO_2 max. An athlete should thus be working at a lower percentage of VO_2 max to travel a given speed when fit than when unfit. Generally speaking the lower the percentage of VO_2 max, the higher the contribution of fat metabolism to total energy expenditure.

While these adaptations explain the potential for enhanced fat oxidation, they do not explain where the increased amount of fat fuels are coming from. Studies using radiolabelled Palmitate (a common long chain fatty acid) have shown that it takes 30-45 minutes after the onset of exercise before plasma free fatty acids reach a maximal rate of oxidation. Even after 45 minutes FFA originating from peripheral sources appears to contribute only 20-30% of the total amount of FFA oxidized. Work in our laboratory has shown that fit dogs reach an RQ of 0.7 within 6 minutes of the onset of low intensity exercise. Since the release of FFA into the bloodstream and their subsequent uptake by muscle cannot respond rapidly enough to support such a low RQ only 6 minutes after the onset of exercise, we concluded that intramuscular sources must provide most of the FFA oxidized during the initial period of an exercise bout. There is substantial evidence to suggest that intracellular fat may actually be the predominant source of FFA throughout events lasting several hours. Work in humans has suggested that intramuscular triglycerides provide most of the FFA oxidized in endurance events as long as 100 kilometers.

Studies by Martin et al have suggested that training may increase intracellular lipid stores in human athletes. Simi et al has shown that rats fed a high fat diet experienced greater increases in regulatory enzyme activity, VO_2 max, and glycogen sparing during exercise than those fed a high carbohydrate diet after the same amount of training. These authors concluded that feeding a high fat diet had an additive effect with training in bringing about to a greater degree the adaptations normally associated with training alone. Abumrad et al has also shown that trained rats fed a high fat diet have greater stores of intramuscular triglycerides than those fed a high carbohydrate diet.

Our earlier work suggested that just as has been demonstrated in rats by Simi et al, feeding high fat diets to sled dogs slowed the rate of glycogen consumption during exercise. We thus became interested in studying whether these diets may affect parameters such as VO_2 max and intramuscular fat stores in our dogs as had been earlier shown in the rats. At the same time, C.R. Taylor and his colleagues were studying the effect of diet on VO_2 max and the maximal rate of fat oxidation in Labrador Retrievers.

Dr. Taylor had trained his Labradors for 3 months while they were fed a high carbohydrate (65% of energy), low fat (25% of energy) diet. He measured oxygen uptake and carbon dioxide production during exercise at 35, 65, 85, and 100% of VO_2 max. From these values he calculated an RQ and from that the rate of fat oxidation at each exercise intensity. Muscle biopsies were also taken from the dogs and evaluated by Hans Hoppeler at the Medical College in Bern, Switzerland. The dogs then continued the same training regimen as before but were switched over to a high fat (65% of energy) low carbohydrate (25% of energy) diet. After 12 weeks on the high fat diet the measurements described above were repeated. Switching the dogs over to the high fat diet (*Figures 6 and 7*) resulted in a nearly 50% increase in both VO_2 max and the maximal rate of fat oxidation! Since training is normally associated with only a 15-20% increase in these parameters, these findings were quite unexpected. To ensure that these were not spurious results the dogs were then placed back on the low fat diet for 12 weeks and retested. Their VO_2 max and maximal fat oxidation rate measurements fell to the values observed during the previous low fat feeding trial (*Figures 6 and 7*).

Analysis of the muscle biopsies yielded information which may in part explain these unexpected results. When sectioned serially and evaluated in three dimensions the percentage of the total volume of each muscle fiber taken up by mitochondria was 35% greater when the dogs were fed the high fat diet than when they were fed the low fat diet (*Figure 8*). It was also observed that each mitochondria appeared as series of membranes wrapped around a lipid droplet core. This lipid droplet was in direct contact with the outer mitochondrial membrane which may explain how intracellular lipids become available so rapidly after the onset of exercise. These workers found that the size of the lipid droplet within each mitochondria does not increase when a high fat diet is fed. However, since the high fat diet supports a 35% increase in mitochondrial volume, it also supports a 35% increase in intracellular lipid stores. Thus feeding a high fat diet to dogs in training increases both the amount of lipid fuel and the number of "furnaces" available to burn that fuel. Since one of the limits on VO_2 max is the rate of substrate utilization, an increase in mitochondrial volume could support an increase in VO_2 max and maximal fat oxidation rate as observed when the high fat diet was fed.

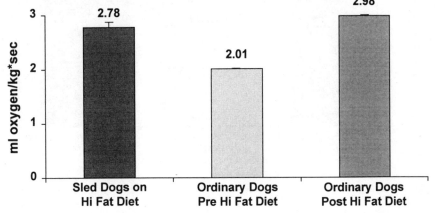

Comparison of VO_2 Max Between Sled Dogs, Ordinary Dogs on Low Fat Diet, and Ordinary Dogs on Hi Fat Diet

Figure 6.

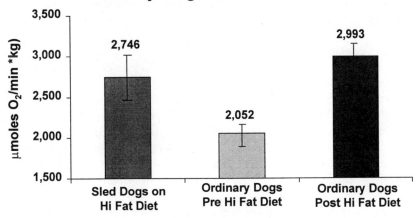

Comparison of Maximal Fat Oxidation in Sled Dogs, Ordinary Dogs on Low Fat Diet, and Ordinary Dogs on Hi Fat Diet

Figure 7.

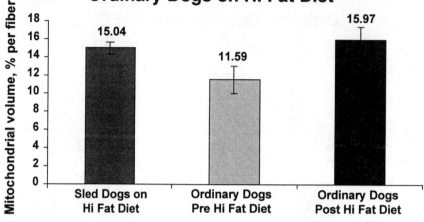

Figure 8.

We have repeated these studies and found identical results with our sled dogs (*Figures 6, 7, 8*). The values for VO$_2$ max and maximal fat oxidation rate in our sled dogs fed the same high fat diet and after six months of training were indistinguishable from those observed in the Labradors studied by Taylor et al. We have also observed the identical drop in value of these parameters after 12 weeks of training on the low fat diet. The conformation, foot structure, hair coat, and innate drive of the sled dog makes it far better suited to its task than a Labrador Retriever. Still these studies suggest the physiological limits of endurance in both breeds may be more influenced by diet and training than by selective breeding.

These studies have yielded insight into some of the mechanisms by which feeding a high fat diet promotes endurance performance in canine athletes. By increasing the availability of lipid fuel and its site of combustion, feeding a high fat diet to trained dogs enhances their VO$_2$ max and the maximum rate at which fat can be burned. These adaptations allow lipid fuels to support a higher proportion of any submaximal exercise intensity and thus spare more limited glycogen stores. Fat-adapted canine athletes can thus run faster and longer than their non-fat adapted comrades. As with any experiment, the results of these studies lead to further questions. The duration of exercise sustainable by intracellular lipid stores has yet to be determined. The timetable for repleting these stores once depleted is also unknown. The molecular mechanisms responsible for enhancing mitochondrial volume can only be speculated upon now. Answers to these questions along with what we have already gleaned may aide us in helping these magnificent athletes better prepare for and recover from the tasks they perform.

The two most important fuels for muscular work are lipids and carbohydrates. Amino acids play a very minor role in the normal, healthy individual. At rest most of the energy generated by myocytes comes from the complete oxidation of free fatty acids. Fat oxidation predominates up until somewhere between 40 and 60% of maximal oxygen uptake (VO_2 max). As the exercise intensity increases above 40% of VO_2 max, carbohydrate metabolism is responsible for an increasingly larger proportion of the energy generated.

What then is the role of muscle glycogen (MG) in exercising dogs? Both the high carbohydrate and high fat fed sled dog groups stored nearly twice as much MG after aerobic training, yet they used very little of this fuel in both aerobic tests (before and after training) (*Figure 3*). These results further support the theory that fat, not carbohydrate, is the most important fuel for low intensity exercise.

Exercise physiologists have shown that even in very low intensity bouts of exercise (such as our aerobic test) small amounts of MG are consumed to permit the continuation of FFA metabolism. The increase in MG storage seen after aerobic training may thus be an adaptation which prolongs the period of exercise sustainable via FFA metabolism.

Unlike the aerobic tests, exercise in the anaerobic tests depended heavily on carbohydrate metabolism. During the first anaerobic test the rate of MG utilization was almost 20 times that observed in both of the aerobic tests. After anaerobic training, both diet groups showed pre-exercise MG levels similar to those measured in carbohydrate loaded human marathoners (*Figure 9*). The high carbohydrate group stored an additional 30% more MG than the high fat group after anaerobic training. Although the high carbohydrate fed dogs stored more MG after interval type training, they also used more to complete the test. If you consider the anaerobic test as a hill or a sprint during a race, the high carbohydrate fed dogs (*Figure 10*) could only perform two such bouts of exercise before they would deplete their MG stores and be unable to fuel high intensity exercise. The high fat fed dogs would be able to perform three or four such bursts before depleting their glycogen stores.

In other words, by feeding a high fat diet while training, you are training your dog's muscles to burn fat more efficiently and to spare the use of carbohydrate. Even the average lean sprint dog has between 10 and 50 times more energy stored in fat reserves than in MG. Strategically it seems better to spare the more limited stores of carbohydrate in favor of the more plentiful deposits of fat whenever possible.

Although glycogen sparing may be a more sound strategy for endurance than glycogen supercompensation in canine endurance athletes, glycogen depletion is still associated with a deterioration in performance.

ANAEROBIC TESTS
Muscle Glycogen Concentrations
(Mean ± SE) in mmoles Glucose/kg Muscle Wet Weight

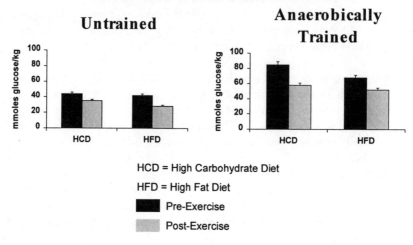

HCD = High Carbohydrate Diet

HFD = High Fat Diet

◼ Pre-Exercise

▨ Post-Exercise

Figure 9.

Muscle Glycogen Concentration vs
Δ Muscle Glycogen Concentration in High
Carbohydrate Fed Dogs
During Both Anaerobic Tests

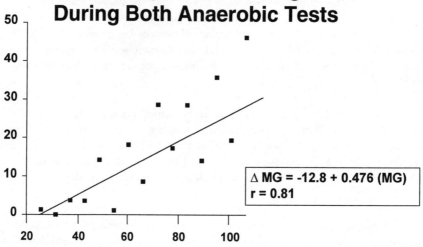

Δ MG = -12.8 + 0.476 (MG)
r = 0.81

Figure 10.

Sled dogs participating in long distance races typically run 4-6 hours, are given a high fat, high protein snack during a 2-4 hour rest period, and then run 4-6 hours again before eating a full meal. This type of running may promote glycogen depletion and since these dogs eat diets which are generally low in carbohydrates (15% of kcal or less during races) it is questionable whether these dogs can replenish glycogen stores between bouts of exercise. We examined the effect of post-exercise carbohydrate supplementation on muscle glycogen repletion in an Iditarod winning sled dog team (*Figure 11*).

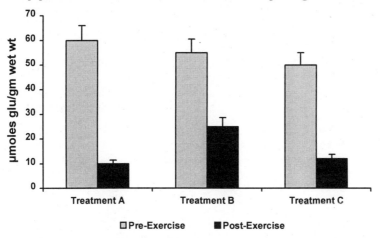

Effect of Post Exercise Carbohydrate Supplementation on Muscle Glycogen Levels

Figure 11. *Treatment* A: Post exercise muscle glycogen levels measured immediately after exercise cessation. *Treatment* B: Supplemented with 1.5 grams glucose/kg body weight immediately post exercise; muscle biopsies obtained 4 hours post exercise. *Treatment* C: No supplementation post exercise; muscle biopsies obtained 4 hours post exercise.

Sled dogs supplemented with 1.5 g/kg of glucose polymers immediately after exercise showed significantly greater muscle glycogen repletion during the first four hours of recovery than non supplemented dogs. Carbohydrate supplementation was also associated with an increase in plasma glucose concentration (*Figure 12*) 100 minutes post-exercise, which may have promoted glycogen storage in these animals. Analysis of PAS staining intensity indicated that post exercise glycogen storage was greater in type II than in type I fibers (*Figure 13*). Since most sled dog races occur over several consecutive days, enhancing the rate of glycogen repletion may increase performance in these animals.

The next question would be how can anaerobic exercise be supported by FFA metabolism when FFA metabolism requires the presence of oxygen? Even in exercise like our anaerobic test where lactic acid levels in the blood stream increased 2-3 times above resting values, more than 50% of the energy generated to support that exercise probably came from aerobic means. The high fat fed dogs were able to supply more of that aerobic energy through FFA metabolism than the high carbohydrate fed dogs.

Effect of Post Exercise Carbohydrate Supplementation on Blood Glucose Levels

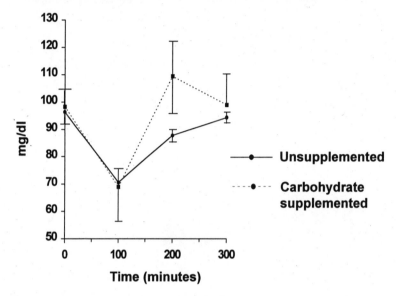

Figure 12.

Effect of Muscle Fiber Type on Relative Glycogen Storage

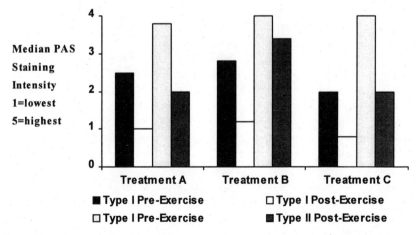

Figure 13.

Interestingly, although the high fat fed dogs received only 15% of their calories as carbohydrates, they were able to more than double their pre exercise MG concentrations as a result of the aerobic and anaerobic training programs. Apparently training is much more important of a stimulus for MG storage than is diet. It was also interesting that the high carbohydrate fed dogs did not produce more lactic acid during the anaerobic tests than the high fat dogs. Exercise intensity, training status and environment probably play more of a role in lactic acid production during exercise than does dietary fat and carbohydrate levels.

An occasional question arises regarding the high fat diet for these athletes and the possibility of pancreatitis. If anything, there was a tendency for the high fat group to have slightly lower concentrations of lipase than the high carbohydrate fed group. This was a non-statistical trend, but definitely not indicative of a potential problem. Pancreatitis is almost unheard of in sled dogs where fat levels representing 50-80% of metabolizable energy calories are fed as fat.

Correct Nutrient Balance

It is important to realize that although emphasizing fat intake is important, it can also be overdone. Oversupplementation of fat or any nutrient will displace the intake of other nutrients and lead to deficiencies. These nutrient deficiencies can manifest themselves in problems such as anemia, inappetence, poor attitude, poor coat quality, and lethargy. Only rations that are complete and balanced for all nutrients should be fed.

The results of these studies do not answer all of our questions, but they do open up new insights into the way that diet and training effect the availability and utilization of muscle fuels in sled dogs. As we enrich our understanding of how these magnificent animals perform, we will improve our ability to provide them with the resources they need to meet their potential.

Acknowledgement

The work discussed under the section entitled "Effects of Diet on VO_2 Max, Mitochondrial Volume, and Maximal Rate of Fat Oxidation" was initiated by Dr. C. Richard Taylor and his colleagues from CFS, Harvard University. Dr. Taylor, along with Dr. Hans Hoppeler and Dr. Ewald Wiebel developed the concept of Symorphism which describes the physiological limits imposed on energy generation in working muscle. These scientists have pioneered investigations into respiratory physiology; most recently their studies have revealed several of the mechanisms by which fat intake affects muscle metabolism. Dr. Taylor would have presented this material himself, but his untimely passing in September of 1995 has left a large void in the field of comparative physiology. He remains an inspiration to all those fortunate enough to have worked with and known him.

References and Suggested Readings

1. Abumrad NA, Sterns SB, Tepperman HM, et al. Studies on serum lipid, insulin, and glucagon and on muscle triglyceride in rats adapted to high fat and high carbohydrate diets. *J Lipid Res* 1978; 19:423-432.

2. Bergstrom J. Muscle electrolytes in man: determined by neutron activation analysis on needle biopsy specimens: a study in normal subjects, kidney patients, and patients with chronic diarrhea. *Scand J Clin Lab Invest* 1967; 71:140-150.

3. Bergstrom J, Hermansen L, Hultman E, Saltin, B. Diet, muscle glycogen, and physical performance. *Acta Physiol Scand* 1968; 71:140-150.

4. Claasen H, Hoppeler H, Tuscher L, Wu XY, Saucedo C, Weber JM. Oxidative substrate pathways and symmorphosis: IV. Relating substrate oxidation to muscle cell structure. *Proc XXXII Congress IUPS*, Glasgow, Scotland 1993; 319.6/0.

5. Conlee RK, Hammer RL, Winder WW, Bracken ML, Nelson AG, Barnett DW. Glycogen repletion and exercise endurance in rats adapted to a high fat diet. *Metabolism* 1990; 39:289-294.

6. Costill DL, Coyle E, Dalsky G, Evans SW, Fink W, Hoopes D. Effects of elevated plasma FFA and insulin on muscle glycogen usage during exercise. *J Appl Physiol* 1977; 43:695-699.

7. Dobson GB, Parkhouse WS, Weber JS, Stuttard E, Harman J, Snow DH, Hochachka PA. Metabolic changes in skeletal muscle and blood of greyhounds during 800m track sprint. *Am J Physiol* 1988; 3:R513-R519.

8. Downey RL, Kronfeld DS, Banta CA. Diet of beagles affects stamina. *J Am An Hosp* 1980; 1980:273-277.

9. Fielding RA, Costill DL, Fink WJ, King DS, Kovaleski JE, Kirwan JP. Effects of pre-exercise carbohydrate feedings on muscle glycogen use during exercise in well-trained runners. *Eur J Appl Physiol* 1987; 56:225-229.

10. Hammel EP, Kronfeld DS, Ganjam VK, Dunlap HL. Metabolic responses to exhaustive exercise in racing sled dogs fed diets containing medium, low, or zero carbohydrate. *Am J Clin Nutr* 1977; 30:409-418.

11. Harvey JW, Calderwood MB, Gropp K, Denaro FJ, Polysaccharide storage myopathy in canine PFK deficiency (Type IV glycogen storage disease). *Vet Path* 1990; 27:1-8.

12. Hickson R, Rennie M, Conlee R, Winder WW, Holloszy JO. Effects of increased plasma fatty acids on glycogen utilization and endurance. *J Appl Physiol* 1977; 43:829-833.

13. Holloszy JO, Coyle EF. Adaptation of skeletal muscle to endurance performance and their metabolic consequences. *J Appl Physiol* 1984; 56:831-838.

14. Hurley B, Nemeth P, Martin W, Hagberg JM, Dalsky GP, Holloszy JO. Muscle triglyceride utilization during exercise: Effect of training. *J Appl Physiol* 1986; 60:562-567.

15. Issekutz B, Miller HI, Paul P. Aerobic work capacity and plasma FFA turnover. *J Appl Physiol* 1965; 20:293-296.

16. Issekutz B Jr, Shaw WA, Issekutz TB. Effect of lactate on FFA and glycerol turnover in resting and exercising dogs. *J Appl Physiol* 1971; 39:349-353.

17. Jacobs I. Muscle glycogen and diet in elite soccer players. *Eur J Appl Phys* 1982; 48:297-302.

18. Jansson E, Kaijser L. Substrate utilization and enzymes in skeletal muscle of extremely endurance-trained men. *J Appl Physiol* 1987; 62:999-1005.

19. Kronfeld DS. Diet and performance in racing sled dogs. *J Am Vet Med Assoc* 1973; 162:470-474.

20. Kronfeld DS, Hammel EP, Ramberg CF, Dunlap HL. Hematological and metabolic responses to training in racing sled dogs fed diets containing medium, low, or zero carbohydrate. *Am J Clin Nutr* 1977; 30:419-430.

21. Martin WH, Dalsky GP, Hurley BF, Matthews DE, Bier DM, Hagberg JM, Rogers MA, King DS, Holloszy JO. Effect of endurance training on plasma free fatty acid turnover and oxidation during exercise. *Am J Physiol* 1993; 265:E708-E714.

22. Miller H, Issekutz, B Rodahl K. Effect of exercise on the metabolism of fatty acids in the dog. *Am J Physiol* 1963; 205:167-172.

23. Miller W, Bryce G, Conlee R. Adaptations to a high fat diet that increase exercise endurance in male rats. *J Appl Physiol* 1984; 56:78-83.

24. Neufer PD, Costill DL, Flynn MG, Kirwan JP, Mitchell JB, Houmard J. Improvements in exercise performance: effects of carbohydrate feedings and diet. *J Appl Physiol* 1987; 62:983-988.

25. Noakes TD, Lambert EV, Lambert MI, McArthur PS, Myburgh KH, Benade AJS. Carbohydrate ingestion and muscle glycogen depletion during marathon and ultramarathon racing. *Eur J Appl Physiol* 1988; 57:482-489.

26. Passonneau JV, Lauderdale VR. A comparison of three methods of glycogen measurement in tissues. *Anal Biochem* 1974; 60:405-412.

27. Paul P, Holmes WL. Free fatty acid and glucose metabolism during increased energy expenditure and after training. *Med Sci Sports* 1975; 7:176-183.

28. Paul P, Issekutz B, Miller HI. Interrelationship of free fatty acids and glucose metabolism in the dog. *Am J Physiol* 1966; 211:1313-1320.

29. Phinney S, Bistrain B, Evans W, Gervino E, Blackburn GL. The human metabolic response to chronic ketosis without caloric restriction: Preservation of submaximal exercise capability with reduced carbohydrate oxidation. *Metabolism* 1983; 32:769-776.

30. Quirion A, Brisson GR, Laurencelle L, DeCarfel D, Audet A, Dulac S, Ledux M, Vogelaere P. Lactate threshold and onset of blood lactate accumulation during incremental exercise after dietary modifications. *Eur J Appl Physiol* 1988; 57:192-197.

31. Rennie MJ, Holloszy JO. Inhibition of glucose uptake and glycogenolysis by availability of oleate in well oxygenated perfused skeletal muscle. *Biochemical Journal* 1977; 168:161-170.

32. Reynolds AJ, Fuhrer L, Dunlap HL, Finke M, Kallfelz FA. Effect of diet and training on muscle glycogen storage and utilization in sled dogs. *J Appl Physiol* 1995; 795(5):1601-1607.

33. Reynolds AJ. Percutaneous muscle biopsy: a new approach. A manuscript submitted to *AJVR* August, 1993.

34. Reynolds AJ, Fuhrer L, Dunlap HL, Finke MD, Kallfelz FA. Lipid metabolite responses to diet and training in sled dogs. *J Nutr* 1994; 124:2754S-2759S.

35. Reynolds AJ, Hoppeler H, Reinhart GA, Roberts, T, Simmerman D, Weyand P, Taylor CR. Sled dog endurance: a result of high fat diet or selective breeding? *FASEB J* 1995; 9(4): A996.

36. Reynolds AJ, Reinhart GA, Carey DP, Swenson RA, Kallfelz FA. The effect of immediate post exercise carbohydrate supplementation on muscle glycogen synthesis in trained sled dogs. *J Applied Physiol*; in press.

37. Martin B, Robinson S, Roberts D. Influence of diet on leg uptake of glucose during heavy exercise. *Am J Clin Nutr* 1978; 31:62-67.

38. Sahlin K, Akatz A, Broberg S. Tricarboxylic acid cycle intermediates in human muscle during prolonged exercise. *Am J Physiol* 1990; 259:C834-C841.

39. Sahlin K. Metabolic changes limiting muscle performance. In: Saltin B, ed. *Biochemistry of Exercise VI 1st ed Vol. 16*. Champaign, Illinois: Human Kinetics Publishers. 1986:323-343.

40. Saltin B, Astrand PO. Free fatty acids and exercise. *Am J Clin Nutr* 1993; 57:S752-S758.

41. Saltin B, Gollnick PD. Skeletal muscle adaptability: significance for metabolism and performance. In: *Handbook of Physiology*. *Skeletal Muscle*. Peach LD, Adrian RH, Geiger SR (eds). Baltimore: Williams and Wilkinson. 1983:555-631.

42. Simi B, Sempore B, Mayet M-H, Favier RJ. Additive effects of training and high-fat diet on energy metabolism during exercise. *J Appl Physiol* 1991; 71:197-203.

43. Terjung RL, Budohoski L, Nazar K, et al. Chylomicron triglyceride metabolism in resting and exercising fed dogs. *J Appl Physiol* 1982; 52:815-820.

44. Vock R, Claasen H, Fryder-Doffey F, Hoppeler H, Ordway GA, Saucedo C, Taylor CR, Tuscher L, Weber JM, Weibel ER. Oxidative substrate pathways and symmorphosis: III. Relating capillary morphometry to O2 and substrate delivery to muscle cells. *Proc XXXII Congress IUPS*, Glasgow, Scotland. 1993:287.7/P.

45. Wasserman K, Beaver WL, Davis JA, Pu JZ, Heber D, Whipp BJ. Lactate, pyruvate, and lactate-to-pyruvate ratio during exercise and recovery. *J Appl Physiol* 1985; 59:935-940.

46. Weber J-M, Brichon G, Roberts T, McClelland G, Hoppeler H. Oxidative substrate pathways and symmorphosis: II. Relative roles of circulatory and intramuscular sources. *Proc XXXII Congress IUPS*, Glasgow, Scotland. 1993:287.13/

Energy Metabolism and Water Turnover in Alaskan Sled Dogs During Running

Kenneth W. Hinchcliff, BVSc, MS, PhD, DACVIM
Associate Professor, Department of Veterinary Clinical Sciences
College of Veterinary Medicine, The Ohio State University, Columbus, Ohio

Gregory A. Reinhart, PhD[a]; John R. Burr, DVM[a];
Curt J. Schreier[a]; Richard A. Swenson[b]
[a]Research and Development, The Iams Company, Lewisburg, Ohio
[b]Lightning Bolt Express Kennels, Two Rivers, Alaska

*"A sledge dog…when hungry, will eat any kind of food, as he needs
must in barren countries…
I have known dogs enjoy a meal of bamboo sticks."*[1]

Sled dogs typically perform heavy muscular work in cold to extremely cold conditions. The performance of physical work, such as pulling a sled, requires the expenditure of energy derived from oxidative metabolism of fat, carbohydrate or protein. Similarly, maintenance of a normal body temperature in cold ambient conditions requires the expenditure of energy above that required for maintenance in a thermoneutral environment. The performance of muscular work in a cold environment increases the amount of energy needed over that required for either activity in a thermoneutral environment or thermoregulation alone. Because of this increased energy need, attention to feeding practices and diet (bamboo is unlikely to be a satisfactory diet for sled dogs) is paramount in maintaining the health and performance of sled dogs.

Introduction

Failure to appreciate the additive effects and magnitude of exposure to cold ambient conditions and physical labor on energy expenditure has had tragic results for human explorers. Perhaps the best documented example is that of Amundsen and Scott during their race to the south pole. Amundsen and his team traveled on cross country skis and used sled dogs to haul supplies and provisions, thus reducing the mens' energy needs. While doing so the men ate a diet of dried milk, biscuits, chocolate, and pemmican (ground meat with added fat), which supplied between 4560 and 5000 kcal/day. Amundsen's team's energy requirements have been estimated to be 4,500 kcal/day. Scott's team ill-advisedly walked on snow shoes, used ponies and then, after the ponies died early in the expedition, man-hauled sleds to the south pole. During the outward journey Scott's team's diet consisted of biscuits, tea, sugar, cocoa, pemmican and butter, and supplied about 4400 kcal/d. On the return journey the ration was reduced and supplied about 4000 kcal/day. Scott's team's energy requirements have been estimated to be 5,500 kcal/day, which is higher than Amundsen's because of the extra work that Scott's men had to perform in hauling their supplies. Scott and his team died on the return journey, Amundsen and all his team completed the round trip in good health.[2] The tragic failure of Scott's team to complete the trip to the south pole and back was at least in part attributable to Scott's failure to appreciate the extreme effect of hard work in a frigid environment on energy requirements.

While Amundsen's men completed the journey, the same cannot be said of his dogs, most of which were eaten during the journey, or died on return to Buenos Aires.[1] However, of those dogs that arrived at the pole, all except the 6 dogs that were killed for food completed the round trip, and indeed are reported to have gained weight on their diet of pemmican and fresh (dog) meat.[3] The dogs hauled sleds with initial weights of between 450 and 500 kg for an average of 25.5 miles per day with at least one ascent to over 10,000 feet.[3] The use of sled dogs for transportation and food (both dog and human) was common in expeditions in the late 19th and early 20th centuries, inspiring one veteran explorer to write that he would like to see "an expedition to one of the poles, or some other difficult place, from which the dogs returned in good condition, as an example of what can be done with proper food and management".[4] Fortunately, events like the Iditarod Trail Sled Dog Race, in which dog deaths are rare and dogs lose minimal (less than 10%) body weight, confirm Dr. Hadwen's speculation that dogs can perform exceptional feats of endurance from which they return in good health.

Energy Requirements of Sled Dogs: An Historical Perspective

Baashuus-Jessen reviewed the accounts of many of the late 19th and early 20th century expeditions that used sled dogs, and concluded that the lack of proper food containing the correct amounts of minerals, vitamins, and fat was the principal cause of malnutrition in the dogs.[5] The Norwegian explorer Nansen is reported to be the first one to have recognized that fat was a necessary component of the diet of men and dogs in polar conditions.[6] However, Inuit and other northern native peoples have eaten, and fed to their dogs, high fat diets for eons. Nansen fed his dogs a pemmican diet of higher fat content than was eaten by the men.[6] Indeed most experienced dog handlers of the 19th and early 20th century recognized the need for supplemental fat in the diet of working sled dogs, although the sometimes stated reason was "to aid the digestion".[7] Others noted that performance of the dogs was sluggish unless an oily food, such as blubber or seal oil was used, a few ounces per day making a great difference.[8]

While fresh or native foods such as blubber, white whale meat, fish, seal, walrus, and/or beaver were preferred over imported diets,[4,8] in many instances logistical concerns dictated that dogs were fed processed diets. The composition of imported diets apparently varied widely, and was a matter of some debate among expeditioners. Rice, corn meal, ground bone, meat (sometimes canned) and tallow were common ingredients. Dogs could be kept alive on a diet of boiled rice to which three quarters of a pound (300 g) of tallow was added, but this diet did not sustain them in good working condition.[8] It was considered preferable to substitute seal oil for tallow.[8] Pemmican was a popular choice for feeding sled dogs.[9] Although the composition of pemmican does not appear to have been rigorously standardized, it was approximately 28% fat and 65% protein and fed at the rate of 1 pound (0.9 kg) per dog per day.[7] This diet was reported to be satisfactory for short journeys, but did not seem to satisfy a dog on a major expedition.[4,7] For long distance travelling, dried or smoked fish (2 to 3 lb [1-1.5 kg] per day) and blubber were recommended.[8]

Thus, the early sled dog drivers found, by trial and error, that active dogs in a cold environment performed best when fed diets with a high fat content. Noticeable by its absence is any attention to vitamin and mineral nutrition. This is surprising given that most writers commented that fresh food was preferable to imported, processed or even cooked local foods. It is interesting to note that on the first Iditarod Trail Sled Dog Races, dogs were fed a variety of feeds ranging from beaver and seal to high protein commercial dog feeds.[10] It was thought that exposure to the cold conditions necessitated a diet heavy with fats and carbohydrates, and tallow was a frequently used feed additive.[10]

Energy Metabolism of Sled Dogs

Consistent with the observations of early dog drivers (described above), careful quantitative studies of the effects of feeding pemmican to sled dogs demonstrated the inadequacy of this mixture as a sole constituent of the diet.[9] Sled dogs fed 1 lb (0.9 kg) of pemmican lost between 0.31 and 0.97 lb (0.14 to 0.43 kg) body weight per day while travelling an average of 5.6 miles (8.9 km) per day in below freezing temperatures. The external work performed by the dogs averaged 122 Cal (0.56 kJ) per day. The pemmican was 66% protein, 28% fat, and 2% carbohydrate of which between 23 and 33% of the fiber, 17 and 39% of the nitrogen, and 3 and 7% of the fat was passed in the feces.[9] The authors recommended a diet of white fish meal, skim milk powder, yeast, starch, margarine, and beef suet that yielded 2800 kcal/lb (25,700 kJ/kg) with a composition of 46% fat, 25% protein, and 18% carbohydrate. Interestingly, seal meat, a common canine feedstuff in both the Arctic and Antarctic regions and on which dogs were maintained while housed at base, contains 39% fat and 18% protein (when fed as meat with skin and blubber attached).[11] Seal blubber is 87% fat and 7% protein.[12]

Wyatt compared several diets, including pemmican, fed to sled dogs and found that during periods when the dogs were in the field dogs lost weight on all diets.[11] The author concluded that for sled dogs performing muscular work, the energy requirement was between 3500 and 4600 kcal/day (15,000 and 19,200 kJ/d). These estimates were based on the observation that sedentary dogs fed 2360 kcal/d (9800 kJ/d) lost weight, and that the most external work a dog can perform in a day is 400 kcal.[11,13] The active dogs in Wyatt's study lost 5.7 lb (2.6 kg) over 10 days of one trial. If we assume that 90% of the weight loss was fat, which represents a caloric deficit of 2340 kcal/d (9700 kJ/d) for the active dogs. The dogs were receiving 2800 kcal/d (11,600 kJ/d) in the diet, indicating a total energy expenditure of 5100 kcal/d (21,000 kJ/d) for light work.

This larger figure is substantiated by Orr who demonstrated that 5000 kcal/d (21,000 kJ/d) was not sufficient to maintain the body weight of dogs pulling heavy sleds over long distances.[12] The dogs pulled sleds weighing 120 lb/dog (55 kg/dog) for 300 miles (480 km) at an average speed of 20 to 30 miles/day (32 to 48 km/d) at a mean daily temperature of -16 degrees F (-27 C). The high energy expenditure is a result of thermoregulation in a cold environment and external work performed.

There are seasonal variations in energy requirements of Alaskan huskies.[14] During winter months the energy intake of sedentary Alaskan huskies was between 79 and 87 kcal/kg/day (330 to 370 kJ/kg/day). In contrast, energy intake during the summer was 49 kcal/kg/day (200 kJ/kg/day).[14] Therefore, a 30 kg dog would require 2700 kcal/d (11,100 kJ/d) for maintenance. Others have measured higher energy intakes of tethered sled dogs in polar conditions. Campbell and Donaldson recorded energy intakes of 4800 kcal/day (25,000 kJ/d) for dogs that did not maintain body weight while housed in polar conditions.[15] Taylor estimated the external work output of sled dogs by attaching strain gauges to the gang line, and running the dogs at various speeds and with sleds of various weights.[13] The greatest work output recorded for any distance greater than 1.8 miles (4 km) was 1100 kcal/h for 9 dogs pulling with a strain of 95 kg at a speed of 3.1 miles/h (5 km/h). A team of 9 dogs pulling a lighter load (100 lb [45 kg]) at 5.0 mph (8.1 km/h) had work outputs of 870 kcal/h (3600 kJ/h).[13] These values represent only the work done by the dog team in pulling the sled, they do not include the energy cost of the dog moving itself. Furthermore, because the maximal efficiency of conversion of chemical (i.e., metabolic) energy into mechanical energy is less than 25%,[16] the metabolic rate the dogs need to support this energy is at least 4 times the measured work output. Therefore, a dog in a team of 9 dogs expending 870 kcal/h per day (3600 kJ/h/day) (the Iditarod is run at an average speed of 7.7 km/h) and with a maintenance requirement of 2700 kcal/d (11,000 kJ/d), would need in excess of 10,000 kcal/d (42,000 kJ/d).

Alaskan sled dogs perform legendary feats of athletic endurance, and it is not unusual for teams of 10 to 20 dogs to pull a driver and laden sled 1600 km in 9 to 12 days at temperatures below 0° C. Previous studies of the energy intake and expenditure of sled dogs have used dogs bred and trained for hauling freight, rather than for distance racing. Typically the freight dogs covered relatively short distances, usually much less than 32 km per day, at slow speed (8 km/h).[11,12,15] Basic adequate rations for the freight dogs provided 4000 to 8000 kcal/d, with dogs fed less demonstrating weight loss and reduced exercise tolerance.[12] Racing sled dogs run for much greater distances (160 km/d) at higher speed (14 km/h) than do freight dogs. Based on our observations of the diets of dogs bred and trained for long distance racing, we believed that values for sustained metabolic rate of these dogs likely exceeded the predicted maximal values for mammals of their size (20-25 kg).

Water
Metabolism
Urinary water loss is related to the obligatory urinary solute load which in turn is directly related to the solute load of the diet.[17] The solute load is related to dietary composition and quantity — diets with high protein concentrations and/or large caloric intake by the dog result in higher obligatory solute loads. Thus,

Alaskan sled dogs consuming 12,000 kcal/day likely have very high solute loads. Even with maximal urine concentration, these high solute loads mandate a large obligatory excretion of water. Given an estimate of the solute load, through dietary records and analysis, and an estimate of the concentration of solutes in the urine, through measurement of urine osmolality, one can estimate the volume of urine (water) excreted over a given period of time.

The potential renal solute load (PRSL, mmol/day) can be calculated from dietary records and composition:[17]

$$PRSL = \frac{N}{28} + 2(Na + K)$$

where N is the intake of nitrogen. The estimated urinary water loss (UWL, l/day) can then be calculated:

$$UWL = \frac{PRSL}{urine\ osmolality}$$

Note that the estimated urinary water loss includes fecal water loss, and that fecal solute and water loss is small compared to urinary water and solute excretion.[17]

While adequate water is recognized to be essential for the health and performance of sled dogs, little information exists regarding the water requirements of these dogs. Taylor and others estimated water intake of dogs eating 2800 kcal/d (11,600 kJ/d) to be one liter.[9] Others, while recognizing the importance of adequate water intake,[4,10] provide no estimate of an adequate water intake. Water turnover of Alaskan sled dogs is anticipated to be high because of their high caloric intake and sustained exertion in very dry atmosphere. This rate of water turnover is likely to be high because of increased water loss by two routes — urinary and respiratory. However, the ratio of the losses by these two routes is unknown. Respiratory water loss is positively related to the temperature and water vapor pressure of inspired air, and negatively related to respiratory frequency and ventilation rate.[18]

Field Studies

We measured energy intake, by feed and dietary record analysis, energy expenditure and body composition, by the doubly labeled water technique (DLW), and water turnover, by deuterium dilution, in highly fit Alaskan sled dogs during a medium distance race, the Copper Basin 300. We also measured energy expenditure and water turnover in similarly fit but sedentary sled dogs housed in a cold environment.[19]

In the first study, dogs completed the 490 km race in 70 h (average speed of 7.0 km/h). Ambient temperatures during the study ranged between -10° and -35° C. Dogs participating in the race ate an average of 890 g of protein, 750 g of fat, and 450 g of nitrogen free extract per 24 hours with a metabolizable energy intake of

10,600 kcal/d (440 kcal/kg/d). Metabolizable energy intake of the untrained sled dogs housed in a thermoneutral environment was 55 ± 1 kcal/kg/d, based on records of dietary intake at a constant body weight. Total energy expenditure (TEE) of the dogs that participated in the race was 11,200 ± 600 kcal/d (460 kcal/kg/d) and was 2500 ± 480 kcal/d (104 kcal/kg/d) in the trained but sedentary dogs.

Water turnover and factors influencing urine volume and composition in 2 groups of highly trained Alaskan sled dogs were measured in a separate study. One group of 12 dogs (EG) ran in a 490 km sled dog race while a second group of 6 dogs (SG) were housed in unheated kennels. Body water turnover was estimated using deuterium oxide. Simultaneous urine and blood samples were collected before, at the midpoint, and immediately after the race. Average ambient temperature was -32 degrees C (range -23 to -40 C). Average water turnover of EG and SG dogs was 5.03 +/- 0.59 and 0.91 +/- 0.1 l/d (*Figure 1*). Serum [Na] and [K] declined during the race, as did the fractional excretion of Na and K. These changes were associated with an increase in plasma aldosterone and atrial natriuretic concentrations and renin activity, and a decrease in vasopressin concentration. These hormonal changes resulted in a decrease in the fractional excretion of Na, K, Cl, and osmoles during the race. These data demonstrate that the high water turnover of Alaskan sled dogs during prolonged exercise is associated with significant changes in serum electrolyte concentrations and tubular reabsorption of Na, K, and Cl, the latter mediated by changes in plasma aldosterone and vasopressin concentrations.

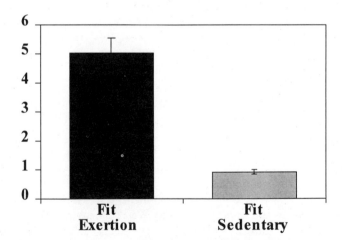

Figure 1.

Discussion

The high metabolizable energy intake and TEE of the exertion group dogs was attributable to the energy requirements of sustained exertion and thermoregulation in subzero temperatures. Also, the high water turnover was mandated by the osmole load associated with the high energy intake.

Previous studies of the energy intake and expenditure of sled dogs have estimated energy expenditure, based on dietary analysis and body weight records, of 4000 to 8000 kcal/d.[7,12] However, these studies used dogs bred and trained for hauling freight, rather than for distance racing. Typically the freight dogs covered relatively short distances, less than 32 km per day, at slow speed (8 km/h).[11-12] Racing sled dogs run for much greater distances (160 km/d) at higher speed (km/h) than do freight dogs. The dogs in the present study completed the 490 km race at an average speed of 7.0 km/h. Assuming that the work output was 92 kcal/h per dog,[13] and that the mechanical efficiency was 25%,[16] the energy expenditure of each dog needed for physical work was 8000 kcal/d. The total calculated daily energy expenditure of the exertion dogs was, therefore, assuming a resting metabolic rate of 90 kcal/kg/d,[14] approximately 11,000 kcal/d. This value closely approximates the actual energy expenditure, measured by the DLW technique of 11,200 kcal/d. Thus, the calculated energy expenditure corresponds closely with those measured by dietary analysis and by the DLW technique and corroborates these estimates of TEE.

The speed of the dogs in this study is similar to the speed at which winning teams complete the 1100 mile Iditarod Trail or Yukon Quest sled dog races.[20] This indicates that the metabolic rates of the dogs in this study are representative of the metabolic rate trained sled dogs are able to maintain for longer than 3 days.

It is likely that the high sustained metabolic rate of these dogs is a consequence of their husbandry and adaptive changes induced by endurance training. The dogs do not have to forage for food, food availability is limited only by what is offered and by what the dogs can consume. Energy density of the food is increased by addition of fat; the diet fed the dogs in this study provided 63% of calories from fat. This ready availability of metabolizable energy is in contrast to most species in which food availability, albeit because of limitations to the volume consumed because of low energy density or the necessity to forage, may be the factor limiting sustainable metabolic rate.

---

1. Hanssen H. Sledge dogs on Amundsen's south polar journey. *Polar Record* 1937; 2(18):57-59.

2. Huntford R. *The last place on earth.* New York: Macmillan. 1983:546-547.

3. Editorial note. *Polar Record* 1937; 2(18):59.

4. Hadwen S. The Canadian sledge dogs to the eastern and western arctic. *Polar Record* 1937; 2(18):59-68.

5. Baashuus-Jessen J. Arctic nervous diseases. *Skandinavisk: Veterinartidskrift.* 1935.

6. Gollnick PD, Saltin B. Fuel for muscular exercise: role of fat. In: Horton ES, Terjung RL (eds) *Exercise, nutrition and energy metabolism.* New York: MacMillan. 1988:72-88.

7. Croft A. West Greenland sledge dogs. *Polar Record* 1937; 2:68-81.

8. Rokeby-Thomas HR. Notes on dogs and sledges in the Queen Maud sea and coronation gulf areas. *Geographical Journal* 1939; 93:424-429.

References

9. Taylor RFJ, Worden AN, Waterhouse CE. The diet of sledge dogs. *Br J Nutr* 1959; 13:1-16.

10. Anon. The Iditarod sled dogs and DVMs. *Mod Vet Pract* 1975; 56:456-461.

11. Wyatt HT. Further experiments on the nutrition of sledge dogs. *Brit J Nutr* 1963; 17:273-279.

12. Orr NWM. The feeding of sledge dogs on Antarctic expeditions. *Brit J Nutr* 1966; 20:1-12.

13. Taylor RFJ. The work output of sledge dogs. *J Physiol* 1957; 137:210-217.

14. Durrer JL, Hannon JP. Seasonal variations in caloric intake of dogs living in an Arctic environment. *Am J Physiol* 1962; 202:375-378.

15. Campbell IT, Donaldson J. Energy requirements of antarctic sledge dogs. *Br J Nutr* 1982; 45(1):95-98.

16. Taylor CR. Relating mechanics and energetics during exercise. In: JH Jones (ed.), *Comparative Vertebrate Exercise Physiology: Unifying Physiological Principles*. *Adv. Vet. Sci. Comp. Med.* 1994; 38A:181-215.

17. Kohn C.W. Composition and distribution of body fluids in dogs and cats. In: DiBartola S. (ed), *Fluid therapy in small animal practice*. Philadelphia: WB Saunders. 1992:1-34.

18. Ferrus L, Commenges D, Gire G, Varene P. Respiratory water loss as a function of ventilatory or environmental factors. *Resp Physiol* 1984; 56:11-20

19. Hinchcliff KW, Olson J, Crusberg C, et al. Serum biochemical changes in dogs competing in a long-distance sled race. *J Am Vet Med Assoc* 1993; 202:401-405.

20. Official race results. Iditarod Trail Committee, Wasilla, Alaska, and Yukon Quest International Sled Dog Race, Fairbanks, Alaska.

Comparison of Biological Changes Before and After Racing, and Between Dogs Competing in Long Distance Sled Dog Races

John R. Burr, DVM
Animal Care Center Veterinarian
Research and Development, The Iams Company, Lewisburg, Ohio

Gregory A. Reinhart, PhD[a]; Richard A. Swenson[b]; Steven F. Swaim, DVM, MS[c];
Dana M. Vaughn, PhD[c,d]; Dino M. Bradley, DVM, MS[c]

[a]Research and Development, The Iams Company, Lewisburg, Ohio
[b]Lightning Bolt Express Kennels, Two Rivers, Alaska
[c]Auburn University, Scott-Ritchey Research Center, Auburn, Alabama
[d]Current address: InnoPet, Inc., Fort Lauderdale, Florida

Summary

Blood samples were collected before and after racing in a team of 17 dogs competing in the 1991 Iditarod sled dog race, and in a second group of 21 dogs running in a simulated 170 mile race. Differences in serum biochemical values between pre-race and post-race values and between dogs that finished the Iditarod and those that were dropped during the race were examined.

Iditarod: Nine of the 17 dogs competing in the Iditarod completed the entire race (finishers). Eight dogs were removed from the team (non-finishers). Serum urea nitrogen and uric acid concentrations increased in response to racing in all dogs, but non-finishers had significantly lower post-race values than finishers (P<.05). All dogs had a slight but significant decrease in serum, sodium, potassium, and calcium in response to racing (P<.05). Significant increases in serum creatine kinase and aspartate aminotransferase occurred in all dogs in response to racing (P<.05). Post-race serum creatine kinase and aspartate aminotransferase means were substantially higher in the non-finisher group compared to the finisher group, but this difference was not significant because of high variability between individual dogs. Lactate dehydrogenase activity increased in response to racing in dogs that finished the race, but decreased in response to racing in those that did not finish.

Simulated race: Post-race means for serum albumin, total protein, hematocrit, hemoglobin, red blood cell count, calcium, and potassium were significantly lower than pre-race values in dogs that ran the simulated race (P<.05). Post-race values for alkaline phosphatase, alanine amino transferase, alkaline phosphatase, alanine aminotransferase, lactate dehydrogenase, and creatine kinase activities, and urea nitrogen, and uric acid levels were significantly higher than pre-race values (P<.05). Elevated creatine kinase and possibly aspartate aminotransferase serum activities may be indicators of performance failure or fatigue in racing sled dogs competing in long-distance races.

Endurance sled dog racing is a popular activity in certain areas of the United States. In recent years, large races such as the Iditarod and the Yukon Quest have received increasing amounts of public and media attention as spectator events. This attention has been accompanied by heightened interest in the humane aspects of sled dog races and the welfare of the dogs that compete. Long distance races may cover more than 1000 miles and entail multiple days of racing for drivers and their teams. During the race, some dogs may be removed from teams because of injury, fatigue, failure to perform, illness, or dehydration.[1] Decisions to remove dogs from the race are made by team drivers and course veterinarians and usually rely upon the presence of injury or subjective assessments of the dog's behavior and performance.

Training and racing result in certain physiological and biochemical adaptations in sled dogs. Energy and water requirements increase dramatically.[2,3] Increases in resting values of packed cell volume and red blood cell count are indicative of the enhanced oxygen transport that is necessary during peak training periods.[4,5] Similarly, fit dogs have lower heart rates and rectal temperatures than unfit dogs in response to exercise.[6] Recent studies of racing sled dogs have also shown that the prolonged periods of exercise that occur during racing are accompanied by specific biochemical changes that can be detected in the blood or serum.[5,7] However, little is known about the significance of these changes and whether they are correlated with performance or onset of fatigue. Such information would be of value to sled dog mushers during periods of training and when selecting dogs for inclusion in a racing team. The identification of a reliable biochemical marker that is associated with strenuous or excessive physical exertion would also be of benefit to course veterinarians who monitor the health and welfare of racing dogs during long distance races.

The purpose of this study was to compare serum biochemical changes between a group of dogs that completed the 1991 Iditarod race and dogs that were dropped from the team at some point during the race. A subsequent race was conducted under conditions which simulated a portion of the Iditarod to provide additional serum biochemical data from racing sled dogs.

A group (team) of 17 Alaskan sled dogs running in the 1991 Iditarod was studied. The Iditarod is an annual race of approximately 1100 miles in length on a course traveling between the cities of Anchorage and Nome, Alaska. The dogs that were studied were all adults, consisting of 13 males and 4 females between the ages of 3 and 11 years. Two groups of dogs were identified. Finishers included the dogs on the team that successfully completed the entire 13 day race. Non-finishers included the dogs that were removed (dropped) from the team at some point during the race. The decision to drop dogs from the team was made by the driver with assistance from race veterinarians. Dogs were dropped at one of 26 possible checkpoints along the route, and were immediately examined by a race veterinarian.

Seven days prior to the race, blood samples were collected from all 17 dogs. The dogs were conditioned for the race but were in a rested state when tested. Blood was taken a second time from each dog after being removed from the team or after completing the race. Logistic and regulatory constraints prevented immediate sampling in some cases, but attempts were made to obtain blood samples as quickly as possible after the dog stopped running. The mean time lapse between the end of the run and sample collection was 6.9 hours, with a range of 2.6 to 11.6 hours.

Blood samples were collected by cephalic venipuncture. Care was taken to prevent the blood from freezing during collection and processing. Samples for CBC analysis were collected in tubes containing sodium EDTA[a] and stored in a cool container for shipment to the processing laboratory. Samples for chemistry profiles were collected in serum separator tubes, allowed to clot for 30 minutes, and then centrifuged at 1500 rpm in a portable AC/DC centrifuge that was carried to each site. Serum was immediately removed, frozen, and shipped in dry ice to the participating laboratory for analysis.

Complete blood counts were determined with a Sysmex F-800 Microcell counter,[b] and chemistry profiles were determined with a Cobas Mira Instrument.[c]

A second study was conducted to obtain biochemical data from dogs under more controlled conditions. A group of 21 dogs ran as a team in the manner of a typical sled dog race, covering a total distance of 170 miles. All of the dogs completed the entire distance. The dogs that were included were all adults, 17 males and 4 females, between the ages of 2 and 13 years. Blood samples were obtained prior to the race when the dogs were in a trained, but rested condition, and again following completion of the race within 30 minutes after the dogs stopped running. Samples were processed in the manner described previously.

Statistical Analysis: Analysis of variance (ANOVA) and simple comparison tests were used to identify differences between means of test values for finishers and non-finishers (status), pre-race and post-race (time), and the interaction between status and time in the 1991 Iditarod race. The Mann-Whitney test (a non-parametric procedure) was used to compare group means of finishers and non-finishers for serum enzymes, hematocrit, and red blood cell count because these variables were found to have unequal variance. The Wilcoxon test was used to compared pre- to post-race values of these parameters. Pre- and post-race values collected in the simulated race were compared using a student's paired t-test or the Wilcoxon test.

1991 Iditarod: Heavy snow conditions occurred for the duration of the 1991 race. The nine dogs that completed the race as a team did so in 12 days, 16 hours, 34 minutes and 39 seconds. Eight dogs were removed from the team at one of six checkpoints along the course. Reasons for removing dogs from the team included: leg or pad injuries (2 dogs), extreme fatigue or failure to perform (5 dogs), or diarrhea (1 dog).

Results

---

[a] Vacutainer™; Beckton, Dickinson and Company, Franklin Lakes, NJ
[b] Tao Medical Electronic, Ltd., Kobe, Japan
[c] Roche Diagnostic Systems, Nutley, NJ

There were no significant differences in post-race values between dogs that finished the race and dogs that were dropped from the race for serum calcium, phosphate, potassium, sodium, chloride, lactate, hemoglobin, or total protein (*Table 1*). Dogs that did not finish the race had significantly lower post-race serum urea nitrogen and uric acid concentrations than those that finished.

Red blood cell count and percent hemoglobin decreased significantly in response to racing in both finishers and non-finishers when pre-race and post-race values were compared (*Table 1*). However, red blood cell count decreased more dramatically in dogs that were dropped than in dogs that finished the race. A similar effect occurred in hematocrit values. There was a slight but significant decrease in serum sodium, potassium, and calcium in response to exercise (pre-race vs post-race) in all dogs. However, these values still remained close to or within the reference range for healthy dogs in both finishers and non-finishers. Serum urea nitrogen and uric acid both increased in response to endurance exercise. No significant changes in serum phosphate or chloride were observed when pre-race and post-race values were compared (*Table 1*).

Table 1. Mean packed cell volume and serum biochemical values of dogs before and after competing in the 1991 Iditarod sled dog race.

VARIABLE	REFERENCE RANGES*	FINISHED		DROPPED	
		Pre-Race	*Post-Race*	*Pre-Race*	*Post-Race*
Red Blood Cell (x 10⁹/ml)	5.65 - 8.49	6.46 ±.15ᵃ (5.8-7.3)	5.60 ±.17ᵇ (4.7-6.6)	6.46 ±.14ᵃ (5.9-7.1)	2.54 ±.66 (0.6-5.5)
Hemoglobin (g/dl)	13.5 - 19.5	15.49 ± .38ᵃ (13.7-17.6)	14.14 ± .34 (12.5-15.8)	15.94 ± .37ᵃ (14.5-17.6)	14.60 ± .33 (13.0-15.9)
Hematocrit (%)	41.0 - 59.0	46.09 ±1.01ᵃ (42.7-51.4)	44.84 ±1.09ᵃ (38.0-49.4)	46.81 ±1.10ᵃ (41.9-51.5)	14.62 ± 4.57 (2.6-37.4)
Total Protein (g/L)	5.5 - 7.1	6.38 ± .09 (5.9-6.7)	5.82 ± .13 (5.1-6.3)	6.64 ± .12 (6.0-7.1)	5.92 ± .14 (5.4-6.5)
Sodium (mEq/L)	146 - 154	150.22 ± .40ᵃ (149-152)	147.33 ± 1.0 (142-152)	151.00 ±.46ᵃ (149-153)	147.25 ± 1.2 (142-152)
Potassium (mEq/L)	3.9 - 5.1	4.69 ± .07ᵃ (4.3-4.9)	4.47 ± .12 (3.8-5.1)	4.64 ± .10ᵃ (4.3-5.2)	4.31 ± .18 (3.7-5.2)
Chloride (mEq/L)	114 - 122	117.11 ± .26 (116-118)	113.67 ± 2.1 (99-120)	116.75 ± .37 (115-118)	117.38 ± .92 (115-122)
Calcium (mg/dl)	9.6 - 11.6	10.49 ± .09ᵃ (9.9-10.7)	9.71 ± .16 (9.2-10.6)	10.53 ± .06ᵃ (10.2-10.7)	9.15 ± .28 (7.5-9.9)
Phosphate (mg/dl)	2.3 - 4.9	4.24 ± .13 (3.6-4.7)	4.22 ± .16 (3.6-5.0)	4.56 ± .19 (3.9-5.7)	4.14 ± .27 (3.4-5.7)
Lactate (mg/dl)	7.97 ± 0.54**	7.89 ± 1.64 (1.0-15.0)	11.44 ± 2.78 (1.0-25.0)	6.75 ± .92 (3.0-11.0)	10.13 ± 1.81 (1.0-17.0)
Urea Nitrogen (mg/dl)	6 - 22	16.00 ± 1.11ᵃ (12.0-21.0)	27.33 ± .99ᵇ (23.0-32.0)	13.00 ± .96ᵃ (8.0-18.0)	22.00 ± 1.84 (16.0-30.0)
Uric Acid (mg/dl)	0.2 - 0.6	.31 ± .1ᵃ (0-.8)	.37 ± .03ᵇ (.2-.5)	.14 ± .05ᵃ (0-.3)	.26 ± .03 (.1-.4)
Creatinine (mg/dl)	0.7 - 1.5	.70 (0.6-0.8)	.60 (0.5-0.7)	.64 (0.5-0.9)	.64 (0.5-0.8)

Mean ± SEM and (range). a = Significant difference (P < .05) between pre and post-race means within groups. b = Significant difference (P < .05) between finishers and non-finishers within time group.
*The Iams Company, Research and Development, Lewisburg, Ohio.
** Control value from a group of rested Greyhound dogs. From: Bjotvedt, G., Weems, C.W. and Foley, K. Strenuous exercise may cause health hazards for racing Greyhounds. *Veterinary Medicine, Small Animal Clinician* 1984; 79:1481-1487.

Serum enzyme activities varied considerably between individual dogs, both before and after racing (*Table 2*). Significant increases in creatine kinase (CK) and aspartate aminotransferase (AST) occurred in all of the dogs in response to racing (pre- vs post-race values). Post-race CK and AST means were substantially higher in the non-finisher group than in the finisher group, but these differences were not statistically significant. Alkaline phosphatase (ALKP) levels increased significantly after racing in dogs that were dropped from the race, but not in dogs that finished the race. Alanine aminotransferase (ALT) levels did not change significantly in either group of dogs in response to racing, although several non-finishers had elevated post-racing levels of this enzyme compared to the laboratory reference range. A significant interaction effect between time and status occurred for lactate dehydrogenase (LDH) activities. Dogs that finished the race had higher post-race LDH values, while those that did not finish had lower post-race LDH values compared to pre-race values (*Table 2*). Gamma glutamyltransferase (GGT) levels did not significantly differ after racing or between dogs that finished or did not finish the Iditarod course.

Table 2. Serum enzyme activity of dogs before and after competing in the 1991 Iditatrod sled dog race.

ENZYME (U/L)	REFERENCE RANGES*	FINISHED		DROPPED	
		Pre-Race	*Post-Race*	*Pre-Race*	*Post-Race*
Creatine Kinase	31 -217	142.89* (85 - 245)	472.89 (157 - 1001)	156.50* (69 - 237)	1565.12 (82 - 4000)
Aspartate Aminotransferase	17 - 43	39.78* (25 - 62)	94.33 (51 - 157)	55.00* (18 - 94)	206.38 (48 - 575)
Alanine Aminotransferase	17 - 73	103.11 (35 - 157)	103.56 (63 - 206)	110.88 (56 - 199)	217.00 (84 - 760)
Alkaline Phosphatase	5 - 53	41.44 (17 - 105)	50.33 (19 - 193)	43.25* (25 - 77)	75.88 (41 - 150)
Lactate Dehydrogenase	20 - 194	39.22* (9 - 92)	94.89 (49 - 188)	61.63* (26 - 174)	42.88 (14 - 61)
Gamma Glutamyltransferase	0 - 6	3.33 (0 - 7)	3.33 (0 - 9)	1.00 (0 - 3)	2.86 (1 - 4)

Mean ± SEM and (range). a = Significant difference (P < .05) between pre- and post-race means within groups.
* The Iams Company, Research and Development, Lewisburg, Ohio.

Simulated Race: The 21 dogs running the simulated race completed the total distance in 2.5 days, covering 70 miles on the first two days and 30 miles on the third day. Post-race values for serum albumin, total protein, hematocrit, hemoglobin, red blood cell count, calcium, and potassium were significantly lower than pre-race values in dogs that ran the simulated race. Post-race values for ALKP, ALT, AST, LDH, and CK activities, and BUN and UA levels were significantly higher than pre-race values (*Tables 3 and 4*).

Table 3. Mean packed cell volume and serum biochemical values of sled dogs before and after completing a 170 mile simulated race.

VARIABLE	REFERENCE RANGES*	PRE-RACE	POST-RACE
Red Blood Cell Count (x 10^9/ml)	5.65 - 8.49	6.39 ± .11[a] (5.8 - 7.3)	5.78 ± .13 (4.6 - 7.0)
Hemoglobin (g/dl)	13.5 - 19.5	16.27 ± .24[a] (14.7 - 18.6)	14.23 ± .33 (11.1 - 17.3)
Hematocrit (%)	41.0 - 59.0	50.49 ± .56[a] (46.5 - 55.3)	43.35 ± .98 (33.7 - 51.4)
Total Protein (g/L)	5.5 - 7.1	6.11 ± .16[a] (4.9 - 7.6)	5.59 ± .16 (4.0 - 7.5)
Sodium (mEq/L)	146 - 154	153.0 ± 1.8 (130 - 164)	151.9 ± 2.6 (132 - 192)
Potassium (mEq/L)	3.9 - 5.1	4.63 ± .08[a] (4.1 - 5.2)	4.33 ± .10 (3.7 - 5.5)
Chloride (mEq/L)	114 - 122	121.1 ± 1.5 (105 - 136)	124.7 ± 1.9 (109 - 155)
Calcium (mg/dl)	9.6 - 11.6	10.52 ± .20[a] (9.0 - 11.9)	9.21 ± .26 (6.2 - 12.1)
Phosphate (mg/dl)	2.3 - 4.9	3.70 ± .12 (2.8 - 4.8)	3.39 ± .10 (2.8 - 4.3)
Lactate (mg/dl)	7.97 ± 0.54**	12.1 ± .79 (5.0 - 18.0)	9.29 ± .71 (5.0 - 16.0)
Urea Nitrogen (mg/dl)	6 - 22	17.24 ± .83[a] (9.0 - 25.0)	33.38 ± 1.7 (22.0 - 50.0)
Uric Acid (mg/dl)	0.2 - 0.6	.26 ± .03[a] (0.0 -0.6)	.72 ± .05 (0.4 - 1.2)
Creatinine (mg/dl)	0.7 - 1.5	.79 (0.6-0.9)	.99 (0.7-1.3)

Mean ± SEM and (range). a = Significant difference (P < .05) between pre- and post-race means.
*The Iams Company, Research and Development, Lewisburg, Ohio.
** Control value from a group of rested Greyhound dogs. From: Bjotvedt, G., Weems, C.W. and Foley, K. Strenuous exercise may cause health hazards for racing Greyhounds. *Veterinary Medicine, Small Animal Clinician* 1984; 79:1481-1487.

Table 4. Serum enzyme activity of sled dogs before and after completing a 170 mile simulated race.

ENZYME (U/L)	REFERENCE RANGES*	PRE-RACE	POST-RACE
Creatine Kinase	31 - 217	96.62[a] (55.0 - 265.0)	3731.62 (121.0 - 47920.0)
Aspartate Aminotransferase	17 - 43	26.86[a] (20.0 - 37.0)	262.76 (32.0 - 2877.0)
Alanine aminotransferase	17 - 73	56.43[a] (22.0 - 113.0)	144.67 (41.0 - 586.0)
Alkaline phosphatase	5 - 53	35.76[a] (9.0 - 74.0)	90.57 (42.0 - 152.0)
Lactate dehydrogenase	20 - 194	65.38 (22.0 - 134.0)	170.43 (75.0 - 1113.0)
Gamma Glutamyltransferase	0 - 6	3.38 (0.0 - 12.0)	5.33 (2.0 - 22.0)

Mean ± SEM and (range). a = Significant difference (P < .05) between pre- and post-race means.
*The Iams Company, Research and Development, Lewisburg, Ohio.

Dogs that compete in long distance sled races undergo intense training and conditioning in preparation for these events. However, despite adequate preparation and good husbandry, dogs are occasionally removed from sled dog teams during long distance sled races. A review of veterinary reports collected from checkpoints on the Yukon Quest between 1987 and 1992 showed that foot and leg injuries, diarrhea, and fatigue were the most frequently cited reasons for veterinary examination, and dehydration was cited as a primary concern.[1] It was also noted that a diagnosis of fatigue or performance failure by the musher and/or attending veterinarian was uniformly accepted as a justifiable reason for dropping a dog from the race. In the present study, foot and leg injuries or diarrhea were responsible for the removal of 3 dogs from the race, while 5 dogs were dropped because of the more subjective assessment of fatigue or performance failure. These results are similar to those reported from a study of dogs running the Yukon Quest in 1993.[8] In that study, more than half of the dogs that did not finish were removed from the race because of fatigue or performance failure.

Although dehydration is discussed anecdotally as a big concern in racing sled dogs, data from this study do not support dehydration as a cause of performance failure. Dogs thermoregulate primarily through evaporative water loss from expired air and secondarily, through convection and radiation.[9,10] During endurance exercise, water turnover is very high due to respiratory losses and to increased urinary water loss. A recent study of racing sled dogs found that dogs running a 300 mile race had an average water turnover rate of 250 ml/kg body weight/day. This high rate appears to be a result of the increased obligatory urinary solute load that is associated with a high energy intake.[3] Exercise induced hemoconcentration (dehydraton) occurs when the amount of water that is lost from the body is not adequately offset by fluid intake. Blood parameters that are indicative of dehydration are increased hematocrit, red blood cell count, and plasma protein concentration.[5,11,12] Increased serum creatinine levels also support a diagnosis of dehydration.[7]

In the present study, pre-race hematology values were within the laboratory's reference range for all dogs. After racing, decreases occurred in red blood cell count, hematocrit, and total protein. The post-race values of dogs that finished the Iditarod and those that ran the simulated race were all within the reference range for healthy dogs, while post-race red blood cell count and hematocrit values of non-finishers were abnormally low. The authors attribute this anomaly to the length of time that passed between whole blood sampling and analysis. Logistics of the race did not allow immediate shipment and processing of whole blood samples that were obtained at checkpoints from non-finishers. This time lapse and extended handling led to hemolysis of some of the samples and is believed to be the cause of the very low values that were recorded. The normal hemoglobin and total protein values in these dogs indicate that the extremely low hematocrit and red blood cell count values were not physiological, but reflected a problem with sample handling. Serum creatinine levels are also a useful biochemical indicator of dehydration. Creatinine is an end product of the metabolism of creatine phosphate in skeletal muscle. Normally, creatinine levels in the blood remain low due to efficient removal by the kidney. Hypovolemia associated with dehydration leads to decreased glomerular filtration rate, which in turn results in an increase in serum creatinine. Both finishers and non-finishers in the 1991 Iditarod and dogs in the simulated race had normal serum creatinine levels before and after racing (*Tables 1 and 4*). Collectively, these results indicate that dehydration was not a common problem in the dogs in this study.

Various disturbances in serum electrolyte concentrations and acid-base balance have been reported as a result of prolonged or intense exercise in humans, horses, and racing Greyhounds.[13,14,15,16] In the present study, serum sodium, potassium, and chloride concentrations remained within the laboratory's reference range for healthy dogs before and after racing in all of the dogs. There was a slight but significant decrease in serum sodium, potassium, and calcium in response to exercise, but no difference was observed in serum electrolytes between dogs that finished the 1991 Iditarod and those that did not finish. These results indicate that electrolyte imbalance was not a significant concern during endurance exercise in these dogs.

Increased serum urea nitrogen and uric acid, like creatinine, can be indicative of decreased glomerular filtration rate and impaired kidney excretion. However, since serum creatinine did not increase in dogs in the present study, the increases in serum urea nitrogen and uric acid were probably due to increased protein catabolism to provide energy for work. During prolonged exercise, protein oxidation can provide up to 10 percent of the energy that is needed by working muscles.[7,17] In the 1991 race, both finishers and non-finishers had increased serum urea nitrogen concentrations in response to exercise. This effect was also observed in the dogs that ran the simulated race. The mean post-race urea nitrogen of non-finishers in the 1991 Iditarod was significantly lower than the post-race mean of finishers, but the ranges of values for each group were similar (*Table 1*). An examination of the data shows that three of the non-finishers were removed after completing only about one third of the race. The urea nitrogen values for these dogs were between 16 and 22 mg/dl and account for the lower mean in that group. It is likely that the shorter period of time that these dogs were working resulted in a decreased need to oxidize amino acids for energy, resulting in lower urea nitrogen and uric acid values. The higher values in dogs that were exercising for prolonged periods of time are consistent with previous reports of increases in serum urea nitrogen concentrations during a long distance sled dog race.[7]

Post-exercise serum lactate levels indicate the level and intensity of exercise that an animal has engaged in, with more intense exercise causing greater lactate concentrations.[14] Twenty-fold increases in serum lactate concentrations have been reported in racing Greyhounds, and up to five-fold increases have been observed in racing sled dogs.[13,14,18,19] While it has been suggested that high serum lactate concentrations may be a factor in performance failure in some racing sled dogs, dramatic increases are not generally observed in these dogs because the aerobic metabolism of fatty acids provides the major source of energy for this type of exercise.[19,20,21,22] In the present study, performance failure was not associated with elevated lactate levels. There were no differences in pre- and post-race serum lactate concentrations between dogs that finished the race and those that did not. These results are supported by data from another recent study of dogs running a long distance sled race.[8]

Physical performance and the onset of fatigue may be related to serum activities of certain enzymes. Muscle enzymes are located within myofibrils and the activity of these enzymes in the serum of healthy, rested dogs is low.[22] Damage to muscle membranes as a result of physical exertion or disease causes the release of certain enzymes into the serum, and measurement of their activity has been used to estimate the degree of muscle damage in many species.[23] The two enzymes that are most commonly evaluated are creatine kinase (CK) and aspartate aminotransferase (AST). An increase in plasma or serum CK activity is accepted as a sensitive index of muscle injury in the dog.[23,24]

Creatine kinase is primarily found in skeletal muscle, the myocardium, and the brain.[25] Because it has a short half-life and serum levels return to normal within 48 hours after muscle permeability ceases, elevated CK levels are indicative of recent, active muscle injury.[26] Serum AST activity is also suggestive of muscle damage, but is less organ specific than CK because a high concentration of AST is also found in the liver.[22] However, AST has a longer half-life (50 hours) than CK, so the measurement of this enzyme is useful in conjunction with CK to indicate whether muscle disease is continuing or resolving.[22] Serum lactate dehydrogenase (LDH) activity has also been shown to increase in humans and horses after strenuous exercise, but inconsistent results have been reported in dogs.[7,8,14,22,27,28]

Serum LDH activity in the dogs in the present study reacted differently in finishers than in non-finishers in response to endurance exercise. Dogs that finished the race had significantly higher post-race LDH activities compared to pre-race values, while the non-finishers had significantly lower post-race serum LDH activity compared to their pre-race values. The dogs that ran in the simulated race had significantly higher post-race LDH activity compared to pre-race levels. Most researchers report an increase in serum LDH activity as a result of strenuous exercise in dogs.[13,14,27,28] However, a recent report of dogs competing in the Yukon Quest found that activities of this enzyme decreased significantly when samples were taken at a checkpoint midway through the race compared to values recorded earlier in the race.[7] It has been postulated that LDH activity is less sensitive to muscle damage than CK or AST activity, and may not increase until greater exercise stress has been attained.[28] This theory is supported by the observation that the four dogs with highest CK and AST activities in the non-finisher group all showed elevated LDH activity compared to their pre-race values. A second possible explanation for lower activity of LDH in non-finishers concerns the catalytic function of the enzyme. Lactate dehydrogenase catalyzes the conversion of pyruvate to lactate for the production of ATP in the glycolytic cycle. This is an anaerobic process, and higher activity of LDH is associated with anaerobic activity. The concluding miles of a long distance sled race always involve a final sprint for the finish line. As a result, it is expected that the dogs that finished the race were exercising very intensely immediately before finishing. In contrast, the dogs that were dropped would have been still working aerobically when they were removed from the team and tested. The lower LDH level in these dogs may reflect a decreased need for this enzyme during aerobic work.

While it is generally accepted that serum CK and AST activities increase in response to strenuous exercise and are indicative of muscle damage, it is not known whether elevated serum CK and AST activities are correlated to the onset of fatigue or impaired performance in a working animal. Moreover, the concentrations of these enzymes in serum that are indicative of pathological muscle damage are not known. Some researchers have suggested that an increase in serum or plasma CK during exercise is related to transient changes in the permeability of muscle cell membranes, and does not indicate pathological damage to muscle fibers.[11,13] A study of racing sled dogs reported only moderate increases in CK and AST during the race.[7] The authors postulated that these small but significant increases were likely to indicate only a mild insult to the skeletal muscle walls, rather than pathological changes.

In the present study, all of the dogs showed a consistent increase in serum activities of CK and AST in response to exercise. Results of the 1991 Iditarod race showed post-race mean values for CK and AST that were substantially higher for the group of non-finishers compared to the group of finishers (*Table 2*). However, because of high inter-individual variation, these differences were not statistically significant. An examination of the CK and AST values of individual dogs shows that six of the eight non-finishers had CK values greater than the laboratory standard after being dropped from the race. Of these six, three had values that were greater than 2000 U/L, a 10-fold increase over the maximum that is considered normal in healthy dogs. In the group of nine dogs that finished the race, eight had CK values that were greater than the laboratory standard, but none of these dogs had values greater than about 1000 U/L.

A comparison of absolute CK values between studies by different researchers is not recommended because absolute values are influenced by the age and sex of the animals and by the method of analysis that is used.[29] However, it is still important to note that the CK activities of some of the dogs in this study were comparable to activities that have been reported in dogs with clinical myocardial disease or primary muscular disease.[22,26] These levels are indicative of severe muscle degeneration, and in racing sled dogs may represent a degree of muscle break down beyond which a dog cannot continue to work. A recent study of necropsy results of eleven dogs that had died suddenly during long distance sled dog races reported severe muscle necrosis in some of the dogs that were similar to the histopathologic lesions seen in animals suffering from exertional rhabdomyolysis.[30,d] There was great

---

[d] Blake JE. A series of eleven case studies of sled dogs who died over the preceding four winters. *Abstract*.

variability among individuals in terms of the location of the damage, and the degree of muscle damage that was observed. It was also noted that the renal failure that is often associated with rhabdomyolysis is not commonly reported in sled dogs.

Results of the present study indicate that markedly elevated CK and possibly AST serum activities may be indicators of performance failure or fatigue in sled dogs competing in long distance races. Other authors have speculated on the possibility of using these enzymes as biochemical markers for estimating performance and/or evaluating the effects of a training program.[5] Moreover, it appears that a syndrome that is similar to exertional rhabdomyolysis and is characterized by performance failure, extremely high CK and AST activities in serum, and normal lactate concentrations occurs in some long distance racing sled dogs. Given the observational nature of the present study, the problems associated with collecting data during long distance race, and the low numbers of animals that were included, it is imperative that further research be conducted on the predictive value of CK and AST activities for racing sled dogs. Additional research is also needed to study the occurrence of a type of exertional rhabdomyolysis that is associated with aerobic endurance activity.

---

1. Long RD. Treatment of common injuries in endurance racing sled dogs. *Compend Cont Ed Pract Vet* 1993; 434-437. *References*

2. Hinchcliff KW, Reinhart GA, Burr JR, et al. Metabolizable energy intake and sustained energy expenditure in Alaskan sled dogs during heavy exertion in the cold. *Submitted for publication*, 1995.

3. Hinchcliff KW. Energy and water expenditure. In: *Proceedings of the Performance Dog Nutrition Symposium*, Colorado State University, Fort Collins, Colorado, April 18, 1995; 4-9.

4. Kronfeld DS, Hammel EP, Ramberg CF Jr, et al. Hematological and metabolic responses to training in racing sled dogs fed diets containing medium, low or zero carbohydrate. *Am J Clin Nutr* 1977; 30:419-430.

5. Querengaesser A, Iben C, Leibetseder J. Blood changes during training and racing in sled dogs. *J Nutr* 1994; 124:2760S-2764S.

6. Sneddon JC, Minnaar PP, Grosskopf JFW, et al. Physiological and blood biochemical responses to submaximal treadmill exercise in Canaan dogs before, during and after training. *J S African Vet A* 1989; 60:87-91.

7. Hinchcliff KW, Olson J, Crusberg C, et al. Serum biochemical changes in dogs competing in a long distance sled race. *JAVMA* 1993; 202:401-405.

8. Hinchcliff KW. Performance failure in Alaskan sled dogs: Biochemical correlates. *Res Vet Sci* (Submitted for publication, 1995).

9. Baker MA. Anatomical and physiological adaptations of panting mammals to heat and exercise. In: Horvath A, Yousef MK, eds. *Environmental Physiology: Aging, Heat and Altitude*. New York: Elsevier North Holland, 1980:121-146.

10. Young DR, Mosher R, Erve P. Energy metabolism and gas exchange during treadmill running in dogs. *J Appl Physiol* 1959; 14:834-838.

11. Snow DH, Kerr MG, Nimmo MA, et al. Alterations in blood, sweat, urine

and muscle composition during prolonged exercise in the horse. *Vet Rec* 1982; 110:377-384.

12. Harrison MH. Effects of thermal stress and exercise on blood volume in humans. *Physiol Rev* 1985; 149-209.

13. Bjotvedt G, Weems CW, Foley K. Strenuous exercise may cause health hazards for racing Greyhounds. *Vet Med: Sm An Clin* 1984; 79:1481-1487.

14. Ilkiw JE, Davis PE, Church DB. Hematologic, biochemical, blood-gas, and acid-base values in Greyhounds before and after exercise. *Am J Vet Res* 1989; 50:583-586.

15. Rose RJ, Purdue RA, Hensley W. Plasma biochemistry alterations in horses during an endurance ride. *Equine Vet J* 1977; 9:122-126.

16. Frizzel RT, Lang, GH, Lowance, DC. Hyponatremia and ultramarathon running. JAMA 1986; 255:772-774.

17. Gollnick PD. Energy metabolism and prolonged exercise. In: Lamb DR, Murray,R, eds. *Perspectives in Exercise Science and Sports Medicine*, Vol 1. Carmel, Ind: Benchmark Press, 1988:1-42.

18. Snow DH, Harris RC, Stuttard E. Changes in haematology and plasma biochemistry during maximal exercise in greyhounds. *Vet Rec* 1988; 123:487-489.

19. Hammel EP, Kronfeld DS, Ganjam VK, et al. Metabolic responses to exhaustive exercise in racing sled dogs fed diets containing medium, low, or zero carbohydrate. *Am J Clin Nutr* 1977; 30:409-418.

20. Paul P, Issekutz B. Role of extramuscular energy sources in the metabolism of the exercising dog. *Am J Physiol* 1967; 22:615-622.

21. Kronfeld DS. Diet and the performance of racing sled dogs. JAVMA 1973; 162:470-473.

22. Scott-Moncrieff JC, Hawkins EC, Cook JR. Canine muscle disorders. *Compend Cont Ed Pract Vet* 1990; 12:31-39.

23. Harris PA. Comparative aspects of exertional myopathy. *Adv Vet Sci: Bicent Symp Series* 1993; 4:115-138.

24. Pennington RJT. Biochemical aspects of muscle disease. In: Walton J, ed. *Disorders of Voluntary Muscle*, 5th ed. Edinburgh: Churchill Livingston, 1988:455-486.

25. Aktas M, Auguste D, Lefebvre HP, et al. Creatine kinase in the dog: a review. *Vet Res Commun* 1993;17:353-369.

26. DiBartola SP, Tasker JB. Elevated serum creatine phosphokinase: A study of 53 cases and a review of its diagnostic usefulness in clinical veterinary medicine. JAVMA 1977; 13:744-753.

27. Sanders TM, Bloor CM. Effects of endurance exercise on serum enzyme activities in the dog, pig and man. *Proc Soc Exp Bio Med* 1975; 48:823-828.

28. Ready AE, Morgan G. The physiological response of Siberian Husky dogs to exercise: effect of interval training. *Can Vet J* 1984; 25:86-91.

29. Bush BM. Enzymes. In: *Interpretation of Laboratory Results for Small Animal Clinicians*. London: Blackwell Scientific Publications, 1993; 311-349.

30. Gannon JR. Exertional rhabdomyolysis (myoglobinuria) in the racing greyhound. In: Kirk RW, ed. *Current Veterinary Therapy*, Philadelphia: W.B. Saunders, 1980:783-787.

Feeding the Cancer Patient

Glenna E. Mauldin, DVM, MS, DACVIM
Staff Veterinarian, The Donaldson-Atwood Cancer Clinic
Director, Nutritional Support Service
The Animal Medical Center, New York, New York

Introduction

The unique form of protein calorie malnutrition which commonly occurs in both human and veterinary cancer patients is called "cancer cachexia."[1-4] Cancer cachexia is characterized by three findings: diminished host nutrient intake, progressive host weight loss, and certain unique host physical and biochemical changes.[1,2,5] These clinical signs are present in up to 80% of the human cancer population;[6] incidence varies with the type of malignancy, and the sensitivity of the means of nutritional assessment.

Cancer cachexia is of great clinical significance because along with tumor type, stage of disease, and performance status, weight loss has been shown repeatedly to be an independent determinant of prognosis in the human cancer patient.[6-8] Severe debilitation and eventual death from malnourishment may result in affected individuals. Thus, the importance of nutrition in the patient with neoplastic disease cannot be overemphasized. The veterinary oncologist must be prepared to utilize the latest nutritional therapies, as well as the newest antibiotics, chemotherapeutics, and recombinant cytokines, in the treatment of the dog or cat with cancer.

This paper will first examine some of the proposed mechanisms of cancer cachexia. It will then discuss the ways in which nutrition may be used to benefit the veterinary cancer patient, focusing on current research being carried out at The Animal Medical Center. It will conclude by considering options for nutritional therapy in those animals with inadequate voluntary food intake.

Theoretical Considerations

Weight loss may occur in cancer patients for two basic reasons. Nutrient intake may be reduced due to physical presence of tumor, or the therapies used to treat it; alternatively or concurrently, there may be changes in metabolism secondary to the malignancy that result in excessive or inefficient energy utilization.[9-12] It is obvious that many tumors have a deleterious effect on host nutrient intake due simply to their location or size: oropharyngeal tumors decrease food intake by interfering with prehension, mastication, or swallowing; gastric masses frequently cause persistent vomiting; diffuse neoplastic infiltration of the small bowel may result in abnormal digestion or absorption of nutrients.[2,13] Equally apparent is the decrease in food intake which can occur secondary to various anticancer therapies. Cancer treatment in human patients can be associated with significant abnormalities in nutrient intake, digestion, and absorption due to the nausea, vomiting, mucositis, and diarrhea caused by radiation or chemotherapy.[14-16] Treatment related anorexia, caused by altered smell and taste perceptions,[17,18] or learned food aversions,[19] may also occur.

Of by far the greatest interest to scientists, however, have been the biochemical alterations associated with the tumor bearing state. Certain specific metabolic abnormalities play an incompletely defined role in the pathogenesis of cancer cachexia: it is hypothesized that they are associated with inefficient energy utilization by the host, which results in weight loss.[9-11] Many investigators have studied both human cancer patients[5,12,20-36] and rodents bearing implanted tumors[37-49] in great detail, in an attempt to further elucidate the mechanisms of cancer cachexia. A number of important principles have emerged from this work. First, tumor tissue is an "obligate glycolytic" tissue, incapable of significant fat oxidation or aerobic glycolysis: it must derive energy from anaerobic glycolysis.[11,20,41,50] Glucose consumed by tumor glycolysis is lost to the host and furthermore, host hepatocytes then resynthesize glucose from the lactate produced.[38,39,41,42] This version of the Cori cycle operates entirely at host energy expense. Second, many tumor cells are characterized by high metabolic activity and rapid growth, which must be supported by continuous input of amino acid nitrogen. Once again, the host is the source of these amino acids, with the tumor acting as a "nitrogen sink."[11,20,31,50] Finally, host hormones and cytokines are released in response to the presence of neoplastic disease, and these compounds can have both local and distant effects on host metabolic processes.[30,51-53] Inefficient energy utilization in wideranging host tissues may be the outcome.

Abnormalities in the intermediary metabolism of all three energy substrates —carbohydrate, protein, and lipid—have been demonstrated in tumor bearing subjects. Each of these changes are ultimately the result of the disruptions in host metabolism described above, and appear to be associated with processes resulting in host weight loss. Lean body mass and adipose stores are both affected.[1,2,5,12,20] Most numerous are alterations in carbohydrate metabolism, including hypo or hyperglycemia;[38-43] increased serum lactate concentrations;[28-31,38-40,42,43] altered serum insulin and glucagon concentrations;[25,26,42] an increased rate of whole body glucose turnover and disposal;[26,27,38-40,44] and, markedly increased rates of gluconeogenesis from lactate and amino acids.[30-33,38,39,41,42] Abnormalities in protein metabolism have also been demonstrated. These include altered serum amino acid concentrations;[30] increased whole body protein turnover;[30-34,45] decreased protein fractional synthetic rates in skeletal muscle;[30,31,33,45] and, increased protein fractional synthetic rates in liver.[34,45-47] Finally, evidence of altered lipid metabolism in the tumor bearing state has included hypertriglyceridemia;[35,43,48] an increased rate of host lipolysis;[36,48] increased serum concentrations of acetoacetate and beta-hydroxybutyrate;[43] increased rates of hepatic triacylglycerol and VLDL synthesis;[35,48] and, suppression of lipoprotein lipase activity.[49]

Theoretically, host energy expenditure should be altered in reflection of the changes in flux through the various metabolic pathways described above. Increased metabolic activity and futile cycling, such as that which may occur through the Cori cycle, should result in increased host energy expenditure. The ultimate result would be host weight loss. Accordingly, many investigators have measured host energy expenditure, primarily by indirect calorimetry, in an attempt to quantify the potential energy lost through these pathways.[21-24,37] Unfortunately, the results of these studies are variable and difficult to interpret. Energy expenditure seems to vary with tumor type and stage of disease. It is increased in some studies, apparently unchanged in others, and actually decreased in still others. Ongoing work in this area will hopefully clarify some of the current inconsistencies; however, one valid conclusion must be that significant variation exists in the manifestations of cancer cachexia between not only tumor types but also between individuals with the same disease.[21-24]

Recent studies by veterinary investigators have revealed that a number of metabolic perturbations similar to those described above are present in dogs with multicentric lymphoma. Canine lymphoma is an attractive model of cancer cachexia, because it is a naturally occurring disease in an outbred patient population. Some caution must be exercised in translating the results of these studies to cachectic human patients, because many of the dogs studied to date do not have significant weight loss. However, weight stable dogs with lymphoma have increased resting serum lactate concentrations;[54] increased lactate production in response to infusion of intravenous dextrose solutions;[54] hyperinsulinism and insulin resistance;[54] altered serum amino acid profiles;[55] increased serum concentrations of triglycerides, nonesterified fatty acids, and VLDL;[56] and, decreased serum concentrations of HDL.[56] Less is known regarding other tumor types, but preliminary results suggest that disruption of normal energy metabolism is likely in dogs and cats with a wide variety of neoplastic diseases, and may contribute to clinically significant weight loss.[57]

Specifically targeted nutritional intervention is intriguing as a possible way to maintain body condition in the severely stressed veterinary cancer patient. Provision of palatable, highly digestible, or energy dense diets could reverse some of the deleterious nutritional effects of neoplastic disease and cancer treatment. Potential benefits to the cancer patient include improved ability to tolerate aggressive antineoplastic therapy, enhanced quality of life, and even increased survival times.[4,10,58-60] Rations can also be designed to take advantage of the metabolic differences between tumor cells and normal host tissues: a diet high in fat and protein but relatively low in carbohydrates should selectively supply energy to the host and meet potentially increased protein requirements, while denying tumor cells the readily available carbohydrate required for continued growth.[58-60] Beneficial effects have been documented in human cancer patients fed such diets, including improved weight gain, improved energy and nitrogen balance, improved preservation of body adipose stores, and decreased glucose intolerance.[61,62]

Nutrition for the Small Animal Cancer Patient

Based on these theoretical considerations, an energy dense, highly palatable ration that is complete and balanced is recommended for use in small animal cancer patients. A commercial pet food produced by a reputable manufacturer is the safest and most convenient way to avoid nutritional deficiencies or excesses. Either canned or dry foods may be appropriate, although it is useful to remember that dry foods are often more energy dense than canned products. In general, the types of rations most likely to fit the outlined profile include "premium" canned or dry products for cats or dogs; canned or dry products designed for use during performance or stress (available products in this category are primarily canine); or, dry or canned kitten or puppy foods. However, before a final choice of ration is made, four factors should be critically evaluated:

1. *Carbohydrate content.* Diets that are high in carbohydrates should be avoided. Readily available sugars may supply additional energy to the tumor; furthermore, host utilization of carbohydrate calories may be inefficient due to insulin resistance.[26,54] As already discussed, high carbohydrate diets may also result in increased production of lactate and a host energy deficit. In this situation, the host not only loses consumed carbohydrate calories to the tumor, but host hepatocytes must also expend energy to resynthesize glucose from tumor-produced lactate.[11,20,38-42,50] Clinically significant acidosis may occur in rare cases.[28,29,63]

2. *Protein content.* The protein content of any ration fed to a cat or dog with cancer must be adequate to meet the potentially increased requirements which may be encountered when neoplastic disease is complicated by systemic conditions such as sepsis. As much as 30 to 50% may be required as protein;[64] this is especially true in feline patients, who have unusually high baseline protein requirements.[65] A diet specifically enriched with certain amino acids, such as glutamine, may also be of benefit. This amino acid has been shown to promote positive nitrogen balance in human and rodent studies.[66-68]

3. *Fat content.* Diets with a relatively high fat content are preferred for feeding small animals with neoplastic disease. High fat diets should preferentially provide energy to the patient.[58-60] High fat diets also tend to be higher in palatability and more energy dense than low fat diets, which may be advantageous in a debilitated cancer patient with decreased food intake.

4. *Vitamin and mineral content.* Adequate quantities of all necessary vitamins and minerals must be present in any ration intended for use in small animal cancer patients.[64] The requirements of many micronutrients can be increased during illness, and particular attention should be paid to these vitamins and minerals.[64,69] In addition, ample quantities of taurine, vitamin A, and the B vitamins must be provided in any diet fed to a feline patient.

Another way in which nutrition may be of benefit to the small animal cancer patient is as primary antineoplastic therapy. The potential antineoplastic effect of energy substrate manipulation has been studied in both human subjects and rodent models, and is currently being examined in the dog. It has been hypothesized that long term ingestion of high fat diets may not only contribute to improved patient energy balance and body condition, but may also "starve" neoplastic cells to death, because they are unable to use fats for energy.[58,60] Glycerol is another energy substrate which cannot be used by the cancer cell, and glycerol infusion during induced hypoglycemia has also been investigated as anticancer therapy.[70] Unfortunately to date, the reported beneficial effects of such treatments have been equivocal or modest at best;[60,70] however, study in the area continues. One point of theoretical concern is the possibility that the use of high fat diets during induction chemotherapy might sufficiently slow the growth rate of the cancer being treated, that response to chemotherapy would be suboptimal. Additional work will help to clarify the role of nutrition in this setting.

Current Studies

Study is currently underway at The Animal Medical Center to assess the utility of a standardized calorie dense, highly digestible diet in the maintenance of tumor-bearing dogs receiving radiation therapy. It is hypothesized that the test diet will be more effective in preventing loss of condition and maintaining lean body mass than the current nutritional standard of care. Subjects for this study have been obtained through the Radiation Therapy Unit of the Donaldson-Atwood Cancer Clinic. Any dog receiving definitive radiation therapy for neoplastic disease is eligible for entry. Potential study subjects are identified prior to initiation of radiation therapy, and all owners must sign an informed consent release.

Baseline testing for clinical and nutritional assessment is first carried out on each animal, to include the following parameters: nutritional history; body weight; mid-triceps skinfold thickness; complete blood count (including lymphocyte count); serum biochemical profile (including serum total protein and serum albumin concentration); serum transferrin, fibrinogen, and IGF-1 concentrations;[71] and, serum creatine kinase concentration.[72] After baseline testing is completed, dogs are stratified by disease category and performance score[73] and randomized to receive one of two nutritional treatments. Dogs in one group receive the test diet, while dogs in the other group continue to receive their regular diets, as fed by their owners. The average analysis of the test diet, as supplied by the manufacturer[a], is as follows:

Crude Protein	36.06%
Crude Fat	26.10%
Crude Fiber	2.10%
Moisture	7.50%
Metabolizable Energy	4,650 kcal/kg

Dogs that are randomized to receive the test diet are allowed a period of adaptation to the new diet of one to two weeks, to minimize gastrointestinal upset. Caloric intake necessary for maintenance of current body weight is calculated using the equation:[74]

$$MER = 132(BW_{kg})^{3/4}$$

---

[a] The Iams Company, Dayton, OH 45414

Some dogs are not consuming all of their maintenance calories exclusively in the form of the test diet until after their radiation therapy has been initiated. However, the adaptation period has not exceeded 7 days in any animal, and courses of radiation therapy as administered at the AMC generally last between 42 and 49 days.

Study subjects are monitored closely during the course of radiation therapy. All owners are asked to fill out and return daily diet history forms. These forms record daily food intake, appetite, and presence or absence of vomiting or diarrhea. All dogs are weighed three times weekly, prior to each radiation treatment. The following tests are repeated on a weekly basis during the course of radiation therapy: mid-triceps skinfold thickness; complete blood count; serum biochemical profile; serum transferrin, fibrinogen, and IGF-1 concentrations; and, serum creatine kinase concentration.

Statistical analysis will be performed to assess potential differences between the two treatment groups. Individual parameters will be compared between the two treatment groups at each time point (i.e., baseline, week 1, week 2, etc.) using a student's t-test or Mann Whitney test. A p value of less than 0.05 will be considered significant. Regression analysis will be utilized to examine correlations between the various assessment parameters and treatment group.

Initiation of Nutritional Support

It is vital to recognize that many of the veterinary cancer patients who would most benefit from the types of dietary therapy outlined above are unwilling or unable to eat for themselves, and have inadequate voluntary food intake. Every effort should be made to encourage animals to eat on their own, including hand feeding of highly palatable foods. Provision of small, frequent meals may also improve food intake in those animals with inconsistent appetites. However, despite these measures caloric intake will still be marginal in many patients. Feeding tubes or catheters should be placed without hesitation in animals with persistent anorexia, to ensure maintenance of optimal nutrient intake. Regardless of the underlying disease or the patient characteristics, there are 5 basic steps involved in the initiation of nutritional support.[64] They are:

1. *Calculation of energy requirement.* The following equations will provide an initial *estimate* of the patient's resting energy requirement (RER) in kilocalories per day:[75]

$$RER = 70 + 30 \, (BW_{kg}) \quad \text{(for patients over 2 kg in weight)}$$
$$RER = 70(BW_{kg})^{3/4} \quad \text{(for all patients)}$$

*(It should be noted that the energy requirements of both healthy and diseased small animal patients are controversial and incompletely defined.[76,77] Studies are being carried out by several investigators that should ultimately help to resolve current debate.)

2. *Illness factor.* The next step is to adjust the RER as calculated above, based on the patient's underlying disease process. The RER is multiplied by an illness factor (IF), which in turn yields the total energy requirement (TER) in kilocalories per day:

$$TER = RER \times IF$$

The appropriate illness factor will depend on the underlying disease process; animals who are relatively healthy will have low illness factors, while those who are critically ill will have much higher illness factors. Generally, illness factors range from 1.25 to 2.0 times the estimated RER in canine cancer patients, and 1.25 to 1.5 times the RER in feline cancer patients. Tables of suggested illness factors have been published.[64,75,78,79] It is important to recognize that overly aggressive supportive alimentation can have deleterious effects, especially in the cat; cholestasis and hepatic lipidosis have been reported.[80]

3. *Proportion protein, fat, and carbohydrate calories.* The optimal distribution of protein, fat, and carbohydrate calories must next be determined. As described above, a formula that is high in fat and low in carbohydrate, but also meets the patient's protein requirements, is recommended for patients with neoplastic disease. Up to 50 or 60% of the total energy requirements can probably be safely met with fat calories in a majority of small animal cancer patients,[74,81] although a reasonable period of gastrointestinal adaptation is certainly required. Protein calories may provide up to 30 to 50% of total calories,[64] especially in feline cancer patients. Any remaining calories can be provided as carbohydrate, but for the reasons given above, readily available sugars should be avoided. Before a final decision on caloric distribution is made, concurrent or underlying disease processes that may affect the patient's ability to tolerate feeding should be considered; i.e., renal or hepatic dysfunction, or significant hyperlipidemia.

4. *Determine adequacy of micronutrients.* The easiest way to ensure that all micronutrient requirements will be met is to use a well-balanced commercial pet food or tube feeding formula that has undergone formalized feed trial testing. A wide variety of human tube feeding formulas are also available, but most of these are inadequate for long term use in cats and dogs.[64] They tend to be very high in carbohydrate calories, relatively low in protein and fat, and deficient in B vitamins and taurine.

5. *Choose a route of delivery.* Supportive alimentation can be delivered parenterally (intravenously) or enterally (into the intestinal tract). The route that is chosen for a particular patient will depend on the underlying disease present, but enteral nutrition is almost always preferred.

A number of reviews describing enteral nutrition in veterinary patients have been published.[64,82-87] With few exceptions, enteral feeding will be superior to parenteral feeding. Enteral nutrition prevents intestinal mucosal atrophy, helps

Enteral Nutrition

prevent bacterial translocation, is cheaper and technically less complex, and has fewer potential complications. Potential disadvantages of enteral nutrition include extended periods of transition, and contraindication in situations where the gastrointestinal tract is nonfunctional.

A number of different types of feeding tubes are available for delivery of enteral nutrition in small animal patients. Nasoesophageal tubes are indicated for relatively short term support in patients who are anorexic but have normal gastrointestinal function, in patients who have oropharyngeal disease preventing normal food intake, and in patients who are too critically ill to tolerate the general anesthesia required for placement of most other types of feeding tubes. Nasoesophageal tubes are contraindicated in those animals with esophageal disease (especially megaesophagus and esophageal stricture), and in situations where gastric dysfunction is significant. Gastrostomy tubes are a better choice for those patients who will be requiring long term nutritional support, because they can often be left in place indefinitely. They are useful in animals who are anorexic but have normal gastrointestinal tract function, and in patients with oropharyngeal disease. Gastrostomy tubes may also be used to feed cats and dogs with esophageal disease, although some care must still be exercised to avoid aspiration of liquid tube feeding formulas in those individuals with megaesophagus.[87]

Gastrostomy tube placement requires general anesthesia, so these tubes are contraindicated in patients who cannot tolerate anesthesia. They are also contraindicated in patients with significant gastric dysfunction, for instance persistent vomiting, or a gastric outflow obstruction. Jejunostomy tubes are generally superior in such cases, because the entire upper gastrointestinal tract, including the stomach and pancreas, can be bypassed. However, disadvantages of jejunostomy feeding include the necessity for general anesthesia and exploratory laparotomy for tube placement, and the close supervision required during feeding. Constant rate infusion of feeding formula rather than bolus feeding techniques must be utilized with jejunostomy tubes.

The ideal tube feeding formula for canine and feline cancer patients will have the same characteristics as the ideal commercial ration: high in fat, ample protein calories, relatively restricted simple carbohydrates, and complete and balanced with regard to micronutrients. A very calorie dense formula (i.e., high fat) will also minimize the volume that must be fed through the tube. Liquid commercial veterinary products designed specifically for tube feeding are generally the best choices for nasoesophageal and jejunostomy tubes, while blenderized canned cat or dog food may be fed through gastrostomy tubes. Initial bolus feeding should be administered every 2 hours, using a small volume of dilute formula. If this is well tolerated, the concentration and volume can gradually be increased, until the patient is finally receiving the full target volume in 4 to 6 daily feedings. This process usually takes at least 5 to 7 days, and in some patients longer than this. As previously stated, jejunostomy tubes should not be used for bolus feeding.

Although tube feeding is generally extremely well tolerated in small animal patients, some complications may be encountered. Tube occlusion is frustrating, and occurs most commonly with small bore tubes such as nasoesophageal and jejunostomy tubes. When tubes do become clogged, they can sometimes be cleared by allowing warm water to sit in the tube for 10 to 15 minutes, and then attempting to flush the tube again. Another fairly common complication of tube feeding is vomiting. Intermittent vomiting is not necessarily a contraindication to tube feeding, and is usually manageable by one or a combination of the following methods: diluting the feeding formula with water, warming the feeding formula to room temperature, feeding smaller volumes more frequently, or changing to a lower fat formulation (to promote gastric emptying). If all these fail, metoclopramide may be administered at 0.2 to 0.4 mg/kg, 2 to 4 times per day. Unrelenting vomiting, however, should prompt discontinuation of tube feeding. Aspiration may result, especially in weak, critically ill patients.

Diarrhea probably develops in most patients at some point during tube feeding. It is seem most commonly immediately after initiation of feeding. In most cases this problem is not severe and will resolve untreated after 2 to 4 days, as the intestinal tract adapts to the tube feeding formula. If it does not, diluting the formula with water is sometimes helpful, as some of the diarrhea associated with tube feeding can be due to hyperosmolarity of tube feeding solutions. The clinician must also recognize that concentrated tube feeding formulas may also contribute to azotemia and hyperglycemia in some patients. Animals receiving tube feedings are force fed a diet high in solutes such as peptides and carbohydrates, yet often have negligible voluntary water intake. Careful attention must always be paid to fluid balance as well as nutrient intake during tube feeding.

The final potential complications of tube feeding that must always be kept in mind are the acute development of life-threatening hypokalemia or hypophosphatemia. These electrolyte abnormalities will usually occur within the first 24 to 72 hours of the initiation of feeding, and are part of the "refeeding syndrome."[88,89] They are probably the result of rapid potassium and phosphate movement into the intracellular space, and must be treated with aggressive intravenous supplementation.

Parenteral nutrition is the only option for nutritional support in those small animal cancer patients who cannot tolerate enteral feeding.[75,78,80,83,90,91] The primary indication for parenteral nutrition is a nonfunctional intestinal tract, such as may occur with intractable vomiting, gastrointestinal obstruction, or severe ileus. Parenteral nutrition is also considered primary therapy for certain types of inflammatory gastrointestinal lesions, such as pancreatitis or severe inflammatory colitis. Coma is another potential indication for parenteral nutrition — the risk of aspiration is significantly decreased when intravenous feeding is used to support such patients. However, regardless of the underlying disease being treated, parenteral nutrition is usually not considered unless a veterinary patient is expected to require support for at least 3 to 5 days, because of its cost and complexity.

Parenteral Nutrition

The primary advantage of parenteral nutrition is that it permits complete rest of the intestinal tract. It can also be utilized in patients who are too critically ill to tolerate general anesthesia for placement of a feeding tube. The major disadvantages of parenteral nutrition are the development of significant intestinal mucosal atrophy after long term use; the necessity for specialized equipment, products, and care; and, increased expense. In addition, there is an increased potential for complications with parenteral nutrition, when compared to enteral feeding. Possible complications include an increased risk of sepsis, mechanical complications such as catheter disconnection and twisted intravenous lines, and biochemical complications such as hyperglycemia and hyperlipidemia, hypokalemia and hypophosphatemia, and increased serum liver enzymes or azotemia.[80,90,91]

The parenteral nutrition prescription for a dog or cat with cancer should be designed to follow the same principles as the enteral diets described above. The dextrose content should be relatively restricted, providing only 30 to 40% of nonprotein calories. The fat content should be relatively increased, providing 60 to 70% of nonprotein calories. Sufficient protein must be supplied to meet requirements, and this level is estimated to be 4 to 6 g/kg/day in canine cancer patients, and 6 g/kg/day in feline cancer patients.[75,78] If parenteral nutrition is continued for longer than 5 to 7 days, appropriate vitamin and mineral supplements should be administered to ensure a complete and balanced nutrient intake.

References

1. Costa G. Cachexia, the metabolic component of neoplastic disease. *Cancer Res* 1977; 37:2327-2335.

2. Theologides A. Cancer cachexia. *Cancer* 1979; 43:2004-2012.

3. Crow SE, Oliver J. Cancer cachexia. *Comp Cont Ed for Pract Vet* 1981; 3:681-686.

4. Ogilvie GK. Metabolic alterations and nutritional therapy for the veterinary cancer patient. In: Withrow SJ, MacEwen EG eds. *Small Animal Clinical Oncology, 2nd ed.* Philadelphia: WB Saunders Company. 1996:117-128.

5. Brennan MF. Uncomplicated starvation versus cancer cachexia. *Cancer Res* 1977; 37:2359-2364.

6. DeWys WD. Weight loss and nutritional abnormalities in cancer patients: incidence, severity and significance. *Clinics in Oncology* 1986; 5:251-261.

7. DeWys WD et al. Prognostic effect of weight loss prior to chemotherapy in cancer patients. *Am J Med* 1980; 69:491-497.

8. Hickman DM et al. Serum albumin and body weight as predictors of postoperative course in colorectal cancer. *JPEN* 1980; 4:314-316.

9. Theologides A. The anorexia-cachexia syndrome: a new hypothesis. *Ann NY Acad Sci* 1974; 230:14-22.

10. Brennan MF. Total parenteral nutrition in the cancer patient. *N Engl J Med* 1981; 305:375-382.

11. DeWys WD. Pathophysiology of cancer cachexia: current understanding and areas for future research. *Cancer Res* 1982; 42(Suppl):721s-726s.

12. Kern KA, Norton JA. Cancer cachexia. *JPEN* 1988; 12:286-298.

13. Lawrence W. Effects of cancer on nutrition. *Cancer* 1979; 43:2020-2029.

14. Kokal WA. The impact of antitumor therapy on nutrition. *Cancer* 1985; 55:273-278.

15. Brennan MF. Metabolic response to surgery in the cancer patient: consequences of aggressive multimodality therapy. *Cancer* 1979; 43:2053-2064.

16. Sloan GM, Maher M, Brennan MF. Nutritional effects of surgery, radiation therapy, and adjuvant chemotherapy for soft tissue sarcomas. *Am J Clin Nutr* 1981; 34:1094-1102.

17. Bernstein IL. Etiology of anorexia in cancer. *Cancer* 1986; 58:1881-1886.

18. Trant AS, Serin J, Douglass HO. Is taste related to anorexia in cancer patients? *Am J Clin Nutr* 1982; 36:45-58.

19. Mattes RD, Arnold C, Boraas M. Learned food aversions among cancer chemotherapy patients: incidence, nature and clinical implications. *Cancer* 1987; 60:2576-2580.

20. Heber D, et al. Pathophysiology of malnutrition in the adult cancer patient. *Cancer* 1986; 58:1867-1873.

21. Lerebours E, et al. Change in energy and protein status during chemotherapy in patients with acute leukemia. *Cancer* 1988; 61:2412-2417.

22. Arbeit JM, et al. Resting energy expenditure in controls and cancer patients with localized and diffuse disease. *Ann Surg* 1984;199:292-298.

23. Dempsey DT, et al. Energy expenditure in malnourished gastrointestinal cancer patients. *Cancer* 1984; 53:1265-1273.

24. Dempsey DT, et al. Energy expenditure in malnourished patients with colorectal cancer. *Arch Surg* 1986; 121:789-795.

25. Schein PS, et al. Cachexia of malignancy: potential role of insulin in nutritional management. *Cancer* 1979; 43:2070-2076.

26. Norton JA, et al. Glucose intolerance in sarcoma patients. *Cancer* 1984; 54:3022-3027.

27. Holroyde CP, et al. Glucose metabolism in cachectic patients with colorectal cancer. *Cancer Res* 1984; 44:5910-5913.

28. Fields ALA, Wolman SL, Halperin ML. Chronic lactic acidosis in a patient with cancer: therapy and metabolic consequences. *Cancer* 1981; 47:2026-2029.

29. Block JB. Lactic acidosis in malignancy and observations on its possible pathogenesis. *Ann NY Acad Sci* 1974; 230:94-102.

30. Burt ME, et al. Peripheral tissue metabolism in cancer-bearing man. *Ann Surg* 1983; 198:685-691.

31. Norton JA, Burt ME, Brennan MF. In vivo utilization of substrate by human sarcoma-bearing limbs. *Cancer* 1980; 45:2934-2939.

32. Eden E, et al. Whole-body tyrosine flux in relation to energy expenditure in weight-losing cancer patients. *Metabolism* 1984; 33:1020-1027.

33. Norton JA, Stein TP, Brennan MF. Whole body protein synthesis and turnover in normal man and malnourished patients with and without known cancer. *Ann Surg* 1981; 194:123-128.

34. Lundholm K, Karlberg I, Schersten T. Albumin and hepatic protein synthesis in patients with early cancer. *Cancer* 1980; 46:71-76.

35. Alexopoulos CG, Blatsios B, Avgerinos A. Serum lipids and lipoprotein disorders in cancer patients. *Cancer* 1987; 60:3065-3070.

36. Eden E, et al. Glycerol dynamics in weight-losing cancer patients. *Surgery* 1985; 97:176-184.

37. Popp MB, Brennan MF, Morrison SD. Resting and activity energy expenditure during total parenteral nutrition in rats with methylcholanthrene-induced sarcoma. *Cancer* 1982; 49:1212-1220.

38. Burt ME, et al. Metabolic alterations in a noncachectic animal tumor system. *Cancer* 1981; 47:2138-2146.

39. Singh J, Grigor MR, Thompson MP. Glucose homeostasis in rats bearing a transplantable sarcoma. *Cancer Res* 1980; 40:1699-1706.

40. Arbeit JM, et al. Glucose metabolism and the percentage of glucose derived from alanine: non-tumor-bearing rats. *Cancer Res* 1982; 42:4936-4942.

41. Roh MS, et al. Gluconeogenesis in tumor-influenced hepatocytes. *Surgery* 1984; 96:427-433.

42. Inculet RI, et al. Gluconeogenesis in the tumor-influenced rat hepatocyte: importance of tumor burden, lactate, insulin and glucagon. *J Natl Cancer Inst* 1987; 79:1039-1046.

43. Alexander HR, et al. Substrate alterations in a sarcoma-bearing rat model: effect of tumor growth and resection. *J Surg Res* 1990; 48:471-475.

44. Lowry SF, et al. Glucose disposal and gluconeogenesis from alanine in tumor-bearing Fischer 344 rats. *J Natl Cancer Inst* 1981; 66:653-658.

45. Norton JA, et al. The influence of tumor-bearing on protein metabolism in the rat. *J Surg Res* 1981; 30:456-462.

46. Warren RS, Jeevanandam M, Brennan MF. Protein synthesis in the tumor-influenced hepatocyte. *Surgery* 1985; 98:275-281.

47. Warren RS, Jeevanandam M, Brennan MF. Comparison of hepatic protein synthesis in vivo versus in vitro in the tumor-bearing rat. *J Surg Res* 1987; 42:43-50.

48. Younes RN, et al. Lipid kinetic alteration in tumor-bearing rats: reversal by tumor excision. *J Surg Res* 1990; 48:324-328.

49. Noguchi Y, et al. Tumor-induced alteration in tissue lipoprotein lipase activity and mRNA levels. *Cancer Res* 1991; 51:863-869.

50. Wesdorp RIC. Role of abnormal metabolism in the aetiology of cancer cachexia. *Clinics in Oncology* 1986; 5:307-316.

51. Beutler B, et al. Identity of tumour necrosis factor and the macrophage secreted factor cachectin. *Nature* 1985; 316:552-554.

52. Oliff A, et al. Tumors secreting human TNF/cachectin induce cachexia in mice. *Cell* 1987; 50:555-563.

53. Norton JA, et al. Parabiotic transfer of cancer anorexia/cachexia in male rats. *Cancer Res* 1985; 45:5547-5552.

54. Vail DM, et al. Alterations in carbohydrate metabolism in canine lymphoma. *J Vet Int Med* 1990; 4:8-11.

55. Ogilvie GK, et al. Alterations in fat and protein metabolism in dogs with cancer. *Proc 8th Annual Vet Cancer Soc* 1988:31.

56. Ogilvie GK, et al. Alterations in lipoprotein profiles in dogs with lymphoma. *J Vet Int Med* 1994; 8:62-66.

57. Noonan M, Mauldin GE, Mauldin GN. Serum lactate concentrations in 120 hospitalized dogs. *Proc 13th Annual Vet Cancer Soc* 1993:130.

58. Rossi-Fanelli F, Cascino A, Muscaritoli M. Abnormal substrate metabolism and nutritional strategies in cancer management. *JPEN* 1991; 15:680-683.

59. Ogilvie GK, Vail DM. Nutrition and cancer: recent developments. *Vet Clin N Amer Small Anim Pract* 1990; 20:969-985.

60. Ogilvie GK, et al. Energy expenditure in dogs with lymphoma fed two specialized diets. *Cancer* 1993; 71:3146-3152.

61. Dempsey DT, Mullen JL. Macronutrient requirements in the malnourished cancer patient. *Ann Surg* 1985; 55:290-294.

62. Shein PS, et al. The oxidation of body fuel stores in cancer patients. *Ann Surg* 1986; 204:637-642.

63. Goodgame JT, Pizzo P, Brennan MF. Iatrogenic lactic acidosis. *Cancer* 1978; 42:800-803.

64. Donoghue S. Nutritional support of hospitalized patients. *Vet Clin N Amer Small Anim Pract* 1989; 19:475-495.

65. Roger QR, Morris JG. Protein and amino acid nutrition of the cat. *Amer Anim Hosp Proc* 1983:333-336.

66. Souba WW, et al. Interorgan glutamine metabolism in the tumor-bearing rat. *J Surg Res* 1988; 44:720-726.

67. Smith RJ. Glutamine metabolism and its physiologic importance. *JPEN* 1990; 14:40s-44s.

68. Souba WW, et al. The role of glutamine in maintaining a healthy gut and supporting the metabolic response to injury and infection. *J Surg Res* 1990; 48:383-391.

69. Inculet RI, et al. Water-soluble vitamins in cancer patients on parenteral nutrition: a prospective study. *JPEN* 1987; 11:243-249.

70. Burt ME, et al. Hypoglycemia with glycerol infusion as antineoplastic therapy: a hypothesis. *Surgery* 1985; 97:231-233.

71. Jeejeebhoy KN. Assessment of nutritional status. In: Rombeau JL, Caldwell MD eds. *Enteral and Tube Feeding, 2nd ed.* Philadelphia: WB Saunders Company 1990:118-126.

72. Fascetti A, Mauldin GE, Mauldin GN. Serum creatine kinase concentrations in anorectic cats. *J Vet Int Med*, in press.

73. Burk RL, Mauldin GN. Use of a performance scale in small animal radiation therapy. *Vet Radiol* 1992; 33:388-391.

74. National Research Council. *Nutrient Requirements of Dogs.* Washington: National Academy Press, 1985.

75. Lippert AC, Armstrong PJ. Parenteral nutritional support. In: Kirk RW, ed. *Current Veterinary Therapy* X. Philadelphia: WB Saunders Company 1989:25-30.

76. Kronfeld DS. Protein and energy estimates for hospitalized dogs and cats. *Purina International Nutrition Symposium Proceedings* 1991:5-11.

77. Walters LM, et al. Repeatability of energy expenditure measurements in normal dogs by indirect calorimetry. *Am J Vet Res* 1993; 54:1881-1885.

78. Remillard RL, Thatcher CD. Parenteral nutritional support in the small animal patient. *Vet Clin N Amer* 1989; 19:1287-1306.

79. Lewis LD, Morris ML, Hand MS. Anorexia, inanition and critical care nutrition. In: *Small Animal Clinical Nutrition, 3rd ed.* Topeka: Mark Morris Associates 1987; 5-1:5-43.

80. Lippert AC, et al. Total parenteral nutrition in clinically normal cats. *J Am Vet Med Assoc* 1989; 194:669-676.

81. National Research Council. *Nutrient Requirements of Cats.* Washington: National Academy Press, 1986.

82. Wheeler SL, McGuire BH. Enteral nutritional support. In: Kirk RW, ed. *Current Veterinary Therapy* X. Philadelphia: WB Saunders Company 1989:30-37.

83. Lippert AC. Enteral and parenteral nutritional support in dogs and cats with gastrointestinal disease. *Sem Vet Med and Surg* 1989; 4:232-240.

84. Crowe DT. Enteral nutrition for critically ill or injured patients: part I. *Comp Cont Ed for Pract Vet* 1986; 8:603-612.

85. Crowe DT. Enteral nutrition for critically ill or injured patients: part II. *Comp Cont Ed for Pract Vet* 1986; 8:719-732.

86. Crowe DT. Enteral nutrition for critically ill or injured patients: part III. *Comp Cont Ed for Pract Vet* 1986; 8:826-838.

87. Armstrong PJ, Hardie EM. Percutaneous endoscopic gastrostomy: a retrospective study of 54 clinical cases in dogs and cats. *J Vet Int Med* 1990; 4:202-206.

88. Silvis SE, Paragas PV. Fatal hyperalimentation syndrome: animal studies. *J Lab Clin Med* 1971; 78:918-930.

89. Justin RB, Hohenhaus AE. Hypophosphatemia associated with enteral alimentation in cats. *J Vet Int Med* 1995; 9:228-233.

90. Mauldin GE. Protein requirements in normal dogs receiving total parenteral nutrition. Master's thesis, Cornell University, 1995.

91. Lippert AC, Fulton RB, Parr AM. A retrospective study of the use of total parenteral nutrition in dogs and cats. *J Vet Int Med* 1993; 7:52-64.

Skin & Hair Coat

Review of Omega-3 Fatty Acids and Dietary Influences on Tissue Concentrations

Gregory A. Reinhart, PhD
Director of Strategic Research, Research and Development
The Iams Company, Lewisburg, Ohio

Introduction

Fatty acid supplements have been used to manage signs of skin inflammation in companion animals for a number of years. Recently, the use of a specific class of these nutrients, the omega-3 fatty acids, has received increased attention. The incorporation of optimal proportions of omega-6 and omega-3 fatty acids into the diet have preventive and therapeutic benefits to pets with certain inflammatory conditions. An understanding of the metabolism of omega-3 fatty acids within the body and the effects of feeding a diet containing an adjusted fatty acid profile is essential when considering the therapeutic or preventative use of dietary fatty acids.

Classification of Polyunsaturated Fatty Acids

Fatty acids are carboxylic acids, varying in length from 2 to 22 carbon chains. The final carbon in the chain opposite the carboxyl group is a methyl group (CH3) and is called the "omega" carbon. This is designated as either the Greek letter (ω) or as "n". Polyunsaturated fatty acids are classified according to the location and number of double bonds that they contain. The omega-3 fatty acids contain a double bond at the third carbon atom from the methyl end of the molecule, while the omega-6 fatty acids contain their first double bond at the 6th carbon atom from the methyl end (*Figure 1*). In addition, the direction of the bend at a double bond in the carbon chain can be either *cis* or *trans*. Cis fatty acids are the form that occur naturally.

Different Types of Fatty Acids

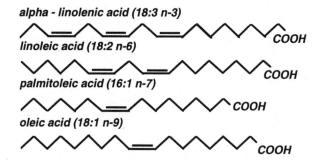

alpha - linolenic acid (18:3 n-3)

COOH

linoleic acid (18:2 n-6)

COOH

palmitoleic acid (16:1 n-7)

COOH

oleic acid (18:1 n-9)

COOH

Figure 1. Adapted from: Reinhart GA. New concepts in fiber nutrition and gastrointestinal disease. *New concepts in nutritional management of dogs and cats: fatty acids and dietary fiber.* TNAVC; 1995:11-15.

Conventional nomenclature for fatty acids designates chain length, the number of double bonds in the molecule, and the location of the first double bond. For example, alpha-linolenic acid is represented as **18:3n-3**. This fatty acid contains 18 carbons with three double bonds, and the first double bond occurs at the third carbon atom from the omega end. An example of an omega-6 fatty acid is arachidonic acid (**20:5n-6**) (*Table 1*). The incorporation of fatty acids into cell membranes and their availability for synthesis of new compounds are affected by chain length, degree of saturation, and position of the first double bond.

Palmitic acid (C16)
$CH_3(CH_2)_{14}COOH$

Stearic acid (C18)
$CH_3(CH_2)_{16}COOH$

Oleic acid (C18:1n-9)
$CH_3(CH_2)_7CH=CH(CH_2)_7COOH$

Linoleic acid (C18:2n-6)
$CH_3(CH_2)_4CH=CHCH_2CH=CH(CH_2)_7COOH$

α-Linolenic acid (C18:3n-3)
$CH_3CH_2CH=CHCH_2CH=CHCH_2CH=CH(CH_2)_7COOH$

γ-Linolenic acid (C18:3n-6)
$CH_3(CH_2)_4CH=CHCH_2CH=CHCH_2CH=CH(CH_2)_4COOH$

Arachidonic acid (C20:4n-6)
$CH_3(CH_2)_4CH=CHCH_2CH=CHCH_2CH=CHCH_2CH=CH(CH_2)_3COOH$

Eicosapentaenoic acid (C20:5n-3)
$CH_3CH_2CH=CHCH_2CH=CHCH_2CH=CHCH_2CH=CHCH_2CH=CH(CH_2)_2COOH$

Docosahexaenoic acid (C22:6n-3)
$CH_3CH_2CH=CHCH_2CH=CHCH_2CH=CHCH_2CH=CHCH_2CH=CHCH_2CH=CH(CH_2)_2COOH$

Table 1. Common naturally occurring fatty acids (common name and structural formula). Adapted from: Carey DP. Introduction: update on the role of fatty acids in veterinary medicine. *Dietary fatty acid supplementation: a new treatment modality.* ACVIM 13th Annual Veterinary Medical Forum; 1995:1-10.

Animals cannot convert one type of fatty acid into another, so certain omega-3 and omega-6 fatty acids must be provided in the diet. However, animals are capable of elongating and desaturating fatty acids towards the carboxyl end of the molecule. For example, the omega-6 fatty acid linoleic acid (18:2n-6), is metabolized through desaturation and elongation to produce arachidonic acid (20:4n-6). The omega-3 fatty acid, alpha-linolenic acid (18:3n-3) is desaturated and elongated to produce eicosapentaenoic acid (20:5n-3). Within the body, linoleic acid and alpha-linolenic acid compete for the same delta-6 desaturase enzymes. As a result, the proportions of omega-6 and omega-3 fatty acids that are available to this enzyme system directly affect the quantity and proportions of arachidonic and eicosapentaenoic acid that are produced.

Essential Fatty Acids (EFAs)

Linoleic acid (18:2n-6) is the only fatty acid that has been proven to be essential in the diet of the dog. The dog synthesizes arachidonic acid from linoleic acid through elongation and desaturation. However, the cat lacks adequate desaturase activity for this process, and so must receive both linoleic acid and arachidonic acid in the diet. Although there is not conclusive evidence available, it is thought that dogs may also have a dietary requirement for alpha-linolenic acid (18:3n-3). It is possible that several other fatty acids may be required in the dog's diet, and may have functions related to the inflammatory process, renal blood flow, nervous system functioning, coronary heart disease, atherosclerosis, and platelet aggregation.

There are numerous dietary sources of omega-6 and omega-3 fatty acids. Safflower and corn oil contain high amounts of the essential fatty acid, linoleic acid (18:2n-6), while cold water fish oils and fish meals contain high levels of omega-3 fatty acids. Flax is a terrestrial plant that is an enriched source of alpha-linolenic acid (18:3n-3). Soy and canola oils contain both alpha-linolenic acid and omega-6 fatty acids. Oils containing high amounts of monounsaturated fats such as olive oil, and saturated animal fats are not enriched in either omega-3 or omega-6 fatty acids.

Eicosanoids are polyunsaturated metabolites of fatty acids which include the prostaglandins, thromboxanes, leukotrienes, and hydroxylated eicosatetraenoic acids. They function as local hormones in the regulation of normal physiology and are also important mediators of inflammation. These compounds are not stored in the body, but are synthesized as needed from polyunsaturated fatty acids that are present in membrane phospholipids. When an inflammatory response is triggered, membrane phospholipases are activated. The injured cells release 20-carbon fatty acids from their membrane phospholipids, which are then metabolized to produce various types of eicosanoids.

Fatty Acids and the Production of Inflammatory Mediators

The type of eicosanoid that is synthesized is dependent upon the type of fatty acid that is released from the cell membrane. The omega-6 fatty acids, such as arachidonic acid, are acted on by the enzymes cyclooxygenase and lipoxygenase to produce the 2-series prostaglandins and thromboxanes and the 4-series leukotrienes (*Figure 2*). In contrast, omega-3 fatty acids, such as eicosapentaenoic acid, are metabolized primarily by lipoxygenase into the 3-series prostaglandins and thromboxanes and 5-series leukotrienes. Eicosanoids that are derived from arachidonic acid are pro-inflammatory, immunosuppressive and pro-aggregatory, and act as potent mediators of inflammation in type I hypersensitivity reactions.[1,2] Eicosanoids that are derived from eicosapentaenoic acid (20:5n-3) are less inflammatory, vasodilatory, anti-aggregatory, and are not immunosuppressive (*Figure 3*). For example, LTB_5, derived from omega-3 fatty acids, is only one tenth as potent as omega-6-derived LTB_4 in neutrophil chemotaxis.[1,3] The end result of these differences is that as the proportion of omega-3 fatty acids that are released from cell membranes increases, the inflammatory potential in the animal concomitantly decreases.

Several factors affect the metabolic pathways that are utilized during an inflammatory response. These include the fatty acid composition of the cell membrane, tissue and individual levels of the two enzymes (cyclooxygenase and lipoxygenase), and the presence or absence of inhibitor substances such as corticosteroids or non-steroidal anti-inflammatory agents. The relationship between LTB_4 and LTB_5 within the body illustrate the interaction between omega-6 and omega-3 membrane fatty acids and their effects upon the inflammatory process. The stimulation of LTB_4 receptors on neutrophils is a primary step in the cyclic cascade of neutrophil recruitment, chemotaxis, degranulation, further leukotriene synthesis, and perpetuation of the inflammatory response. The presence of newly formed LTB_5, derived from omega-3 fatty acids in membranes, serves to competitively inhibit LTB_4-induced neutrophil activation, and diminishes LTB_4-mediated allergic or inflammatory conditions.[4] A second way in which the omega-3 fatty acids may decrease the pro-inflammatory effects of LTB_4 is through inhibition of LTB_4 synthesis. Eicosapentaenoic acid is metabolized to LTB_5 by one of the same enzymes as arachidonic acid (leukotriene A hydrolase). Therefore, the presence of increased amounts of eicosapentaenoic acid competitively inhibits the production of LTB_4. There is also evidence that LTB_5 may be a weak inhibitor of a second enzyme, 5-lipoxygenase.[5]

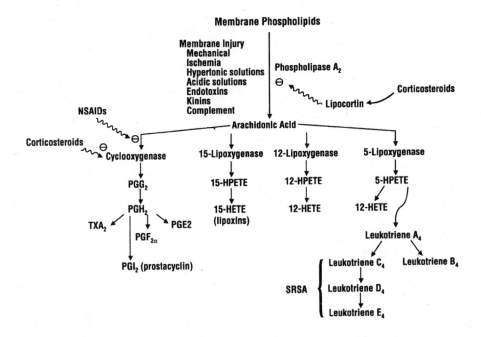

Figure 2. Arachidonic acid cascade. Adapted from: Carey DP. Introduction: update on the role of fatty acids in veterinary medicine. *Dietary fatty acid supplementation: a new treatment modality*. ACVIM 13th Annual Veterinary Medical Forum; 1995:1-10

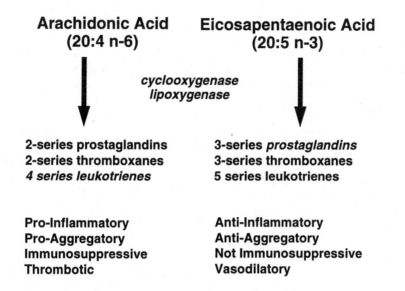

**Arachidonic Acid
(20:4 n-6)**

**Eicosapentaenoic Acid
(20:5 n-3)**

*cyclooxygenase
lipoxygenase*

2-series prostaglandins
2-series thromboxanes
4 series leukotrienes

3-series *prostaglandins*
3-series thromboxanes
5 series leukotrienes

Pro-Inflammatory
Pro-Aggregatory
Immunosuppressive
Thrombotic

Anti-Inflammatory
Anti-Aggregatory
Not Immunosuppressive
Vasodilatory

Figure 3. Adapted from: Reinhart GA. New concepts in fiber nutrition and gastrointestinal disease. *New concepts in nutritional management of dogs and cats: fatty acids and dietary fiber.* TNAVC; 1995:11-15.

The manipulation of the dietary ratio of omega-6 to omega-3 fatty acids has the potential to change tissue concentrations of these fatty acids and to ultimately affect the inflammatory response. Studies have shown that feeding diets that are enriched in omega-3 fatty acids results in their incorporation into tissue and cell membranes with a corresponding decrease in concentrations of omega-6 fatty acids.[6,7] For example, supplementation of dogs' diets with fish oil-derived omega-3 fatty acids resulted in increased proportions of omega-3 fatty acids in cell membrane phospholipids of the skin and neutrophils.[8] Another study reported that dogs fed diets containing soy oil had higher serum and cutaneous levels of oleic acid and arachidonic acid than dogs fed diets containing poultry fat.[9]

Effect of Dietary Omega-3 Fatty Acids on Tissue Concentrations

Results of research in humans and in dogs also indicates that the entire fatty acid profile of the diet is important. Specifically, fatty acid therapy appears to be most successful in suppressing pro-inflammatory LTB_4 and producing increased amounts of the less inflammatory LTB_5 when the ratio of dietary omega-6 to omega-3 fatty acids is controlled.[10,11] This effect occurs because the omega-6 and omega-3 fatty acids compete for the same enzyme systems. As a result, the ratio between these two types of fatty acids determines the relative proportions of the respective omega-6 (pro-inflammatory) and omega-3 (less inflammatory) metabolites that are produced.

The optimal balance of omega-6 to omega-3 fatty acids in the diets of dogs is between 5:1 and 10:1. This ratio was determined from a study with adult beagles in which 30 dogs were fed diets containing ratios of 5:1, 10:1, 25:1, 50:1 or 100:1 for a period of 12 weeks.[12] Effects of feeding the diets on plasma and skin fatty acid concentrations, and leukotriene B synthesis in lipopolysaccharide-stimulated skin cells and neutrophils were evaluated at 0, 6 and 12 weeks. Plasma fatty acids generally reflected dietary fatty acid distribution at 6 and 12 weeks. Total omega-3 fatty acids, including eicosapentaenoic acid, docosapentaenoic acid, and docosahexaenoic acid, increased in the plasma of dogs fed diets containing ratios of 5:1 and 10:1. In contrast, arachidonic acid levels decreased in the plasma of dogs fed the diet containing the lowest ratio (5:1). Although the level of response was not as great in skin as in plasma, skin fatty acid concentrations were also influenced by diet. Significant correlations between plasma and skin compositions were found for linoleic acid, arachidonic acid, and eicosapentaenoic acid after feeding the diets for 12 weeks. Similar observations have been observed following dietary supplementation of eicosapentaenoic acid and docosapentaenoic acid.[8]

Similar changes were observed in gastrointestinal tract cells.[13] Dietary omega-6:omega-3 fatty acid ratios of 5:1 and 10:1 resulted in increases of certain long chain omega-3 fatty acids in both small intestinal and colonic mucosa, and decreases in arachidonic acid levels. Regional differences were observed, with small intestinal mucosa having a greater concentration of stearic acid (18:0) and linoleic acid (18:2n-6) than colonic mucosa, and colonic mucosa having greater concentrations of eicosatrienoic (20:3n-3) and arachidonic acids (20:4n-6) than small intestinal mucosa.

The production of inflammatory agents in neutrophils and skin were significantly affected by the diet's fatty acid composition in this study. The neutrophils of dogs fed diets with omega-6 to omega-3 fatty acid ratios of 5:1 and 10:1 synthesized 30-33% less LTB_4 and 370-500% more LTB_5 at 6 and 12 weeks. Skin samples of dogs fed diets with these ratios synthesized 48-62% less LTB_4 and 48-79% greater LTB_5 at 12 weeks.

Although detrimental effects are associated with over-supplementation of omega-3 fatty acids, ratios of between 5:1 and 10:1 do not alter blood clotting, neutrophil reactivity, or wound healing parameters in dogs.[14] The absolute levels of fatty acids that were included in the diets in this study also met the dog's dietary requirement for essential fatty acids (*Table 2*).

Table 2. Dietary omega-6:omega-3 ratios and percentages of omega-6, omega-3, and linoleic acid.

Targeted Omega-6:Omega-3 Dietary Fatty Acid Ratio	Percentage of Total Dietary Fatty Acids as Omega-6 Fatty Acids	Percentage of Total Dietary Fatty Acids as Omega-3 Fatty Acids	Percentage of Total Dietary Energy as Linoleic Acid
5:1	18.1	3.4	8.27
10:1	18.7	1.8	8.55
25:1	19.3	0.8	8.82
50:1	25.8	0.5	11.79
100:1	38.3	0.4	17.50

Adapted from Reinhart GA. Canine dietary fatty acid ratios and tissue fatty acid content. *Dietary fat acid supplementation: a new treatment modality.* ACVIM 13th Annual Veterinary Medical Forum; 1995:22-25.

Supplementing a dog's regular diet with omega-3 fatty acids may not be effective in decreasing inflammatory potential because the exact quantities and ratio of fatty acids in the dog's regular diet are usually not known. As a result it is very difficult to achieve an effective fatty acid profile through supplementation. Fatty acid supplements are quite expensive, are occasionally associated with undesirable side effects, and have been shown to be effective in decreasing clinical signs of allergic pruritus in only about 10% of dogs.[15] Reported side effects of fatty acid supplementation in dogs include lethargy, pruritus, vomiting, diarrhea, and urticaria.[16,17] Supplementation of omega-3 and omega-6 fatty acids to a complete and balanced diet may result in unbalanced ratios, poor client compliance, and inconsistent or low-level responses to therapeutic treatment of allergic conditions.[11,14] An added risk of supplementation with omega-3 fatty acids is over-supplementation, which can lead to decreased platelet aggregation and increased blood clotting time.

The Total Dietary Approach vs. Supplementation

It is more efficacious to achieve optimal levels of omega-3 and omega-6 fatty acids through feeding a diet that is specifically formulated to achieve the proper ratio. Benefits of a total dietary approach include improved client compliance, achievement of a specifically targeted omega-6:omega-3 ratio, and safety (no danger of over-supplementation). Because omega-3 fatty acids are unstable, they require adequate antioxidant protection and necessitate increased levels of vitamin E in the diet. A complete and balanced diet can supply these added requirements.

While fatty acid therapy was initially used only for aiding in the control of pruritus, recent research indicates that dietary fatty acid manipulation may also be beneficial for patients with other types of inflammatory disorders. The practical use of diets with optimized quantities and proportions of omega-6 and omega-3 fatty acids may include prevention or adjunctive treatment for atopy (allergic inhalant dermatitis) and flea bite hypersensitivity. A balanced omega-3 to omega-6 ratio may also reduce the incidence or severity of carcinogenesis and of chronic degenerative diseases such as colitis or arthritis. Fatty acid therapy may also have effects upon renal blood flow, hyperlipidemia, thromboembolic disease, autoimmune disease, and neoplasia. As research into this exciting new area continues, more information will become available concerning the potential benefits of omega-3 fatty acids in preventative health care and in the treatment of disease.

Preventive and Therapeutic Uses of Diets with Adjusted Omega-6:Omega-3 Fatty Acid Ratios

1.   Goetzl EJ. Oxygenation products of arachidonic acid as mediators of hypersensitivity and inflammation. *Med Clin North Am* 1981; 65:809-828.

2.   Lewis PA, Austen KF, Soberman RJ. Leukotrienes and other products of the 5-lipoxygenase pathway: Biochemistry and relation to pathobiology in human diseases. *N Eng J Med* 1990; 323:645-655.

3.   Samuelsson B. Leukotrienes. Mediators of allergic reactions and inflammation. *Int Arch Allergy Immunol* 66(Suppl 1) 1991; 98-106.

References

4. Logas D. Potential clinical benefits of dietary supplementation with marine-life oil. *JAVMA* 1991; 199:1631-1636.

5. Nathaniel DJ, Evans JF, LeBlanc Y, et al. Leukotriene A$_5$ is a substrate and an inhibitor of rat and human neutrophil LTA$_4$ hydrolase. *Biochem Res Commun* 1985; 131(2)827-835.

6. Ziboh VA, Chapkin RS. Biological significance of polyunsaturated fatty acids in the skin. *Arch Dermatol* 1987; 123(12):1686-1690.

7. Ziboh VA, Miller CC. Essential fatty acids and polyunsaturated fatty acids: Significance in cutaneous biology. *Annu Rev Nutr* 1990; 10:433-450.

8. Savic MS, Yager JA, Holub BJ. Effect of n-3 and n-6 fatty acid dietary supplementation on canine neutrophil and keratinocyte phospholipid composition. *Proc Sec World Congr Vet Derm* 1992:77.

9. Campbell KL, Czarnecki-Maulden GL, Schaeffer DJ. Effects of animal and soy fats and proteins in the diet on concentrations of fatty acids in the serum and skin of dogs. *Am J Vet Res*, accepted for publication, 1995.

10. Scott DW et al. Nonsteroidal management of canine pruritus: Chlorpheniramine and a fatty acid supplement (DVM dermcaps) in combination, and the fatty acid supplement at twice the manufacturer's recommended dosage. *Cornell Vet* 1990; 80:381-387.

11. Miller WH, Scott DW, Wellington JR. Efficacy of DVM DermCaps liquid in the management of allergic and inflammatory dermatoses of the cat. *JAAHA* 1993; 29:37-40.

12. Vaughn DM, Reinhart GA, Swaim SF, Lauten SD, Garner CA, Boudreaux MK, Spano JS, Hoffman CE, Conner B. Evaluation of dietary n-6 to n-3 fatty acid ratios on leukotriene B synthesis in dog skin and neutrophils. *Vet Derm* 1994; 5(4):163-173.

13. Reinhart, GA, Vaughn DM. Dietary fatty acid ratios and tissue fatty acid content. *Proc. 13th ACVIM Forum*, Lake Buena Vista, Florida. 1995:466-469.

14. Vaughn DM, Reinhart GA. Dietary fatty acid ratios and eicosanoid production. *Proc 13th ACVIM Forum*, 1995.

15. Griffin CE. Atopic disease. *Semin Vet Med (SA)* 1991; 6:290-295.

16. Scott DW, Buerger RG. Nonsteroidal and anti-inflammatory agents in the management of canine pruritus. *JAAHA* 1988; 24:425-428.

17. Landhmore EW, Cameron CA, Sheridan BL. Reduction of intimal hyperplasia in canine autologous vein grafts with cond liver oil and dipryidamole. *Can J Surg* 1986; 29:357-358.

Influence of Dietary Fatty Acid Ratios on Tissue Eicosanoid Production and Blood Coagulation Parameters in Dogs

Dana M. Vaughn, PhD
Scott-Ritchey Research Center, Auburn University, Auburn, Alabama
Current address: InnoPet, Inc., Fort Lauderdale, Florida

Gregory A. Reinhart, PhD
Research and Development, The Iams Company, Lewisburg, Ohio

Introduction

During the past decade, serious attention has been focused on the use of dietary omega-3 (n-3) fatty acid supplementation to modify eicosanoid production. Fish oil sources of n-3 fatty acids have been successfully used to decrease the incidence of cardiopulmonary disease, cancer, diabetes, and inflammatory or allergic skin and bowel disease in humans.[1-6] It is believed that diets supplemented with a combination of omega-6 (n-6) and omega-3 polyunsaturated fatty acids could also benefit the health and appearance of domestic animals such as the dog. A variety of pruritic skin conditions in dogs and cats have shown favorable response with the addition of n-3 fatty acids in the diet.[7-11] A pronounced improvement was seen in 4 dogs with idiopathic seborrhea when their diets were supplemented with an n-3 fatty acid.[12] Another study has indicated the use of fatty acids may be beneficial for dogs with hip arthritis.[13] Other suggestions for n-3 fatty acids have included treatment of hyperlipidemia, thromboembolic disease, and neoplasia.[8]

Eicosanoids are the metabolic products of 20-carbon fatty acids; they include leukotrienes, thromboxanes, prostaglandins, and hydroxylated eicosatetraenoic acids. These chemical mediators have varying inflammatory, vasodilatory, and metabolic activity and are produced by the actions of cylooxygenase and lipoxygenase on arachidonic acid (n-6) and eicosapentaenoic acid (n-3).

Arachidonic acid, which is the primary substrate in eicosanoid biosynthesis, can be found in serum and plasma and as a component of cell membrane phospholipids. Arachidonic acid (20:4n-6) is a 20-carbon fatty acid with four double bonds; the last double bond is on the sixth carbon from the omega (tail) end of the molecule, hence the name omega-6 fatty acid.

In contrast, n-3 polyunsaturated fatty acids, such as the 20-carbon eicosapentaenoic acid (20:5n-3), have an additional double bond on the third to the last carbon from the tail end of the molecule. This additional double bond decreases the molecular reactivity of the eicosanoids made from polyunsaturated n-3 fatty acids. The normal metabolism of the n-3 and n-6 families of fatty acids is shown (*Figure 1*). The n-3 fatty acids are converted into isomers of leukotriene B, prostaglandin E, and thromboxane A that are much less pro-inflammatory than their corresponding n-6 fatty acid isomers. It is reported that the n-3 derived leukotriene B_5 (LTB_5) is 30-100 times less active at stimulating the leukotriene B receptor than the corresponding n-6 derived leukotriene B_4 (LTB_4).[14,15,16,17,18]

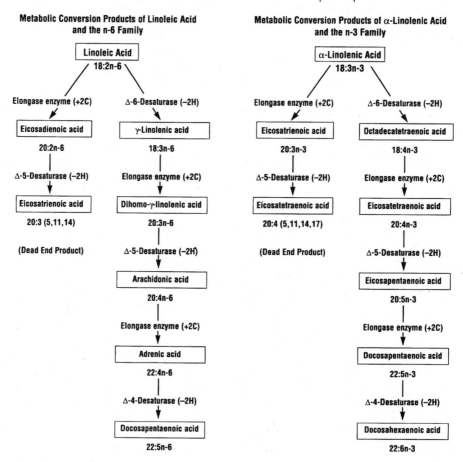

Figure 1. Metabolic conversion products of linoleic acid and the n-6 family and α-linolenic acid and the n-3 family.

Stimulation of LTB_4 receptors on neutrophils is one of the primary steps in the cyclic cascade of neutrophil recruitment, chemotaxis, degranulation, further leukotriene B synthesis, and the perpetuation of an inflammatory response.[14] Selectively increasing the amount of LTB_5 synthesized would competitively inhibit this LTB$_4$-induced neutrophil response and would subsequently diminish LTB$_4$-mediated inflammation.[15]

Omega-3 fatty acids may also serve to decrease the pro-inflammatory effects of LTB$_4$ by inhibiting its synthesis. The n-3 eicosapentaenoic acid is metabolized into LTB$_5$ by leukotriene A hydrolase and 5-lipoxygenase. Eicosapentaenoic acid acts as a competitive substrate against n-6 arachidonic acid for leukotriene A hydrolase.[1,19,20] Additionally, LTB$_5$ may be a weak inhibitor of 5-lipoxygenase.[21]

Eicosanoids are not stored in tissues. Instead, they are synthesized from polyunsaturated fatty acids in membrane phospholipids in response to various stimuli. Dietary supplementation with the n-3 lipids eicosapentaenoic acid (20:5n-3) and docosahexaenoic acid (22:6n-3) resulted in the insertion of these n-3 fatty acids into membrane phospholipids of tissues and circulating cells,[22,23] with a corresponding decrease in concentrations of n-6 fatty acids.[6,24,25]

High levels of n-3 fatty acid consumption in humans have also been noticed to variably affect bleeding time and platelet function.[26,27] The mechanism(s) explaining these effects may involve changes in membrane fluidity,[28] platelet procoagulant activity,[29] and platelet eicosanoid products.[30] No studies have investigated similar responses in dogs to n-3 fatty acid supplementation or to adjustments in the ratio of n-6 to n-3 fatty acids.

Commercial dog foods contain polyunsaturated fats with both n-6 and n-3 fatty acids. Dogs and cats cannot convert n-6 fatty acids to n-3 fatty acids or vice versa. Boudreau and associates suggested that not only is the absolute amount of n-3 fatty acids in the diet important to suppress arachidonic acid metabolism, but that the n-6:n-3 ratio of fatty acids in the diet should be optimized.[31] We conducted the present study to determine the ratio of n-6:n-3 fatty acids required to suppress pro-inflammatory n-6 LTB$_4$ and to produce anti-inflammatory n-3 LTB$_5$ in dogs. The effects of diets supplemented with increasing ratios of n-6:n-3 polyunsaturated fatty acids on leukotriene B synthesis in canine skin and neutrophils were evaluated. Leukotriene B synthesis in skin was evaluated because the skin is the target organ for most canine allergic reactions.[10,32] To determine the dermal effects of different ratios of dietary n-6:n-3 fatty acids, a model of skin eicosanoid metabolism was developed that involved intradermal injections of bacterial lipopolysaccharide (LPS), a known stimulant of leukotriene B synthesis.

Materials and Methods

Animals and Diets. Thirty, purpose-bred, one year old beagles were housed individually in concrete-floored kennels.[a] The dogs had free access to water and were fed ad libitum once each morning during preconditioning. All of the dogs were preconditioned for 8 weeks on a complete diet made of chicken, chicken by-product meal, corn, rice and chicken fat. The ratio of omega-6 to omega-3 fatty acids was 28.1:1.

[a] Marshall Farms, North Rose, NY

After the 8 week preconditioning period, each of five groups of six dogs received one of five experimental diets. The protein, carbohydrate and fat sources and relative amounts in these diets were very similar to those of the preconditioning diet. The fat source was chicken fat with additional lipid sources added to adjust the fatty acid composition (*Table 1*). Refined menhaden oil[b] added eicosapentaenoic acid (20:5n-3) and docosahexaenoic acid (22:6n-3); flax oil provided alpha-linolenic acid (18:3n-3); safflower oil was used to add a concentrated source of linoleic acid (18:2n-6). The diets were formulated to contain n-6 to n-3 ratios of: 5:1 (diet A), 10:1 (diet B), 25:1 (diet C), 50:1 (diet D) and 100:1 (diet E). The actual ratios and total amount of n-3s and n-6s are shown (*Table 1*).

Table 1. Dietary omega-6:omega-3 ratios and percentage of omega-6, omega-3, and linoleic acid.

Targeted Omega-6:Omega-3 Dietary Fatty Acid Ratio	Percentage of Total Dietary Fatty Acids as Omega-6 Fatty Acids	Percentage of Total Dietary Fatty Acids as Omega-3 Fatty Acids	Percentage of Total Dietary Energy as Linoleic Acid
5:1	18.1	3.4	8.27
10:1	18.7	1.8	8.55
25:1	19.3	0.8	8.82
50:1	25.8	0.5	11.79
100:1	38.3	0.4	17.50

Adapted from Reinhart GA. Canine dietary fatty acid ratios and tissue fatty acid content. *Dietary fat acid supplementation: a new treatment modality.* ACVIM 13th Annual Veterinary Medical Forum; 1995:22-25.

All procedures were approved by the Auburn University Animal Care and Use Committee.

Skin biopsies. Preliminary research conducted in our laboratory showed canine LTB_4 levels in the skin to be low or undetectable. However, a skin biopsy taken 90 minutes after intradermal injection of 0.1 mg bacterial lipopolysaccharide (LPS)[c] will show a predictable LTB_4 response. All clipping was done 24 hours prior to collecting the biopsy to avoid preparation induced LTB_4. Skin biopsies and plasma samples were taken at the end of the preconditioning period (week 0) and after six and twelve weeks on the experimental diets. All samples were collected after a 20 hour fast. Intravenous xylazine HCl (1 mg/kg)[d] was used for analgesia and sedation following intramuscular pretreatment with atropine sulfate (0.4 mg/kg).[e]

All blood and subcutaneous tissue was removed from each sample which was then immediately frozen on dry ice. Sample vials were flushed with argon gas and stored at -80° C.

Isolation, separation, and measurement of leukotriene B isomers from skin biopsies. Frozen skin samples were weighed, minced, placed in 1.5 ml ethyl acetate and homogenized for one minute.[f] The microtip probe was rinsed with 1.5 ml ethyl acetate which was added to the homogenate. The mixture was kept on ice until centrifuged at 500g for 10 minutes at 4° C. The supernatant was collected by

[b] Zapata Haynie Corporation
[c] E. Coli J5, Rc mutant, Sigma Chemical Co., St. Louis, MO.
[d] Rompun®, Miles, Inc., Shawnee Mission, KS.
[e] Vedco, Inc., St. Joseph, MO.
[f] Polytron, Brinkman Inst, Westbury, NY.

pipette and dried then resuspended in 200 μl acidic methanol, vortexed, flushed with argon gas and stored at -80° C.

The leukotrienes in acidic methanol were dried and resuspended in 200 μl d-H$_2$O. The suspensions were passed through 360 mg columns under vacuum.[g] The leukotriene isomers were eluted with methanol which was then removed by drying[h] and resuspended in 100 ml acidic methanol. The suspensions were flushed with argon gas and stored at -80° C. The methods of von Schacky et al[33] and Gallon and Barcelli[34] were modified and used to separate the isomers. Using LTB standards, recovery was approximately 78%.

Leukotriene B concentrations were determined by radioimmunoassay as previously described.[35,36]

Platelet isolation and function tests. Blood samples collected from the jugular vein with 1 ml 3.8% trisodium citrate was assayed to determine mean platelet volume before separation of the platelet rich plasma (PRP). Platelet rich plasma was collected by multiple centrifugations at 21° C for 3-4 minutes at 6-700g and eluted to 300,000 μl with autologous platelet poor plasma.

Platelet aggregation was performed as previously described using adenosine diphosphate (25, 10 and 5 μM final) and collagen (12, 6 and 3 μg/ml final) at each sampling period.[37,38] Concurrent to platelet aggregation measurement, platelet release was evaluated using a modified method of Jerushalmy and Zucker.[39]

Coagulation tests. Antithrombin III activity was determined with an automated chemical analyzer[i] using a chromagenic substrate.[j] Activated partial thromboplastin[k] , prothrombin time[l] and thrombin time[m] were performed on citrated plasma using a fibrinometer. Samples and controls were evaluated in duplicate.

Neutrophil oxidative burst. The respiratory burst of purified nuetrophils was characterized by monitoring the reduction of oxidized cytochrome C to reduced cytochrome C at 550 nM in a dual beam spectrophotometer. Neutrophils were collected and evaluated from day 0 and weeks 6 and 12. Respiratory burst was measured as previously described.[36] The results are reported as nmoles superoxide produced per million neutrophils.

Statistical analysis. The data were statistically evaluated by analysis of variance or with a two-tailed Student's t-test with significance set at P<0.05 between group means. The data are expressed as the mean ± standard error of the mean (SEM) for *n* = 6 dogs/group.

The 5:1 and 10:1 diets had two effects on LTB synthesis in the canine skin: LTB$_4$ decreased and LTB$_5$ increased at weeks 6 and 12 compared to time 0 (*Figures 2*

Results

[g] Sep-Pak Classic C18 extraction columns, Waters/Millipoer Corp., Milford, MA.

[h] Speed-Vac Concentrator, Savant Instruments Inc., Farmingdale, NY.

[i] Cobas Mira, Roche Diagnostic Systems, Nutley, NJ.

[j] S-2238, COATEST antithrombin, Helena Laboratories, Beaumont, TX.

[k] Actin, American Dade, Aquada, Puerto Rico.

[l] Activated thromboplastin, American Dade, Aquada, Puerto Rico.

[m] Fibrinogen, Sigma Chemical Co., St. Louis, MO.

and 3). After 12 weeks, the 5:1 diet decreased LPS-induced skin synthesis of LTB$_4$ by 62% compared to baseline (P<0.05). The 10:1 diet resulted in a 48% reduction in the same time period. The 25:1, 50:1 and 100:1 diets did not result in any change versus baseline in LTB$_4$ production.

Effects of Dietary Omega-6:Omega-3 Fatty Acid Ratios on LTB$_4$ Synthesis in Dog Skin

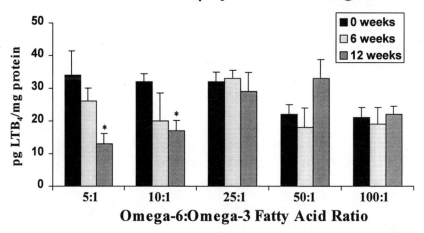

Figure 2. Effects of dietary omega-6 to omega-3 fatty acid ratios on lipopolysaccharide-induced LTB$_4$ synthesis in dog skin 90 min post-lipopolysaccharide injection. The values are the means ± SEM of six dogs per group. * P<0.05, indicates a significant difference from 0 time concentrations.

Effects of Dietary Omega-6:Omega-3 Fatty Acid Ratios on LTB$_5$ Synthesis in Dog Skin

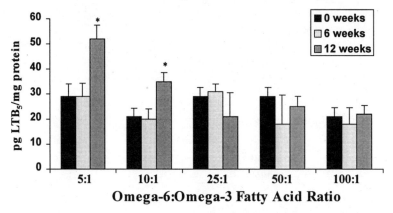

Figure 3. Effects of dietary omega-6 to omega-3 fatty acid ratios on lipopolysaccharide-induced LTB$_5$ synthesis in dog skin 90 min post-lipopolysaccharide injection. The values are the mean ± SEM of six dogs per group. * P<0.05, indicates a significant difference from 0 time concentrations.

Leukotriene B_5 synthesis in the skin induced by LPS increased in the 5:1 and 10:1 diets by 79% and 48%, respectively (*Figure 3*). The remaining dietary treatments did not significantly alter LTB_5 synthesis.

No LTB_3 was detected in the skin samples.

Dog neutrophils stimulated with isoproterenol readily generated superoxide anions (*Table 2*). The oxidative burst generated superoxide concentrations from 8.5 ± 0.9 to 13.2 ±1.5 nmoles superoxide per one million neutrophils. None of the diets with varied n-6 to n-3 fatty acid ratios significantly altered this measurement.

Table 2. Influence of n-6/n-3 fatty acids on neutrophil respiratory burst.

Diet	Baseline	6 weeks	12 weeks
5:1	8.7 ± 1.9	8.5 ± 0.9	8.6 ± 1.1
10:1	11.2 ± 1.2	12.5 ± 1.5	12.8 ± 0.8
25:1	11.6 ± 0.7	10.9 ± 1.2	12.1 ± 2.4
50:1	9.7 ± 2.4	13.2 ± 1.5	9.2 ± 0.9
100:1	9.2 ± 1.8	10.7 ± 1.0	10.5 ± 1.0

The units are nmoles superoxide generated per million neutrophils during the 10-20 min interval after stimulation with 30 μm isoproterenol. The data are the means ± SEM of n = 6 dogs per group. Adapted from 36.

There were no statistically or clinically significant changes in platelet function or coagulation tests.

General. All dogs remained healthy throughout the study.

The use of products enriched with omega-3 fatty acids has become popular in the management of canine inflammatory skin disorders. Modulation of skin eicosanoid metabolism via dietary mechanisms has been suggested as a possible method of controlling pruritic skin conditions in dogs.[7,8,10,11] The use of fatty acid supplements has met with variable success in many studies, suggesting that some other factor(s) may be involved in modifying the arachidonic acid cascade and eicosanoid production. A ratio effect could explain the variable results in earlier studies because the dietary contribution of fatty acids (either n-6 or n-3) was not reported and, presumably, not considered. Had the dietary fatty acid intake been known, a correlation between response to fatty acid supplementation and total intake and ratio of n-6 and n-3 could have been made. This study was conducted to determine if changes in the ratios of dietary n-6 to n-3 fatty acids would alter LTB_4 and LTB_5 synthesis in canine tissues. A combination of in vivo (skin) and in vitro (neutophil) models of acute inflammatory responses were used to evaluate the effects of various experimental diets.

Discussion

Previous studies have shown leukotriene B is not stored in neutrophil granules,[35,40] but is synthesized from neutrophil membrane phospholipids in response to a stimulatory agent such as A23187. The in vitro neutrophil model of acute inflammatory response used in this study was able to indirectly show that the dietary n-3 fatty acids had been incorporated into the membrane phospholipids of neutrophils. After incubation of the isolated neutrophils with A23187, calcium-stimulated phospholipase A_2 cleaved the ester bonds of the neutrophil membrane phospholipids and free eicosapentaenoic acid was mobilized and then metabolized into leukotriene B_5 by leukotriene A hydrolase and 5-lipoxygenase. Nonstimulated neutrophils were evaluated for the presence of LTB_5 and the findings were negative. This suggests that LTB_5, like LTB_4, is synthesized in response to stimulation, but is not stored within neutrophil granules.

Of the diets tested, those with n-6:n-3 ratios of 5:1 and 10:1 positively altered eicosanoid metabolism in tissues. After feeding the experimental diets for 6 weeks, neutrophils obtained from dogs fed the 5:1 and 10:1 ratios were isolated and incubated with calcium ionophore and were found to synthesize 30 and 33 per cent less LTB_4, respectively, than control neutrophils. Increased concentrations of LTB_5 were cosynthesized from these same neutrophil suspensions. The amount of LTB_5 (33-36 pg per 1.2×10^{-6} neutrophils) released from neutrophils of dogs fed the 5:1 and 10:1 diets for 6 weeks is physiologically relevant when compared to the amount of LTB_4 (77 pg per 1.2×10^{-6} neutrophils) released from control neutrophils. Leukotriene B measurements obtained after continued feeding of the 5:1 and 10:1 diets for 12 weeks demonstrate average total decreases in neutrophil LTB_4 concentrations which were not statistically different ($P>0.05$) from the 6-week values. Although leukotriene B metabolism was obviously altered by increased proportions of n-3 polyunsaturated fatty acids, neutrophil function was not compromised as shown in the respiratory burst response data. Canine neutrophils stimulated with isoproterenol readily generated superoxide anions. None of the diets significantly altered the relative amount of superoxide released from purified neutrophils. When choosing a therapeutic modality for treating canine inflammatory dermatologic disease, an ideal agent would modulate the inflammatory component of the disease, but would not precipitate immune system dysfunction. The omega-3 fatty acids appear to meet this criteria when used in diets providing these optimum ratios of n-6:n-3 fatty acids.

There is evidence to suggest that n-6 and n-3 polyunsaturated fatty acids compete for insertion into membrane phospholipids.[22,23,41] However, there is no evidence the total phospholipid pool available for eicosanoid metabolism increases due to changes in the n-6:n-3 ratio. This may explain why increases in the relative proportion of n-6 fatty acids in the 50:1 and 100:1 diets did not result in increased LTB_4 synthesis in stimulated neutrophils or skin. Although plasma concentrations of LTB_4 and LTB_5 paralleled the neutrophil response to increased ratios of dietary n-3 fatty acids, increasing proportions of n-6 fatty acids in the diet also failed to produce increased plasma LTB_4 concentrations. The existence of a homeostatic mechanism to control the concentration of polyunsaturated fatty acids in membrane phospholipids may explain why increases in n-6 fatty acids above a given amount may result in no further increases in eicosanoid metabolism.

The in vivo portion of this experiment substantiated the ability of variations in the dietary n-6:n-3 polyunsaturated fatty acids to alter LTB_4 generation in canine skin. Intradermal injections of bacterial lipopolysaccharide were used to produce a model of controlled inflammatory response that would stimulate leukotriene B_4 synthesis in the skin of dogs. The rationale for this model was found in the human medical literature. Lipopolysaccharide has been used to stimulate LTB_4 production in human macrophages and monocytes.[42,43,44] Of the diets tested, those with n-6:n-3 ratios of 5:1 and 10:1 produced significant decreases in leukotriene B_4 concentration and increases in leukotriene B_5 immunoreactivity after provocation with lipopolysaccharide. A decrease in tissue LTB_4 equal to or greater than 50 per cent is considered to be large enough to attenuate the lipid component of an inflammatory response in clinical situations.[45,46] The magnitude of change of LTB_4 and LTB_5 concentrations produced in this phase of the study was approximately 50 percent and was, therefore, physiologically significant. Twelve weeks of feeding the test diets were required to produce the reported changes in eicosanoid metabolism in the skin of dogs. This time frame is in contrast with the six weeks required to produce similar changes in the leukotriene B synthesis in neutrophils. These findings indicate it may take longer to achieve the same consistent ratios of n-6:n-3 fatty acids in the membranes of stationary skin cells than in the circulating blood cells. The clinical implication for veterinarians and dog owners is that adjusting the ratio of n-6:n-3 fatty acids in the diet may not result in a therapeutic response for several weeks. In fact, this study suggests twelve weeks may be a reasonable duration of initial trial therapy when omega-3 fatty acids are used to treat canine dermatologic disease. A subsequent report suggests responses in 7 to 21 days.[47]

Although concern has been verbally expressed regarding potential effects of n-3 intake adversely affecting platelet function and coagulation profiles, no evidence of such an effect could be found in this study. The levels of n-3 fatty acids used in this study were carefully controlled. Levels of n-3 fatty acid intake greater than these or at ratios below 5:1 have not been investigated. Suggestions of platelet or coagulation effects are speculative. Additionally, none of the dietary treatments had an effect on neutrophil function as measured by oxidative burst. No adverse effects were noted in either the in vitro or the in vivo portions of this study.

Research from several laboratories has demonstrated that allergic or inflammatory skin conditions are associated with increased arachidonic acid metabolism and proinflammatory eicosanoid concentration.[4,24,25,48-50] It is also well established that n-3 fatty acids, when administered through the diet or as pharmacologic supplements, can attenuate some atopic or inflammatory skin conditions with a concomitant decrease in skin n-6 eicosanoid concentrations and increase in n-3 eicosanoid concentrations.[2,4,6,51-54] The data from the present study indicated a dietary n-6:n-3 ratio of 5:1 to 10:1 decreased the concentration of pro-inflammatory LTB_4 and competitively increased the concentration of LTB_5. The 5:1 and 10:1 ratios of the tested diets also met canine essential fatty acid requirements.

Determining the fatty acid ratio of a specific commercial diet consumed by an individual patient and attempting to use polyunsaturated fatty acid supplements to achieve this optimum ratio of n-6:n-3 fatty acids would be a difficult and impractical proposition for dog owners and veterinarians. The most convenient method of ensuring that the proper fatty acid ratio is delivered to a patient is by the use of specifically formulated diets. Such diets are potentially useful in the treatment or prevention of inflammatory skin conditions in dogs, such as atopy, allergic dermatitis, and flea bite hypersensitivity.[7,8,10,11] Improved coat condition has also been reported as an additional benefit in dogs supplemented with eicosapentaenoic acid.[32,52]

In summary, skin and blood tissues obtained from dogs that were fed diets with 5:1 and 10:1 ratios of n-6 to n-3 polyunsaturated fatty acids for 6 and 12 weeks contained decreased levels of pro-inflammatory LTB_4 and increased concentrations of the less inflammatory LTB_5. Incorporating these optimum ratios of omega-6 and omega-3 fatty acids in the diet of dogs holds promise in the treatment of a variety of inflammatory skin conditions.

Acknowledgement   The author acknowledges and appreciates the efforts of Mary K. Boudreaux, Department of Pathobiology, College of Veterinary Medicine, Auburn University, for her work in conducting the blood coagulation parameter experiments discussed above.

References   1.   Bjerve KS, Brubakk AM, Fougner KJ, Johnsen H, Midthjell K, Vik T. Omega-3 fatty acids: essential fatty acids with important biological effects, and serum phospholipid fatty acids as markers of dietary omega-3 fatty acid intake. Am J Clin Nutr 1993; 57 (Suppl.):8018-8068.

2.   Hertog JM, Lamers JMJ, Achterberg PW, Van Heuven D, Nijkump FP, Verdouw PD. The effects of dietary mackerel oil on the recovery of cardiac function after acute isochemic events in the pig. Basic Res Cardiol 1987; 82:223-234.

3.   Hornstra G, van Houwelingren AC, Kivita GA, Fisher S, Uedelhoven W. Dietary fish and prostanoid formation in man. Advanc Prostaglandin Thromboxane Leukotriene Res 1991; 21(A):225-228.

4.   Kojima T, Terano T, Tanabe E, Okamoto S, Tamura Y, Yoshida S. Long-term administration of highly purified eicosapentaenoic acid provides improvement of psoriasis. Dermatologica 1991; 182(4):225-230.

5.   Simopoulos AP. Omega-3 fatty acids in health and disease and in growth and development. Am J Clin Nutr 1991; 54(3):438-463.

6.   Ziboh VA. Implications of dietary oils and polyunsaturated fatty acids in the management of cutaneous disorders. Arch Derm 1989; 125:421-445.

7.   Codner EC, Thatcher CD. Nutritional management of skin disease.

Compend Cont Ed Pract Vet 1993; 15(3):411-423.

8.   Logas D, Beale K M, Bauer JE. Potential clinical benefits of dietary supplementation with marine-life oil. *JAVMA* 1991; 199(22):1631-1636.

9.   Miller WH, Scott DW, Wellington JR. Efficacy of DVM derm caps liquid in the management of allergic and inflammatory dermatoses of the cat. *J Amer Anim Hosp Assoc* 1993; 29:37-40.

10.   Scott DW, Miller WH. Nonsteroidal management of canine pruritis: chlorpheniramine and a fatty acid supplement (DVM derm caps) in combination, and the fatty acid supplement at twice the manufacturer's recommended dosage. *Cornell Vet* 1990; 80:381-387.

11.   White PD. Essential fatty acids: use in management of canine atopy. *Compend Cont Ed Pract Vet* 1993; 15(3):451-457.

12.   Miller WH. Fatty acid supplements as anti-inflammatory agents. In: Kirk RW, ed. *Current Veterinary Therapy* X. Philadelphia: WB Saunders Co, 1989:563-565.

13.   Miller WH, Scott DW, Wellington JR. Treatment of dogs with hip arthritis with a fatty acid supplement. *Canine Pract* 1992; 6-8.

14.   Charleston S, Evans JF, Zamboni RJ, et al. Leukotriene B_3, leukotriene B_4 and leukotriene B_5: binding to leukotriene B_4 receptors on rat and human leukocyte membranes. *Prostaglandins* 1986; 32(4):503-516.

15.   Kragballe K, Voorhess J J, Goetzl EL. Inhibition by leukotriene B_5 of leukotriene B_4-induced activation of human keratinocytes and neutrophils. *J Invest Derm* 1987; 88(5):555-558.

16.   Lee TH, Sethi T, Crea AE, et al. Characterization of leukotriene B_3 : comparison of its biological activities with leukotriene B_4 and leukotriene B_5 in complement receptor enhancement, lysozyme release and chemotaxis of human neutrophils. *Clin Sci* 1988; 74(5):467-475.

17.   Seya A, Terano T, Tamura Y, Yoshida S. Comparative effect of leukotriene B_4 and leukotriene B_5 on calcium mobilization in human neutrophils. *Prostaglandins, Leukotrienes, Essential Fatty Acids* 1988; 34(1):47-50.

18.   Lagarde M. Metabolism of fatty acids by platelets and the functions of various metabolites in mediating platelet function. *Prog Lipid Res* 1988; 27:135-152.

19.   Iversen L, Fogh K, Kragballe K. Effect of dihomogamma-linolenic acid and its 15-lipoxygenase metabolite on eicosanoid metabolism by human mononuclear leukocytes in vitro: selective inhibition of the 5-lipoxygenase pathway. *Arch Derm Res* 1992; 284:222-226.

20.   O'Keefe SF, Lagarde M, Grandgirard A, Sebedio JL. *Trans* n-3 eicosapentaenoic and docosahexaenoic acid isomers exhibit different inhibitory effects on arachidonic acid metabolism in human platelets compared to the respective *cis* fatty acids. *J Lipid Res* 1990; 31(7):1241-1246.

21.   Nathaniel DJ, Evans JF, LeblancY, et al. Leukotriene A_3 is a substrate and an inhibitor of rat and human neutrophil LTA_4 hydrolase. *Biochem Res Comm* 1985; 131(2):827-835.

22.   Charnock JS, Abeywardena MY, McLennan PL. Comparative changes in the fatty acid composition of cardiac phospholipids after long-term feeding of sun seed oil or tuna oil-supplemented diets. *Ann Nutr Metab* 1986; 30:393-406.

23. Fletcher MP, Ziboh VA. Effects of dietary supplementation with eicosapentaenoic acid or gamma-linolenic acid on neutrophil phospholipid fatty acid composition and activation responses. *Inflammation* 1990; 14(5):585-597.

24. Ziboh VA, Chapkin RS. Biological significance of polyunsaturated fatty acids in the skin. *Arch Derm* 1987; 123(12):1686-1690.

25. Ziboh VA, Miller CC. Essential fatty acids and polyunsaturated fatty acids: significance in cutaneous biology. *Ann Rev Nutr* 1990; 10:433-450.

26. Ahmed AA, Holub BJ. Alteration and recovery of bleeding times, platelet aggregation and fatty acid composition of individual phospholipids in platelets of human subjects receiving a supplement of cod-liver oil. *Lipids* 1984; 19:617-624.

27. von Schacky C, Fischer S, Weber PC. Long-term effects of dietary marine n-3 fatty acids upon plasma and cellular lipids, platelet function and eicosanoid formation in humans. *J Clin Invest* 1985; 76:1626-1631.

28. Hornstra G, Rand ML. Effect of dietary n-6 and n-3 polyunsaturated fatty acids on the fluidity of platelet membranes in rat and man. *Prog Lipid Res* 1986; 25:636-638.

29. Nordoy A. The role of dietary fatty acids in thrombosis. *Prog Lipid Res* 1986; 25:455-459.

30. Goodnight SH Jr, Harris WS, Connor WE, Illingworth DR. Polyunsaturated fatty acids, hyperlipidemia and thrombosis. *Arteriosclerosis* 1982; 2:87-113.

31. Boudreau MD, Chanmugam RS, Hart SB, Lee SH, Hwang DH. Lack of dose response by dietary n-3 fatty acid at a constant ratio of n-3 to n-6 fatty acid in suppressing eicosanoid biosynthesis from arachidonic acid. *Am J Clin Nutr* 1991; 54:111-117.

32. Lloyd DH. Essential fatty acids and skin disease. *J Sm Anim Pract* 1989; 30:207-212.

33. von Schacky C, Fahrer C, Fisher S. Catabolism of leukotriene B_5 in humans. *J Lipid Res* 1990; 31:1831-1838.

34. Gallon LS, Barcelli UO. Measurement of prostaglandin E_3 and other eicosanoids in biological samples using high pressure liquid chromatography and radioimmunoasay. *Prostaglandins* 1986; 31:217-225.

35. Amalsadvala TM, Vaughn DM. Characterization of leukotriene B_4 synthesis in Greyhound polymorphonuclear leukocytes. *Prost Leuk and Essential Fatty Acids* 1992; 45:283-288.

36. Vaughn DM, Reinhart GA, Swaim SF, Lauten SD, Garner CA, Boudreaux MK, Spano JS, Hoffman CE, Conner B. Evaluation of dietary n-6 to n-3 fatty acid ratios on leukotriene B synthesis in dog skin and neutrophils. *Vet Derm* 1994; 5:163-173.

37. Born G. Aggregation of blood platelets by adenosine diphosphate and its reversal. *Nature* 1962; 194:927-929.

38. Boudreaux MK, Dillon AR, Spano JS. Enhanced platelet reactivity in heartworm-infected dogs. *Am J Vet Res* 1989; 50:1544-1547.

39. Jerushalmy Z, Zucker M. Some effects of fibrinogen degradation products (FDP) on blood platelets. *Thromb Diath Haemorrh* 1966; 15:413-419.

40. Iversen L, Fogh K, Ziboh VA, Kristensen P, Schmedes A, Kragballe K. Leukotriene B_4 formation during human neutrophil keratinocyte interactions:

evidence for transformation of leukotriene A_4 by putative keratinocyte leukotriene A_4 hydrolase. *J Invest Derm* 1993; 100:293-298.

41. Chanmugam PS, Boudreaux MD, Hwang DH. Dietary (n-3) fatty acids alter fatty acid composition and prostaglandin synthesis in rat testis. *J Nutr* 1991; 121:1173-1178.

42. Takahashi H, Abe M, Hashimoto S, Takayama K, Miyazaki M. *In vivo* effect of lipopolysaccharide on alveolar and peritoneal macrophages of rats: superoxide anion generation and 5-lipoxygenase metabolism of arachidonic acid. *Amer J Resp Cell Molecular Biol* 1993; 91:526-531.

43. Conti P, Panara MR, Barbacane RC, Bongrazio M, Dempsey RA, Reale M. Human recombinant IL-1 receptor antagonist (IL-1Ra) inhibits leukotriene B_4 generation from human monocyte suspensions stimulated by lipopolysaccharide (LPS). *Clin Exper Immun* 1993; 91:526-531.

44. Rankin JA, Sylvester I, Smith S, Yoshimura T, Leonard EJ. Macrophages cultured in vitro release LTB_4 and neutrophil attractant/activation protein (interleukin-8) sequentially in response to stimulation with lipopolysaccharide and zymosan. *J Clin Invest* 1990; 86:1556-1564.

45. Aked D, Foster SJ, Howarth A, McCormick ME, Potts HC. The inflammatory response of rabbit skin to topical arachidonic acid and its pharmacological modulation. *Brit J Pharmacol* 1986; 89:431-438.

46. Aked D, Foster SJ. Leukotriene B_4 and prostaglandin E_2 mediate the inflammatory respone of rabbit skin to intradermal arachidonic acid. *Brit J Pharmacol* 1987; 92:545-552.

47. Scott DW, Miller WH. Efficacy of an omega-3 omega-6 fatty acid containing commercial dog food in the management of atopy. *Proc 12th Europ Soc Vet Derm* 1995:163.

48. Ruzicka TS, Ring J. Enhanced releasability of prostaglandin E_2 and leukotrienes B_4 and C_4 from leukocytes of patients with atopic eczema. *Acta Dermatologica Venereology (Stockholm)* 1987; 67:469-475.

49. Iwarnoto I, Tomoe S, Yoshida S. Role of leukotriene B4 in substance P-induced granulocytic infiltration in mouse skin. *Regulatory Peptides* 1993; 46:225-227.

50. Ruzicka T, Simmet T, Peskar BA, Ring J. Skin levels of arachidonic acid-derived inflammatory mediators and histamine in atopic dermatitis and psoriasis. *J Invest Derm* 1986; 86:105-108.

51. Hamazaki, T. Intravenous infusion of n-3 polyunsaturated fatty acids. *Proc Soc Exper Biol and Med* 1992; 200:171-173.

52. Lloyd DH, Thomsett LR, Essential fatty acid supplementation in the treatment of canine atopy: a preliminary study. *Vet Derm* 1989; 1:41-44.

53. Miller CC, Yamaguchi RY, Ziboh VA. Guinea pig epidermis generates putative anti-inflammatory metabolites from fish oil polyunsaturated fatty acids. *Lipids* 1989; 24:988-1003.

54. Miller CC, Zoboh VA, Wong T, Fletcher MP. Dietary supplementation with oils rich in (n-3) and (n-6) fatty acids influence in vivo levels of epidermal lipoxygenase products in guinea pigs. *J Nutr* 1990; 120:36-44.

Effects of Various Proteins in the Diet on Fatty Acid Concentrations in the Skin, Cutaneous Histology, Clinicopathology, and Thyroid Function in Dogs

Stephen D. White, DVM, DACVD
Associate Professor, Department of Clinical Sciences
College of Veterinary Medicine and Biomedical Sciences
Colorado State University, Fort Collins, Colorado

Rod A. W. Rosychuk, DVM, MS[a]; Kathryn V. Scott, DVM[b]; Daniel P. Carey, DVM[c];
Curtis Longardner[c]; Patricia C. Schultheiss, DVM, PhD[d]; Mowafak Salman, DVM, PhD[a]

[a]Department of Clinical Sciences, Colorado State University, Fort Collins, CO
[b]Veterinary Teaching Hospital, Colorado State University, Fort Collins, Colorado
[c]Research and Development, The Iams Company, Lewisburg, Ohio
[d]Department of Pathology, Colorado State University, Fort Collins, Colorado

Summary

Twelve dogs were fed each of six diets for 12 weeks. Diets differed only in protein source: chicken, pork, lamb, fish, beef, and soy. Dogs were evaluated via CBC, serum chemistry profile, urinalysis, TSH response test, and skin biopsy. Skin biopsy was evaluated both histologically and for determination of cutaneous fatty acid concentrations. The fatty acids evaluated were linolenic acid, gamma linolenic acid, alpha linolenic acid, arachidonic acid, eicosatetraenoic acid, and eicosapentaenoic acid. Dogs were also evaluated subjectively for hair regrowth at biopsy sites and presence or absence of scale.

Results showed no difference in CBCs, histologic findings, or cutaneous fatty acid values between dogs fed the various diets. Three of 12 dogs fed the beef diet had hypercholesterolemia, 9 of 12 dogs fed the soy diet had alkaline urine, and 4 of 12 dogs fed pork had a subjective increase in scale and a decrease in regrowth of hair. Three of 12 dogs developed hypothyroidism during the study.

Introduction

The importance of protein in the proper development and maintenance of the skin has been well documented in dogs from the standpoint of protein deficiency.[1] Proteins have also been implicated as allergens in cases of food hypersensitivity.[2-5] Proteins may affect lipid metabolism. Plant proteins have been shown to be hypocholesterolemic, compared with animal proteins when fed to rats and monkeys,[6,7] although not when fed to dogs.[8] Rabbits fed diets for either 12 or 24 weeks differing in type of protein showed differences in serum and liver cholesterol levels and, by implication, lipid metabolism.[9,10]

Fatty acid supplements have been evaluated in clinical trials for treatment of allergic dermatitis.[11-14] However, the potential role of the various proteins in the diets being consumed by the dogs in the development and treatment of the disease (in particular the fatty acid concentrations of the diets) has not been considered.

The purpose of this study was to assess the effect of different dietary proteins on fatty acid concentration and histology, clinicopathology, and thyroid function in dogs. Twelve dogs were fed complete, balanced diets that differed only in their protein source. The skin was monitored for gross morphologic and histopathologic changes. Special attention was given to assessment of changes in cutaneous fatty acid concentrations that could potentiate inflammation.

Materials and Methods	*Dogs* — Twelve mixed breed, hound-type dogs, all approximately one year of age, were utilized for this study. There were five females and seven males. All dogs were housed individually.

Diets — Prior to starting the diet trial, all dogs were fed a commercial corn- and soy-based dog food (Dealer's Choice®, St. Louis, Missouri, USA) for a period of 10 weeks. During the diet trial, six diets were used, differing only in their protein sources: chicken, pork, lamb, fish, beef and soy. The chicken, pork, beef and lamb proteins were derived from skeletal muscle; the fish was herring, as fish meal. The dogs were fed each diet for 12 weeks. The dogs were randomized in regard to which diet they were being fed. All diets were blinded to the investigators.

Clinicopathology	At the initiation of the study and every 12 weeks (i.e., at the end of each diet), all dogs had blood drawn for a CBC and serum chemistry profile, and urine was collected by cystocentesis for urinalysis.

Histopathology	Two skin 6 mm punch biopsies were obtained every 6 weeks from hair-clipped areas along the dorsal midline approximately between the scapulae, 1 for histologic examination and 1 for determination of fatty acid values. Subcutaneous fat was not removed from the samples. Biopsy samples for histopathology were placed in 10% buffered formalin, routinely processed and stained with hematoxylin and eosin. Histology of the skin biopsies was reviewed noting any changes in the epidermis, dermis, subcutis, and adnexae; and for the presence of inflammation.

Cutaneous Fatty Acid Analysis	Biopsy samples for cutaneous fatty acid determination were put in sterile dry glass tubes and kept frozen at -18° Centigrade until assayed. The fatty acids evaluated were linoleic acid, gamma linolenic acid, alpha linolenic acid, arachidonic acid, eicosatetraenoic acid and eicosapentaenoic acid. In brief, each skin biopsy was placed into a 5 ml reaction vial and hydrolyzed for three minutes at 110°C with 33% HCL. The sample was then thoroughly vortexed to break up the

skin matter. The sample was allowed to cool, 1 ml of LC grade hexane added and then vortexed for 30 seconds. The sample was then centrifuged at 2400 rpm for 15 minutes. This ensured that the fatty acids were in the hexane layer and no skin matter was esterified. The upper hexane layer was carefully transferred to a clean 5 ml reaction vial and was esterified with 3 ml of 15% boron tri-fluoride methanol solution from Supelco. The hexane was separated from the methanol by adding 1 ml of saturated NaCl solution, vortexing for 10 seconds and then centrifuging the mixture at 310 rpm for two minutes. The upper hexane layer was then transferred to an auto-sampler vial.

The equipment used to analyze the fatty acid esters consisted of the following:

- Varian 3400 GC with a 1077 split/splitless injector and a FID detector
- Varian 8100 autosampler
- J & W DB-23; 30 meters in length, 25 mm ID, with a 25 microns film thickness
- Water's MAXIMA 825 Chromatography workstation

Helium was used as the carrier gas with a flow rate of 20 cm/second and a split ratio of nearly 100:1. The GC parameters were as follows:

- Injector at 270 degrees C
- Detector at 280 degrees C
- Oven program starts at 160 and holds for 1 minute. It then ramps up to 220 at 1.7 degrees a minute and holds for 8 minutes.

Statistical analysis was performed using the Kurskal-Wallis procedure[15] to determine the significant difference of medians of fatty acid values between the different diets fed. Our significance level was $P \leq 0.05$. Fatty acid values were statistically analyzed at six weeks (mid diet), 12 weeks (end of diet) and in combination.

Thyroid function — A thyroid stimulating hormone (TSH) response test was performed at the initiation of the study and every 12 weeks thereafter (i.e., at the end of each diet). Each dog was given 1 unit of TSH, IV, with serum T_4 concentrations measured at time zero (pre or basal T_4) and six hours post injection.

Recently, researchers substantiated the finding that serum antithyroglobulin antibody (ATA) titers closely correlated with the presence of lymphocytic thyroiditis in the dog.[16] With this knowledge, ATA titers were examined retrospectively in serum samples taken from all dogs during the second to last diet. Serum ATA titers were also evaluated at the end of each diet trial in all dogs with evidence of thyroid dysfunction based on the TSH response test, and in all dogs with a significant ATA titer on the second to last diet sample. Where possible, all dogs with significant thyroid dysfunction based on the TSH response tests or with significant ATA titers had a thyroid biopsy performed with standard surgical technique.

Criteria for interpretation of thyroid hormone data — Normal "pre" basal or resting T_4; 0.8 to 3.6 µg/dl. The relative frequency with which these values fell into low normal, borderline, borderline low, and low ranges was reported and used when comparing the effects of various diets on thyroid function.

Pre T_4:		
	> 1.5 to 2.0	low normal
	1.0 to 1.5	borderline
	0.8 to 1.0	borderline low
	< 0.8	low

Normal response to TSH stimulation was considered if the dog showed an incremental increase of ≥ 2.0 µ T_4 from baseline and/or a post $T_4 \geq 3.0$ µg/dl (absolute value). A post TSH stimulation of $T_4 < 3.0$ µg/dl was considered a decreased response; incremental increases in T_4 were graded as > 1.5 to 2.0 µg/dl = moderate decrease, < 1.5 µg/dl = marked decrease. Interpretation of ATA titers: < 3 RAU (relative antibody units) = negative; 3 to 10 RAU = suspect; > 10 RAU = lymphocytic thyroiditis.

Subjective examination — At every six weeks, the dogs were subjectively examined for hair regrowth at previous biopsy sites, as well as presence or absence of scale.

Results

No differences between dogs fed the various diets were noted in CBCs. Serum cholesterol levels were high (> 300 mg/dl) in three dogs. In all three, this occurred after being fed the beef diet. One of these dogs also became hypercholesterolemic after being fed the fish diet, and another also after being fed the chicken diet. This latter dog was also hypercholesterolemic immediately prior to beginning the diet trials.

Nine of the 12 dogs fed with soy diet had alkaline urine (pH ≥ 7.0). Histology showed variable (but within normal limits) thickness of the stratum corneum and a decrease in the nonsuppurative inflammation seen in some dogs on the baseline (pre-diet trial) biopsy. Fatty acid values (expressed as percentage of total fat) are shown in *Table 1*. Statistical analysis of the fatty acid values revealed no significant differences between the various diets.

The only consistent trend noted subjectively on physical examination was that 4 of the 12 dogs fed pork had an increase in scale and a decrease in regrowth of hair following clipping for the biopsies. These did not include any of the hypothyroid dogs.

Table 1.

	Chicken	Pork	Lamb	Fish	Beef	Soy
Linoleic	10.5-34.7 (25.1)	13.6-34.2 (25.2)	12.0-35.3 (22.6)	13.9-33.3 (24.8)	6.3-35.4 (24.1)	14.6-37.1 (26.2)
gamma-Linolenic	0.5-1.7 (1.3)	0.7-1.7 (1.2)	0.6-1.7 (1.1)	0.7-1.6 (1.2)	0.3-1.7 (1.15)	0.6-1.8 (1.35)
Arachidonic	0.1-0.5 (0.3)	0.1-0.5 (0.2)	0.1-0.4 (0.2)	0.1-0.3 (0.2)	0.1-0.4 (0.2)	0.1-0.5 (0.3)
alpha-Linolenic	0.2-0.6 (0.4)	0.2-0.5 (0.4)	0.2-0.5 (0.35)	0.1-0.4 (0.4)	0.1-0.4 (0.35)	0.1-0.7 (0.4)
Eicosatetraenoic	0.1	0.1	0.1	0.1	0.1-0.2 (0.15)	0.1-0.3 (0.1)
Eicosapentaenoic	0.1	0.1	0.1	0.1	0.1	0.1

Values are presented with the range first and median in parentheses. Where no range is given, the only value was 0.1.
Values expressed as percent of total fat in the sample.

Thyroid function test results — Three dogs developed test results consistent with hypothyroidism. One dog developed a lack of response to TSH while on the pork diet (sixth diet fed), and a thyroid biopsy showed idiopathic follicular atrophy. The ATA titers were negative. Another dog developed a moderate decrease in response to TSH while being fed the pork diet (fourth diet fed), which progressed to a markedly decreased response after being fed the last diet (fish). Biopsy was not done, and the ATA titers were negative. An attempt to "super" stimulate this dog's thyroid with five units IV TSH still showed a markedly decreased response. The third dog developed a markedly decreased response to TSH on the lamb diet (second diet fed). Thyroid biopsy showed lymphocytic thyroiditis, and ATA titers were consistent with this diagnosis ranging during the remainder of the study from 10 to 364 RAU.

Of the other nine dogs, transient (diet-specific) changes in thyroid function were seen in three dogs. A moderately decreased response to TSH was seen in two dogs, one while being fed the lamb diet, and one while being fed the fish diet. This latter dog also had a transient markedly decreased response to TSH while fed the beef diet. One dog showed a low baseline T_4 while being fed the soy diet.

Two dogs, other than the aforementioned three hypothyroid dogs, had elevated ATA titers ranging from 63 to 845 RAU prior to initiation of the diet trials, which were persistently elevated throughout the study. One of these was the dog with the transient, moderately decreased response to TSH while fed the lamb diet; the other dog had no other thyroid abnormality noted. Both dogs had thyroid biopsies performed, which showed no abnormalities.

Discussion   Food hypersensitivity has been well described in the dog.[1-5] Various authors have documented food proteins as allergens.[3,4] No differences in histologic or gross evidence of inflammation or pruritus, or in fatty acid levels were found between the dogs fed the various diets in our study. This would suggest the allergenicity of a protein in the dog is related more to individual susceptibility and exposure rather than any change affected in fatty acid values or skin architecture. Conversely, proteins previously designated as "hypoallergenic" probably were less likely to have been included in a dog's previous diet rather than have any lesser intrinsic allergenicity.[17]

The high level of sulfur amino acids in meats results in a urine-acidifying effect. The oxidation of these amino acids results in the excretion of sulfate in the urine and a decrease in urine pH. Thus, the urinary pH of dogs fed soy-based rather than meat-based diets would trend towards an alkaline pH as observed in this trial. We do not have a ready explanation for the increase in scale and decrease in post-clipping hair regrowth in some of the dogs fed the pork diet. This latter finding may suggest avoidance of pork in formulating diets for seborrheic dogs, although the observations were subjective, not documented on histopathology, and more research would need to be done to confirm these findings.

The decrease, following the initial pre-diet trial biopsy, of inflammation seen on histologic examination may have been due to the dietary change from the pre-diet trial food to the formulations utilized in the six trial diets. Alternatively, this decrease may have been an ongoing process, starting when the dogs came into our care; we did not biopsy them upon their arrival, so this is conjectural.

A number of reports have suggested that essential fatty acids (EFAs) play a role in regulation of inflammation in the skin of dogs.[11-14,18,19] These reports have generally focused on supplemental administration of the EFAs, particularly in dogs with atopy. A recent report emphasizes supplying a ratio of omega-6 to omega-3 fatty acids of 5 to 10:1 in the food as a way to manipulate less production of inflammatory leukotrienes.[19] While fatty acids are derived from fat intake,[20] protein source might affect cutaneous fatty acid values by fat contamination. This is less likely when skeletal muscle, as opposed to liver for example, is used as the protein source. Protein sources may also alter fat metabolism. Rabbits fed diets for either 12 or 24 weeks differing in type of protein showed differences in serum and liver cholesterol levels and, by implication, lipid metabolism.[9,10] While changes in protein have altered serum cholesterol in rats and monkeys,[6,7] these findings have not been duplicated in dogs. In a recent study,[8] no significant differences in dogs fed soy protein versus "meat" meal as protein sources were seen in serum cholesterol, and only marginal changes in serum and cutaneous fatty acid concentrations. That study (like ours), had a duration of diet fed of 12 weeks (84 days). In our study we chose to compare six different proteins (one plant, five animals in origin). We did find that three dogs (25%) became hypercholesterolemic when fed the beef diet. However, two of these dogs were hypercholesterolemic on other diets. While beef fat has cholesterol-raising properties in humans,[21] lean beef meat does not, and is interchangeable with chicken meat in diets seeking to control or lower serum cholesterol levels.[22] This finding deserves further study.

Unfortunately the actual fatty acid concentrations of each diet were not determined. However, as the proteins were the only components of each diet changed, and each dog was fed each diet, each dog served as its own control.

Thyroid function — Of the various tests of thyroid function available at the time of this study, the assessment of incremental increases in serum T_4 following TSH stimulation was considered most accurate.[23] Using this criteria, the pork and lamb diets may have had deleterious effects on the thyroid gland.

While feeding the lamb diet, one dog had a transient decrease in response to TSH stimulation. In one other dog, thyroid deficiency was first noted following the feeding of this diet and persisted during the rest of the study. Thyroid biopsy showed lymphocytic thyroiditis. This dog also developed an elevated ATA titer while on the lamb diet.

While feeding the pork diet, two dogs developed decreased responses to TSH stimulation. In one of these dogs a total lack of response to TSH was noted. Thyroid atrophy (non-inflammatory) was confirmed by the thyroid biopsy in the dog. The other dog developed a subnormal decrease in response to TSH, which worsened through the end of the study. At the end of the study, an attempt was made to "super" stimulate this dog with a high dose of TSH (5 U) but response remained marginal. The dog's thyroid was not biopsied. The ATA values of both these dogs were negative.

The two dogs with persistent elevated ATAs from the beginning of the study but with normal thyroid biopsy results could have represented those apparently healthy dogs which have been found to have elevated ATAs.[16] Alternatively, the thyroid biopsy may have missed any active pathology.

Changes in basal or resting T_4 concentrations are considered more difficult to interpret when assessing thyroid function because they may be more significantly affected by extrathyroidal influences, such as intercurrent diseases or drugs. These changes are thought to be mediated in part by changes in thyroid hormone protein binding or thyroid hormone building protein concentrations, etc. Lowered basal T_4 concentrations can, of course, be associated with the development of hypothyroidism, but usually after the disease is well advanced. In our experience, a failure to respond adequately to TSH stimulation is a much earlier indicator of thyroid dysfunction. Only one dog (other than the three hypothyroid dogs) had below normal values of T_4, and this only once, on the soy diet.

When transient abnormalities in thyroid function are noted, this would seem to be more reasonably attributed to diet. However, when thyroid dysfunction and/or ATA titers are noted to develop and persist, the question of idiopathic thyroid "injury" vs diet-induced changes is presented. An argument against the serendipitous occurrence is the fact that three of the 12 dogs in this random population were documented to develop hypothyroidism by biopsy and/or abnormal TSH stimulation tests. The relative incidence of spontaneous hypothyroidism in the dog population has been variably reported to be 1:156 to 1:500. Also, these dogs were all less than 3 years of age when the hypothyroidism occurred; the risk of this disease peaks in an age range of 5 to 9 years, dependent on breed.[24] This would argue for a potential role for diet in the development of the hypothyroidism noted above.

References

1. Scott DW, Miller WH, Griffin CE. Muller and Kirk's *Small Animal Dermatology, 5th ed*, Philadelphia: WB Saunders, 1995:894.

2. White SD. Food hypersensitivity in 30 dogs. *J Am Vet Med Assoc* 1986; 188:695-698.

3. Carlotti DN, Remy I, Prost C. Food allergy in dogs and cats. A review and report of 43 cases. *Veterinary Dermatology* 1990; 1:55-62.

4. Jeffers JG, Shanley KJ, Meyer EK. Diagnostic testing of dogs for food hypersensitivity. *J Am Vet Med Assoc* 1991; 198:245-250.

5. Rosser EJ. Diagnosis of food allergy in dogs. *J Am Vet Med Assoc* 1993; 203:259-262.

6. Terpstra AHM, West CE, Fennis JTCM, et al. Hypocholesterolemic effect of dietary soy protein versus casein in rhesus monkeys. *Am J Clin Nutr* 1984; 39:1-7.

7. Vahoung GV, Adamson I, Chalcarz W, et al. Effects of casein and soy protein on hepatic and serum lipids and lipoprotein lipid distribution in rats. *Atherosclerosis* 1985; 56:127-137.

8. Cambell KL, Czarnecki-Maulden GL, Schaefer DJ. Effects of animal and soy fats and proteins in the diet on fatty acid concentrations in the serum and skin of dogs. *Am J Vet Res* 1995; 56:1465-1469.

9. Bauer JE, Covert SJ. The influence of protein and carbohydrate type on serum and liver lipids and lipoprotein cholesterol in rabbits. *Lipids* 1984; 19:844-850.

10. Bauer JE. Lipids, lipoproteins and hepatic 3-hydroxy-3-methylglutaryl CoA reductase activities in rabbits during adaptation to atherogenic semi-purified diets. *Artery* 1988; 15:140-162.

11. Lloyd DH, Thomsett LR. Essential fatty acid supplementation in the treatment of canine atopy: a preliminary study. *Vet Derm* 1989; 1:41-44.

12. Miller WH, Griffin CE, Scott DW, Angarano DK, Norton AL. Clinical trial of DVM DermCaps in the treatment of allergic disease in dogs: A nonblinded study. *J Am Anim Hosp Assoc* 1989; 163-168.

13. Logas D, Beale KM, Bauer JE. Potential clinical benefits of dietary supplementation with marine-life oil. *J Am Vet Med Assoc* 1991; 199:1631-1636.

14. Bond R, Lloyd DH. Randomized single-blind comparison of an evening

primrose oil and fish oil combination and concentrates of these oils in the management of canine atopy. *Vet Derm* 1992; 3:215-219.

15. Schott S. *Statistics for Health Professionals.* Philadelphia:WB Saunders 1990:252-253.

16. Beale KM, Halliwell REW, Chen CL. Prevalence of antithyroglobulin antibodies detected by enzyme-linked immunosorbent assay of canine serum. *J Am Vet Med Assoc* 1990; 196:745-748.

17. Ackerman L. Adverse reactions to foods. *J Vet Algy Clin Immun* 1993; 1:18-22.

18. White PD. Essential fatty acids used in management of canine atopy. *Comp Cont Ed Pract Vet* 1993; 15:451-457.

19. Vaughn DM, Reinhart GA, Swaim SF, et al. Evaluation of dietary n-6 to n-3 fatty acid ratios in leukotriene B synthesis in dog skin and neutrophils. *Vet Derm* 1994; 5:163-173.

20. Lewis LD, Morris ML, Hand MS. *Small Animal Clinical Nutrition III.* Topeka, Kansas: Mark Morris Associates. 1987:1-17.

21. Denke MA. Role of the beef and beef fallow, an enriched source of stearic acid, in a cholesterol-lowering diet. *Am J Clin Nutr* 1994; 60:10445-10495.

22. Scott LW, Dunn JK, Pownall HJ, et al. Effects of beef and chicken consumption on plasma lipid levels in hypercholesterolemic men. *Arch Intern Med* 1994; 154:1261-1267.

23. Ferguson DC. Update on diagnosis of canine hypothyroidism. *Vet Clin North Am Sm Anim Pract* 1994; 24:515-539.

24. Scarlet MJ. Epidemiology of thyroid disease of dogs and cats. *Vet Clin North Am: Sm Anim Pract* 1994; 24:467-486.

The Role of Polyunsaturated Fatty Acids In the Canine Epidermis: Normal Structural and Functional Components, Inflammatory Disease State Components, and as Therapeutic Dietary Components

Mary P. Schick, DVM
Robert O. Schick, DVM, DACVD
Atlanta Animal Allergy and Dermatology, Roswell, Georgia

Gregory A. Reinhart, PhD
Research and Development, The Iams Company, Lewisburg, Ohio

Polyunsaturated Fatty Acids in Normal Epidermal Structure and Function

Dietary fatty acids have been shown to be absorbed by the intestinal tract and utilized by the body in several ways. They can be immediately metabolized as an energy source, incorporated into cell membranes, or become a substrate for metabolic synthetic pathways for the production of steroids such as cholesterol or estrogen. To be incorporated into the lipid-protein bilayer of the cell membrane, fatty acids are elongated to 20 carbons and combined with glycerol phosphate to become membrane phospholipids. These fatty acids may subsequently be released when the cell membrane is inflamed.[1,2,3]

Variations in epidermal lipid composition influence the keratinocyte proliferation-desquamation processes of the skin as well as maintain its normal water permeability barrier function.[4] Polyunsaturated fatty acids are incorporated into what is considered the most important constituent of the water permeability barrier, the ceramide component of the epidermal lipids. The omega-6 family of fatty acids, in particular, are required to maintain normal keratinocyte membrane structure and function and especially the intact ceramide permeability barrier of the skin (as well as healthy haircoat in the dog).[5] Ceramides are highly concentrated in intercellular lipid lamellae and covalently attach to the cornified cell envelope in the stratum corneum.

In humans, a molecular lesion in the ceramide structure, caused by chronic essential fatty acid deficiency disrupts normal skin barrier function, producing clinical disease. Interestingly, when a dietary essential fatty acid deficiency becomes chronic, non-essential omega-9 polyunsaturated family (oleic acid derived) members substitute for the missing essential fatty acids in epidermal cells, resulting in clinical disease. These omega-9 non-essential fatty acids, are abundant in the diet for direct absorption by keratinocytes from the blood or can be synthesized from glucose by the liver.[6, 7]

Two other families of polyunsaturated fatty acids, the omega-6s and omega-3s, are of major importance in maintaining normal skin structure and function. Since the keratinocytes of the epidermis lack delta-5 and delta-6 desaturase enzymes, the epidermis is incapable of directly synthesizing the longer chain omega-6 polyunsaturated fatty acids (such as arachidonic acid from linoleic acid) or omega-3 polyunsaturated fatty acids (such as eicosapentaenoic from alpha linolenic acid). Dietary precursors are absorbed and then hepatically biosynthesized into most of the fatty acids which are subsequently transported by the blood stream and delivered to the epidermal keratinocytes.[8, 9, 10, 11] (*Figure 1*)

Eicosanoid Production

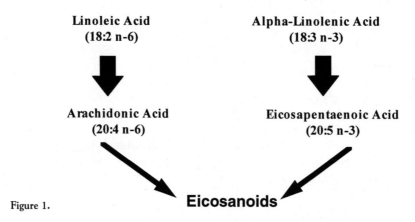

Figure 1.

One omega-6 essential polyunsaturated fatty acid in the dog that is classified as "essential" is cis-linoleic acid. The cis-isomer (the trans-form is biologically inactive) of linoleic acid cannot be hepatically synthesized from precursors in the body and must be provided exclusively in its original structure from the diet for direct absorption and incorporation into keratinocyte cellular membranes.[11] Cis-linoleic acid must be absorbed at a required nutritional level to maintain normal basal metabolism in healthy epidermal cells.[12, 13] A nutritional requirement of alpha-linolenic acid has been theorized but has not yet been proven.[13]

Arachidonic acid is a polyunsaturated fatty acid synthesized from linoleic acid that binds to the phospholipid portion of cell membranes in the canine epidermis. Arachidonic acid does not provide any barrier protection effects, but plays an important role in membrane fluidity and stability.[14]

Membrane-bound arachidonic acid is the most important precursor for the production of eicosanoids. The eicosanoids as a group are considered to be autocoids, hormones that exert local biologic effects and then are metabolized rapidly. Since the eicosanoids are metabolites of both the lipoxygenase and cyclooxygenase enzyme cascades that break down arachidonic acid and other polyunsaturated fatty acids during the inflammatory response, it is not surprising that there is a large group of approximately 270 metabolic derivatives of the 20-carbon polyunsaturated fatty acids in the cell membrane.

Polyunsaturated Fatty Acids in Inflammatory Disease States of the Epidermis

Inflammation is an extremely complex reaction, of which arachidonic acid metabolites play a major but not singularly causative role. Research efforts have proven that allergic or inflammatory skin conditions are associated with epidermal and blood cell injury that initiates arachidonic acid metabolism causing vascular changes mediated by kinins, histamine, and eicosanoids (specifically prostaglandins) as well as chemotactic changes mediated by complement fragments, immune complexes, and eicosanoids (specifically leukotriene B_4).[8, 15, 16]

In inflammatory skin disease, hydrolysis of cell membrane phospholipids triggers the arachidonic acid cascade. Arachidonic acid is released from the keratinocyte, mast cell, macrophage, leukocyte, platelet, fibroblast, or vascular endothelial cell membranes by phosphorylases after immunologic stimulation or cell injury. Metabolism of arachidonic acid produces eicosanoids including cyclooxygenase metabolites (prostaglandin E_2, thromboxane A_2) and lipoxygenase metabolites (leukotriene B_4, 12-HETE, 15-HETE) that are considered to be highly proinflammatory.[17] The eicosanoids produce various effects, such as proinflammatory activity of prostaglandin E_2; leukocyte chemoattraction, stimulation of lysosomal enzymes, and increased vascular permeability caused by leukotriene B_4; and proinflammatory, potent neutrophil and mononuclear cell chemoattractant, anti-inflammmatory activity of 15-HETE.[17] A type of "cellular cascade effect" occurs when leukotriene B_4 receptors are stimulated on the neutrophil (and probably other cell types as well) cell surface. This binding process initiates neutrophil recruitment, chemotaxis, degranulation, and more leukotriene B_4 synthesis which perpetuates the inflammatory response.[18]

When fatty acids are released by membranes, the enzyme pathway by which they are metabolized is determined by whether they are omega-6 or omega-3 fatty acids. Omega-6 fatty acids are metabolized primarily by cyclooxygenase which produces metabolites that are pro-inflammatory. Omega-3 fatty acids are metabolized primarily by the lipoxygenase pathway and form mediators with much less inflammatory activity. The pathway is influenced not only by the fatty acid composition of the cell membrane, but by the tissue levels of the enzymes and the presence and/or absence of inhibitors such as corticosteroid and non-steroidal anti-inflammatory drugs.[19]

As the relative amounts of membrane bound omega-6 and omega-3 fatty acids change, the relative amounts of the eicosanoid mediators that are produced also change.[19] Increasing omega-3s leads to decreased production of the pro-inflammatory eicosanoids and increased amounts of the less inflammatory metabolites.

*Polyunsaturated
Fatty Acids as
Therapeutic
Dietary
Supplements*

Dietary supplements containing eicosapentaenoic acid (precursor for docohexaenoic acid) and gamma-linolenic acid (precursor for dihomo-gamma-linolenic acid) can modulate inflammation associated with Type 1 hypersensitivity reactions.[20] Since the epidermal keratinocytes lack delta desaturase enzymes, dihomo-gamma-linolenic acid is not further metabolized into arachidonic acid, but rather it is incorporated into epidermal keratinocyte membranes. When a traumatic or immunological insult occurs to the cell membranes, the eicosapentaenoic acids and dihomo-gamma linolenic are metabolized by lipoxygenase and cyclooxygenase enzymes (in direct competition with arachidonic acid for these enzyme substrates). This results in a relative decreased amount of arachidonic acid-derived eicosanoids and increased amounts of less inflammatory eicosanoids (prostaglandin E_1, thromboxane A_1, and 15-HETE). Theoretically, the anti-inflammatory activity of 15-HETE lies in its ability to block potent proinflammatory activity of eicosanoid leukotriene B_4, while prostaglandin E_1 competitively inhibits arachidonic acid release from damaged cell membranes.[19, 20]

With respect to the omega-3 polyunsaturated fatty acid family, alpha-linolenic acid is the precursor that is absorbed and metabolized into important epidermal metabolites such as eicosapentaenoic acid (which is also directly available from dietary sources such as certain cold marine fish oils) and docosahexaenoic acid. Eicosapentaenoic acid metabolites have been found to decrease inflammation associated with Type 1 hypersensitivity reactions.[21, 22] Eicosapentaenoic acid competes with arachidionic acid to bind to 5-lipoxygenase and 15-lipoxygenase enzymes, resulting in increased production of leukotriene B_5 and 15-hydroxyeicosapentaenoic acid (15-HEPE). These metabolic isomers competitively inhibit the production of leukotriene B_4 (30 - 100 times more potent inflammatory metabolite than leukotriene B_5). Eicosapentaenoic acid also binds to cyclooxygenase to limit the production of prostaglandin E_2 by increasing production of less inflammatory metabolite prostaglandin E_1. Docosahexaenoic acid is a strong inhibitor of leukotriene B_4 production.[19]

Delta-6-desaturase is the rate limiting enzyme in the metabolism of linoleic acid into arachidonic acid. Research has shown a decreased activity of the delta-6-desaturase enzyme in human patients with atopic dermatitis.[23] Dietary supplementation with eicosapentaenoic acid and/or gamma-linolenic acid have been shown to decrease clinical signs of pruritus, erythema, and inflammation associated with atopic dermatitis in humans and dogs. [22, 23, 24]

Research studies show that large doses of an 80% evening primrose oil which contains gamma linolenic acid, an omega-6 fatty acid, and 20% cold water marine fish oil which contains eicosapentaenoic acid, an omega-3 fatty acid, prescription product (Efa Vet Regular®; Efamol Vet®) were needed to attenuate the clinical signs associated with atopy in dogs.[25]   In another study, high-dose marine fish oil dietary supplementation alone was found to be effective and apparently safe for short-term relief of the signs of canine allergic skin disease.[26]

It became apparent that these studies had not been designed to assess the therapeutic importance of relative ratios of omega-6 to omega-3 fatty acids. The rationale for using an adjusted omega-6:omega-3 fatty acid ratio enriched diet was based on several postulates. Since linoleic acid is an essential dietary requirement for dogs, it was necessary to determine the optimal ratio to concurrently meet the basal linoleic acid requirement as well as produce a potentially less-inflammatory fatty acid metabolic profile. Also, the enriched diet would insure that the dog would receive the appropriate amount of fatty acids without owner compliance problems associated with oral supplements.

A scientific study was performed by researchers to determine the effects of combined omega-6 and omega-3 fatty acids in defined dietary ratios on canine in vivo eicosanoids production.[19] The experimental diets were composed of menhaden oil (concentrated source of eicosapentaenoic acid, 20:5n-3, and docosahexaenoic acid, 22:6n-3), flax (concentrated source of alpha-linolenic acid, 18:3n-3), and safflower oil (concentrated source of linoleic acid, 18:2n-6).[19] The chronic feeding studies (12 weeks in duration) using 5 groups of healthy laboratory beagles were fed with omega-6:omega-3 ratios of 5:1, 10:1, 25:1, 50:1, and 100:1. Eicosanoids were measured in the skin, plasma, and neutrophils at 0, 6, and 12 weeks.

The results of marker eicosanoids showed decreased concentrations of proinflammatory leukotriene B_4 and increased concentrations of less inflammatory leukotriene B_5 in dogs fed diets containing the 5:1 and 10:1 omega-6 to omega-3 fatty acid ratios. Alterations of leukotriene B_4 synthesis in the canine epidermis did not occur until 12 weeks into the dietary trial. At that time, both the 5:1 and 10:1 omega-6 to omega-3 fatty acid ratio diets produced significant decreases in leukotriene B_4 and increases in leukotriene B_5 in plasma and skin samples. Theoretically, leukotriene B synthesis in the skin results from alterations in the membrane phospholipid compositions of various stationary cells (i.e., keratinocytes) and circulating blood cells (i.e., mast cells, neutrophils, macrophages, etc.), to produce inflammatory disease of the skin. This data has direct clinical applications for long-term feeding of specially formulated diets with balanced omega-6:omega-3 fatty acid ratios. It indicates that decreases in pro-inflammatory derivatives of arachidonic acid metabolism in the skin can aid in control of inflammatory conditions (such as allergic inhalant dermatitis and flea allergic dermatitis) in dogs.[19]

Some researchers postulate that even though an extended time period may be necessary to incorporate "new fatty acids" into the cellular membrane phospholipids of epidermal and other tissues, (detectable by HPLC separation techniques), clinical improvement may precede changes in cutaneous fatty acid levels. [27]

*Efficacy
of an Omega-6:
Omega-3
Polyunsaturated
Fatty Acid
Adjusted Diet in
Pruritic Dogs*

The purposes of this clinical trial were to: (1) evaluate the clinical condition of canine pruritic patients pre-, during, and post-dietary omega-3 polyunsaturated fatty acid supplementation (as provided through an enriched veterinary therapeutic diet); (2) examine serum fatty acid profile changes during the course of the trial; and (3) evaluate palatability, any untoward gastrointestinal side-effects and owner compliance using the therapeutic diet in canine patients.

Thirty one clinical patients with either confirmed inhalant allergies, adverse reactions to foods or a combination of both diseases were fed exclusively Eukanuba® Veterinary Diets® Response Formula FP™ For Dogs (*Table 1*).

Table 1. Fatty acid profile of Eukanuba Veterinary Diets Response Formula FP used in the 8 week clinical trial.

Fatty Acid	Isomer	Symbol	Percentage (by weight)
Caprylic	none	8:0	0.0
Capric	none	10:0	0.0
Lauric	none	12:0	0.0
Myristic	none	14:0	1.4
Myristoleic	cis	14:1n-5	0.0
Pentadecanoic	none	15:0	0.1
Palmitic	none	16:0	13.5
Palmiteladic	trans	16:1n-7	0.5
Palmitoleic	cis	16:1n-7	2.8
Hexadecadienoic	unkn.	16:2	0.1
Hexadecatetranoic	unkn.	16:4	0.1
Margaric	none	17:0	0.1
Margaroleic	cis	17:1	0.1
Stearic	none	18:0	3.7
Elaidic	trans	18:1n-9	0.0
Oleic	cis	18:1n-9	37.8
Vaccenic	trans	18:1n-7	1.9
Octadecenoic	cis	18:1n-7	0.1
Linoleic	cis	18:2n-6	19.9
gamma-Linolenic	cis	18:3n-6	0.2
alpha-Linolenic	cis	18:3n-3	1.0
Stearidonic	cis	18:4n-3	0.2
Arachidic	none	20:0	0.2
Gondoic	cis	20:1n-9	2.6
Eicosenoic	cis	20:1n-7	0.2
Eicosadienoic	cis	20:2n-6	0.6
Eicosatrienoic	cis	20:3n-6	0.5
Eicosatrienoic	cis	20:3n-3	0.1
Arachidonic	cis	20:4n-6	0.4
Eicosatetraenoic	cis	20:4n-3	0.1
Eicosapentaenoic	cis	20:5n-3	1.2
Behenic	none	22:0	0.1
Cetoleic	unkn.	22:1n-11	2.4
Erucic	cis	22:1n-9	0.3
Docosatetraenoic	cis	22:4n-6	0.1
Docosapentaenoic	cis	22:5n-3	0.3
Docosahexaenoic	cis	22:6n-3	2.3
Lignoceric	none	24:0	0.1
Nervonic	cis	24:1n-9	0.2
Omega-3 Fatty Acids			**5.2**
Omega-6 Fatty Acids			**21.7**

The clinical patient dogs participated in the 8 week enriched diet that conveniently achieved a total dietary intake of a 5:1 ratio of omega-6 to omega-3 polyunsaturated fatty acids. Concurrent intensive flea control was maintained throughout the trial period. No changes in hyposensitization immunotherapy injection protocols, bathing schedules, or additional antipruritic medications were allowed. Hyposensitization immunotherapy in all allergic inhalant dogs had been for a minimum of one year and was currently in force. No oral treats were allowed to be fed for the duration of the trial feeding. Every patient was examined at 0, 4, and 8 weeks after enrollment into the clinical trial. At each visit, a complete clinical examination to evaluate for pruritus, erythroderma, alopecia or other changes in skin and coat conditions were performed by a veterinary dermatologist. At each clinical visit, blood was drawn and submitted for complete blood counts as well as serum fatty acid evaluation. In addition, owners were required to keep daily logs with evaluation of pruritus, palatability, and other clinical signs such as stool consistency, form, or any gastrointestinal side-effects.

Twenty eight dogs completed this dietary trial, with three dogs removed for palatability or owner compliance issues. Fourteen (45%) dogs were judged to have good to excellent response to dietary change as evaluated by both the owner and dermatologist. Dietary change during the 8 week trial did not have any effect on complete blood counts (including platelet counts, which were all within numerical normal range), or eosinophil counts. Increases in serum omega-3 fatty acids were observed after feeding the omega-3 fatty acid adjusted diet.

This clinical data provides support for the biochemical data which indicates that it may take several weeks of omega-3 fatty acid administration to result in therapeutic steady state levels for the treatment of pruritic dermatological diseases of the dog.

Eukanuba and Eukanuba Veterinary Diets are registered trademarks of The Iams Company. Response Formula FP is a trademark of The Iams Company.

References

1. Fly AD, Johnston PV. Tissue fatty acid composition, prostaglandin synthesis, and antibody production in rats fed corn, soybean, or low erucic acid rapeseed oil (canola oil). *Nutr Res* 1990; 10:1299-1310.

2. Lands WEM. Biochemistry and physiology of n-3 fatty acids. *FASEB J* 1992; 6:2530-2536.

3. Hwang D. Essential fatty acids and the immune response. *FASEB J* 1989; 3:2052-2061.

4. Downing DT, Stewart ME, et al. Lipids of the epidermis and the sebaceous glands. In: Fitzpatrick, TB, Eisen, AZ, et al. (ed). *Dermatology in General Medicine,* 4th ed. New York: McGraw-Hill, 1993:210-221.

5. White PD. Essential fatty acids: use in management of canine atopy. *The Compend of Small Ani Med* 1993; 3:451-457.

6. Hou SYE, Mitra AK, et al. Membrane structures in normal and essential fatty acid-deficient stratum corneum: characterization by ruthenium tetroxide

staining and X-ray diffraction. *J of Invest Dermatol* 1991; 96:215-223.

7. Lands WEM. Renewed questions about polyunsaturated fatty acids. *Nutr Rev* 1986; 44:189.

8. Ziboh VA, Chapkin RS. Biological significance of polyunsaturated fatty acids in the skin. *Arch of Dermatol.* 1987; 123:168a-190a.

9. Ziboh VA, Cohen KA, Ellis CN, et al. Effects of dietary supplementation of fish oil on neutrophil and epidermal fatty acids: modulation of clinical course of psoriatic subjects. *Arch Dermatol* 1986; 122:12277.

10. Horrobin DF. Essential fatty acids in clinical dermatology. *J Amer Acad of Dermatol* 1989; 20:1045-1053.

11. Lloyd DH, Thomsett LR. Essential fatty acid supplementation in the treatment of canine atopy: a preliminary study. *Vet Dermatol* 1989; 1:41-44.

12. National Research Council. *Nutrient Requirements of Dogs.* Washington DC: National Academy Press, 1985:7.

13. Simpson JW, Anderson RS, Markwell PJ. *Clinical nutrition of the dog and cat.* Oxford: Blackwell Scientific Publication, 1993:22-23.

14. Elias PM, Brown BE, Ziboh VA. The permeability barrier in essential fatty acid deficiency: evidence for a direct role for linoleic acid in barrier function. *J Invest Dermatol* 1980; 74:230-233.

15. Kojima T, Terano T, Tanabe E, et al. Long term administration of highly purified eicosapentaenoic acid provides improvement in psoriasis. *Dermatologica* 1991; 182(4):225-230.

16. Ziboh VA, Miller CC. Essential fatty acids and polyunsaturated fatty acids: significance in cutaneous biology. *Ann Rev Nutri* 1990; 10:433-450.

17. Kwochka KW. Review article. The structure and function of epidermal lipids. *J Vet Derm* 1993; 4(4):151-159.

18. Charleson S, Evans JF, Zamboni RJ, et al. Leukotriene B_3, leukotriene B_4 and leukotriene B_5; binding to leukotriene B_4 receptors on rat and human leukocyte membranes. *Prostaglandins* 1986; 32(4):503-516.

19. Vaughn DM, Reinhart GA, Swaim SF, et al. Evaluation of dietary n-6 to n-3 fatty acid ratios on leukotriene B synthesis in dog skin and neutrophils. *J Vet Derm* 1994; 5(4):163-173.

20. Lands WEM. Biochemistry and physiology of n-3 fatty acids. *FASEB J* 1992; 6:2530-2536.

21. Ziboh VA. Biochemical basis for the anti-inflammatory action of gamma-linolenic acid. In: Horrobin, DF. (ed.) *Omega-6 essential fatty acids. Pathophysiology and roles in clinical medicine.* New York: Alan R. Liss, 1990:55-65.

22. Logas D, Beale KM, Bauer JE. Potential clinical benefits of dietary supplementation with marine-life oil. *J AVMA* 1991; 199:1631-1636.

23. Bordoni A, Biagi PL, Masi M, et al. Evening primrose oil in the treatment of children with atopic eczema. *Drugs and Exper Clin Res* 1988; 14:291-297.

24. Wright, S. Atopic dermatitis and essential fatty acids: a biochemical basis for atopy? *Act Dermato-Vener Stockholm* 1985; 114:143-145.

25. Bond R, Lloyd DH. A double blind comparison of olive oil and a combination of evening primrose oil and fish oil in the management of canine atopy. *Vet Rec* 1992; 131:558-560.

26. Logas D, Kunkle GA. Double-blind crossover study with marine oil supplementation containing high-dose eicosapentaenoic acid for the treatment of canine pruritic skin disease. *Vet Derm* 1994; 5(3):99-104.

27. Campbell KL. Review article: Clinical use of fatty acid supplements in dogs. *Vet Derm* 1993; 4(4):167-173.

A Controlled Dietary Omega-6:Omega-3 Ratio Reduces Pruritus in Non-Food Allergic Atopic Dogs

Gregory A. Reinhart, PhD
Director of Strategic Research, Research and Development
The Iams Company, Lewisburg, Ohio

Danny W. Scott, DVM, DACVD
William H. Miller, Jr., VMD, DACVD
New York State College of Veterinary Medicine
Cornell University, Ithaca, New York

Allergic skin diseases are common in companion animals. Flea bite hypersensitivity accounts for the largest number of cases that are reported, with atopic disease (allergic inhalant dermatitis) ranking second.[1] It has been estimated that approximately 10 to 15 percent of the canine population is affected by this disorder.[2,3] Clinical signs include variable pruritus, self trauma to the skin, and secondary bacterial infections. Most dogs are sensitive to more than one allergen, which may include house dust mites or dust, molds, weeds, grasses, or trees.[1] Observations of breed and family predilections along with results of limited breeding trials indicate that atopy is genetically programmed in the dog.[3,4] Breeds that are at increased risk include Chinese Shar Peis, Dalmatians, Irish Setters, Golden Retrievers, Boxers, Labrador Retrievers, Belgian Tervurens, and several terrier and toy breeds.[5,6]

Clinical signs of atopic disease occur when the animal is exposed to the offending antigen and sensitized mast cells present in the skin degranulate and release inflammatory agents. In the dog, these compounds include histamine, heparin, proteolytic enzymes, chemotactic factors and vasoactive metabolites of membrane fatty acids.[1] It is the final category of inflammatory agents, those derived from membrane fatty acids, that is of interest when examining the dietary management of atopy. The oxidative products of membrane fatty acids that are involved in the inflammatory response are called eicosanoids. These 20-carbon compounds are mediators of inflammation in most tissues in the body, including skin. They include prostaglandins, thromboxanes, hydroxyeicosatetraenoic acids and leukotrienes.[7]

The types of fatty acids that are present in cell membranes dictate the types of eicosanoids that are produced during an inflammatory response. Two series of fatty acids that are of recent interest in the treatment of inflammatory skin disorders are the omega-3 and the omega-6 fatty acids. Recent research has shown that manipulation of these fatty acids in the diet results in changes in the levels found in both plasma and tissues, and may affect the inflammatory response.[8,9,10]

Role of Membrane Polyunsaturated Fatty Acids in Cutaneous Inflammation

Polyunsaturated fatty acids are classified into several series, based upon the distance of the first double bond in the carbon chain from the terminal methyl group. The omega-6 fatty acids have the first double bond located at the sixth carbon. The omega-3 fatty acids have the first double bond located at the third carbon atom from the methyl end. Algae synthesize high amounts of omega-3 fatty acids. As a result, most marine animals contain high concentrations of omega-3 fatty acids in their tissues. Sources of omega-3 fatty acids in pet foods include fresh, cold water fish oils, and whole fat flax (an enriched source of alpha-linolenic acid). Land animals, in contrast, have high concentrations of the omega-6 fatty acids because most plants that are consumed by terrestrial animals contain greater amounts of omega-6 than omega-3 fatty acids. Enriched sources of omega-6 fatty acids in pets foods include corn, safflower, sunflower, cottonseed, and soy oils.

The essential fatty acids that are most important in cutaneous homeostasis in the dog are linoleic acid of the omega-6 family (18:2n-6) and alpha-linolenic acid of the omega-3 family (18:3n-3). Arachidonic acid (20:4n-6) is synthesized from linoleic acid by the dog, but must be supplied in the diet of the cat. Arachidonic acid is a major cellular membrane fatty acid that is incorporated into membranes as a phospholipid and contributes to membrane fluidity and stability. Alpha-linolenic acid is a precursor of eicosapentaenoic acid (20:5-n3). While animals are capable of elongating and further desaturating omega-6 and omega-3 fatty acids after they have been consumed, interconversion between the two series is not possible within the body. However, the metabolism of these fatty acids to eicosanoids do share and compete for the same enzyme systems.

Arachidonic acid and eicosapentaenoic acid are the most biologically active membrane fatty acids. When cells are subjected to a chemical or physical insult (i.e., exposure to an antigen), phospholipase A_2 is activated. This enzyme releases polyunsaturated fatty acids from the membrane, making them available for eicosanoid production. Arachidonic acid is metabolized via the cyclooxygenase system to the 2-series prostaglandins and thromboxane A_2, and via lipoxygenase pathways to the 4-series leukotrienes and hydroxyeicosatetraenoic acid (HETE). The prostaglandins of this series alter vascular permeability, potentiate effects of other vasoactive substances (including the 4-series leukotrienes), and modulate lymphocyte function.[1,11,12,13] The 4-series leukotrienes act as chemotactic factors for neutrophils and eosinophils, modify lymphocyte function, and alter vascular permeability.[14,15] The end products of arachidonic acid are predominantly pro-inflammatory and are believed to contribute to the pathologic process of atopy in dogs.[16] Eicosapentaenoic acid, on the other hand, is converted primarily via cyclooxygenase pathways to the 3-series prostaglandins and thromboxane A_3 and via lipoxygenase pathways to the 5-series leukotrienes and hydroxyeicosapentaenoic acid (HEPE). These compounds have different biological activities than the metabolites of arachidonic acid. Most importantly, their effects are less inflammatory than those of the 2-series prostaglandins and 4-series leukotrienes.[17] Two end products of eicosapentaenoic acid that are of importance are leukotriene B_5 and 15-hydroxyeicosapentaenoic acid. There is evidence that these compounds inhibit leukotriene B_4, the potent pro-inflammatory end product of arachidonic acid metabolism.[18]

Medical management of atopy usually involves various combinations of avoidance of the offending antigens, drug therapy, and in some cases, hyposensitization (immunotherapy). Glucocorticoids and several types of antihistamines are most commonly used. However, the acute and chronic side effects of these drugs, the presence of concurrent diseases which make glucocorticoid use inappropriate, and many owners' reluctance to use long-term drug therapy make these medications unsatisfactory for many dogs. As a result, alternative methods of treatment for atopic pets are continually being investigated.

Fatty Acid Supplements as Adjunct Therapy

In recent years, fatty acid supplements have been investigated and used as adjunctive treatment for atopic disease in dogs and cats. The dietary manipulation of fatty acid metabolism is usually aimed at decreasing the proportion of omega-6 fatty acids and increasing the proportion of omega-3 fatty acids in cell membranes. Early studies examined the efficacy of administering fatty acid supplements containing combinations of omega-3 and omega-6 fatty acids for reducing pruritus in allergic animals. A review of five separate clinical tests of a commercial supplement (DVM Derm Caps™) showed that fatty acid supplementation was effective in controlling pruritus in 11 to 27 percent of the dogs that were treated.[19,20,21,22,23] In one study, 93 dogs diagnosed with atopic dermatitis were treated with a commercial fatty acid supplement containing 15 mg of eicosapentaenoic acid per capsule.[21] A dose of one capsule per 9 kg (20 lb) body weight was given. One-third of the dogs showed good to excellent response to the supplement, but only 17 dogs (18%) required no additional therapy. Another study using the same supplement reported that after only one week of treatment, 11 percent of dogs with atopy, food allergy, or flea bite allergy were adequately controlled by the supplement alone with no other treatment necessary.[20] Many variables affect the effectiveness of a fatty acid supplement, and it is estimated that anywhere from 10 to 80 percent of atopic pets will show varying degrees of responsiveness to dietary supplementation.[24]

The mechanism of action of omega-3 fatty acids, and specifically of eicosapentaenoic acid, appears to be a change in the type of eicosanoid that is produced. Providing increased amounts of dietary omega-3 fatty acids results in their incorporation into cell membranes with a corresponding decrease in concentrations of omega-6 fatty acids.[25,26] Because arachidonic acid and eicosapentaenoic acid compete for the same enzymes, when the level of omega-3 fatty acids are increased in cell membranes, competitive inhibition leads to increased production of the less inflammatory three and five-series eicosanoids and decreased production of the two- and four-series eicosanoids.[10,27] This shift in eicosanoid production has the potential to diminish the inflammatory response.

While a proportion of allergic dogs has been shown to require no additional therapy when provided with a dietary fatty acid supplement, most dogs still required concurrent administration of antihistamines or low dosages of corticosteroids to control pruritus.[23,28,29] Therefore, it appears that fatty acid supplementation as a treatment for allergic dermatitis may allow reduction in the dose and/or frequency of other anti-inflammatory drugs that are being used, but does not completely control the disorder in most cases. There are several possible reasons for the variable responses that have been observed. First, there are a number of different agents which mediate inflammation and pruritus in dogs with allergic dermatitis. There- fore, the manipulation of fatty acids would not be expected to work in all cases. A second factor may involve the manner in which fatty acid therapy is administered. Supplementing a dog's diet with a fatty acid-containing capsule does not account for the levels or proportions of fatty acids that are present in the dog's regular diet. The effectiveness of fatty acid therapy relies upon competitive inhibition between omega-6 and omega-3 fatty acids and their metabolites. Therefore, if the pet's regular diet already contains high levels of omega-6 fatty acids, providing an omega-3 fatty acid supplement may not effectively change the proportion of the two types of fatty acids present in tissues. Lastly, many questions still remain regarding appropriate doses of fatty acid supplements. Several studies have shown that allergic pruritus is not controlled in dogs using recommended doses of omega-3 fatty acid supplements.[28,30] Others have reported that doses of 2 to 10 times the recommended dose may be necessary to achieve results in pruritic dogs.[31,32]

Recent research indicates that using a total dietary approach, in which both the quantity and the ratio of omega-6 and omega-3 fatty acids are controlled, is an effective means of altering tissue eicosanoid profiles in the body.[10] Specifically, feeding a diet which contains an omega-6 to omega-3 ratio between 5:1 and 10:1 results in desired changes in skin leukotriene concentrations. Clinical studies are underway to study the effectiveness of this approach in treating allergic animals. The results of a study of atopic dogs are presented here.

Clinical Study: The Total Dietary Approach

A clinical study to determine the efficacy of using a diet formulated to provide therapeutic levels of fatty acids to treat pruritus in atopic dogs was under- taken. A group of 18 non-food allergic, atopic dogs were identified for inclusion in the prospective, single-blinded study. Eleven of the eighteen dogs had previously been treated with a commercial fatty acid supplement containing a combination of omega-3 and omega-6 fatty acids, but no reduction in pruritus was seen after treatment with this supplement at recommended dosages for 3 to 6 weeks.

Fatty acid profile analyses were performed on samples of each dog's regular diet and on the test diet. The test diet was a commercial lamb and rice dog food

(Eukanuba® Natural™ Lamb and Rice For Dogs) containing both omega-6 and omega-3 fatty acids, with a ratio of 5.3:1. Dogs were fed this diet exclusively for a period of 8 weeks. Blood and skin samples were obtained prior to the start of the study (pre-test) and at the end of the 8-week feeding period (post-test). The dogs' responses to the test diet were based upon the owner's and veterinarian's observations and were grouped into three categories: excellent, good or poor. An excellent response was one in which pruritus was either completely eliminated or reduced to a level at which no additional therapy was needed. A good response indicated a reduction in pruritus of at least 50%, but residual itching was such that other modes of therapy were still necessary. A poor response indicated that there was little or no change in pruritus. Dogs that received either a good or excellent rating during the study period were refed their previous diets and observed for a return of clinical signs. When pruritus returned, the dogs were again fed the test diet to determine if pruritus was reduced or eliminated a second time.

Forty four percent of the dogs (8/18) demonstrated a good to excellent response to the test diet within 7 to 21 days of the 8-week period. All 8 dogs were subsequently refed their original commercial diets, and pruritus returned in all of the dogs within 3 to 14 days. Pruritus was again alleviated by reintroduction of the test diet in all 8 dogs. The dogs' sex, skin test reactivity (≤ 10 vs. > 10 positive intradermal reactions), nature of regular diet, or duration of disease did not significantly influence the dogs' responsiveness to the test diet. However, dogs that were positive to flea antigen were found to be less likely to respond to the test diet than those that were not.

Fatty acid analyses showed that plasma omega-3 fatty acid levels were higher in post-test samples than in pre-test samples for the majority of dogs. Changes in omega-6 fatty acids, on the other hand, were less consistent. A comparison of the eight responders to the 10 non-responders showed that the group of responders had significantly greater increases in plasma arachidonic acid and eicosapentaenoic acid in response to the test diet, compared to the group of non-responders.

An important result of this study was the positive response of dogs that had previously been non-responsive to a dietary fatty acid supplement containing omega-3 and omega-6 fatty acids. Of the 11 dogs that had been previously treated with a fatty acid supplement, seven had a good to excellent response to the test diet (64%). Fatty acid profile analysis of the test diet showed that the omega-3 fatty acid levels were 4 to 7 times higher than the levels consumed by these dogs when their original diets were being supplemented with a fatty acid product. These data indicate that the addition of a fatty acid supplement to a dog's regular diet may not raise omega-3 fatty acids to levels that are effective in the control of pruritus.

Recent research in the dog indicates that a dietary omega-6 to omega-3 fatty acid ratio of between 5:1 and 10:1 is optimal for reducing the production of   *Conclusions* pro-inflammatory agents in the skin and neutrophils of some dogs.[10] The present study indicates that a diet containing an omega-6 to omega-3 ratio of 5.3:1 is efficacious in reducing pruritus in dogs suffering from atopic disease. The fatty acid content of this diet meets the essential fatty acid requirements of dogs and does not alter blood clotting parameters.[33] Enriched sources of omega-3 fatty acids that can be included in such diets are marine oils and certain terrestrial plant oils such as flax. Sources of omega-6 fatty acids include corn, safflower, canola, and soy oils, and animal fats. Further clinical uses for these diets may include preventive treatment for allergic inhalant dermatitis, flea bite hypersensitivity, and other inflammatory disorders in dogs and cats. More clinical studies are required to fully explore these applications.

Eukanuba is a registered trademark of The Iams Company. Natural is trademark of The Iams Company.

References

1. Scott DW, Miller WH, Griffin CE. *Muller and Kirk's Small Animal Dermatology.* 5th ed., Philadelphia, PA: WB Saunders, 1995:500-518.

2. Chalmers SA, Medleau L. An update on atopic dermatitis in dogs. *Vet Med* 1994; 89:326.

3. Scott DW, Paradis M. A survey of canine and feline skin disorders seen in a university practice: Small animal clinic, University of Montreal, Saint-Hyacinthe, Quebec (1987-1989). *Can Vet J* 1990; 31:830-835.

4. Schwartzman RM. Immunologic studies of progeny of atopic dogs. *Am J Vet Res* 1984; 45:375-379.

5. Reedy LM, Miller WH, Jr. *Allergic Skin Diseases of Dogs and Cats.* Philadelphia, PA: W.B. Saunders Co., 1989.

6. Scott DW. Observations on canine atopy. *J Am Anim Hosp Assoc* 1981; 17:91-100.

7. Crawford MP. Background to essential fatty acids and their prostanoid derivatives. *Br Med Bulletin* 1983; 39:210-213.

8. Savic MS, Yager JA, Holub BJ. Effect of n-3 and n-6 fatty acid dietary supplementation on canine neutrophil and keratinocyte phospholipid composition. *Proc Sec World Congr Vet Derm* 1992:7.

9. Campbell KL, Czarnecki-Maulden GL, Schaeffer DJ. Effects of animal and soy fats and proteins in the diet on concentrations of fatty acids in the serum and skin of dogs. *Am J Vet Res,* accepted for publication, 1995.

10. Vaughn DM, Reinhart GA, Swaim SF, Lauten SD, Garner CA, Boudreaux MK, Spano JS, Hoffman CE, Conner B. Evaluation of dietary n-6 to n-3 fatty acid ratios on leukotriene B synthesis in dog skin and neutrophils. *Vet Dermatol* 1994; 5(4):163-173.

11. Samuelsson B. Leukotrienes: mediators of immediate hypersensitivity reactions and inflammation. *Science* 1983; 220:568-575.

12. Kragballe K. Voorhees JJ. Arachidonic acid and leukotrienes in dermatology. *J Invest Derm* 1983; 81:293-296.

13. Tolman EL, Mezick JA, Rosenthale ME. The arachidonic acid cascade and

skin disease. In: Stone J, ed. *Dermatologic Immunology and Allergy*, St. Louis, Mosby Co., 1985: 53-62.

14. Lewis GP. Immunoregulatory activity of metabolites of arachidonic acid and their role in inflammation. *Br Med Bulletin* 1983; 39:243-248.

15. Voorhees JJ. Research on inflammation spotlights leukotrienes role. *Derm Focus* 1984; 2:1-3.

16. Kietzman M. Eicosanoid levels in canine inflammatory skin diseases. In: vonTscharner C, Halliwell REW, eds. *Advances in Veterinary Dermatology*, vol 1, London, Baillier Tindall, 1990:211-220.

17. Voorhees JJ. Leukotrienes and other lipoxygenase products in the pathogenesis and therapy of psoriasis and other dermatoses. *Arch Derm* 1983; 119:541-547.

18. White P. Essential fatty acids: use in management of canine atopy. *Comp Cont Educ* 1993; 15:451-457.

19. Miller WH Jr., Scott DW, Wellington JR. Investigation on the antipruritic effects of ascorbic acid given alone and in combination with a fatty acid supplement to dogs with allergic skin disease. *Canine Pract* 1992; 17(5):11-13.

20. Scott DW, Buerger RG. Nonsteroidal anti-inflammatory agents in the management of canine pruritus. *J Am Anim Hosp Assoc* 1988; 24:425-428.

21. Miller WH, Griffin GE, Scott DW, Angarano DK, Norton AL. Clinical trial of DVM Dermcaps in the treatment of allergic disease in dogs: a non-blinded study. *J Am Anim Hosp Assoc* 1989; 25:163-168.

22. Scott DW, Miller WH, Decker GA, Wellington JR. Comparison of the clinical efficacy of two commercial fatty acid supplements (EfaVet® and DVM Derm Caps®). Evening primrose oil, and cold water marine fish oil in the management of allergic pruritus in dogs: A double- blinded study. *Cornell Vet* 1992; 82:319-329.

23. Paradis M, Lemay S, Scott DW. The efficacy of clemastine (Tavist), a fatty acid-containing product (DVM Derm Caps®) and the combination of both products in the management of canine pruritus. *Vet Derm* 1991; 2:17-20.

24. Scott DW, Miller WH, Griffin CE. *Muller and Kirk's Small Animal Dermatology*. 5th ed., Philadelphia, PA: WB Saunders, 1995:214-217.

25. Ziboh VA, Chapkin RS. Biological significance of polyunsaturated fatty acids in the skin. *Arch Dermatol* 1987; 123(12):1686-1690.

26. Ziboh VA, Miller CC. Essential fatty acids and polyunsaturated fatty acids: Significance in cutaneous biology. *Annu Rev Nutr* 1990; 10:433-450.

27. Savic MS, Yager JA, Holub BJ. Effect of n-3 and n-6 fatty acid dietary supplementation on canine neutrophil and keratinocyte phospholipid composition. *Proc Sec World Congr Vet Derm*, 1992:77.

28. Scott DW, Miller WH. Nonsteroidal management of canine pruritus: chlorpheniramine and a fatty acid supplement (DVM Derm Caps) in combination, and the fatty acid supplement at twice the manufacturers' recommended dosage. *Cornell Vet* 1991; 80:381-387.

29. Paradis M, Scott DW. Further investigation on the use of nonsteroidal and steroidal anti-inflammatory agents in the management of canine pruritus. *J Am Anim Hosp Assoc* 1991; 27:44-48.

30. Lloyd DH, Thomsett LR. Essential fatty acid supplementation in the treatment of canine atopy. A preliminary study. *Vet Derm* 1989; *1:41-44.*

31. Bond R, Lloyd DH. A double-blind comparison of olive oil and a combination of evening primrose oil and fish oil in the management of chronic atopy. *Vet Rec* 1992; 131:558-562.

32. Bond R, Lloyd DH. Randomized single-blind comparison of an evening primrose oil and fish oil combination and concentrates of these oils in the management of canine atopy. *Vet Derm* 1992; 3:215-221.

33. Vaughn DM, Reinhart GA. Dietary fatty acid ratios and eicosanoid production. *Proc 13th ACVIM Forum,* 1995.